TRANSFORMING CURRICULUM FOR A CULTURALLY DIVERSE SOCIETY

TRANSFORMING CURRICULUM FOR A CULTURALLY DIVERSE SOCIETY

Edited by

Etta R. Hollins
Washington State University

LEA **LAWRENCE ERLBAUM ASSOCIATES, PUBLISHERS**
1996 **Mahwah, New Jersey**

Lawrence Erlbaum Associates, Inc., Publishers
10 Industrial Avenue
Mahwah, New Jersey 07430

Library of Congress Cataloging-in-Publication Data

Transforming curriculum for a culturally diverse society / edited by
Etta R. Hollins.
p. cm.
Includes bibliographical references and indexes.
ISBN 0-8058-8033-X (pbk. : alk. paper)
1. Education—United States—Curricula. 2. Multicultural education—United States—Curricula. 3. Curriculum planning—Social aspects—United States. 4. Curriculum change—United States.
5. Curriculum evaluation—Social aspects—United States.
I. Hollins, Etta R., 1942–
LB1570.T68 1996
375'.00973—dc20 95-44515
CIP

Books published by Lawrence Erlbaum Associates are printed on acid-free paper, and their bindings are chosen for strength and durability.

Printed in the United States of America
10 9 8 7 6 5 4 3 2 1

Dedicated to the collective efforts and energies of those who deliberate, collaborate, and actively participate in transforming school practices for a culturally diverse society—and to all who benefit

Contents

Preface

The purpose of this book is to facilitate transforming the public school curriculum for a culturally diverse society. This means raising fundamental issues concerning the ideologies that presently undergird school practices; revealing the ways in which the actualized curriculum is differentiated on the basis of the perceived attributes and status of particular populations; expanding the unit of analysis for assessing the outcomes of schooling to include the relationship between school practices and societal structures and between the planned curriculum and students' experiences within and outside of school; and presenting an inclusive structure for decision making where diverse groups experience equity in representation and power in determining the purpose, values, and outcomes of school practices. Transforming the curriculum for a culturally diverse society means more than including knowledge about diverse populations. It means reconceptualizing school practices through debate, deliberation, and collaboration involving the diverse voices that comprise the nation.

In this book, *culturally diverse* refers to all of the identifiable cultural or ethnic groups living in the United States (including European Americans) and other groups of people who have lived together over extended periods of time where those features characteristic of culture that influence their beliefs, perceptions, and responses to the sociological, spiritual, and physical environment are shared and transmitted from one generation to the next. This may include social class groups or other configurations. Transforming the curriculum for a culturally diverse society requires thoughtful deliberation on highly salient aspects of school practices, including how they influence students' perceptions and responses within and outside of school and how they impact the larger society. The members of the group engaged in deliberation should be representative of a culturally diverse society. The authors in this book address critical perspectives from which a framework is constructed for a discourse on planning curriculum for a culturally diverse society.

HOW THIS BOOK IS ORGANIZED

In Part I, the ideologies and values that form the basis of school practices are discussed from three perspectives, which include (a) the context of education for Native Americans at the turn of the century, (b) different societal and educational responses to cultural and ethnic pluralism, and (c) multiculturalism as an essential premise for a democratic society. This discussion reveals the complexity of ideas, motives, and values that influence the purpose and practice of schooling. The authors present different perspectives on the purpose of schooling in a culturally diverse society.

In Part II, the authors address issues related to the process and participants in curriculum planning. Central issues in planning curriculum for a culturally diverse society include who should have the power to decide what knowledge and which practices are of the greatest value and what processes or approaches should be employed in curriculum planning. Responses to these issues are proposed, corroborated, and challenged with examples from practice.

In Part III, the authors introduce curriculum differentiation based on culture and social class. Identifiable outcomes of curriculum differentiation may include (a) reproducing existing societal structures that maintain inequalities, (b) facilitating learning, (c) transmitting culture, (d) promoting cross-cultural acceptance and understanding, and (e) supporting personal and reference group identity. These examples of possible outcomes of curriculum differentiation are presented to illustrate the importance of understanding potential differences between the planned and actualized curriculum and how different students may experience the same curriculum differently.

Part IV is about curriculum evaluation. Here, the authors review the practices and functions of assessment and evaluation. They discuss individual and group assessment employing standardized tests as well as the more recent performance-based assessment. The traditional discussion of individual academic achievement is expanded to include evaluation of the social meanings of the curriculum and the potential societal impact of school practices on promoting a more equitable and democratic society.

Specific features are included in this book to facilitate its use as a textbook. The critical questions at the beginning of each part assist the reader in identifying complex issues to be examined. The chapters in each part are not intended to provide complete and final answers to the questions posed, but rather, to generate discussion, critical thinking, and further investigation. The overview for each part of the book provides an introduction and summary of the main issues addressed and the relationship among ideas presented by different authors. The suggested learning experiences have been selected as examples of ways to expand the reader's understanding of specific issues, practices, and questions addressed in each part. The included references may also be used to expand the reader's knowledge in specific areas.

INTENDED USES OF THIS BOOK

This book is primarily designed for graduate courses in curriculum development and theory, although it may be used in other courses concerned with issues of cultural diversity. The authors address substantive and complex issues concerning school practices in a culturally diverse society. The issues covered and the examples provided have been limited in order to preserve depth and quality in the discussion.

This book can be used to facilitate scholarly inquiry. Scholarly inquiry is an important aspect of transforming public school curriculum for a culturally diverse society. Although interest in the relationship between culture, cognition, and school learning has increased in recent years, there is still a need for more extensive research on ways to transform schooling for a culturally diverse society. The issues and questions raised in this book identify areas of inquiry and theorizing that may be useful to researchers.

This book can be used by practitioners to facilitate collaboration, deliberation, and decision making in curriculum planning. This book provides insights into such questions as: What should be the purpose of schooling in a culturally diverse society? Who should be involved in curriculum planning and what process should be used? How is the actualized curriculum differentiated? What is the relationship between school practices and the structure of the larger society? How should the curriculum be evaluated? These questions take the practitioner beyond contemporary practices in multicultural education to examine broader questions of social and educational equity in planning the school curriculum.

In summary, this book provides important insight into the need for transforming the curriculum for a culturally diverse society and enhances the reader's ability to identify approaches likely to facilitate enduring systemic change.

ACKNOWLEDGMENTS

This book is an outgrowth of my own teaching and the need to provide students in the courses I teach with the most exemplary thinking in curriculum studies. I am especially grateful for the thoughtful deliberation and insight that characterizes the efforts of the scholars whose work is included in this book and to the students whose dialogue during class meetings directed my search for exemplary scholarship.

I wish to thank the faculty, administration, and staff at California State University, Hayward, for providing the time, support, and opportunities for me to engage in the planning, reflection, and study that have facilitated my own professional growth and ability to contribute to improving the preparation of public school educators.

I am grateful to Naomi Silverman, a terrifically insightful, sensitive, and skilled editor, from whom I have learned to share my work with a broader audience.

I am particularly indebted to my daughters, Kimberly and Karla, who have their own careers and lives, yet find the time to share interest and support for my work.

—Etta R. Hollins

Acknowledgment is given to the following sources for permission to reprint selected chapters and tables:

Adams, David Wallace, "Fundamental Considerations: The Deep Meaning of Native American Schooling, 1880–1900," *Harvard Educational Review*, 58:1, pp. 1–28. Copyright © 1988 by the President and Fellows of Harvard College. All rights reserved.

Smolicz, Jerzy, "Multiculturalism and an Overarching Framework of Values: Some Educational Responses for Ethnically Plural Societies," *European Journal of Education*, 19:1 (1984), pp. 11–23. Reprinted with permission of Carfax Publishing Company, 875-81 Massachusetts Avenue, Cambridge, MA 02139.

Banks, James A., "Multicultural Education: For Freedom's Sake," *Educational Leadership*, 49:4 (1991), pp. 32–36. Reprinted with permission of the Association for Supervision and Curriculum Development. Copyright © 1991 by ASCD. All rights reserved.

Schwab, Joseph J., "The Practical 4: Something for Curriculum Professors to Do," *Curriculum Inquiry*, 13:3 (1983), pp. 239–265. Reprinted with permission of Blackwell Publishers. Copyright © 1983 by the Ontario Institute for Studies in Education.

Schwartz, Henrietta, "Dialogue: Schwab's 'Practical 4' and Its Corroboration in Recent History," *Curriculum Inquiry*, 14:4 (1984), pp. 437–463. Reprinted with permission of Blackwell Publishers. Copyright © 1983 by the Ontario Institute for Studies in Education.

Cornbleth, Catherine, "Curriculum In and Out of Context," *Journal of Curriculum and Supervision*, 3:2 (1988), pp. 85–96. Reprinted with permission of the Association for Supervision and Curriculum Development. Copyright © 1988 by ASCD. All rights reserved.

Anyon, Jean, "Social Class and the Hidden Curriculum of Work." Reprinted from *Journal of Education*, Boston University School of Education (1980), Vol. 162, with permission from The Trustees of Boston University (copyright holder) and the author.

Lipka, Jerry, "Toward a Culturally Based Pedagogy: A Case Study of One Yup'ik Eskimo Teacher." Reproduced by permission of the American Anthropological Association from *Anthropology and Education Quarterly*, 22:3, September 1991. Not for further reproduction.

Spears-Bunton, Linda A., "Welcome to My House: African American and European American Students' Responses to Virginia Hamilton's *House of Dies Drear*," *The Journal of Negro Education*, 59:4 (1990), pp. 566–576. Copyright © 1990 by Howard University.

Darling-Hammond, Linda, "Performance-Based Assessment and Educational Equity," *Harvard Educational Review*, 64:1 (1994). Copyright © 1993 by the Ford Foundation. All rights reserved. Reprinted with permission.

Apple, Michael W., and Beyer, Landon E. "Social Evaluation of Curriculum," *Educational Evaluation and Policy Analysis*, 5:4 (1983), pp. 425–434. Copyright © by 1983 by the American Educational Research Association. Reprinted by permission of the publisher.

Table 1.1 (Principles of Good Subject-Matter Teaching): Adapted from "Probing the Subtleties of Subject-Matter Teaching," Jere Brophy, *Educational Leadership*, 49:7 (1992), pp. 4–8. Reprinted with permission of the Association for Supervision and Curriculum Development. Copyright © 1992 by ASCD. All rights reserved.

Table 1.2 (Curriculum Guidelines for Multicultural Education): Adapted from "Curriculum Guidelines for Multicultural Education," *Social Education*, September 1992, pp. 279–281. Reprinted by permission of the publisher.

CHAPTER ONE

Introduction

Etta R. Hollins

This chapter describes how this book may be used as a framework for discourse on curriculum planning in a culturally diverse society. It is organized into four parts that address the purpose of schooling, curriculum planning, curriculum differentiation, and curriculum evaluation. The framework presented here addresses (a) the impetus for curriculum change, (b) representative participation, (c) systematic inquiry, and (d) informed practice. Each of the areas discussed includes examples and, where possible, supporting research and theory.

The perspectives presented in this book address different aspects of the curriculum including the explicit or planned, the implicit or hidden, and the null or omitted. *Curriculum* is defined as all of the learning, routines, and interactions that occur among all participants as a function of schooling, whether planned or not, which inform and shape responses to the environment within and outside of school. This definition is predicated on the premise that there is (a) a reciprocal and constitutive relationship between the practices and values in school and those found in the larger society and (b) at least a contributory relationship between the students' home-culture and productive school practices.

The school curriculum legitimates knowledge, perspectives, values, and interactions and relationships among people and institutions. The planned curriculum is overt and intentional in what is legitimated. History, English, and science content are examples of the planned curriculum. The implicit curriculum is indirect in that what is legitimated is culturally, socially, and institutionally embedded and may be incorporated into school practices without planning or thought. For example, competition and individualism are values held in the larger society that permeate school practices without requiring much thought or planning. The null curriculum mainly consists of knowledge valued by marginalized groups and may be omitted from the curriculum as a matter of routine. The null curriculum helps to maintain and perpetuate the existing societal structure. The omission of the history and culture of ethnic minorities is an example of the null curriculum. Historically, this omission has been part of the acculturation or Americanization process aimed at eliminating cultural identities and practices that are not "mainstream middle-class European American." The authors in this book make various aspects of the curriculum explicit, thereby providing opportunities to examine critical issues important to transforming the curriculum for a culturally diverse society.

IDENTIFYING THE IMPETUS FOR CHANGE

Curriculum change is usually aimed at improving the academic, psychological, or social outcomes of schooling. The desire to improve the outcomes of schooling may be motivated by (a) local or national economic needs or changes in technology, (b) specific societal concerns or issues such as health and public safety, and (c) internal or external threats of a political nature. For example, recent technological advances in the computer industry have had a significant influence on the school curriculum. Many high schools and some elementary schools have the latest computer hardware and software. Computer programs direct academic study in many areas including language arts, science, and social studies. Students use computers for compiling and organizing data for a variety of purposes, for communicating with other students at different locations, and for general word processing. Much planning has been done to ensure that the school curriculum adequately prepares young people for the information age in which computers are expected to be indispensable.

An example of societal concerns with health issues involves AIDS education. Some public interest groups and school districts have developed curriculum guides and information packets for educators and students about AIDS. Some groups such as health care workers and educators may be more concerned with preventing the spread of AIDS than with social or cultural values and practices and may advocate controversial practices such as the dissemination of condoms to high school students or needles to confirmed drug addicts. Other groups may be more concerned with morality than with preventing the spread of this disease and may be opposed to such practices as the dissemination of condoms or needles to drug addicts. Tension over curriculum content resulting from differences in value perspectives is common in public education. In this instance, the conflict is over whether to include the null curriculum (AIDS education) as part of the explicit curriculum. The values inherent in the implicit curriculum are in opposition to practices advocated by some groups.

Differences in value perspectives and the increased tension produced may be more evident in situations involving a potential internal political threat. For example, cultural pluralism, a concept that emerged as a social and political response to the influx of immigrants from southern and eastern Europe during the colonial period, was revitalized during the Civil Rights Movement of the 1960s (Pratte, 1979). Each case represented a political threat of civil unrest and in each case the concept was controversial. The conceptualization of multicultural education as we know it today is an outgrowth of the Civil Rights Movement and is based on the earlier concept of cultural pluralism.

The multiculturalists contend that national unity can co-exist with cultural pluralism where diverse groups retain visible aspects of their original cultural heritage. They advocate a multicultural curriculum that includes multiple perspectives and the accomplishments of all groups within the society (Banks, 1991/1992). Traditionalists argue that an emphasis on ethnicity is a threat to national unity. They advocate a common curriculum that includes noteworthy contributions from different groups (Ravitch, 1991/1992). The multiculturalists argue that the common culture is the dominant culture and excludes the fair representation of ethnic minorities. Despite the debate between the traditionalists and the multiculturalists, multicultural education has influenced all areas of the public school curriculum.

The impetus for change in the school curriculum may come from many different sources. Cultural diversity within the society is a significant impetus for curriculum change, although the topic is too general to develop a vision for planning. The authors in this book present issues that when synthesized in deliberation, collaboration, and planning have the potential for generating a vision for enduring systemic change, which will transform the curriculum to meet the needs of a culturally diverse society.

REPRESENTATIVE PARTICIPATION

Once the decision is made to change or alter the curriculum a planning or study group is formed. In the first chapter in Part II, Schwab (1983) describes in detail the composition of the planning group along with the attributes, roles, and responsibilities. In summary, Schwab's planning group includes the following:

1. teachers with innovative ideas who represent the area of the curriculum to be addressed, and at least one who represents an area that may be directly or indirectly affected by the proposed changes;

2. the principal;
3. a chairperson;
4. community representation;
5. student representation;
6. an academic advisor who is a professional academic with extensive knowledge of the field being addressed (occasional attendance at meetings);
7. a research advisor (occasional attendance at meetings); and
8. a social science consultant such as a psychologist, sociologist, or ethnographer (occasional attendance at meetings).

Schwab describes four commonplaces in curriculum planning including the teacher, the student, the subject matter, and the milieu. Each member of the planning group should have expertise in at least one of the four commonplaces of curriculum planning. Schwab recommends that the size of the planning group should be about nine regular members, although the size may vary depending on the size of the school and the availability of individuals for membership. For example, in small schools all of those who will use the curriculum may be involved in the planning process. In large schools, involving two or three teachers who will use the curriculum may be sufficient.

The chairperson of the curriculum group is primarily responsible for facilitating collaboration, deliberation, and decision making. The chairperson helps group members overcome both biases and stereotypes in their interactions with each other and limitations in their knowledge and awareness related to the task at hand. He or she also supports and ensures equal participation of all group members in collaboration, deliberation, and decision making.

In describing the composition of the curriculum planning group, Schwab does not address the representation of those from culturally and ethnically diverse backgrounds, different social class levels, those with different physical or intellectual attributes, or a balance in gender. In transforming the school curriculum for a culturally diverse society it is important to develop an inclusive structure for curriculum planning where diverse groups experience equity in representation and power in determining the purpose, values, and outcomes of schooling. Individuals representing different populations served by the school should be knowledgeable about the group's aspirations, expectations, experiences, perceptions, practices, and values. These individuals may be members of the groups represented or closely associated with these groups in ways that provide similar insights. Including culturally diverse populations need not increase the size of the curriculum planning group. Cultural diversity can be represented within the categories of group membership Schwab describes. For example, some of the teachers participating in the curriculum group may come from different cultural or social class backgrounds and may be able to represent the values and interests of these groups.

SYSTEMATIC INQUIRY

Systematic inquiry entails the use of multiple approaches and multiple sources to gather data related to school practices and their impact on the students served, their teachers, and the larger society. This includes qualitative and quantitative research and a thorough review of the research and theoretical literature. Inadequate or inappropriate inquiry or data gathering can result in curriculum planning based on inaccurate or incomplete information. Thus, the design of the curriculum may be seriously flawed and the desired outcomes may be inappropriate or unattainable.

Schwab's four commonplaces are important areas for inquiry. For example, it is important to understand how teacher perception and other factors such as social interactions and relationships in the classroom influence the actualized curriculum; how students respond to the subject matter presented and to the learning experiences provided by teachers; how subject matter is framed and whether this varies from one student population to another; and how classroom and school practices are related to the values and practices in the students' home-cultures and communities. Ethnographic techniques of inquiry can produce important insights into relationships among the four commonplaces. Existing ethnographic data related to the curriculum project should be reviewed. Ethnographic techniques may be employed to collect additional data needed for curriculum decision making.

Approaches and Sources

Part III provides examples of reports from ethnographic studies that provide important insights for curriculum planning, which are directly related to Schwab's four commonplaces. For example, the study by Anyon (1980) addresses all four commonplaces. Observations in elementary school classrooms serving students from five different social class levels show how teachers' perceptions of children's social status influences the presentation of the curriculum. In this case the teachers take into consideration the social milieu from which the children come to reframe the curriculum in a way that denies access to socially valued knowledge and skills. Lipka (1991) reports a case study that also addresses all four of Schwab's commonplaces. Extensive observation of a Yup'ik Eskimo teacher whose students share his culture reveals the relationship between values and practices in this classroom and those in the students' home-culture and community. Lipka shows how the teacher reframes the curriculum to include content that is familiar to the students and how social interactions in the classroom are consistent with values and practices in the Yup'ik culture. The interactions in this classroom are friendly and mutually supportive for the teacher and the students. In contrast, the European-American teacher unknowingly imposes her own culture and perceptions on the children, which results in conflict and disruptions in class. This case study points to the importance of the relationship between cultural practices and values, the framing of the curriculum, and the social interaction among teachers and students.

The third chapter in Part III presents a case study reported by Spears-Bunton (1990) involving a European-American English teacher with students from poor and working-class African-American and European-American backgrounds. This teacher takes it upon herself to integrate African-American literature into the traditional English curriculum. Initially, it is an uncomfortable situation that erupts in racial conflict. Finally, the students read Virginia Hamilton's *House of Dies Drear.* Reading this provides a shared experience of common understanding that allows the students to move beyond their personal biases and stereotypes.

Spears-Bunton's study deals with Schwab's four commonplaces, but with a slightly different approach. This English teacher reframes the curriculum to address larger societal issues of cultural inclusion, racism, and stereotypes, while simultaneously addressing issues of personal and group identity. This study more directly brings forth the question of the purpose of school learning and how school practices may be related to larger societal structures, values, and practices. This study also provides insights into students' responses to certain types of curriculum content and strategies that help resolve conflicts.

The first author in Part III, Branch, presents a discussion of the competing curriculum, which he describes as "unwritten influences that intrude on the parameters of the classroom" (p. 172, this volume). The competing curriculum, which is difficult to document, is projected through the attitudes and behaviors of educators. Branch uses the ecological systems theory to describe educators' background experiences and early socialization as sources in the development of the competing curriculum. Branch's discussion of the competing curriculum provides a reference for better understanding of the research reports presented by the other authors in this part.

The studies presented in Part III identify some of the most profound issues and problems in transforming curriculum for a culturally diverse society. Although they are not exhaustive, they do point to the importance of inquiry in the process of curriculum planning. A more extensive review of the research literature will reveal additional studies that are equally relevant to curriculum planning.

Other important sources of data on students include interviews, questionnaires, and standardized achievement tests and performance assessments as well as other school records. Sources for additional data on teachers include employment records that provide background information such as years of experience and educational attainment. It is also important to gather demographic data on the community served by the school. Data gathered from these sources can provide important insights for curriculum planning.

Data Analysis

The analysis of data will depend on the types of data gathered and the conceptual framework employed. In transforming curriculum for a culturally diverse society it may be beneficial for curriculum planners to focus on salient practices in schools and classrooms and salient conditions within and outside of school (Schwab's milieu) in analyzing data. Examples of salient practices are contained in the research reports in Part III of this book. One example is the curriculum differentiation on the basis of social class reported by Anyon (1980). These research studies also identify salient conditions within and outside of school. Salient conditions may include social interactions and relationships among students and teachers in school and the structural inequalities that exist in the larger society outside of school.

An example of a data analysis tool that includes practices and values is Schwartz's (1984) matrix combining Schwab's four commonplaces and Heskovitz's nine cultural universals. Schwartz illustrates how discrepancies may exist among the four commonplaces regarding the nine cultural universals. Such an analysis may be used to identify suitable points for curriculum improvement efforts.

Conclusions and inferences drawn from the analysis of ethnographic data can be used to generate statements of purpose, policy, and guidelines for curriculum efforts. Cornbleth (1988), in the final chapter in Part II, emphasizes the importance of including policymaking as part of curriculum planning. The use of the results from ethnographic inquiry will be influenced by the perceptions and values of the members of the curriculum planning group. Data gathering and analysis provide information about what exists; however, thoughtful deliberation on the findings can facilitate the creation of a vision of what schools should or can be like.

INFORMED PRACTICE

Informed practice involves the use of the findings from systematic inquiry in developing a vision or mission, planning the curriculum, designing the assessment, and formulating policy. Each aspect of informed practice is interrelated and interdependent.

Developing a Vision

Ponder and Holmes (1992) define a *vision* as "an operating model of all aspects of the organization and the actual steps necessary to make that model a reality" (p. 408). These researchers conducted a study to develop a holistic vision of the ideal school for the 21st century. The Ponder and Holmes study involved 29 individuals with demonstrated leadership in school restructuring and whose ideas were disseminated through published works, seminars and workshops, the media, or were apparent in practice to develop a holistic vision of an ideal 21st-century school. The individuals participating in this study included university professors, journalists, school administrators, and corporate executives.

The themes dominating the vision that emerged in the study conducted by Ponder and Holmes (1992) are as follows:

1. relationships that are positive, supportive, and personally meaningful among members of the learning community;
2. democracy in action, which is apparent in the daily practices in the school;
3. conserving and developing human resources that are actualized in communal efforts to ensure maximum growth and development of all members of the learning community;
4. problem solving that is directly related to real-life situations and concerns as the central focus for learning; and
5. educational flexibility that embraces shared planning among all participants in the learning community and that also embraces change, innovation, and new knowledge.

From these themes emerged the clear purpose of the ideal school as stated by Ponder and Holmes: "to create global citizens capable of peaceful, productive interaction with multicultural, multiethnic community team members; to create citizens whose every action is congruent with democratic principles; to create people capable of not only solving the thorny issues of 21st-century life, but of inventing exciting and enriching new realities" (p. 416).

The study conducted by Ponder and Holmes (1992) is an important contribution to the discussion of the vision and purpose of schooling. However, it is important to examine the extent to which the themes and purpose of the ideal school for the 21st-century address the deep societal values discussed in Part I of this book. For example, how do the themes and purpose of this ideal school avoid the cultural hegemony described by Adams (1988) as manifested in schools for Native Americans at the turn of the century in the form of conversion to Protestantism, individualization, and Americanization? Smolicz (1984) points out that solutions to pluralism have included assimilation, separatism, and five different interpretations of multiculturalism. Which approach to pluralism is embraced in the ideal school? What will students learn about how to perceive and respond to potentially negative aspects of democracy such as capitalism and competition? A clear vision and statement of purpose for schooling is an essential prerequisite for the more detailed work of deciding what knowledge and skills are of the greatest value and identifying the most meaningful and productive school practices.

Planning the Curriculum

The discussions in Parts II and III provide some impressions of aspects of the curriculum. In some instances the planned and actualized curriculum are described in detail and the null curriculum can be inferred. For example, Spears-Bunton's (1990) discussion of the English teacher who revised the traditional curriculum to include African-American literature provides insight into the planned and actualized curriculum. The planned curriculum was traditional. The actualized curriculum was adapted to include African-American literature. Anyon's discussion of the curriculum, differentiated according to social class, reveals the implicit or hidden curriculum. The planned curriculum was similar for all social class groups; however, the hidden curriculum included a relationship to capital that was different for each group. These variations in the curriculum suggest a need to make clear linkages between curriculum planning and the vision for the school. This linkage is important because of the need for consistency between ideology and practice.

Curriculum content in specific subject-matter areas and approaches to teaching should be directly related to the vision statement. Brophy (1992) draws from the research on teaching school subjects for understanding and higher order applications to develop principles for good subject-matter teaching (see Table 1.1). These principles identify examples of approaches to instruction and characteristics of knowledge, skills, and attitudes for subject-matter learning that may be considered by the curriculum planning committee in designing the specific objectives and learning experiences for the curriculum in a specific subject-matter area. These principles can serve as a vehicle for discussion; however, the planning committee must determine whether they are consistent with the vision statement.

Another resource to use in identifying specific objectives for curriculum in a particular subject-matter area are the curriculum guidelines for multicultural education developed for the National Council for Social Studies (see Table 1.2). These guidelines provide additional examples of approaches to instruction and characteristics of knowledge, skills, and attitudes for subject-matter learning that may be considered by the curriculum planning group in designing the specific objectives and learning experiences for the curriculum in a specific subject-matter area. These guidelines, the principles

TABLE 1.1
Principles of Good Subject-Matter Teaching

1. The curriculum is designed to equip students with knowledge, skills, values, and dispositions useful both inside and outside of school.

2. Instructional goals underscore developing student expertise within an application context and with emphasis on conceptual understanding and self-regulated use of skills.

3. The curriculum balances breadth and depth by addressing limited content but developing this content sufficiently to foster understanding.

4. The content is organized around a limited set of powerful ideas (key understandings and principles).

5. The teacher's role is not just to present information but also to scaffold and respond to students' learning.

6. The students' role is not just to absorb or copy but to actively make sense and construct meaning.

7. Activities and assignments feature authentic tasks that call for problem solving or critical thinking, not just memory or reproduction.

8. Higher-order thinking skills are not taught as a separate skills curriculum. Instead, they are developed in the process of teaching subject-matter knowledge within application contexts that call for students to relate what they are learning to their lives outside of school by thinking critically or creatively about it or by using it to solve problems or make decisions.

9. The teacher creates a social environment in the classroom that could be described as a learning community where dialogue promotes understanding.

Note. Adapted from Brophy, J. (1992). Probing the subleties of subject-matter teaching. *Educational Leadership*, *49*(7), 4-8.

TABLE 1.2
Curriculum Guidelines for Multicultural Education

1. Ethnic and cultural diversity should permeate the total school environment.

2. School policies and procedures should foster positive multicultural interactions and understandings among students, teachers, and the support staff.

3. A school's staff should reflect the ethnic and cultural diversity within the United States.

4. Schools should have systematic, comprehensive, mandatory, and continuing staff development programs.

5. The curriculum should reflect the cultural learning styles and characteristics of the students within the school community.

6. The multicultural curriculum should provide students with the continuous opportunity to develop a better sense of self.

7. The curriculum should help students understand the totality of the experiences of ethnic and cultural groups in the United States.

(Continued)

TABLE 1.2
(Continued)

8. The multicultural curriculum should help students understand that a conflict between ideals and realities always exists in human societies.

9. The multicultural curriculum should explore and clarify ethnic and cultural alternatives and options in the United States.

10. The multicultural curriculum should promote values, attitudes, and behaviors that support ethnic pluralism and cultural diversity as well as build and support the nation-state and the nation's shared national culture. E pluribus unum should be the goal of the schools and the nation.

11. The multicultural curriculum should help students develop their decision-making abilities, social participation skills, and sense of political efficacy as necessry bases for effective citizenship in a pluralistic democratic nation.

12. The multicultural curriculum should help students develop the skills necessary for effective interpersonal, interethnic, and intercultural group interactions.

13. The multicultural curriculum should be comprehensive in scope and sequence, should present holistic views of ethnic and cultural groups, and should be an integral part of the total school curriculum.

14. The multicultural curriculum should include the continuous study of the cultures, historical experiences, social realities, and existential conditions of ethnic and cultural groups, including a variety of racial compositions.

15. Interdisciplinary and multidisciplinary approaches should be used in designing and implementing the multicultural curriculum.

16. The multicultural curriculum should use comparative approaches in the study of ethnic and cultural groups.

17. The multicultural curriculum should help students to view and interpret events, situations, and conflict from diverse ethnic and cultural perspectives and points of view.

18. The multicultural curriculum should conceptualize and describe the development of the United States as a multidirectional society.

19. Schools should provide opportunities for students to participate in the aesthetic experiences of various ethnic and cultural groups.

20. The multicultural curriculum should provide opportunities for students to study ethnic group languages as legitimate communication systems and help them develop full literacy in at least two languages.

21. The multicultural curriculum should make maximum use of experiential learning, especially local community resources.

22. The assessment procedures used with students should reflect their ethnic and cultural experiences.

23. Schools should conduct ongoing, systematic evaluations of the goals, methods, and instructional materials used in teaching about ethnic and cultural diversity.

Note. Adapted from Curriculum guidelines for multicultural education. (September, 1992). *Social Education*, 274-294.

of good subject-matter teaching, and the vision of the ideal school all point out the importance of relating curriculum content to the larger society outside of school, providing experientially based learning, and creating a supportive social context for learning. Each curriculum planning group should utilize the findings from their own inquiry to determine the significance of these factors in their curriculum planning effort.

Designing the Assessment

Part IV describes different approaches, perspectives, and purposes for assessing and evaluating the outcomes of schooling. Traditional approaches to evaluation focused on using standardized tests to measure the academic achievement of individuals and groups. Contemporary approaches emphasize performance-based assessment focused on demonstrating the ability to apply or use learning from a sequence of planned experiences. These different approaches and perspectives on assessment and evaluation give rise to several questions that curriculum planners will need to answer including: What aspects or impacts of schooling should be assessed, how, and for what purposes? To what extent should the internal reliability and validity of school practices be examined? Should the outcomes of schooling be measured on the basis of individual student's academic achievement or social or psychological development; the achievement of groups of students and the relationships among them; the impact on the larger society, the environment, and the world; or all of these factors?

Internal Reliability and Validity. Issues of internal reliability and validity include two important questions: Do school practices consistently generate the intended outcomes or meet predetermined objectives? and To what extent do school practices contribute to the preparation of students for full active, productive, and meaningful or satisfying participation in the economic, political, and social life within the larger society?

It is a well-documented fact that students from low-income and certain ethnic minority backgrounds are categorically underserved in the nation's public schools. This fact alone challenges the reliability and validity of school practices for these populations of students, however, the problem is seldom addressed in this fashion. The study presented in this volume by Lipka (1991) compares the classroom practices of a Yup'ik Eskimo teacher with Yup'ik students to that of a European-American teacher with Yup'ik students. Lipka documents the incorporation of Yup'ik culture in the Yup'ik teacher's classroom and the imposition of European-American culture in the other classroom. The validity of learning in the Yup'ik teacher's classroom is based on the apparent relationship between what is learned within and outside of school, and the applicability of what is learned within school to the larger society outside of school. This factor of validity is absent in instruction in the European-American teacher's classroom. The fact that the children cooperate with their Yup'ik teacher and meet the intended learning objectives supports the reliability of this teacher's classroom practices. This factor of reliability is absent in the European-American teacher's classroom practices and the actualized curriculum.

A critical aspect of curriculum planning is assessing the reliability and validity of school practices. Contemporary and traditional practices in evaluation can be used to assess reliability. Students' scores on standardized achievement tests and the new performance assessment tools can provide information on whether school practices consistently generate the intended outcomes. For example, in inner-city schools where such assessments consistently show poor academic performance, it is apparent that school practices are not reliable for this population. This indicates a need to examine and redesign approaches to school learning, rather than blaming the students' life conditions for school failure.

Assessing the validity of school practices requires more than data produced from standardized tests and performance portfolios. It requires careful examination of the relationship between school learning and what students experience and need for functioning in the larger society. School learning is accepted as valid to the extent that it provides all students with a wide range of opportunities for full and active participation in the economic, political, and social life in the larger society.

Anyon (1980), in her study of schools serving students from different social class backgrounds, documented differences in the preparation received for participating in the larger society. Only students from the most elite group received schooling that provided multiple opportunities for full and meaningful participation in the larger society and for influencing the future. These students' schooling enabled them to select from among a wide range of choices as to how they would structure their own lives. The students from the elite school viewed their schoolwork as valid and were usually willing participants. Schooling for students from a lower social class status provided access to a limited range of opportunities within the larger society. These students viewed their school learning as invalid and often resisted their schoolwork.

The central purpose for assessing reliability and validity of school practices is to identify those conditions and experiences that provide equitable access to high-quality school learning for all students regardless of their culture, ethnicity, race, social class status, gender, or physical or intellectual attributes. As schools presently exist, students are usually expected to benefit equally from the same learning conditions and experiences. However, not all students enter school with the same life experiences, values, ways of learning and perceiving, or ways of interacting with others. The significance of these factors may be revealed in assessments of the reliability and validity of school practices.

Individual and Group Performance. Traditional assessments of the outcomes of schooling have relied on standardized achievement tests to measure individual and group performance. These types of assessments have served multiple purposes. Eisner (1993) identifies five functions of assessment which include (a) *temperature-taking*, where the academic achievement of individuals and groups of students, as measured by standardized tests, is used to determine how well schools are performing; (b) *gate-keeping*, where individual student's performance on specific tests such as the SAT or ACT is used to determine the adequacy of their preparation for advanced study or professional or occupational responsibility; (c) determining whether course objectives have been met; (d) providing feedback to teachers on the productivity of their work; and (e) providing information on the quality of the school program provided. Eisner concludes that "programme evaluation, teacher evaluation and student evaluation are the major areas of focus for any form of educational assessment" (p. 225).

Program evaluation and teacher evaluation are addressed under the rubric of reliability and validity of school practices. The term *program evaluation* may be too ambiguous for designing an assessment that will inform practice. For example, more information may be generated by examining specific school practices that extend through a variety of programs. Similarly, the term *teacher evaluation* may be too ambiguous. Determining the validity and reliability of specific classroom practices may be a prerequisite to assessing the quality of the application by individual teachers.

The use of standardized tests to assess the outcomes of schooling or to serve the functions identified by Eisner (1993) has been deemed inadequate by many contemporary critics. However, Darling-Hammond (1994), in this volume, differentiates between testing and assessment. The purpose of testing is described as selection, placement, and predicting learning potential prior to instruction. Testing practices have been plagued by biases in content and outcomes that tend to support existing inequities in the larger society. The purpose of assessment is to measure the outcomes of instruction. Data from assessments can be used to improve school practices.

Darling-Hammond (1994) points out that "current standardized tests are widely criticized for placing test-takers in a passive, reactive role . . . , rather than one that engages their capacities to structure tasks, produce ideas, and solve problems. Based on out-moded views of learning, intelligence, and performance, they fail to measure students' higher order cognitive abilities or to support their capacities to perform real-world tasks" (p. 251). The criticism of testing has supported increasingly widespread use of various performance-based assessment approaches. Rather than relying solely on multiple-choice tests, these new performance assessments rely on a variety of techniques that may include oral presentations, debates, exhibits, collections of students' written products, videotapes of performances and different learning situations, projects, problem-solving approaches, laboratory experiments, and other demonstrations of the knowledge acquired from a sequence of learning experiences that are related to real-world tasks.

The results from performance assessments should provide important feedback for learners, teachers, curriculum designers, and policymakers that will inform the improvement of school practices. Darling-Hammond (1994) warns that "If performance-based assessments are used for the same purposes as traditional tests have been, the outcomes for undeserved students are likely to be unchanged" (p. 13).

Societal Impact. The impact of the outcomes of school practices on the larger society is often overlooked in assessment and evaluation. That is, little attention is given to the relationship between schools and other social institutions and the fundamental ideologies that direct their practices and organization. The importance of these relationships is discussed in Adams (1988) and Apple and Beyer (1983), both included in this volume. The purpose for assessing the impact of the outcomes of school practices on the larger society is to determine the relationships promoted among people and institutions, the distribution of benefits, and the validity and value of the legitimated knowledge and the supporting ideologies to the larger society. The study included in this volume by Anyon (1980) provides insights into the validity of each of these purposes.

Apple and Beyer (1983) advocate an ethnographic approach to investigating the impact of the outcomes of school practices on the larger society. Ethnographic techniques can provide a broad base of information without the constraints of standardized tests used alone. However, this approach also has potential limitations and pitfalls. Ethnographic data analysis is very subjective or qualitative rather than objective or quantitative. The analysis of ethnographic data is influenced by the skill, insight, perception, academic knowledge, and background experiences of the researcher. The analysis of similar data can vary significantly from one researcher to the next. In spite of these limitations, the data gathered using ethnographic techniques can provide valuable insights that may not be extracted from quantitative approaches alone. Ideally, curriculum planners will employ both techniques to assess the societal impact of school practices.

Testing and assessment are quantitative sources of data that can provide information on the societal impact of schooling; however, certain standards need to be met (see Table 1.3). Darling-Hammond (1994) identifies content validity and consequential validity as important emerging standards for assessment approaches and instruments. *Content validity* refers to the ability

TABLE 1.3
Criteria for Evaluating New Assessments

1. Access to educational opportunity: Assessments should be designed to survey possibilities for student growth, rather than to designate students as ready or not ready to profit from standard instruction.

2. Consequential validity: Assessments should be interpreted and evaluated on the basis of their instructional effects; that is, their effectiveness in leading teachers to spend time on classroom activities conducive to valuable learning goals and responsive to individual student learning styles and needs.

3. Transparency and openness: Knowledge and skills should be measued so that the processes and products of learning are openly displayed. The criteria of performance must be transparent rather than secret so that they can motivate and direct learning.

4. Self-assessment: Because assessment and instruction will be integrally related, instructional situations should provide coaching and practice in ways that help students to set incremental standards by which they can judge their own achievement, and develop self-direction for attaining higher performance levels.

5. Socially situated assessment: Assessment situations in which the student participtes in group activity should increase. In this context, not only performance, but also the facility with which a student adapts to help and guidance can be assessed.

6. Extended tasks and contextualized skills: Assessment should be more representative of meaningful tasks and subject matter goals. Assessment opportunities will themselves provide worthwhile learning experiences that illustrate the relevance and utility of the knowledge and skills tasks entail, as well as their content.

7. Scope and comprehensiveness: Assessment will attend to a greater range of learning and performance processes, stimulating analysis of what students can do in terms of the cognitive demands and performance skills tasks entail, as well as their content.

Note. Glaser (1990) as cited by Darling-Hammond (1994).

to describe the nature of performance that results from learning. *Consequential validity* refers to the extent to which an assessment tool and the ways in which it is used produce positive consequences both for the teaching and learning process and for students . . . [Consequential validity] places a much heavier burden on assessment developers and users to demonstrate that what they are doing works to the benefit of those who are assessed and to the society at large. Both of these types of validity are important in analyzing data that will inform curriculum planning.

Policymaking

Adams' (1988) description of the process of Native-American education makes clear the economic, political, and social context of educational policymaking and the resulting school curriculum. He points out the interrelatedness of the perception of Native Americans held by the settlers, the predominant ideology of the time (Protestantism), and political and economic motives in the formulation of educational policy at the turn of the century. The primary purposes of schooling for Native Americans derived from the prevailing ideology and motives of the settlers were manual or industrial training, conversion to Christianity, and Americanization. The purposes and ideology undergirding school practices for Native Americans at the turn of the century required a curriculum consisting of the English language, citizenship education, religious training, political recitations, patriotic rituals and celebrations, and manual or industrial training. In historical perspective, the interrelatedness of the prevailing ideology, the purposes of schooling, and the curriculum is evident.

Cornbleth (1988), included in this volume, warns contemporary curriculum developers of the pitfalls of decontextualizing curriculum by isolating it from its sociocultural and political context and separating curriculum planning and policymaking. A similar warning is given by Johnston (1993) in describing the context of educational policy related to the recent focus on the global economy and the domestic economic crisis when he points out that:

> Attempts to respond to economic crisis associated with declining competitiveness and productivity have driven the development of educational reform during the 1980s. Meliorative strategies have centered on human capital development of the labor force. Review of industrial, occupational, and organizational restructuring reveals, however, that general attributes of the labor force have little direct influence on economic outcomes. The primary difficulty is one of structural and ideological discontinuity associated with transformation to a service-based society. School policy development is thus located within the broader arena of cultural politics, in which the power to define the meaning of social events is at stake. Emerging school policy needs to place examination of structures of accumulation and legitimation at the center of curricular and pedagogical reform and to prepare all students to participate in the social reconstruction of the social and economic life-world. (p. 39)

These warnings emphasize the need for curriculum planning groups to participate in policymaking in order to allay disruptive tensions from competing societal forces that influence school practices and outcomes.

The relationship between teachers' perceptions of students' social class statuses and the curriculum content and learning experiences presented is an example of the influence of societal forces on contemporary school practices. This is poignantly portrayed in research studies by Anyon (1980) and Spears-Bunton (1990). These authors clearly identify the need to have educational policy focused on ensuring equity and excellence in the preparation of all students for full and active influence and participation in the economic, political, and social life within the United States and the world.

This means preparing students to meet their own economic and social needs and those of their families, and for participation in improving the economic, political, and social conditions of the nation and the world.

Prudent statements of policy need to be supported by precisely delineated guidelines for decision making and planning. The curriculum guidelines for multicultural education put forth by the National Council for Social Studies and the principles of good subject-matter teaching (Brophy, 1992) may be resources for generating both policy and the supporting guidelines.

SUMMARY

Important considerations in planning curriculum in a culturally diverse society include (a) the purpose of schooling, (b) processes and approaches to curriculum planning, (c) how the actualized curriculum may be differentiated, and (d) what aspects of schooling should be assessed and how. The content in this book can be used by the reader in multiple ways. One way to use this book is as a framework for discussing curriculum planning for a culturally diverse society. This framework addresses the impetus for curriculum change, representative participation, systematic inquiry, and informed practice.

REFERENCES

Adams, D. W. (1988). Fundamental considerations: The deep meaning of Native American schooling, 1880–1900. *Harvard Educational Review, 58*(1), 1–28.

Anyon, J. (1980). Social class and the hidden curriculum of work. *Journal of Education, 162*(1), 67–92.

Apple, M. W., & Beyer, L. F. (1983). Social evaluation of curriculum. *Educational Evaluation and Policy Analysis, 5*(4), 425–434.

Banks, J. A. (December 1991/January 1992). Multicultural education: For freedom's sake. *Educational Leadership*, 32–36.

Brophy, J. (1992). Probing the subtleties of subject-matter teaching. *Educational Leadership, 49*(7), 4–8.

Cornbleth, C. (1988). Curriculum in and out of context. *Journal of Curriculum and Supervision, 3*(2), 85–96.

Curriculum guidelines for multicultural education. (1992, September). *Social Education*, 274–294.

Darling-Hammond, L. (1994). Performance-based assessment and educational equity. *Harvard Educational Review, 64*(1), 5–30.

Eisner, E. W. (1993). Reshaping assessment in education: Some criteria in search of practice. *Journal of Curriculum Studies, 25*(3), 219–233.

Johnston, B. J. (1993). The transformation of work and educational reform policy. *American Educational Research Journal, 30*(1), 39–65.

Lipka, J. (1991). Toward a culturally based pedagogy: A case study of one Yup'ik Eskimo teacher. *Anthropology & Education Quarterly, 22*, 203–223.

Ponder, G. A., & Holmes, K. M. (1992). Purpose, products, and visions: The creation of new schools. *The Educational Forum, 56*(4), 405–418.

Pratte, R. (1979). *Ideology & education.* New York: David McKay.

Ravitch, D. (1991/1992). A culture in common. *Educational Leadership, 49*(4), 8–11.

Schwab, J. J. (1983). The Practical 4: Something for curriculum professors to do. *Curriculum Inquiry, 13*(3), 239–265.

Schwartz, H. (1984). Dialogue: Schwab's "Practical 4" and its corroboration in recent history. *Curriculum Inquiry, 14*(4), 437–463.

Smolicz, J. (1984). Multiculturalism and an overarching framework of values: Some educational responses for ethnically plural societies. *European Journal of Education, 19*(1), 11–23.

Spears-Bunton, L. A. (1990). Welcome to my house: African American and European American students' responses to Virginia Hamilton's "House of Dies Drear." *Journal of Negro Education, 59*(4), 566–576.

PART ONE

THE PURPOSE OF SCHOOLING

CRITICAL QUESTIONS

1. What should be the purpose of schooling in a culturally diverse society?
2. The three articles in this section describe contending visions of relationships between different cultural and ethnic groups within the society, contending value perspectives between different groups, and contending motives for the practice of schooling. What do you believe should be the role of schooling in a culturally diverse society where such differences exist?
3. Traditionalists perceive a conflict between national cohesion and ethnic cultural identity. Multiculturalists deny the validity of the traditionalists' perception which fuels the debate described by James Banks. Jerzy Smolicz and David Adams describe national or social cohesion as an issue that supports attempts to eradicate or suppress ethnic cultural identity. What do you believe should be the role of schooling in supporting national cohesion and ethnic cultural identity?
4. According to Henry Giroux and Roger Simon (1984) ". . . institutionally legitimated knowledge organizes and disorganizes experience and educators must know whose experience and whose interests are supported by different forms of education" (p. 228). How should educators use information about "whose experience and whose interests are supported by different forms of education" in determining the purpose

and process of schooling? How should we determine whether, or to what extent, schooling should legitimate both particularistic and common experiences and interests of different cultural and ethnic groups?

OVERVIEW

> Education is more than the means to economic success. The United States historically and consistently has been committed to universal education for all its citizens for several reasons: maintenance of an educated populace in a democratic society, promotion of individual growth and development, the inculcation of new groups into the society, and the transmittal of a common culture. (Ducharme, 1988)

The purposes of schooling Ducharme described are well established and accepted by many educational researchers and practitioners. However, the national goal of high-quality universal education has not been realized. Although school attendance is mandatory for youngsters under 16 years of age, the quality of outcomes vary based on social class, race/ethnicity, gender, and physical and intellectual attributes. Statements of the purposes of schooling do not always reveal the existing deep structure (the interaction between the predominant ideology, the prevailing social paradigm, and educational policy). The deep structure underlying the purposes of schooling have significant influence on the practices and outcomes. Relating this deep structure to curriculum decision making is a relatively new phenomenon.

The analysis of the deep structure of U.S. education raises new questions about the content and process of schooling appropriate to maintain an educated populace in a democratic society, the direction individual growth and development should take, how cultural diversity should be addressed, and what constitutes the common culture. Revealing the ideological and cultural forms that serve to maintain the existing social order provides avenues for conscious decision making concerning the roles schools might play in the evolution of an ideal democracy characterized by justice, equality, and full participation of citizens regardless of race, ethnicity, gender, or social class status.

The deep structure of U.S. education is poignantly revealed by the first author in this part, David Adams, in a description of Native American schooling at the turn of this century. Adams' discussion introduces assimilation as one of several societal approaches to cultural pluralism. He describes the Protestant ideology, the civilization-savagism paradigm, and the quest for land by the European immigrants as the deep structure shaping policies and practices for Native American schooling at the turn of the century. The central purpose of schooling was to assimilate Native Americans into the

White population and eliminate cultural cohesion within tribes. The approaches used to accomplish these goals included instituting boarding schools that removed students from their parents and communities and a curriculum that focused on language and re-socialization to the ways of the European-American culture. The students were taught the Protestant values of Bible reading, individual salvation, and personal mortality, which were linked to the secular values of capitalism, including personal industry, private property, and the idea of individual success. The outcome was that assimilation was not successful and the lives of Native American students were disrupted. David Adam's paper invites the reader to analyze and compare the policies and practices for schooling Native Americans at the turn of this century with what exists today for ethnic minorities.

Jerzy Smolicz, the second author in this part, describes three approaches to cultural pluralism—assimilation, separatism, and multiculturalism. Smolicz bases much of his analysis on changes that have taken place in Australia, supported by examples from societies existing in other nations.

The perspective from which Smolicz discusses responses to pluralism is that of the proximal relationship between ethnic group values and societal norms as reflected in social policies and practices. For example, in cases of assimilation one ethnic group's values *are* the societal norms and those of all other ethnic groups are subject to obliteration. In cases of separatism, each group retains its own values and there is limited contact between groups with different ancestral origins. Smolicz identifies two types of separatism: *mono-cultural homogeneity* where domination is absent and *dominated separatism* such as that in South Africa.

Perhaps the most important contribution Smolicz makes to this volume is his careful and detailed discussion of multiculturalism. He delineates five categories of multiculturalism and describes corresponding educational responses to diversity that shape policies and practices. The five categories of multiculturalism he describes are (a) co-existence and synthesis (the blending, exchanging, and sharing of values from different cultural groups in constructing a personal lifestyle); (b) core values (such as language and religion that are directly related to ethnic identity); (c) residual multiculturalism (the elimination of core values and the denigration of ethnic minority cultures to subcultural status); (d) stable multiculturalism for maintenance (cultural accommodation in which all cultures share common values related to governance of the nation yet retain chosen aspects of their own core values); and (e) tolerance ratio and compatibility of values ("a balance between the overarching framework and the various ethnic values" taking into consideration the variation in compatibility between core values among different ethnic groups).

In discussing how educational systems reflect differing ideologies related to ethnicity, Smolicz emphasizes the cultural transmission function of education. He contends that "the importance of the educational process is grounded in its function of transmitting culture from generation to generation and reflecting changes that occur in the overarching framework, as well as in ethnic values, resulting from cultural interaction at all levels in society's life" (p. 68, this volume). An examination of the role of core values, such as language, is at the heart of Smolicz's description of educational responses to ideologies related to cultural pluralism. For example, in the case of residual multiculturalism, ethnic minority languages are relegated to intimate or home use only and in Smolicz's thinking "such cultures cease to stimulate any significant intellectual activity." Smolicz presents a global view of multiculturalism that permits the classification of different responses to cultural pluralism and illuminates designs of schooling corresponding to a particular societal ideology.

The final challenge in Part I is to determine how the ideological perspectives described in Adams' and Smolicz's chapters relate to contemporary perspectives on cultural pluralism and the practice of schooling in the United States. The third author in Part I, James Banks, refocuses our attention on national issues. Banks describes the pluralism ideologies undergirding the curriculum debate between the Western traditionalists who want to maintain the status quo and the multiculturalists who seek the inclusion of people of color and women. In relating Banks' description of Western traditionalists and multiculturalists to Jerzy Smolicz's categorization, the traditionalists' perspective seems to have attributes of assimilationism and residual multiculturalism, whereas the multiculturalists' perspective seems more akin to Smolicz's depiction of stable multiculturalism for maintenance. The traditionalists, consistent with assimilationism and residual multiculturalism, call for a curriculum based on a common culture. The multiculturalists criticize this view as one in which the common culture is synonymous with the dominant culture rather than one that incorporates core values that have been mutually agreed upon by all groups in the society. Banks' calls for an educational system that "affirm[s] and help[s] students understand their home and community cultures . . . [and equips them with] . . . skills they need to participate in civic action to make society more equitable and just" (p. 75, this volume). This is consistent with aspects of stable multiculturalism for maintenance described by Smolicz.

According to Banks, educational policies and practices in the United States today are characterized by an assimilationist ideology in which the core values of one ethnic group are pervasive and others are invalidated. This is an ideological perspective that seems curiously related to that underpinning the politics and practices of education for Native Americans at the turn of the century.

In the final analysis, Banks calls for the alignment of educational practices with democratic ideology. Smolicz is surprisingly silent on the role of democratic ideology in education, whereas Adams' discussion of the deep meaning of Native American schooling clearly represents outcomes of assimilationism and residual multiculturalism.

The three chapters in Part I clearly have implications for curriculum decision making. Curriculum decision makers consciously or unconsciously subscribe to a particular pluralism ideology and will implicitly or explicitly promote a particular purpose for schooling based on the preferred ideology. The critical question is: How will curriculum decision makers determine an appropriate purpose for schooling in a culturally diverse society?

REFERENCES

Ducharme, E. R. (1988). The purpose of American education today: Concerns and assertions. In D. Corrigan (Ed.), *The purposes of American education today: Conceptions of schooling.* College Station, Texas: College of Education, Texas A & M University.

Giroux, Henry A., & Simon, Roger (1984). Curriculum study and cultural politics. *Journal of Education, 166*(3), 226–238.

CHAPTER TWO

Fundamental Considerations: The Deep Meaning of Native American Schooling, 1880–1900

David Wallace Adams

In the mid-nineteenth century, U.S. policymakers held two conflicting visions of the Indian's future: one, that Indians as a race were doomed to extinction, and two, that Indians were capable of being "civilized" and assimilated into White society. By the end of the century, in light of the Indians' loss of land and traditional ways of life, policymakers undertook an intense campaign to assimilate Indians through schooling. David Adams argues that to see this process of schooling simply as a means of assimilating the Indian into White culture is to rob this historic fact of its deeper meanings. Adams examines three perspectives and fundamental considerations that were at work at that time: the Protestant ideology, the civilization-savagism paradigm, and the quest for land by Whites, and explores how these translated into concrete educational policy. In the end the author argues that these three perspectives reinforced each other and were essential factors in the history of Indian schooling.

This they tell, and whether it
happened so or not I do not know;
but if you think about it,
you can see that it is true.
—from *Black Elk Speaks* by John Neihardt

"These are great evils; and it must be added that they appear to me to be irremediable." Alexis de Tocqueville used these terms to characterize the ways that the young republic treated its native peoples in his now classic *Democracy in America.* Tocqueville's judgment was not the result of casual speculation. In his tour of America he had observed firsthand the tragic consequences that occurred when Indian societies stood in the path of "the most grasping nation on the globe."

> At the end of the year 1831, while I was on the left bank of the Mississippi, at a place named by Europeans Memphis, there arrived a numerous band of Choctaws. . . . These savages had left their country and were endeavoring to gain the right bank of the Mississippi, where they hoped to find an asylum that had been promised them by the American government. It was then the middle of winter, and the cold was unusually severe; the snow had frozen hard upon the ground, and the river was drifting huge masses of ice. The Indians had their families with them, and they brought in their train the wounded and the sick, with children newly born and old men upon the verge of death. They possessed neither tents nor wagons, but only their arms and some provisions. I saw them embark to pass the mighty river, and never will that solemn spectacle fade from my remembrance. No cry, no sob, was heard among the assembled crowd; all were silent. Their calamities were of ancient date, and they knew them to be irremediable. The Indians had all stepped into the bark that was to carry them across, but their dogs remained upon the bank. As soon as these animals perceived that their masters were finally leaving the shore, they set up a dismal howl, and plunging all together into the icy waters of the Mississippi, swam after the boat.[1]

Tocqueville understood all too well that removal was at best only a temporary solution to the "Indian problem." As White settlers pushed ever westward, oblivious and contemptuous of Indian ways and treaty agreements, the same uneven confrontation between the two races would be repeated on succeeding frontiers, and with the same results. Indian removal only postponed the long-term question of what place, if any, the Native American would have in the American empire. The keen-eyed Frenchman was pessimistic: "I believe that the Indian nations of North America are doomed to perish, and that whenever the Europeans shall be established on the shores of the Pacific Ocean, that race of men will have ceased to exist."[2]

Throughout the nineteenth century, two visions of the Indian's future struggled for dominance in the minds of policymakers. One of them predicted, as Tocqueville's did, that the Indian was doomed to extinction. In this vision Indians, like characters in a Cooper novel, would retreat ever deeper into the forest in an attempt to live out their last days as a dying race in accordance with ancestral customs. According to this view, even if

---

[1]Tocqueville, *Democracy in America*, Vol. 1 (1835; rpt., New York: Alfred A. Knopf, 1980), p. 340.

[2]Tocqueville, *Democracy*, p. 342.

the hand of philanthropy were extended by a beneficent government, the "Red Man" would be either unable or unwilling to grasp it. Reinforced by the frontier mentality of Indian-hating and the continued call for land concessions, this attitude prevailed all too often in the councils of Washington. But a second and contradictory vision is also evident throughout the course of Indian-White relations. From this perspective, Indians, like most other members of the human family, were creatures of environmental and historical circumstance, fully capable of being transformed and assimilated once exposed to the "superior" influences of White society. This was clearly the view of the Congress in 1819, when it created a "civilization fund" to support missionaries on the frontier. The House Committee on Indian Affairs exhorted the Congress thus: "Put into the hands of their children the primer and the hoe, and they will naturally, in time, take hold of the plow; and as their minds become enlightened and expand, the Bible will be their book, and they will grow up in habits of morality and industry, leave the chase to those of minds less cultured, and become useful members of society."[3]

By midcentury, the Indian's fate was still unresolved, and, by 1880, the time for postponement had run out. The earlier policies of removal had now reached their logical conclusion in the form of the Indian reservation. Now, with the near extinction of the buffalo, with renewed demands by Whites for Indian land, and with the iron rails of the locomotive snaking their way across the vast stretches of prairie, it was clear that the days of the Indian were numbered. Census figures told the story. The Indian population continued to decline with each decade: 1850—400,764; 1860—339,421; 1870—313,712; 1880—306,543; 1890—248,253.[4] It was in this context that policymakers moved aggressively to assimilate the Indian into the mainstream of American life. Their efforts were greatly aided by the rise of several organizations devoted specifically to the reform of Indian policy, notably the Indian Rights Association, the Lake Mohonk Conference, and the

[3]For an overview of nineteenth-century Indian-White relations, see Francis Paul Prucha, *The Great Father: The United States Government and the American Indians* (Lincoln: University of Nebraska Press, 1984), vol. 1; Wilcomb E. Washburn, *The Indian in America* (New York: Harper & Row, 1975), pp. 146–249; Arrell Morgan Gibson, *The American Indian: Prehistory to the Present* (Lexington, MA: D. C. Heath, 1980), pp. 249–484; Robert M. Utley, *The Indian Frontier of the American West, 1846–1890* (Albuquerque: University of New Mexico Press, 1984); Robert F. Berkhofer, Jr., *The White Man's Indian: Images of the American Indian from Columbus to the Present* (New York: Alfred A. Knopf, 1978); and Brian W. Dippie, *The Vanishing American: White Attitudes and U.S. Indian Policy* (Middletown, CT: Wesleyan University Press, 1982), pp. 3–196. The House Committee on Indian Affairs quotation is taken from Henry Warner Bowden, *American Indians and Christian Missions: Studies in Cultural Conflict* (Chicago: University of Chicago Press, 1981), p. 167.

[4]Dippie, *The Vanishing American*, p. 200.

Women's National Indian Association. These groups, together with the older Board of Indian Commissioners, led a well-coordinated effort to solve the "Indian problem" along the humanitarian lines.[5]

Much of this assimilation campaign focused on education. Annual congressional appropriations for Indian education rose from $75,000 in 1880 to nearly $3 million in 1900.[6] In 1891 Congress declared that school attendance for Indian children should be compulsory. Two years later it added teeth to the measure by authorizing the Indian Bureau to "withhold rations, clothing, and other annuities" from those parents who resisted sending their children to school.[7] While these measures held weight only where schools were in existence, they provided the legal basis for stricter enforcement of school attendance. In fact, between 1880 and 1900 the number of Indian children enrolled in school more than quadrupled from 4,651 to 21,568, the latter figure representing over one-half of all Indian children of school age.[8] By 1900, Congress had created a network of Indian schools composed of 147 reservation day schools, 81 reservation boarding schools, and 25 off-reservation boarding schools.[9]

---

[5]The assimilation campaign is examined in Francis Paul Prucha, *American Indian Policy in Crisis: Christian Reformers and the Indian, 1865–1900* (Norman: University of Oklahoma Press, 1976); Loring Benson Priest, *Uncle Sam's Stepchildren: The Reformation of United States Indian Policy, 1865–1887* (New Brunswick, NJ: Rutgers University Press, 1942); Frederick E. Hoxie, *A Final Promise: The Campaign to Assimilate the Indians, 1880–1920* (Lincoln: University of Nebraska Press, 1984); Henry E. Fritz, *The Movement for Indian Assimilation, 1860–1890* (Philadelphia: University of Pennsylvania Press, 1961); and Robert Winston Mardock, *The Reformers and the American Indian* (Columbia: University of Missouri Press, 1971). For the role of reform organizations, see, in addition to the above, William T. Hagan, *The Indian Rights Association: The Herbert Welsh Years, 1882–1904* (Tucson: University of Arizona Press, 1985); Vine Deloria, Jr., "The Indian Rights Association: An Appraisal" in *The Aggressions of Civilization: Federal Indian Policy Since the 1880's*, ed. Sandra L. Cadwalder and Vine Deloria, Jr. (Philadelphia: Temple University Press, 1984), pp. 3–18; Larry E. Burgess, " 'We'll Discuss It at Mohonk'," *Quaker History, 60* (Spring 1971): 14–28; Larry E. Burgess, "The Lake Mohonk Conferences on the Indian, 1883–1916," Diss., Claremont Graduate School, 1972; Helen M. Wanken, " 'Women's Sphere' and Indian Reform: The Women's National Indian Association, 1879–1901," Diss., Marquette University, 1981. The role of the Board of Indian Commissioners is assessed in Robert H. Keller, Jr., *American Protestantism and United States Indian Policy, 1869–1882* (Lincoln: University of Nebraska Press, 1983), chap. 4; and Henry E. Fritz, "The Board of Indian Commissioners and Ethnocentric Reform, 1878–1893," in *Indian-White Relations*, ed. Jane Smith and Robert Kvasnicka (Washington, DC: Howard University Press, 1976), pp. 57–78.

[6]*Annual Report of the Secretary of the Interior*, 1913, Administrative Reports, Vol. II, p. 183.

[7]The legislative history on compulsory education for Indians during this period is traced in Theodore Fischbacher, *A Study of the Role of the Federal Government in the Education of the American Indian* (San Francisco: R and E Research Associates, 1974), pp. 125–131.

[8]*Annual Report of the Commissioner of Indian Affairs*, 1900, House Doc. No. 5, 56th Cong., 2nd sess., 1900–1901, serial 4102, p. 643; and Laurence F. Schmeckebier, *The Office of Indian Affairs* (Baltimore: Johns Hopkins Press, 1927), p. 209.

[9]Schmeckebier, *The Office of Indian Affairs*, p. 214.

This dramatic growth in Indian schooling reflects the sublime faith that Americans in general, and reformers in particular, placed in schools as agencies for social cohesion and assimilation. The extent of that faith is captured by Annie Beecher Scoville, a missionary to the Sioux, in her remarks at Lake Mohonk in 1901. Having observed the government's feverish efforts to construct schools among the Sioux, she observed:

> If there is an idol that the American people have, it is the school. What gold is to the miser, the schoolhouse is to the Yankee. If you don't believe it go out to Pine Ridge, where there are seven thousand Sioux on eight million acres of land incapable of supporting these people, and find planted over that stretch of territory thirty-two schoolhouses, standing there as a testimony to our belief in education. There is something whimsical in planting schoolhouses where no man can read, far from the highways, unneighbored by farms, and planted, not at the request of the Sioux, but because we believed it was good for them! It is a remedy for barbarism we think, and so we give the dose. Uncle Sam is like a man setting a charge of powder. The school is the slow match. He lights it and goes off whistling, sure that in time it will blow up the old life, and of its shattered pieces he will make good citizens.[10]

My purpose in this article is to reveal the fundamental considerations that underlay the late nineteenth-century campaign for the establishment of Indian schools. To characterize this campaign as merely another use of the common school as an instrument for assimilation misses, in my view, the deeper historical significance of the determined crusade to school the Native American in the ways of White society. I will examine the subject from three interpretive vantage points, and while I will occasionally discuss life in Indian schools for the purpose of illustration, my primary focus will be on the rhetoric of reform. This article, then, is largely a study of reformers' motives and how those motives were translated into educational policy.

THE PROTESTANT IDEOLOGY

The first interpretive perspective I will utilize is that of the so-called Protestant ideology.[11] In the work of John Higham, Carl Kaestle, and David Tyack and Elizabeth Hansot, ideology is seen as a set of interconnected and mutually

---

[10] *Proceedings of the Nineteenth Annual Meeting of the Lake Mohonk Conference*, 1901, pp. 17–18.

[11] John Higham, "Hanging Together: Divergent Unities in American History," *Journal of American History, 61* (June 1974): 5–28; Carl F. Kaestle, *Pillars of the Republic: Common Schools and American Society, 1780–1860* (New York: Hill & Wang, 1983), chap. 5; Carl F. Kaestle, "Ideology and American Educational History," *History of Education Quarterly, 22* (Summer 1982): 123–138; and David Tyack and Elizabeth Hansot, *Managers of Virtue: Public School Leadership in America, 1820–1980* (New York: Basic Books, 1982), pt. 1.

reinforcing beliefs and values that provide members of a given society with a sense of who they are as a collective cultural enterprise and where they fit into the historical scheme of things.

Using this broad definition, historians have undertaken the difficult task of sorting out the various strands of American ideology that gave rise to the common school in the first half of the nineteenth century. The result has been an emerging consensus around the importance of three seminal elements in American thought: Protestantism, capitalism, and republicanism. Briefly stated, the thesis is that the pan-Protestant values of common-school reformers—the importance of Bible reading, individual salvation, and personal morality—were conveniently linked to the secular values inherent in nascent capitalism; namely, the emphasis on personal industry, the sanctity of private property, and the ideal of "success." The fusion of religious and economic values made the dominant ideology powerful enough, but when these ideals were incorporated into a larger vision of national destiny—an aspect of republican thought that went beyond idealizing constitutional democracy as a form of government—the ideology assumed truly mythic proportions. As Higham notes: "America began to be seen as the spiritual center of Christendom. Thus, the Protestant ideology, instead of enshrining a single creed, exalted a sacred place."[12] By providential intention, America had a millennial destiny to impose its system onto those who stood in the path of its march to the Pacific. And if Protestantism, capitalism, and republicanism constituted the core of the ideology, the common school was seen as the natural instrument for transmitting it to rising generations of American youth.[13]

The question before us is the following: Can the Protestant ideology, which played such an important role in defining the goals of the common-school movement in the first half of the nineteenth century, also aid us in understanding the aims of Indian education in the last two decades of that century? At first, one might think not. Higham argues, for instance, that in the late nineteenth century the integrating force of the Protestant ideology

---

[12]Higham, "Hanging Together," p. 10; Kaestle, *Pillars of the Republic*, p. 76.

[13]Kaestle argues that the Protestant ideology was largely composed of ten interlocking propositions:

> "the sacredness and fragility of the Republican polity (including ideas about individualism, liberty, and virtue); the importance of the individual character in fostering social morality; the central role of personal industry in defining rectitude and merit; the delineation of a highly respected but limited domestic role for women; the importance for character building of familial and social environment (within certain racial and ethnic limitations); the sanctity and social virtues of property; the equality and abundance of economic opportunity in the United States; the superiority of American Protestant culture; the grandeur of America's destiny; and the necessity of a determined public effort to unify America's polyglot population, chiefly through education." See Kaestle, "Ideology and American Educational History," pp. 127–128.

gradually began to wane and give way to the more intensified and cohesive force of "technical unity."[14] Tyack and others have clearly established how this development manifested itself in the sphere of education, where a new generation of educational leaders labored to apply the principles of centralization, specialization, standardization, and meritocracy to all aspects of school life.[15] The quest for the "one best system" makes for an important story, yet it would be a misreading of the period to assert that the rise of educational bureaucracies somehow condemned evangelical Protestants to playing bit parts in the new educational drama. Quite the contrary. As demonstrated by Robert T. Handy, Protestantism in post–Civil War America continued to be an "aggressive dynamic form of Christianity that set out confidently to confront American life at every level, to permeate, evangelize, and Christianize it."[16] Most important, Protestants continued to wield immense influence over the course of the nation's schools. William J. Reese argues correctly that "American Evangelical Protestants of the turn of the century could still rejoice that the schools were safely theirs."[17]

Particularly significant to this story is the fact that those involved in reshaping the nation's Indian policy were firmly rooted in the Protestant tradition and, more to the point, were thoroughly imbued with the three cardinal elements of that ideology: Protestantism, capitalism, and republicanism. Indeed, by slightly recasting these three themes into Protestantism, individualization, and Americanization, we are provided with a useful angle for understanding late nineteenth-century Indian schooling. As it turns out, all three themes figured prominently in discussions concerning Indian education.

The importance placed on individualization stemmed from the belief that the greatest barrier to the Indians' assimilation was their attachment to the tribal community over and above their own individual advancement. This attachment reflected two aspects of Indian society that reformers viewed as particularly loathsome: the Indians' longstanding adherence to communal values and their general disdain for the White man's work ethic. The problem was especially acute given the fact that many reservations were almost totally dependent upon government rations for day-to-day subsistence.

---

[14]Higham, "Hanging Together," p. 23.

[15]Tyack and Hansot, *Managers of Virtue*, pp. 94–180; Tyack, *The One Best System: A History of American Urban Education* (Cambridge: Harvard University Press, 1974), pts. 2, 4.

[16]Handy, "The Protestant Quest for a Christian America, 1830–1930," *Church History, 22* (March 1953): 10. See also Handy, *A Christian America: Protestant Hopes and Historical Realities* (New York: Oxford University Press, 1971), chaps. 3–4; and Winthrop S. Hudson, *American Protestantism* (Chicago: University of Chicago Press, 1961), pp. 109–127.

[17]Reese, "The Public Schools and the Great Gates of Hell," *Educational Theory, 32* (Winter 1982): 14. See also David B. Tyack and Thomas James, "Moral Majorities and the School Curriculum: Historical Perspectives on the Legalization of Virtue," *Teachers College Record, 86* (Summer 1985): 513–535.

With the eradication of the buffalo and the rise of the reservation system, hunting-oriented economies all but collapsed. Young warriors who had once been honored for their hunting skill were now reduced to gathering at the agency for biweekly distributions of flour, sugar, coffee, and periodically, beef. What was particularly infuriating to reformers was that, in the face of such humiliating dependency, all too many Indians remained contemptuous of what Whites saw as the only path to self-respecting manhood; namely, the endless toil associated with eking out an existence from the soil. The situation was even more complicated by the Indian's lack of desire to accumulate more wealth than his neighbors; and indeed, once he did accumulate it, to squander it in elaborate gift-giving ceremonies.[18] It followed that a major objective of policymakers was to convert the Indian child to the ideal of the self-reliant man. This effort took two forms: industrial training and the inculcation of values.

In boarding schools, which accounted for a majority of Indians enrolled, half of the student's day was devoted to some form of manual or industrial training. This practice followed from the belief, as expressed by one school superintendent, that "the best education for the aborigines of our country is that which inspires them to become producers instead of remaining consumers." He maintained that although acquiring rudimentary academic skills was surely important, it was even more fundamental to teach the Indian child how to work: "A string of textbooks piled up in the storehouses high enough to surround a reservation if laid side by side will never educate a being with centuries of laziness instilled in his race."[19] Because policymakers believed that the Indian's future depended upon the schools' success at transforming hunters into farmers, it followed that boys were taught those skills required for self-sufficient farming: plowing, planting, harvesting, fence-building, stock-raising, wagon-making, harness-making, carpentry, and blacksmithing. Likewise, Indian girls were taught skills deemed appropriate for the rural housewife and mother: cooking, cleaning, and sewing.[20]

---

[18]Reformers' assessments of the Indian's economic value system were both exaggerated and misinformed. Still, the sharing and cooperative tradition of most Indian societies is richly documented in ethnographic literature. See, for instance, De Mallie, "Pine Ridge Economy, Cultural and Historical Perspectives" in *American Indian Economic Development*, ed. Sam Stanley (The Hague: Monton Publishers, 1978), p. 250; Royal B. Hassrick, *The Sioux* (Norman: University of Oklahoma Press, 1964), pp. 36–37, 296; Edward P. Dozier, *Hano: A Tewa Indian Community in Arizona* (New York: Holt, Rinehart & Winston, 1966), pp. 88–89; Malcolm McFee, *Modern Blackfeet: Montanans on a Reservation* (New York: Holt, Rinehart & Winston, 1972), p. 46; and E. Adamson Hoebel, *The Cheyennes: Indians of the Great Plains* (New York: Holt, Rinehart & Winston, 1962), p. 94.

[19]*Annual Report of the Commissioner of Indian Affairs*, 1886, House Exec. Doc. No. 1, 49th Cong., 2nd sess., 1886–1887, Serial 2467, pp. 221–222.

[20]"Rules for Indian Schools," *Annual Report of the Commissioner of Indian Affairs*, 1890, House Exec. Doc. No. 1, 51st Cong., 2nd sess., 1890–1891, Serial 2841, pp. CXLVI, CLII.

Individualization also entailed persuading the student to embrace a cluster of related values and beliefs that, taken together, served to portray capitalism as a model social order and the rugged individualist as an ideal personality. For U.S. Senator Henry Dawes, the solution to the Indian problem was to "teach him to stand alone first, then to walk, then to dig, then to plant, then to hoe, then to gather, and then to *Keep*"—the last step being a vital one.[21] Similarly, Merrill Gates reminded those at Lake Mohonk in 1896 that the primary challenge to philanthropy was to awaken "wants" in the Indian. Then, and only then, Gates argued, could the Indian be coaxed "out of the blanket and into trousers and trousers with a *pocket that aches to be filled with dollars*"! [emphasis added][22] Commissioner of Indian Affairs John Oberly believed that the Indian student should be taught the "exalting egotism of American civilization, so that he will say 'I' instead of 'We,' and 'This is mine' instead of 'This is ours.' "[23] Thus did educators seek to create in the Indian student's mind the mental and moral concept of possessive individualism. In textbooks, classrooms, workshops, and sermons, the importance of the key American values of industriousness, thrift, perseverance, and acquisitiveness was continually drummed home. For the students at Phoenix Indian School, the message of individualism came in the form of a poem, "There's Always a Way," printed in the school newspaper:

There's always a way to rise, my boy,
Always a way to advance;
Yet the road that leads to Mount Success
Does not pass by the way of chance
But goes through the stations of Work and Strife,
Through the valley of Persevere.
And the man that succeeds, while others fail,
Must be willing to pay most dear.[24]

The Protestant ideology also required that the Indian child be Christianized and, ideally, Protestantized. Reformers invariably dismissed the Indian's native religion as a hodgepodge of barbaric rites and ceremonies totally devoid of any moral content. Beyond this, native beliefs were condemned for encouraging in Indians a naive and childish tendency to seek spiritual meanings and truth in the natural world, for their failure to acknowledge any associa-

[21] *Journal of the Thirteenth Annual Conference with Representatives of Missionary Boards*, in the *Annual Report of the Board of Indian Commissioners*, 1883, House Exec. Doc. No. 1, 48th Cong., 2nd sess., 1883–1884, Serial 2191, pp. 731–732.

[22] *Proceedings of the Fourteenth Annual Meeting of the Lake Mohonk Conference*, 1896, pp. 11–12.

[23] *Annual Report of the Commissioner of Indian Affairs*, 1888, House Exec. Doc. No. 1, 50th Cong., 2nd sess., 1888–1889, Serial 2637, p. 89.

[24] *Native American*, September 13, 1902, p. 1.

tion between religious activity and material advancement, and finally, for their acceptance of polygamous marriage and extended kinship relationships as legitimate and desirable social arrangements.[25] What reformers were objecting to was the fact that Native American religions reinforced and reflected the values and cultural patterns of Indian life, something they were committed to erasing.[26]

It followed that the religious aims of Indian schooling fell into two categories. On the one hand, reformers believed that Indian children should be introduced to essential Christian doctrine, and in the process come to feel the "pulsing life-tide of Christ's life." On the other hand, they should be subjected to a rigorous program of moral training. It was in this realm that the religious and acquisitive values of Protestant America were to be given complementary expression. Indian children must be taught to love their neighbor, but they must also be told about "the road that leads to Mount Success."[27]

The Christian message was communicated in a number of ways. In day schools, it came in the form of *McGuffey Readers*, classroom prayers, and hymn singing. In boarding schools, it was expressed in the form of Sunday church services, nightly prayer meetings, and a host of religious clubs. Native American autobiographies from this period clearly show that the Protestant impulse profoundly influenced life in Indian schools. For instance, Jason Betzinez, an Apache, tells us that his introduction to Christianity came at Carlisle Indian School in Pennsylvania, where, as a result of attending church on Sundays and frequent prayer meetings, the "influence became stronger and stronger as I came to understand English better. It changed my whole life."[28] Similarly, Thomas Wildcat Alford, a Shawnee, who on the eve of departure for a distant boarding school was instructed by tribal chiefs not to listen to the White man's preaching, also fell under the spell of the

---

[25]The Protestant missionary effort has been examined in Robert F. Berkhofer, Jr., *Salvation and the Savage: An Analysis of Protestant Missions and American Indian Response, 1787–1862* (New York: Atheneum, 1972); Bowden, *American Indians and Christian Missions*; and Keller, *American Protestantism and United States Indian Policy.*

[26]Hopelessly ethnocentric, reformers had little appreciation for the richness and diversity of Native American religious life. For an introduction to this aspect of Indian societies, see Joseph Epes Brown, *The Spiritual Legacy of the American Indian* (Crossroad: New York, 1982); Ake Hultkrantz, *Belief and Worship in Native North America* (Syracuse: Syracuse University Press, 1981); Hultkrantz, *The Religions of the American Indians* (Berkeley: University of California Press, 1979); Hartley Burr Alexander, *The World's Rim: Great Mysteries of the North American Indians* (Lincoln: University of Nebraska Press, 1953); Sam D. Gill, *Native American Religions: An Introduction* (Belmont, CA: Wadsworth Publishing Co., 1982).

[27]See the remarks of Merrill Gates in the *Proceedings of the Eleventh Annual Meeting of the Lake Mohonk Conference*, 1893, pp. 11–12; and Daniel Dorchester, "Moral Training in Indian Schools," *Annual Report of the Commissioner of Indian Affairs*, 1891, House Exec. Doc. No. 1, 52nd Cong., 1st sess., 1891–1892, Serial 2934, p. 542.

[28]Betzinez, *I Fought with Geronimo* (Harrisburg, WV: Stackpole Co., 1959), p. 156.

evangelical promise. At first, Alford was able to resist the religious onslaught, "but as time passed," he explains, "and the interest of my teachers became stronger, their pleas more insistent, I could not ignore the subject. I began to consider the religious beliefs and to study the Gospel of Jesus Christ." In time, he wrote, he came to know "deep in my soul that Jesus Christ was my Savior."[29] Don Talayesva, a Hopi boy who attended an off-reservation school in Riverside, California, tells us of being torn between his ancestral Hopi beliefs and the White man's religion. He remembers conjuring up this sermon for the school YMCA meeting:

> Well, my partners, I am asked to speak a few words for Jesus. I am glad that I came to Sherman and learned to read and cipher. Now I discover that Jesus was a good writer. So I am thankful that Uncle Sam taught me to read in order that I may understand the Scriptures and take my steps along God's road. When I get a clear understanding of the Gospel I shall return home and preach it to my people in darkness. I will teach them all I know about Jesus Christ, the Heavenly Father, and the Holy Ghost. So I advise you boys to do your best and pray to God to give us a good understanding. Then we will be ready for Jesus to come and take us up to heaven. I don't want any of my friends to be thrown into the lake of hell fire where there is suffering and sorrow forever. Amen.[30]

These passages should not be taken as representative responses to the Christian message; many students, to the exasperation of school officials, stubbornly adhered to their native beliefs. These passages simply illustrate the extent to which the evangelical spirit permeated the atmosphere of Indian schooling.

When policymakers turned to the third aim of Indian schooling—Americanization—they were primarily addressing the issue of the Indian's future political status. Two issues were involved here: the status of the tribal unit as a collective political entity (that is to say, tribal sovereignty), and the individual Indian's citizenship status. In the minds of reformers the two issues were inextricably linked: the elimination of tribal sovereignty would facilitate the individual Indian's entry into citizenship. The political sovereignty of Indian tribes had, in fact, been eroding steadily throughout the nineteenth century. By 1871, when Congress declared that the government would no longer conduct its relations with Indians by treaty, the process was nearly complete; henceforth, Indians were to be regarded as mere "wards" of the government.[31] Meanwhile, the Indian reservation was an

---

[29]Alford, *Civilization, as Told to Florence Drake* (Norman: University of Oklahoma Press, 1936), pp. 105–106.

[30]Leo W. Simmons, ed., *Sun Chief: The Autobiography of a Hopi Indian* (New Haven: Yale University Press, 1942), pp. 116–117.

[31]The changing legal status of the American Indian during this period is reviewed in Prucha,

anomaly in the American system. Only when Indians were separated from the larger tribal unit, the government held, would they be truly fit for citizenship. Congress could simply declare them citizens, but was hesitant to do so. Most policymakers agreed with Commissioner of Indian Affairs Ezra Hayt, who contended that Indians needed "a long tutelage before launching them into the world to manage their own affairs."[32] On two questions, then, reformers were in agreement: First, the Indians' connections to their tribal unit and the reservation had to be severed if they were to be absorbed into the larger body politic; and second, the government had a special responsibility to prepare them for citizenship. In this matter the schools would have a special role to play.

Education for citizenship focused on language instruction and political socialization. The connection between language and citizenship stemmed from the belief that, along with all citizens, the Indian child should be compelled to read, write, and speak the English language. As Commissioner of Indian Affairs J. D. C. Atkins argued in 1887: "If we expect to infuse into the rising generation the leaven of American citizenship, we must remove the stumbling blocks of hereditary customs and manners, and of these language is one of the most important elements." According to Atkins, "no unity or community of feeling can be established among different peoples unless they are brought to speak the same language and thus become imbued with the like ideas of duty."[33] That same year, John Riley, Superintendent of Indian Schools, echoed the sentiments of his superior. Teaching English to the Indian, he argued, would reduce the Indian's prejudice toward the White man's ways, would enhance the Indian's understanding of the "spirit of the laws and institutions under which they are to live," and finally, would lessen their vulnerability to "unprincipled white men."[34] The bottom line was that Indians, as a colonized people, could legitimately be expected to take on the tongue of their conquerors. Again, according to Atkins, citizenship required a certain amount of cultural absorption and "nothing so surely and perfectly stamps upon an individual a national characteristic as language." Besides, Atkins

---

American Indian Policy in Crisis, chap. 11; Walter L. Williams, "From Independence to Wardship: The Legal Process of Erosion of American Indian Sovereignty, 1810–1903," *American Indian Culture and Research Journal,* 7 (1984): 5–32; and Alvin J. Ziontz, "Indian Litigation," in Cadwalder and Deloria, *Aggressions of Civilization,* chap. 7.

[32]*Annual Report of the Commissioner of Indian Affairs,* 1878, House Exec. Doc. No. 1, 45th Cong., 3rd sess., 1878–1879, Serial 1850, p. 444. All Indians were granted citizenship by an Act of Congress in 1924. See Gary C. Stein, "The Indian Citizenship Act of 1924," *New Mexico Historical Review,* 47 (July 1972): 257–274.

[33]*Annual Report of the Commissioner of Indian Affairs,* 1887, reprinted in Francis Paul Prucha, *Americanizing the American Indians: Writings by the "Friends of the Indian," 1880–1900* (Cambridge: Harvard University Press, 1973), pp. 201–203.

[34]*Annual Report of the Commissioner of Indian Affairs,* 1887, House Exec. Doc. No. 1, 50th Cong., 1st sess., 1887–1888, Serial 2542, p. 763.

continued, "this language, which is good enough for a white man and a black man, ought to be good enough for the red man."[35]

If the issue of language was largely instrumental, the real focus of citizenship education was the Indian's political socialization. On the one hand, this meant instruction in the rights and duties of citizenship and in the principles of the U.S. Constitution. No less important, however, was the need to awaken a "fervent patriotism" in Indian students. They should, according to Commissioner Morgan, "be taught to look upon America as their home and upon the United States Government as their friend and benefactor."[36] The campaign to win the Indian's political allegiance was in part carried out in the traditional U.S. History course.[37] Beyond textbook instruction, schools were encouraged to teach students patriotic songs, political recitations, and, perhaps most important, involve them in patriotic rituals, including the celebration of national holidays.

Since boarding-school students wore special government uniforms and were subjected to a daily routine of marching and drilling, these patriotic rituals occasionally assumed elaborate proportions. When President William McKinley visited Phoenix Indian School in 1901, for example, the entire student body performed a highly disciplined marching routine before lining up in front of the President, who looked on from the reviewing stand. "There they stood for an instant, 700 pairs of eyes gazing sharply and intently at the 'great father,' " the school newspaper reported, and then at the sound of a bugle, the Indians roared in unison: "I give my head and my heart to my country; one country, one language, and one flag."[38]

In remote outposts, patriotic rituals were more modest, but equally pointed. A Hopi memoir describes an observance at a reservation boarding school in the Southwest: "In May we had a decoration celebration. We stuck little flags in our caps, took bunches of flowers, and marched out to the graves of two soldiers who had come out here to fight the Hopi and had died."[39] In another school, students were asked to participate in a political pageant celebrating

---

[35]*Annual Report of the Commissioner of Indian Affairs*, 1887, reprinted in Prucha, *Americanizing the American Indians*, pp. 200–203.

[36]*Annual Report of the Commissioner of Indian Affairs*, 1889, reprinted in Prucha, *Americanizing the American Indians*, p. 233; and "Instructions to Indian Agents in Regards to Inculcation of Patriotism in Indian Schools," *Annual Report of the Commissioner of Indian Affairs*, 1890, House of Exec. Doc. 1, 51st Cong., 2nd sess., 1890–1891, Serial 2841, p. CLXVII.

[37]For the belief system of U.S. history texts during this period see Ruth M. Elson, *Guardians of Tradition: American Schoolbooks of the Nineteenth Century* (Lincoln: University of Nebraska Press, 1964); and Laurence M. Hauptman, "Mythologizing Westward Expansion: Schoolbooks and the Image of the American Frontier before Turner," *Western Historical Quarterly*, 8 (July 1977): 269–282.

[38]Quoted in *Annual Report of the Commissioner of Indian Affairs*, 1901, House Exec. Doc. 5, 57th Cong., 1st sess., 1901–1902, Serial 4290, p. 524.

[39]Simmons, *Sun Chief*, p. 99.

the day that Europeans first set foot on the shores of the New World. An Indian student, dressed as Columbus, recited the lines:

Then boomed the Pinta's signal gun!
The first that ever broke
The sleep of the new world—the sound
Echoing to forest depths profound,
A continent awoke![40]

A continent awoke? From what? This question suggests another line of investigation, one that explores the idea that reformers, in their discussion of Indian policy in general and Indian schooling in particular, were forced to draw upon images more fundamental than those generated by the Protestant ideology, images at least as old as that fateful day in 1492, when Columbus and his band of voyagers first confronted not only a New World, but, as Tzvetan Todorov has put it, "the question of the other," the people Columbus called *Indios*.[41]

THE CIVILIZATION–SAVAGISM PARADIGM

When Europeans, and later, European-Americans, first encountered the Native American's "otherness," they made a distinction between Indians and Whites that by the late eighteenth century had become the central reference point for explaining the cultural chasm that separated the two races. The basic idea was that peoples on the globe were at various stages in their evolution from "savagism" to "civilization." As the theory went, while the Whites were for the most part civilized, Indians were still largely savages. There was room for minor variations where particular groups or societies were involved, but the generalization was said to be true in the main. Because Indians—and here the images came flooding forth—indulged in barbaric religious practices, relied on hunting and gathering for subsistence, were disdainful of private property and wealth, and generally lived out their lives in pagan ignorance of all things civilized, they were culturally worthless. Sometimes noble, sometimes ignoble, they were nevertheless savages.[42]

---

[40]*Southern Workman*, March 1892, p. 42.

[41]Todorov, *The Conquest of America: The Question of the Other*, trans. Richard Howard (New York: Harper & Row, 1984).

[42]Nineteenth-century images of the Indian are examined in Ray Allen Billington, *Land of Savagery, Land of Promise: The European Image of the American Frontier* (New York: W. W. Norton, 1981); Elemire Zolla, *The Writer and the Shaman: A Morphology of the American Indian* (New York: Harcourt Brace Jovanovich, 1969), chaps. 4–7; Berkhofer, *The White Man's Indian*, pts. 1–3; Roy Harvey Pearce, *The Savages of America: A Study of the Indian and the Idea of Civilization* (Baltimore: The Johns Hopkins Press, 1965); Reginald Horsman, *Race and Manifest: The Origins of American Racial Anglo-Saxonism* (Cambridge: Harvard University Press, 1981), chaps. 6–10; and Thomas F. Gossett, *Race: The History of an Idea in America* (New York: Schocken, 1965), chaps. 3–4, 10.

Central to the civilization–savagism paradigm was the concept of historical process. History was seen as the story of man's progressive movement toward the ideal of civilization. If one wished to see the process unfold, one had only to look at America. Near the end of his life Jefferson wrote to a friend:

> Let a philosophic observer commence a journey from the savages of the Rocky Mountains, eastwardly towards our sea-coast. These he would observe in the earliest stage of association living under no law but that of nature, subsisting and covering themselves with the flesh and skins of wild beasts. He would next find those on our frontiers in the pastoral state, raising domestic animals to supply the defects of hunting. Then succeed our own semi-barbarous citizens, the pioneers of the advance of civilization, and so in his progress he would meet the gradual shades of improving man until he would reach his, as yet, most improved state in our seaport towns. This, in fact, is equivalent to a survey, in time, of the progress of man from the infancy of creation to the present day.[43]

Just as savagery must give way to civilization, Jefferson and his contemporaries reasoned, so Indian ways must give way to White ways. Whether Indians as a people would survive remained an open question. Jefferson seems to have genuinely hoped and believed that they would. In any event, traditional Indian ways were destined to perish. The alternatives before them were clear: civilization or extinction.[44]

Throughout the nineteenth century, the idea of civilization remained a fixed reference point in all discussions of the Indian question. Coincidentally, in 1877, just as the movement to reform Indian policy was getting under way, the idea received impressive scholarly support with the appearance of Lewis Henry Morgan's *Ancient Society*.[45] A cultural evolutionist, Morgan identified seven stages in the path to human progress: lower savagery, middle savagery, upper savagery, lower barbarism, middle barbarism, upper barbarism, and civilization. On Morgan's scale, North American Indians fell somewhere between middle savagery and middle barbarism, depending upon the particular attributes of a given culture. Numerous factors determined where Morgan placed various societies on his categorical scale, but three were deemed to be of particular importance in the passage to civilization: the acceptance of monogamous marriage and the nuclear family as the basic unit in society, the reliance on agriculture as the basis for subsistence, and a firm belief in private property as the proper basis for economic and social organization. Morgan found Indian societies wanting in one or

---

[43]Quoted in Pearce, *The Savages of America*, p. 155.

[44]The philanthropic tradition in early federal Indian policy is treated in Bernard W. Sheehan, *Seeds of Extinction: Jeffersonian Philanthropy and the American Indian* (Chapel Hill: University of North Carolina Press, 1973); and Prucha, *The Great Father*, vol. 1, chapter 5.

[45]Lewis Henry Morgan, *Ancient Society* (New York: Henry Holt & Co., 1877).

more of these criteria. Nevertheless, he was convinced that Indians, with proper guidance from a benevolent government, were fully capable of acquiring civilized ways and eventually being absorbed into the mainstream of American life.[46]

Late nineteenth-century reformers subscribed not only to the law of civilized progress, but also to its corollary, that the Indians' only hope for survival depended upon their assimilation into mainstream American society. According to Commissioner of Indian Affairs Henry Price: "Savage and civilized life cannot live and prosper on the same ground. One of the two must die."[47] As Secretary of the Interior Carl Shurz pointed out, time was of the essence: "To civilize them, which was once only a benevolent fancy, has now become an absolute necessity, if we mean to save them." Indians were a dying race.[48]

Since Indians were on the brink of extinction, the civilization–savagism paradigm posed a question that was of immense importance to the Indians' destiny: Must the process of social evolution be as painstakingly slow for Indians as it had been for Whites? No, reformers answered; where human progress was involved, historical time was to be measured in relative rather than absolute terms. Moreover, the school could be the instrument for hastening the evolutionary process. As Commissioner Morgan pointed out, a civilizing education was capable of carrying a single generation of Indian youth across "the dreary chasm of a thousand years of tedious evo-

---

[46]For a discussion of Morgan's ideas see Dwight W. Hoover, *The Red and the Black* (Chicago: Rand McNally, 1976), pp. 157–160; Berkhofer, *The White Man's Indian*, pp. 52–54; and Gossett, *Race*, pp. 248–251. The idea of social evolution also figured prominently in the works of sociologists Herbert Spencer and William Graham Sumner and historian Frederick Jackson Turner. However, in the hands of these writers there was little room for a happy resolution to the Indian story. See Richard Hofstadter, *Social Darwinism in American Thought* (Philadelphia: University of Pennsylvania Press, 1944; rpt. ed., Boston: Beacon Press, 1962), chaps. 2–3; David A. Nichols, "Civilization over Savage: Frederick Jackson Turner and the Indian," *South Dakota History, 2* (Fall 1972): 383–405; and Robert F. Berkhofer, "Space, Time, Culture and the New Frontier," *Agricultural History, 38* (January 1964): 21–30.

[47]*Annual Report of the Commissioner of Indian Affairs*, 1881, House Exec. Doc. No. 1, 47th Cong., 1st sess., 1881–1882, Serial 2018, pp. 1–2.

[48]Shurz, "Present Aspects of the Indian Problems," *North American Review*, No. 133 (July 1881): 7. See also *Annual Report of the Secretary of the Interior*, 1886, House Exec. Doc. No. 1, 49th Cong., 2nd sess., 1886–1887, Serial 2467, p. 4; and *Annual Report of the Commissioner of Indian Affairs*, 1888, House Exec. Doc. 1, 50th Cong., 2nd sess., 1888–1889, Serial 2637, p. 262. While reformers' statements on the possibility of Indian extinction may reflect the rising tide of social Darwinism, I would argue that they were much more rooted in the Jeffersonian tradition that hoped for a philanthropic resolution of the Indian question. For the impact of social Darwinism on American thought, see Hofstadter, *Social Darwinism in American Thought*; and Robert Bannister, *Social Darwinism: Science and Myth in Anglo-American Social Thought* (Philadelphia: Temple University Press, 1979). This is also an underlying theme in Stephen Jay Gould's *The Mismeasure of Man* (New York: W. W. Norton, 1981).

lution."[49] Addressing the Lake Mohonk Conference, U.S. Commissioner of Education William Torrey Harris concurred:

> But shall we say to the tribal people that they shall not come to these higher things unless they pass through all the intermediate stages, or can we teach them directly these higher things, and save them from the slow progress of the ages? In the light of Christian civilization we say there is a method of rapid progress. Education has become of great potency in our hands, and we believe that we can now vicariously save them very much that the white race has had to go through. Look at feudalism. Look at the village community stage. . . . We have had our tribulation with them. But we say to lower races: we can help you out of these things. We can help you avoid the imperfect stages that follow them on the way to our level. Give us your children and we will educate them in the Kindergarten and in the schools. We will give them letters, and make them acquainted with the printed page. With these comes emancipation from mere personal authority, from the authority of the master, from the authority of the overseer and the oracle. With these comes the great emancipation, and the school will give you that.[50]

Schools, then, could not only civilize; they could civilize quickly.

It should be clear by now that where the education of Indians was concerned, fundamental and unique considerations come into play that are unaccounted for in the Protestant ideology. To be sure, there is nothing in the first interpretation that contradicts the one emerging here. Indeed, one might reasonably argue that nineteenth-century discussions on the fate of the Indian were simply the by-product of the historical forces unleashed by one of the most consequential strands in the Protestant ideology; namely, the belief that it was America's destiny to extend European-American institutions and ways of life across the continent. Moreover, the doctrine of progress was certainly as deeply embedded in the tradition of evangelical Protestantism as it was in the Enlightenment tradition of Jefferson. The fact remains, however, that when policymakers turned their attention to the Indian question, they invariably shifted to a frame of reference and a descriptive language tailor-made for the occasion—they shifted to the civilization–savagism model. Needless to say, to define the Indian's "otherness" in terms of savagery was more than a little self-serving. To dismiss the Indian as a savage was surely a convenient means of legitimizing the history of Indian-White relations, a history that, if viewed objectively, might cast a shadow over the righteous pretensions of the American empire.

---

[49] *Annual Report of the Commissioner of Indian Affairs,* 1891, House Exec. Doc. No. 1, 52nd Cong., 1st sess., 1891–1892, Serial 2934, p. 5.

[50] *Proceedings of the Thirteenth Annual Meeting of the Lake Mohonk Conference of Friends of the Indian,* 1895, pp. 36–37.

It should be noted that the Protestant ideology, including its educational prescriptions (Protestantization, individualization, and Americanization), was certainly relevant to the discussion of what it would take to civilize the Indian. When policymakers spoke of Christianizing Indians, they always assumed that their conversion would be an important step in civilizing them as well. Thus, Merrill Gates proclaimed at Lake Mohonk that introducing the Indian to Christianity could "do in one generation most of that which evolution takes centuries to do."[51] And although the reformers preferred that Protestantism prevail over Catholicism in the battle for the Indian's heart and soul, most saw the Indian's conversion from paganism to any Christian faith as progress. Even Herbert Welsh, well known for his anti-Catholic sentiment, could appreciate the fact that "the great religious bodies, the Roman communion on the one side, and the Protestant communions on the other, should try to recognize the value of each other's work, at least as an instrument of civilization."[52] Citizenship education was regarded as a civilizing force as well. Instruction in the rights and duties of citizenship would prepare the Indian child for full participation in the political life of one of the most civilized nations on earth. As for language instruction, Commissioner Atkins was convinced that "the first step to be taken toward civilization, toward teaching the Indians the mischief and folly of continuing in their barbarous practices, is to teach them in the English language."[53] Finally, the Indian's individualization would surely advance the cultural elevation process. "There is an utter barbarism in which property has almost no existence," claimed Merrill Gates. "The tribal organization tends to retain men in such barbarism. It is a great step gained when you awaken in an Indian the desire for the acquisition of property of his own, by his own honest labor."[54] In this respect, as in others, the Protestant ideology shaped reformers' thinking as to what they must teach the Indians if they were to civilize them.

The idea of civilization, however, remained a fundamental frame of reference for discussions on Indian education. Its impact on the overall direction of Indian schooling can be illustrated in three ways. First, it set the boundaries

---

[51]*Proceedings of the Fourteenth Annual Meeting of the Lake Mohonk Conference of Friends of the Indian*, 1900, reprinted in Prucha, *Americanizing the American Indians*, p. 339. See also Herbert Welsh, *Four Weeks Among Some of the Sioux Tribes of Dakota and Nebraska Together with a Brief Consideration of the Indian Problem* (Philadelphia: Horace F. McCann, 1882), p. 21.

[52]Welsh, "The Meaning of the Dakota Outbreak," *Scribner's Magazine*, April, 1891, p. 452. Welsh's anti-Catholicism came through in his efforts to end the government's support for contract schools (missionary schools supported by congressional funds) when Catholics began to capture an increasing percentage of appropriations. See Francis Paul Prucha, *The Churches and the Indian Schools, 1888–1912* (Lincoln: University of Nebraska Press, 1979), chap. 3.

[53]*Annual Report of the Commissioner of Indian Affairs*, 1887, reprinted in Prucha, *Americanizing the American Indians*, p. 203.

[54]*Annual Report of the Secretary of the Interior*, 1885, House Exec. Doc. No. 1, 49th Cong., 1st sess., 1885–1886, Serial 2378, p. 777.

for one of the most troublesome questions confronting the Indian Bureau: What type of institution—the day school, the reservation boarding school, or the off-reservation boarding school—was best suited to accomplish the Indian child's transformation? This question forced policymakers to return to first principles. In time, they would conclude that the civilizing process could be carried out most effectively if it were conducted in an environment isolated from the countervailing influence of savagery, that is, at a distance from the tribal community. By the late 1870s, this resulted in a general preference for the reservation boarding school over the day school. The problem with the day school, officials in the field complained, was that although children were taught the curriculum of civilization during the day, they were instructed in the ways of savagery at night. By removing children from the camp and cloistering them in a boarding school for nine months of the year, the civilizing process could be carried on much more efficiently.[55]

By the early 1880s, however, the enthusiasm for reservation boarding schools had begun to wane. Students, it seemed, still felt the pull of traditional life beyond the school fence, and they frequently ran away. Furthermore, during the annual summer vacation, many students suffered severe cases of "relapse." More than one Indian agent would observe "how soon they seem to forget all they have been taught, after they return to camp."[56] According to another agent:

> Immediately following the close of the school the children laid aside the clothing furnished them and donned the kind the camp Indians wear. A number of them continue to come about the agency, but not a word can one be induced to speak in English. They attend our Sabbath services, but they can not be prevailed upon to sing, while in school the majority of them sing elegantly. These are some of the reasons why the results of the school are not satisfactory to me. I really believe that one year's schooling away from the influence of the camp Indians would do the child more good than four at the agency.[57]

A good number of policymakers and reformers agreed. The result was the creation of a new institution, the off-reservation boarding school, where students were schooled in the ways of Whites for an uninterrupted period of five years before returning home. As it turned out, both types of boarding schools, reservation and off-reservation, would remain the cornerstone of the Indian school system for years to come. One thing remained certain: in order for savagism to be countermanded, the Indian child had to be educated

[55]*Annual Report of the Secretary of the Interior*, 1880, House Exec. Doc. No. 1, 46th Cong., 3rd sess., 1880–1881, Serial 1959, p. 7.

[56]*Annual Report of the Commissioner of Indian Affairs*, 1879, House Exec. Doc. No. 1, 46th Cong., 2nd sess., 1879–1880, Serial 1910, p. 174.

[57]*Annual Report of the Commissioner of Indian Affairs*, 1889, House Exec. Doc. No. 1, 51st Cong., 1st sess., 1889–1890, Serial 2725, p. 119.

in an isolated environment. Hence, by 1900 close to 85 percent of Indian children enrolled in school were attending boarding schools.[58]

A second impact of the idea of civilization on Indian schooling can be seen by examining the nature of the educational program itself; namely, the sheer comprehensiveness of it. A close examination of the institutional life of Indian schools reveals that they were waging an all-out assault on the child's "otherness." For the war against savagery to be successful, reformers decided, it must be waged uncompromisingly on every aspect of the child's being. Thus, while their bronze skin would never wash white, the Indian children could otherwise be taught to look, dress, eat, walk, and think like civilized Whites. The alteration process can be seen in the following account of the opening day at Pine Ridge boarding school in South Dakota, about 1880. The description was written by Julia McGillycuddy, wife of the government's agent, Valentine McGillycuddy.

> On the opening day, hundreds of curious Indians—bucks, squaws, and children—hung about the building wondering just what was going to happen to the 200 youngsters sequestered within it. McGillycuddy advised pulling down the shades at the windows in the large bathroom on the ground floor to exclude the gaze of the inquisitive.
>
> The first step toward civilizing these primitive children was to purge them of various uncleanliness. The several bathrooms as well as the laundry were the scenes of activity, the hair-cutting to be accomplished first, followed by a bath which would include washing the heads as a labor-saving device.
>
> In each bathroom a teacher armed with shears was prepared to begin operations. Curious peepers stood close to the windows on the ground floor, deeply regretful of the drawn shades which barred their observation of the activities carried on behind them. There the matron seated a small boy and taking a lousy braid in one hand, raised the shears hanging by a chain from her waist. A single clip and the filthy braid could be severed. But unfortunately, at that moment a breeze blew back the shade from the window. The previously baffled effort of a youngster plastered against the casing on the outside of the window was now rewarded by a fleeting glimpse of his playmate seated

[58]*Reports of the Department of Interior*, 1909, Administrative Reports, Vol. II, p. 89. For selected aspects of the boarding school story see David Wallace Adams, "Schooling the Hopi: Federal Indian Policy Writ Small, 1887–1917," *Pacific Historical Review, 48* (August 1979): 335–356; Wilbert H. Ahern, "The Returned Indians: Hampton Institute and Its Indian Alumni, 1879–1893," *Journal of Ethnic Studies, 10* (Winter 1983): 101–124; Robert A. Trennert, "From Carlisle to Phoenix: The Rise and Fall of the Indian Outing System, 1878–1930," *Pacific Historical Review, 52* (August 1983): 267–291; Trennert, "Educating Indian Girls at Nonreservation Boarding Schools, 1878–1920," *Western Historical Quarterly, 13* (July 1982): 271–290; Margaret Connell Szasz, "Federal Boarding Schools and the Indian Child: 1920–1960," *South Dakota History, 7* (Fall 1977): 371–384; and Sally J. McBeth, *Ethnic Identity and the Boarding School Experience of West-Central Oklahoma American Indians* (Washington, DC: University Press of America, 1983).

in the chair and a tall lean woman with a pair of shears in her hand prepared to divest the boy of his hair—Delilah bringing calamity upon an embryo Samson.

Like a war whoop rang out the cry: "*Pahin kaksa, pahin kaksa!*" The enclosure rang with alarm, it invaded every room in the building and floated out on the prairie. No warning of fire or flood or tornado or hurricane, not even the approach of an enemy could have more effectively emptied the building as well as the grounds of the new school as did the ominous cry. "They are cutting the hair!" Through doors and windows the children flew, down the steps, through the gates and over fences in mad flight toward the Indian villages, followed by the mob of bucks and squaws as though all were pursued by a bad spirit. They had been suspicious of the school from the beginning; now they knew it was intended to bring disgrace upon them.

McGillycuddy's raised hands, his placating shouts, and his stern commands were less effective than they had been on occasions of threatened outbreak. He was impotent to stem the flight. He calmed the excited teachers, assuring them that the schoolhouse would soon again be filled with children. But their faces expressed disappointment as well as chagrin over the apparent failure of his attempt to civilize the Sioux.[59]

All this was necessary, we are expected to understand, because Indians were too savage to know what was good for them. This leads us to a third implication of the civilization ideal—namely the belief that the student must be made to embrace the essential elements of the civilization–savagism paradigm. The Indian child must come to know what Whites already knew—that Whites were civilized and Indians were savages. The entire boarding school experience, of course, implied this message, but occasionally the point had to be made outright. At Hampton Institute in Hampton, Virginia, for instance, where Indians were educated along with Blacks, it appears to have permeated the entire curriculum.[60] Thus, the following section of a student's examination was published in the school newspaper under the heading "Work and Fun in the Geography Class":

9. To what race do we all belong?
9. The Human race.

---

[59]McGillycuddy, *McGillycuddy, Agent: A Biography of Dr. Valentine T. McGillycuddy* (Stanford: Stanford University Press, 1941), pp. 205–206.

[60]Hampton's Indian work is examined in Frances Greenwood Peabody, *Education for Life: The Story of Hampton Institute* (New York: Doubleday, Page and Co., 1918); David Wallace Adams, "Education in Hues: Red and Black at Hampton Institute, 1878–1893," *South Atlantic Quarterly*, 76 (Spring 1977): 159–176; William H. Robinson, "Indian Education at Hampton Institute," in *Stony the Road: Chapters in the History of Hampton Institute*, ed. Keith L. Schall (Charlottesville: University of Virginia Press, 1977), pp. 1–33; and Joseph Willard Tingey, "Indians and Blacks Together: An Experiment in Biracial Education at Hampton Institute, 1878–1923," Ed.D. Diss., Teachers College, Columbia University, 1978.

10. How many classes belong to this race?
10. There are five large classes belonging to the Human race.
11. Which are the first?
11. The white people are the strongest.
12. Which are the next?
12. The Mongolians or yellows.
13. The next?
13. The Ethiopians or blacks.
14. Next?
14. The Americans or reds.
15. Tell me something of the white people.
15. The Caucasian is away ahead of all of the other races—he thought more than any other race, he thought that somebody must made the earth, and if the white people did not find that out, nobody would never know it—it is God who made the world.[61]

An underlying assumption of the civilization–savagism paradigm was that although Indians were at the bottom of the ladder of civilization, the ladder could eventually be climbed. The proper note to be struck, then, was one that simultaneously inspired both humiliation and hope in the student. In 1893, Philip Garrett, an influential member of the Indian Rights Association, attempted to strike just this note when addressing the graduating class of Carlisle Indian School. Garrett began by reminding his audience that their race had been "thrown by the providence of God in the pathway of a mighty and resistless tide of civilization." Since the only path of survival was to adopt civilized ways, Garrett continued, the Indian would have to make the best of a difficult situation. Indeed, they ought to be thankful for their situation. Left to their own resources and the painstakingly slow process of social evolution, they might have been mired in the backwaters of savagery for several generations. Instead, a benevolent government was offering them a different and brighter prospect: Students had a "unique opportunity to show the marvelous change that can be wrought in a single generation by the aid of good schools, and the lessons of centuries."[62]

As one considers these statements, the question comes to mind: What were the ultimate concerns that drove reformers to make such statements? The answer, in part, no doubt lies in the fact that they truly believed them. As philanthropic spokesmen for Protestant America, they appear to have been utterly convinced that the Indian's only hope for survival lay in em-

[61] *Southern Workman*, February, 1885, p. 20.
[62] *Red Man*, March–April, 1893, p. 4.

bracing White civilization. But there was another, perhaps more fundamental, consideration at work as well. And this leads us to still another perspective on the meaning of Indian schooling.

TAKING THE LAND

This third perspective begins with the rude fact that in the beginning Indians possessed the land and Whites desperately wanted it. On the proposition that Indian land would eventually become White land there was never any serious debate. Both the Protestant ideology and the civilization–savagism paradigm presupposed and demanded it. In the meantime, the question of how the great transfer of real estate might be managed loomed large.[63]

The problem facing policymakers in Jefferson's time was how to dispossess Indians of large tracts of land without doing undue violence to their philanthropic ideals. Their ingenious solution to this dilemma was rooted in the conviction that it required much more land to support a nomadic hunting society than a like-sized population of sedentary farmers. Thus, the willingness of Indians to sell their land would be directly proportionate to their ability to acquire civilized ways. Moreover, in the civilizing process, they would be drawn inevitably into the White economy; they would come to hunger for the goods of Whites just as the White man hungered for Indian land. The pieces of the puzzle began to fall into place. "When [Indians] shall cultivate small spots of earth, and see how useless their extensive forests are," Jefferson wrote, "they will sell from time to time, to help out their personal labor in stocking their farms, and procuring clothes and comforts from our trading houses."[64] On another occasion he remarked: "While they are learning to do better on less land, our increasing numbers will be calling for more land, and thus a coincidence of interests."[65] The so-called "coincidence of interests" between the two races amounted to this: Indians possessed the land and needed civilization; Whites, on the other hand, had civilization but needed land. The philanthropic solution to the Indian question was now clear: a fair exchange whereby Whites would give the Indians civilization in return for land cessions—land the Indians would no longer

[63]See Wilcomb E. Washburn, "The Moral and Legal Justifications for Dispossessing the Indians," in *Seventeenth-Century America: Essays in Colonial History*, ed. James Morton Smith (Chapel Hill: University of North Carolina Press, 1959), pp. 15–32; and Arrell Morgan Gibson, "Philosophical, Legal, and Social Rationales for Appropriating the Tribal Estate, 1607 to 1980," *American Indian Law Review, 12* (1985): 3–37. The link between dispossession and education is briefly but perceptively analyzed by Lawrence A. Cremin in his *American Education: The National Experience, 1783–1876* (New York: Harper & Row, 1980), pp. 230–242.

[64]Quoted in Gibson, "Philosophical, Legal, and Social Rationales," p. 14.

[65]Quoted in Gibson, *The American Indian*, p. 272.

require once they were civilized. This was the basis for an Indian policy characterized by one historian as "expansion with honor."[66]

As it turned out, there was very little honor to be had. The White hunger for land was far in excess of congressional willingness to fund civilization programs. Moreover, Native Americans proved to be less enthusiastic about committing cultural suicide than the Jeffersonians had surmised. The result was that Indian nations were first simply moved farther West, and in time were concentrated on reservations so that Whites might circumvent them in their rush across the continent. But the march of civilized progress was not to be stopped; eventually, even the reservation itself was looked upon as a new source of land. As Henry Pancoast, cofounder of the Indian Rights Association, noted in 1882: "The rush of Western settlement grows more and more; an enormous army pours forth continually into our Eastern seaports to spread itself over the West. How can we keep these still places in the midst of the current, a bit of stone age in the crush and fever of American enterprise?"[67] The answer, of course, was that it would be impossible; the only solution was civilization, which, once accomplished, would free up more land. As Commissioner Morgan reminded philanthropists in 1892: "A wild Indian requires a thousand acres to roam over, while an intelligent man will find a comfortable support for his family on a very small tract."[68]

Thus, while reformers were earnestly striving to save Indians from extinction by a process of assimilation, they were also mindful of the fact that under the reservation system Indians still possessed more land than they would ever need once they were transformed into farmers. Some reformers were even willing to challenge the idea that the Indians really owned the land to begin with. In the words of Lyman Abbott:

> It is sometimes said that the Indians occupied this country and that we took it away from them; that the country belonged to them. This is not true. The Indians did not occupy this land. A people do not occupy a country simply because they roam over it. They did not occupy the coal mines, nor the gold mines, into which they never struck a pick; nor the rivers which flow to the sea, and on which the music of a mill was never heard. The Indians can scarcely be said to have occupied this country more than the bisons and the buffalo they hunted. Three hundred thousand people have no right to hold a continent and keep at bay a race able to people it and provide the happy homes of civilization. We do owe the Indians sacred rights and obligations, but one

---

[66]Berkhofer, *The White Man's Indian*, pp. 134–145.

[67]Pancoast, *Impressions of the Sioux Tribes in 1882 with Some First Principles in the Indian Question* (Philadelphia: Franklin Printing House, 1883), pp. 6–7.

[68]Thomas J. Morgan, "A Plea for the Papoose," reprinted in Prucha, *Americanizing the American Indians*, p. 249.

> of those duties is not the right to let them hold forever the land they did not occupy and which they were not making fruitful for themselves or others.[69]

Not all reformers went as far as Abbott, but all were convinced that the reservation system should be abandoned.

I do not mean to create the impression that reformers were primarily motivated by their desire to dispossess Indians of their land. Their opposition to the reservation system was rooted in several factors, not the least of which was the fact that it forestalled the Indian's absorption into national life. As we can see from the discussion above, however, the issues of land and national economic growth clearly figured into their considerations. In any event, the reservation system came under increasing attack in the 1880s from reformers, and, not surprisingly, from Western land interests, who had their own reasons for wanting to abolish the Indian reservation.

The result of this unholy alliance was one of the most important and devastating pieces of Indian legislation of the late nineteenth century—the General Allotment Act of 1887, more commonly called the Dawes Act after its chief sponsor, Senator Henry Dawes of Massachusetts. The Dawes Act authorized the President to select those reservations he deemed suitable for allotment, after which the following provisions came into effect: First, the reservation would be divided into individual allotments, the head of each family receiving 160 acres, with smaller allotments made to unmarried women and orphans. Second, to protect the new landholders from land-hungry Whites, title to the land would be held by the government for a period of twenty-five years, after which it would pass to its lawful owner. Third, holders of allotments would be granted U.S. citizenship. Finally, the surplus, unalloted lands would be sold off to Whites, the funds gained therefrom to be spent for the Indians' benefit, mainly for education.[70] Reformers looked upon the Dawes Act as a major milestone in their crusade to solve the Indian problem. In a single piece of legislation they believed they had found the mechanism to smash tribalism, transform hunters into

[69] *Proceedings of the Third Annual Meeting of the Lake Mohonk Conference*, 1885, reprinted in Prucha, *Americanizing the American Indians*, pp. 33–34.

[70] The literature on the Dawes Act is especially rich. See Prucha, *The Great Father*, vol. 2, chap. 26; Prucha, *American Indian Policy in Crisis*, chap. 8; Hoxie, *A Final Promise*, pp. 70–81, chap. 5; Priest, *Uncle Sam's Stepchildren*, pt. 4; D. S. Otis, *The Dawes Act and the Allotment of Indian Lands*, ed. Francis Paul Prucha (Norman: University of Oklahoma Press, 1973); Leonard A. Carlson, *Indians, Bureaucrats, and Land: The Dawes Act and the Decline of Indian Farming* (Westport, CT: Greenwood Press, 1981). Two excellent case studies are Donald J. Berthrong, *The Cheyenne and Arapaho Ordeal: Reservation and Agency Life in the Indian Territory, 1875–1907* (Norman: University of Oklahoma Press, 1976); and William T. Hagan, *United States–Comanche Relations: The Reservation Years* (New Haven: Yale University Press, 1976), chaps. 9–12.

farmers, and grant the Indians U.S. citizenship. Even the selling of the surplus lands would facilitate the process; as White settlers established productive homesteads on the available lands, they would inevitably prove to be positive role models for their Indian neighbors.[71]

Against this background, the campaign to educate the Indians takes on new meaning. First, allotment enables us to understand why educators placed so much emphasis on individualization and citizenship training—both were essential if the Indians were going to survive in their new citizen-farmer roles. Without such preparatory education, reformers pointed out, allotment would prove to be a cruel hoax. "Put an ignorant and imbruted savage on land of his own, and he remains a pauper, if he does not become a vagrant and a thief," claimed Lyman Abbott.[72] Charles Painter, lobbyist for the Indian Rights Association, agreed: "The reservation walls being down" he said, "and the retraining power of the agent broken, he [the Indian] and his children will become a race of wanderers and beggars, unless they are met . . . with influences wise enough and large enough to teach them the nobility of manhood and the uses of freedom." Painter then added: "There is now scope and hope for the schoolmaster."[73] The Dawes Act, then, helped to remind educators of what they must teach Indians if they were to survive and prosper as citizens.

A second connection between education and allotment stems from the fact that, in theory, the allotment process was to be set into motion on a given reservation only when the President, with the advice of the Indian Bureau, deemed a given Indian population capable of making the transition to a freeholding agricultural economy. Since surplus lands could not be sold until allotment was completed, it followed that educating Indians was a necessary preliminary to divesting them of excess lands. The connection between education and surplus lands would provide Commissioner Morgan with one of his most effective arguments for funding Indian education.

> [The] great economical fact is that the lands known as Indian reservations now set apart by the Government for Indian occupancy aggregate nearly 190,000 square miles. This land, for the most part, is uncultivated and unproductive. When the Indians shall have been properly educated they will utilize a sufficient quantity of those lands for their own support and will release the remainder that it may be restored to the public domain to become the foun-

[71]In 1881, Indians owned 155,632,312 acres. By 1900, the number had dwindled to 77,865,373. Prucha, *American Indian Policy in Crisis,* p. 257.

[72]*Proceedings of the Sixth Annual Meeting of the Lake Mohonk Conference of Friends of the Indian,* 1888, reprinted in *Annual Report of the Commissioner of Indian Affairs,* 1888, House Exec. Doc. No. 1, 50th Cong., 2nd sess., 1888–1889, Serial 2637, p. 780.

[73]*Proceedings of the Fifth Annual Meeting of the Lake Mohonk Conference of Friends of the Indian,* 1887, reprinted in *Annual Report of the Commissioner of Indian Affairs,* 1887, House Exec. Doc. No. 1, 50th Cong., 1st sess., 1887–1888, Serial 2542, p. 959.

> dation for innumerable happy homes, and thus will be added to the national wealth immense tracts of farming land and vast mineral resources which will repay the nation more than one hundred fold for the amount which it is proposed shall be expended in Indian education.[74]

Third, the issue of Indian land loss was inextricably connected to the school's efforts at citizenship education. The point here is that school officials occasionally felt compelled to address the issue that was at the heart of so much Indian–White conflict—the fact that Whites had nearly succeeded in dispossessing the Indians of the entire continent. The objective was to persuade the students to accept the idea that it was inevitable and entirely justified that the Indians lose their ancestral lands to a more progressive people. Some students did in fact come to internalize this point of view, as evidenced by this account of Indian–White relations by a Hampton pupil:

> Centuries ago we undoubtedly held full control over this fair land—this vast domain from east to west. Bodily we were free to roam, but our freedom of thought lay dormant as we slumbered heavily by the camp-fires of prosperity. What did the fertile valleys, the rich plain, the mineral treasures concealed in the hillsides mean to us? They simply told us that here was a good hunting ground, and there a good site for temporary habitation. But when the white man came he put everything in a new light. He saw how everything in nature could render him a service. 'Twas not long before we saw his engines making their way across our domains west-ward. Mountains were in his way, but he climbed them. Rivers were there, but he crossed them. When he was killed by our arrows, he, as it were, sprang up from his own ashes. He brought with him civilization and freedom. These constituted the power which made him a most formidable adversary. Our wanderings along his track proved a hindrance to his progress and we were driven away until finally we found ourselves penned on reservations with nothing to do and nothing to expect. . . . Since then we have entered upon a stage of civilization which brings with it problems hard for us to handle. This is our past.[75]

One suspects that such sentiments were relatively rare among Indian students, but this passage illustrates the ultimate political purpose to which the civilization theme might be applied. The civilization–savagism paradigm called for establishing political and cultural hegemony over Indians as a first step to their incorporation into American life. In the instance above, the process may be said to have merely reached its logical conclusion.[76]

---

[74]*Annual Report of the Commissioner of Indian Affairs,* 1889, reprinted in Prucha, *Americanizing the American Indians,* p. 237.

[75]*Talks and Thoughts,* February, 1904, p. 4.

[76]T. J. Jackson Lears, "The Concept of Cultural Hegemony: Problems and Possibilities," *American Historical Review, 90* (June 1985): 567–593.

School officials also made concerted efforts to win student support for the Dawes Act. Just two years after its enactment, Commissioner Morgan instructed school superintendents to observe annually the anniversary of the law's passage, along with other national holidays. The occasion might be used, explained Morgan, "to impress upon Indian youth the enlarged scope and opportunity given them by this law and the new obligations which it imposes."[77] For the next decade or so, especially at larger off-reservation schools, special efforts were made to celebrate the day with speeches, dramatic sketches, and elaborate pageants. In 1890, the Carlisle celebration of "Franchise Day" required students to listen to a recitation of a poem titled "A Message from Carlisle Students to the Indians." Apparently written by one of the school staff, but read by a student, the purpose of the poem was to dispel Indian fears that the Dawes Act, despite its promise of citizenship, was in reality nothing but a scheme to dispossess the Indian of more real estate. As the poem admits, taking land from the Indian was an old American story.

> You say we are poor, though a splendid dominion
> Of forests and rivers and mountains of gold
> Were ours, e'er the greed of the white man detained it;
> You are sorry and grumble that now it is sold.

The poem continues by pointing out that the government was now offering the Indian redress:

> Redress in this way, that though we as a Nation
> No more may hold sway o'er a boundless domain,
> Though tribes may be scattered like leaves of the maple
> And the pipes of our councils be smoked not again.
>
> Yet prospects more pleasant than these in the future
> And riches far better, our people may see,
> When learning, shall bring us a wealth more resplendent
> Than title to millions can possibly be.

Education, then, would compensate for the past dispossession of Indian lands, and presumably for those lost as a consequence of the Dawes Act as well.

> But welcome the ruin, if now by our losses,
> We gain thousand fold in a better estate.

---

[77] "Instructions to Indian Agents in Regard to Inculcation of Patriotism in Indian Schools," p. CLXVII.

> A man may be chief in the empire of reason.
> Education, not land, makes a citizen great.[78]

Celebrations of the Dawes Act were intended to evoke in students a genuine enthusiasm for the provision of the bill that awarded citizenship to allottees. One student responded:

> Now we are citizens
> We give him applause;
> So three cheers, my friends,
> To Senator Dawes![79]

For those students converted to the idea of civilization and the Protestant ideology, the Dawes Act indeed gave them something to celebrate. For others, those still not won over to the White man's way of thinking, the price of citizenship must have appeared too severe: the further loss of the tribal estate.[80]

---

[78]*The Red Man*, March, 1890, p. 5.

[79]Quoted in Cora Folsom, "Memories of Old Hampton," Cora Folsom Papers, Hampton Institute.

[80]While the focus of this paper is essentially on the meaning behind policymakers' assimilation efforts, it should be noted that students responded to these efforts in a variety of ways. While some cooperated with the educational program, others resisted. In the latter instance, arson, running away from school, and subtle forms of passive resistance all proved effective. Another response was to selectively embrace some aspects of the program while rejecting other strands, thereby constructing a kind of personal syncretic resolution of potentially conflicting value systems, all the while attempting to maintain a sense of personal and ethnic identity. The subject of student response is treated in Michael C. Coleman, "The Mission Education of Francis La Flesche: An Indian Response to the Presbyterian Boarding School in the 1860's," *American Studies in Scandinavia, 18* (1986): 67–82; Coleman, "The Responses of American Indian Children to Presbyterian Schooling in the Nineteenth Century: An Analysis through Missionary Sources," *History of Education Quarterly* (forthcoming); Sally J. McBeth, *Ethnic Identity and the Boarding School Experience of West-Central Oklahoma American Indians* (Washington, DC: University Press of America, 1983), esp. pp. 127–134; David Wallace Adams, "The Federal Indian Boarding School: A Study of Environment and Response, 1879–1918," Ed.D. Diss., Indiana University, 1975, chaps. 5–6; and Wilbert H. Ahern, "The Returned Indians: Hampton Institute and Its Indian Alumni, 1875–1893," *Journal of Ethnic Studies, 10* (Winter, 1983): 101–124. An important perspective can be gained from consulting Indian autobiographies. Especially good are Luther Standing Bear, *My People the Sioux* (1928; rpt. Lincoln: University of Nebraska, 1975); Simmons, *Sun Chief*; Louise Udall, ed., *Me and Mine: The Life Story of Helen Sekaquaptewa* (Tucson: University of Arizona Press, 1965); Francis La Flesche, *The Middle Five: Indian Schoolboys of the Omaha Tribe* (Madison: University of Wisconsin Press, 1963); Jim Whitewolf, *The Life of a Kiowa Apache Indian* ed. Charles Brandt (New York: Dover, 1969); and Harold Courlander, *Big Falling Snow: A Tewa-Hopi Indian's Life and Times and the History and Traditions of His People* (Albuquerque: University of New Mexico Press, 1978).

CONCLUSION

This essay has been an attempt to peel away the layers of meaning behind the late nineteenth-century effort to school Native Americans in the ways of Whites. My investigations have caused me to conclude that while the Protestant ideology tells us a great deal about the aims of Indian schooling during this period, it leaves a good deal unexplained as well. In particular, it leaves unexplained reformers' preoccupation with the concept of civilization and its counterpart, savagism. It also fails to make any direct connection between the objectives of Indian schooling and the most fundamental fact of Indian–White conflict, the fact that Whites were aggressively dispossessing Native Americans of their land. It might be argued that I have engaged in a bit of hairsplitting: that while the Protestant ideology failed to address the Indian question directly, its glorification of the American empire certainly implied the cultural inferiority of people who stood in its path; and that the Indian's loss of land was always rather blatantly assumed—in short, the handwriting was on the wall. Perhaps so, but this does not explain away the fact that when policymakers went about the business of designing an Indian school system, both the civilization–savagism paradigm and the issue of land possession became the fundamental points of reference for discussion. It is entirely understandable that this should be so. Although Protestant ideology might provide the necessary spiritual and ideational energy to propel the American empire westward, ever deeper into Indian country, it could not address in precise terms what it was about the Indians' "otherness" that justified systematic political and cultural subjugation, including the taking of their land. Still, it was not irrelevant either. The Protestant ideology helped shape policymakers' ideas of what it meant to be civilized, of what Indians must become if they were to be saved from extinction. In the end, I would argue, the Protestant ideology, the civilization–savagism paradigm, and the White hunger for Indian land were all mutually reinforcing and hopelessly intertwined as factors influencing the educational campaign to assimilate the Indian.

A visual depiction of historical forces at work can be seen in George A. Crofutt's chromolithograph "American Progress," published in 1873 after an earlier painting by John Gast, and issued with an accompanying text, in which Crofutt sought to capture the quintessential spirit and meaning of the American experience.[81] At center stage is one of the most powerful icons of nineteenth-century America, Columbia, who, with the "Star of the Empire"

[81]The text is reprinted in Wilcomb E. Washburn, ed., *The Indian and White Man* (Garden City: Anchor Books, 1964), pp. 128–130. Charles Burgess has used the Gast painting as a point of departure for his discussion of the late nineteenth-century compulsory school-attendance movement in "The Goddess, the School Book, and Compulsion," *Harvard Educational Review, 46* (May 1976): 199–216.

on her forehead, drifts majestically westward over the American landscape. In one hand she carries the "talking wires" of the telegraph, a symbol of American progress, and in the other a large volume, which one would expect to be the Bible. Closer inspection, however, reveals the inscription "Schoolbook."

Crofutt's print can be read at several levels. On the one hand, it is an attempt to dramatically show a persistent strain in the Protestant ideology—the idea that America is a sacred place with a millennial destiny. But "American Progress" is about the idea of civilization as well; it is about the triumph of civilization over Indian savagism. Indeed, one can scarcely look at it without calling to mind Jefferson's vision of America as a panoramic representation of "the progress of man from the infancy of creation to the present day." In fact, the accompanying text relates:

> On the right of the picture is a city, steamships, manufactories, schools, and churches, over which beams of light are streaming and filling the air—indicative of civilization. The general tone of the picture on the left declares darkness, waste and confusion. From the city proceed the three great continental lines of railway, passing the frontier settlers' rude cabin, and tending toward the Western Ocean. Next to these are the transportation wagons, overland stage, hunters, gold seekers, pony express, the pioneer emigrant and the war-dance of the "noble red man." Fleeing from "Progress," and towards the blue waters of the Pacific, which shows itself on the left of the picture beyond the snow-capped summits of the Sierra Nevadas, are the Indians, buffaloes, wild horses, bears, and other game, moving Westward—ever Westward the Indians, with their squaws, papooses, and "pony lodges," . . . as they flee from the presence of the wondrous vision. The "Star" is *too much for them.*[82]

And finally, of course, there is the land. As the Indian is pushed off the canvas of American life, the land remains for the taking.

Crofutt's print is a depiction of the national myth of the day. But let us imagine that he had issued the print several years later, let us say 1883. Would the vision have been altered? Probably little would have been changed, except that now Columbia, with an outstretched arm, would be seen offering the "Schoolbook" to the "vanishing American." For the schoolbook contained within it the Americanizing lessons of Christianity, capitalism, and republicanism. The schoolbook would save the Indian from extinction. If only Indians would accept the gift of the book, they would come to enjoy the blessings of civilized progress. But even then—and this was always clearly understood—they must continue to give up the land. Such was the deep meaning of Indian education.

---

[82]Washburn, *The Indian and the White Man*, p. 129.

CHAPTER THREE

Multiculturalism and an Overarching Framework of Values: Some Educational Responses for Ethnically Plural Societies

Jerzy Smolicz

In a society composed of more than one ethnic group, there can exist a variety of relationships between the dominant (frequently the majority) group and the minorities (Smolicz, 1979). If such a society is governed by a degree of consensus, rather than coercion, there must have evolved a set of *shared* values that *overarch* the various ethnic groups. Within such a cultural 'umbrella', ethnic groups may retain certain core values, such as a distinct language, family tradition or religion (Smolicz, 1981a).

We thus have a dynamic equilibrium established between the overarching or shared values of the country, on the one hand, and ethnic core values on the other. The dominant group exhibits its own set of majority values, many of which have percolated into the overarching framework. Such shared values should not be regarded, however, as the majority's own 'private domain', but as the common possession of all the citizens.

To take an example, the overarching framework that has evolved in Australian society relates to the upholding of the western democratic political tradition; the concept of man as worthy of freedom and respect; economic pluralism whereby individuals can advance themselves according to merit; and the English language as the basic value for all Australians. Although these shared values may largely originate in the heritage of the Anglo-Saxon group, they ultimately become the property of all groups. There is, for example, an accumulation of research evidence that ethnic groups recognize the importance of English as an overarching value, in the sense that it is indispensable for communication among all Australians and the principal vehicle for the political, economic, and legal activities of society (Marjoribanks, 1979, 1980; Smolicz & Secombe, 1977, 1983). However, the acceptance of English by all the ethnic groups is based upon the understanding that, for those who wish to preserve their native tongue, English represents an *additional* language, rather than the sole and unique means of communication.

SOLUTIONS TO PLURALISM

Assimilation

Under the conditions of *assimilation*, the overarching framework has the lion's share of its values derived from the dominant group, while minority ethnic components are but remnants that are obliterated as far as possible. In such a situation even 'ethnic food' is suspect, while literacy in ethnic tongues is actively devalued and presented as intellectually confusing, socially disadvantaging and politically divisive.

In Australia, the direct support for assimilation of this type has abated since the early 1970s, when all major political parties began to espouse a policy of 'multiculturalism'. The nature of that kind of 'official' multiculturalism is, however, far from clear and will be analysed later. It should also be noted that thinking more or less in favour of assimilation has not been wholly eradicated and that it continues to be heard from a fairly small but persistent group of writers who equate minority languages and traditions with a whole spectrum of subcultural variations that exist *within* the majority group, such as the rural/urban, social class and life-style differences based upon geographical factors, economic circumstances and sexual preferences. In this way ethnic cultures are reduced to subcultural variants of the majority culture.

One possible consequence of 'assimilationist' policy that has not been sufficiently analysed is the frequent inconsistency of the demand for cultural assimilation, with the simultaneous rejection of the assimilated minority in terms of social interaction, usually at primary, but occasionally even at the secondary (including the occupational) level. Certain specific markers of minority ethnicity (such as colour, hair texture, surname or some cultural fragments) can hardly ever be completely expurgated. Thus ethnic labels may continue to be used to keep minorities socially apart; having had their culture destroyed, minority members may suffer the indignity of rejection from those they have been persuaded (or forced) to imitate. This underlines the danger of alienation among culturally dispossessed and socially rejected ethnic groups (Smolicz, 1983).

Separatism

The opposite of assimilation is held to be separatism, when the overarching framework is only vestigial and each ethnic group is encrusted within its own value system, with little interaction between different groups whose members have constructed personal cultural systems almost entirely from their ancestral mono-ethnic constituents. There are, however, two very different kinds of separatism in society. One form of separatism does not automatically mean the complete domination of the segregated groups by one single ruling entity with values that are almost automatically held to be superior over those of other groups. In Switzerland, for example, several cantons show a high degree of monocultural homogeneity without dominating each other.

In contrast, the *domain separatism* which prevails in South Africa does not even attempt to parade as a relationship of equals. Separatism of that kind not only places restrictions upon interaction, but also imposes the overwhelming political control of the European-descended group upon the rest of the population. The latter example shows that ruling groups, at times, may favour separatism since they remain 'uncontaminated' by the culture and social infusion of the 'inferior' minorities, while dominating them economically and politically.

A variant of this approach is discussed by Bullivant (1980, 1981, 1982) who postulates the existence in Australia of a ruling group labelled significantly as *Staatsvolk*, or 'people of the state'. The *Staatsvolk* is said to be

> concerned to maintain control over political power [and since in Australia] there is also an intimate relationship between the political and economic system [. . . the latter] too is controlled by the majority ethnic group. (1982, p. 25)

According to this view, to espouse the idea that all Australians are 'people of the state' would be sheer 'naivety'. Such a 'polyethnic' model appears a static one, with 'core domination' by the Staatsvolk creating "a cultural division of labour that serves to block the peripheral groups' full political integration."

The consequence is that 'multicultural education', which is currently being implemented in a number of Australian schools is made to appear as a waste of time and resources, since it cannot affect children's life chances or give adults any influence in the economic or political domains. By generating hopes of structural and institutional changes, such educational provisions may, in the long run, lead to inflated expectations and encourage the 'ethnics' to demand political and economic rights which the ruling *Staatsvolk* would have no intention of satisfying. This exclusion of minorities from the mainstream of society's life implies a refusal by the majority to alter its overarching framework. The effect is to place the minorities outside the polity that is circumscribed by such a framework.

Multiculturalism

In between the 'assimilationist' and separatist approaches lies the vast area that is covered by the label of 'multiculturalism'. This involves some form of an on-going interpenetration between the overarching or shared values of the country, on the one hand, and ethnic values of the constituent groups, on the other.

(a) *Co-existence and Synthesis*

As long as the ethnic cultural variation continues to exist, individuals will be able to draw upon more than one cultural model in the construction of their personal cultural worlds. This will mean that the cultural and social life of the country will be enriched, as individuals can choose from a number of cultural options. One possibility is that of cultural *co-existence* when they can construct a *dual* system of values. (In the sphere of language this will lead to bilingualism, and in the Anglo-Saxon influenced societies, to the use of English in conjunction with some other community ethnic language.) In the case of other forms of interaction, some *synthesis* or *blend* or in-between position may be achieved in personal life-styles, as individuals draw, for example, upon the Italian or Greek collectivist family traditions of *inter*-dependence and extended network of primary relations, on the one hand, and the Anglo-Saxon ideal of individualism, self-reliance, independence and personal autonomy, on the other (Smolicz, 1984a).

The distinction between interaction resulting in synthesis and that based upon co-existence of alternating systems helps to counteract facile talk of 'integration' in relation to language, since this either denies the significance of linguistic diversity (in the tacit expectation of the eventual extinction of minority languages), or assumes the unrealistic stance of 'linguistic hybridisation'. (The latter situation is mostly encountered among illiterate populations, but is hardly an alternative for people with established literary traditions.)

The continuing growth of overarching values provides one of the best guarantees of the cohesion of society. Should at some future date ethnic variation within a particular plural society disappear altogether, the expansion of overarching values would have claimed exclusive application to virtually all aspects of life. Cultural synthesis would then have reached the final stage of "hybrid monism" (Smolicz, 1979; Smolicz & Secombe, 1977) or the "permissive melting pot" (Ramirez & Castaneda, 1975).

It would seem that this situation is rare, but it could be argued that it is currently being approached in Israel among its Jewish population, and that people of Polish, German, Dutch, American, as well as Moroccan, Libyan and Yemeni backgrounds are increasingly relying on Hebrew alone as their newly acquired everyday mother tongue, inter-marrying among people of different origins, and adopting a steadily evolving set of *Jewish-Israeli* values. This synthesis, however, is underpinned by the already shared set of traditional Jewish core values of religion, peoplehood, and historical continuity. However, despite additional inducements to homogenisation, such as hostile neighbours and separatist or even cessionist tendencies along some of its Arabic minority, the differences between 'Western' and 'Oriental' Jews have not yet disappeared completely, as evidenced by recent disagreements especially in the field of 'political culture'. Hence it can be assumed that, in most plural societies, although some blending will proceed in selected areas of life, we have to expect a continuing cultural diversity, even if there exists a well articulated overarching system of values that is supported by the vast majority of the population involved in the process of interaction.

(b) *Core Values and Multiculturalism*

In relation to multiculturalism, one needs to consider not only the *process* by which the phenomenon manifests itself in society, but also the cultural *content* of any such process. In this connection, it is important to distinguish between different types of multiculturalism, since while members of minority ethnic communities often view their own position in society from the standpoint of a *stable* multiculturalism (for maintenance), a number of official agencies, in countries such as the USA and Australia, appear to think and act, whether consciously or unconsciously, in terms of a process that has other outcomes. One of them is *transition*, when minority languages and cultures are dismantled like some kind of useless scaffolding and phased out as soon as the dominant language is deemed to have been acquired; the other outcome is that of the *multiculturalism of residues* (Smolicz, 1981b, c).

The theory of core values (Smolicz, 1981a) enables one to distinguish among these different kinds of approaches, and especially to explain the characteristics of residual multiculturalism. The theory argues that every culture has certain core element(s) which represent its heartland, and act as identifying values for its members. For most cultures, this core value is represented by the native tongue, although there are cultures where, at least during present times, the core element is primarily located in religion (as in the Irish or Malay groups), family network (Italian), or clan and race (Chinese). This is not to say that language is of no consequence for these groups and, in certain situations, one should speak of a hierarchy of core values, rather than of single value alone, although one could hardly argue that ability to speak Irish Gaelic is an indispensable element of Irish identity. Nor should one assume that core values are like some kind of 'crystal ball' and static for all times. It has already been mentioned, for example, that in modern Israel, Hebrew as a spoken tongue has acquired the new function of another core value while the concept of the land where Jewish values can be practised has gained a new dimension. Indeed, no culture and hence no core value can be assumed to be static since a tradition must be continually re-shaped and revalued to meet the changing situation of the group, if it is to survive as a tradition (Szacki, 1969).

In modern times, at least, in cultures such as Greek, Polish, French, Latvian or Lithuanian, the supremacy of language as the rallying call of ethnic identity, can hardly be disputed. It is only fair to add that the English language plays the role of one of the most important core elements not only of the English group, but also of the overwhelming majority of the British people, and of the great number of their descendants in the former possessions of the British Empire (and even among British minority groups in such countries as Argentina and Chile where it has been preserved as a mother tongue after several generations of settlement in a Spanish-dominated environment).

For minority groups that are language-centred, the preservation of their linguistic core is indispensable for the continuation of their cultures as viable entities that can be transmitted to the next generation. Hence the defence of their mother tongue is seen by many cultural minorities as their first priority (Clyne, 1982). In this light, the struggle for language maintenance is not some kind of abstract or 'high culture' phenomenon, but an effort by a group of people to preserve their ethnic identity within a plural society which already sanctions a variety of life-styles. For such language-centred ethnic groups there is hardly any doubt that language and culture are highly political phenomena since they are concerned with people deciding their own destiny.

It should also be stressed that the question of language is no less political from the point of view of those dominant groups which attempt to suppress the cultures of the minorities in the name of 'social cohesion' (a favoured catchword for those on the 'right' of the political spectrum), or 'equality for all' (the slogan most usually appealed to by those on the 'left'). It is ironical that the dominant group may 'arrange' the social and educational systems to suit its own language and culture, and later argue that parents who teach their children their own tongue as an *additional* language are handicapping them in socio-economic advancement which has been attuned to the needs and expectations of dominant group. (Indeed, children from the latter group may themselves be studying Latin, with the comfort of knowing that Romans, as an 'extinct species', cannot be rivals in the occupational sphere, nor act as models of the way that the language should be pronounced.)

(c) *Residual Multiculturalism*

Attitudes to minority languages are usually good pointers to official intentions with respect to the continued existence of multiculturalism. The destruction of linguistic core values reduces most cultures to residues, which represent only segments of the cultural activities of the individual. Such an individual is forced to adopt the core values of the majority. When ethnic cultures have been degraded to ethnic residues through the loss of their native tongues, we have the phenomenon of *residual multiculturalism*.

Under this condition minority cultures are reduced to a subcultural status on the lines of other subcultural variations within the majority group (such as regional or social class differences). Such cultures cease to stimulate any significant intellectual activity, as the languages concerned become more restricted in usage and thus relegated to the intimacy of the family; they then lose their ability to express abstract notions and elevated ideas or to evoke the contemporary realities of an advanced culture. The most important phenomenon resulting from this loss of domains of usage is the growing number of ethnic speakers who lose confidence in the future of their language and only have recourse to it for domestic needs and as a secret language (Harris, 1982).

Such cultural residualism may appear to be the tacit aim of at least some proponents of Australian or American multiculturalism, in relation to community languages other than English. 'Multiculturalism' of this kind seems to pander to a limited range of 'ethnic issues', while giving insufficient consideration to the diffusion of non-British-derived cultural elements into the mainstream of social life and its system of overarching values.

(d) *Stable Multiculturalism for Maintenance*

The concept of stable multiculturalism does not require that cultures be transplanted 'as wholes' into a new setting. The insistence on the need to preserve core values in order that cultures can retain their integrity does not mean that one can expect, say, European or Asian cultures to be incorporated *in toto* into societies such as those of Canada, Australia, or the United States. National cultures are concerned not only with languages or life-styles, but also with institutional structures that are of political, economic, or legal significance. It is these institutional forms that all ethnic cultures would be expected to shed or modify in a plural society in favour of the overarching values that are acceptable to ethnic majorities and minorities alike.

In a modern multicultural state, the modifications or even loss of certain institutional forms is inevitable. In this connection one should correct the purists who assume that the word 'multiculturalism' requires that each ethnic culture within a given state should retain the full complement of the institutions and norms which it displays (or displayed in some past era) in its original homeland. In this way such writers ignore the development of a shared framework of values that overarch all groups, in conjunction with the retention of other values that are characteristic of specific ethnicities. By stretching the meaning of multiculturalism to these absurd limits, the concept is defined out of existence.

According to this type of argument not only any loss of ethnic cultural elements, but even any evolution of new forms common to all, negates either the 'culture' or the 'multi' part of 'multiculturalism'. The use of that term then comes to be reserved for unusual situations where, for example, territorially distinct groups wish to establish some form of loose confederation, or where a benevolent imperial power rules over conquered natives, allowing them to retain the full panoply of local autonomy in legal and internal political matters, while retaining the overall control in such matters as foreign affairs and defence. If one were to adopt such extreme criteria, most modern societies which display some degree of cultural diversity in their midst would presumably be destined either for fragmentation and eventual disintegration of the state or, alternatively, for assimilation to the dominant culture, with or without subjugation of the ethnic minorities to a modern kind of serfdom.

Fortunately in between such extreme solutions there are a number of other alternatives, including a stable kind of multiculturalism that is characterised by the acceptance of shared institutions by all the groups, and consequent modifications in the culture of each group. This adaptation is, however, of an entirely different order from the excision of core values that are fundamental to the survival and development of each constituent ethnic culture. The boundary between cultural accommodation to plurality, on the one hand, and assimilation to the ways of the dominant majority on the other, is provided by the distinct cores of each culture.

The stress on development of an ethnic culture, rather than simply on its maintenance, means that it would not become fossilised within its core boundary. Ethnic cultures must change in order to survive, but the change must be at their own pace, while due deference is paid to the natural caution of a minority group to guard itself against any process that could carry assimilationist undertones. Cultures in a minority setting are often more conservative than in the homeland, since their members are so preoccupied with the importance of preservation that any radical alteration may be interpreted as a prelude to assimilation. This must be acknowledged as one of the facts of minority cultural existence, and allowance made for it, without at the same time precluding the need for adaptation on account of changing patterns both in the plural society itself and in the home country. Such a model of 'stabilised' multiculturalism stresses both the preservation of ethnic cultures and their adjustment to the overarching values of society as a whole.

Of the various overarching values that have evolved in different plural societies, the one involving the desirability of multiculturalism itself is still perhaps insufficiently understood or appreciated. Nevertheless, without the acceptance of cultural diversity as a shared value by the majority group, and by society as a whole, there can be no multicultural society. Instead, the way is left open for the pitfalls of assimilation or separatism.

In summary, the following two complementary points can be reiterated in relation to overarching and ethnic core values:

(i) the retention and development of ethnic cultures may be perfectly compatible with the evolution and acceptance of overarching values for the whole society. This holds even though not all cultures interact or overlap equally readily;

(ii) the modification of national cultures and their fitting into the general framework of shared values is not equivalent to their reduction to residues.

(e) *Tolerance Ratio and Compatibility of Values*

In arriving at a balance between the overarching framework and the various ethnic values, one has to accept the fact that, since cultures differ in their core values, the compatibility between cultures will also vary, and that some cultures will interact more readily than others. There is ample evidence, for example, that in Australia at least, Dutch-Australians 'fit in' linguistically and culturally more readily with the majority group than almost any other group from a non-English speaking background (Clyne, 1982). There is also evidence that groups from most parts of Southern and Eastern Europe uphold family values which are more collectivist than the individualistically oriented people from Northern and Western Europe, and those who originate in Great Britain in particular (Smolicz, 1984a; Smolicz & Piesiewicz, 1983). Such variations increase the dimension and complexity of Australian pluralism without undermining its foundations, or threatening the stability of the state, since the differences concerned can be encompassed within the existing and still developing overarching framework of values.

In general terms, however, the greater variety of ethnic value systems suggests the necessity to establish some kind of 'tolerance ratio' for each society, whereby members of certain specific ethnic groups are accepted provided that the number of their members does not exceed a certain proportion of the whole. It is to be expected that for a given society such a tolerance ratio would differ from group to group. Such a ratio is not, of course, to be assumed as constant and groups that would have found it difficult to fit in at one time may later find acceptance, at least up to some new and more flexible 'tolerance limit'. For example, while Baltic immigrants in Australia were received with suspicion in the early post-war years as the first non-Anglo-Saxon groups to be actively encouraged to emigrate to Australia, they are now regarded as virtually model immigrants, anxious to preserve their cultures, while accommodating to the overall Australian framework.

In the current ideological climate whereby the earlier expectations of effecting assimilation of minorities are recognised as impractical, cultural diversity assumes even greater importance than in the past. As long as Americans and Australians were hopeful that cultural differences could be eliminated in subsequent generations through the assimilation of the descendents of 'foreigners', time was seen as exercising the benign function of value homogenisation. With this faith gone, much more attention is likely in the future to be focussed upon the cultural values of the new arrivals, and the way they are likely to fit (or not to fit) both the overarching values of society, and the ethnic values of some of the existing groups (this refers not only to the way minorities fit into the values of the Anglo-Saxon majority, but also, for example, to the possibility of discord between Australians of Jewish and Arabic backgrounds, or between those of Greek and Turkish, or of Lebanese Christian and Palestinian origins).

Hence the paramount importance of education, both for the dominant group and the minorities which are *already in the country* and which must be accommodated as fellow citizens. In such a situation there is virtually no choice in the matter. For example in Germany, most Germans appear to show no desire for the guest workers and their children to become simply German (i.e. they have no desire to assimilate all the minorities); at the same time, the minorities may also be unwilling to become assimilated into 'plain' Germans, yet they may refuse to return to their ancestral homelands. When such permanent ethnic minorities are 'built' into a society, the task of education is to build bridges, with the aim of strengthening and developing the overarching values, without at the same time obliterating the intrinsic cultural features of either the majority or the minorities. Hence the overarching framework has to develop in harmony with the core values of all ethnic groups. Education planning in such instances is a matter of necessity, and even of survival.

EDUCATIONAL RESPONSES TO ETHNIC DIVERSITY

The cultural complexion of society and its future development in the face of ethnic plurality is fundamentally dependent upon the nature of the education that children from all ethnic backgrounds receive in schools. The importance of the educational process is grounded in its function of transmitting culture from generation to generation and reflecting changes that occur in the overarching framework, as well as in ethnic values, resulting from cultural interaction at all levels in society's life.

Since schools are in their essence ideological agencies, the educational programmes that they adopt will reveal the ideological orientation that is accepted at the time as the basis for the development of society. In the discussion which follows, the basic orientations to pluralism are applied to education, with special reference to Australia. In that country, a variety of approaches has been tried in the wake of post-war migrations, and these illustrate the inter-dependence between ideologies towards ethnicity and their educational consequences. However, although Australia is used as an example documenting changing policies to minorities and educational responses, the theoretical principles involved can equally well be applied to other countries, such as Germany, with its large ethnic minorities (for this is what the 'guest workers' really are), or Great Britain, with its newly injected cultural and racial variety.

Education and Assimilation

If a society's ruling ethnic group were determined to put into effect the policy of cultural assimilation of the minorities, it could effectively take no educational action, by ignoring the existence of cultural differences and allowing minority children to settle down in the mainstream institutions. They could then either 'swim' to salvation through assimilation, or become overwhelmed by the alien curriculum and 'sink' to the bottom of the school, and ultimately, to the bottom of the socio-economic pyramid. This policy of 'sink or swim' was practised by Australia in the two post-war decades despite the extremely heavy inflow of immigrants from non-English speaking backgrounds.

Since 1971 this indifference to the welfare of migrants and their children has been arrested by a series of measures designed to teach English (labelled 'migrant English') to the new arrivals. This new enthusiasm may have been caused by a genuine concern for migrants' educational chances, or possibly by a greater need for skilled labour; alternatively, it may have been prompted by a sudden fear that insufficient knowledge of English would undermine the 'cohesion' of society. Whatever the reason, in the Australia of the 1970s and 1980s there is an almost obsessive fear among some prominent spokesmen of the majority group that 'migrants' (a term frequently used not only for non-Anglo-Saxon newcomers, but also for their Australian-born children or even grandchildren) may not have sufficient knowledge of English, and that they somehow need to be enticed to learn it. Preoccupations of this kind are still indicative of the ideology of assimilation, except that the majority culture is made more accessible to the minorities (at least at its basic level).

Education and Transitional Multiculturalism

During the 1970s in Australia we also witnessed the modest dawn of the ideology of multiculturalism, although some aspects of multicultural or bilingual education, both in Australia and America carry with them the undoubted stamp of transitional multiculturalism, or 'assimilation in disguise'.

In the United States, funds for bilingual education have generally been made available only if one could plead the children's ignorance of English, and hence the need for their native tongues to be used in teaching, say, mathematics or science. Such funds were to be automatically withdrawn when such children had mastered English. In California, for example, during 1982 great debates ensued as to the time when the child was deemed to have acquired a mastery of English. Those suspicious of bilingualism 'for maintenance', rather than 'for transition', accused the school authorities of giving in to the pressure of minorities, and artificially raising the standards required to pass in English so as to keep the minority children permanently within the bilingual programmes. This strategy, it was pointed out, had the effect of maintaining the children's mother tongues, rather than using their languages as a temporary educational expedient adopted solely for the transitional period on the way towards the acquisition of English.

Education and Residual Multiculturalism

In Australia over the past decade 'multiculturalism' has received probably more open support from the governments (Federal and State) than in most Western plural societies. Leaders, from the Prime Minister down, made statements supporting the ideology of maintaining a diversity of cultures, provided that social cohesion was not endangered by ethnic fragmentation and divisiveness. In this connection it is significant that it is not separate ethnic schools that have been selected as a potential danger to society's overarching framework. Instead, the focus of the Anglo–Australian backlash has been directed usually against the maintenance of ethnic community languages (other than English) and especially against their teaching in the systemic or relatively conventional Australian schools.

The ostensible support for multicultural education on the one hand, and simultaneous attacks on languages, on the other, make one uncomfortably aware that, despite the florid phrases and multicultural rhetoric, what administrative authorities had in mind was multiculturalism of residues (Hodges, 1982). From this perspective, multicultural education is regarded essentially as involving positive attitudes and tolerance to other cultures, in the belief that they would in fact dissolve in the near future, or at least lose their distinctive cores, leaving behind a sediment of food, folklore, some surnames and other cultural remnants.

The focus of attack on minority community languages has been fuelled by the Australian tradition of monolingualism and the virtual disbelief in the ability to speak, read and write in more than one language. Knowledge of Greek, German or Polish has been somehow perceived as a threat, or even a slight upon English. This linguistic ethnocentrism has frequently been camouflaged by protestations of the 'unfairness' of ethnic parents to their own children, because of their insistence on burdening them with learning their mother tongues. The majority's claim has been that in this way such parents have been handicapping their children, both educationally and in their subsequent socio-economic advance. Such arguments, however, carry little credibility in view of the continuing approval of 'foreign' school languages, such as French (in the virtual absence of French migrants!). Such languages are considered as educationally broadening for the children of the majority, in contrast to the disapproval of 'migrant' languages, such as Greek or Italian which are assumed to confuse minority children when they study them in addition to English.

Education and Stable Multiculturalism

Despite the ideology of residualism that seems incipient in many multicultural programmes, some progress has already been made in Australia in the recognition accorded to minority languages in the conventional State and Catholic schools. The establishment of a multicultural television channel and state aid to part-time ethnic Saturday schools should also be noted (Smolicz, 1984a; Smolicz & Secombe, 1984). Among these measures, it is the more widespread introduction of minority languages and cultures into schools attended by *all* Australians that would herald the acceptance of the ideology of stable multiculturalism. Only when cultural maintenance for the minorities is combined with the opening up of their cultures to the children of the majority can we expect genuine cultural dialogue, and a more substantial, rather than purely cosmetic, transformation of the overarching framework of values that would take account of the cultures of the minorities.

Such a juxtaposition of cultures at school level, where it occurs, demonstrates the complexity of the interaction process, in that at times it may involve intermingling of cultures within one and the same lesson, while in other cases elements of a particular culture have to be taught in their intrinsically distinct and separate forms. For example, in a geography or social studies lesson one may make use of more than one cultural heritage but, in the sphere of language, the phenomenon of *dualism* or *co-existence* is essential. The latter terms are used to signify that the learning of a language, such as Italian, has to be an independent activity which parallels the child's acquisition of English, and possibly some other languages as well. In this way majority children are made to realise an obvious, if frequently misunderstood fact, namely that Arabic, Chinese or Portuguese cannot be treated on a par with English regional or class dialects, but that they are fully autonomous forms of cultural expression which cannot be reduced to intellectually subordinate elements of the majority culture. The comprehension of this fact has been sufficiently successful in Australia as to affect the views of at least a few prominent public servants who now argue for a national language policy and an appreciation of the need to study languages other than the dominant English (Menadue, 1981).

Education and Separatism

Despite such promising indications of the gradual acceptance that the overarching framework of values can no longer be simply a direct copy of the values of the majority group alone, some recent trends almost inexplicably favour the ideology of separatism. This would almost suggest that at least a section of the dominant group, discouraged by its inability to assimilate the minorities, or to residualise them, as it were, into insignificance, would prefer such groups to be incarcerated in, so to speak, their own little ethnic cauldrons, provided these were on the periphery of economic and political life, and did not impinge either on the distribution of power, or on the essentially Anglo-Saxon character of the overarching framework of values. According to this view that seems associated with supporters of 'privatisation' of education, it is even preferable to allow minorities to run their own separate schools, and even provide some state funding for that purpose, rather than risk a more fundamental transformation of the overarching framework that could result from the expansion of multicultural programmes in Australian schools as a whole, whereby all children would be exposed to the cultures of the minorities.

The moves against an expansion of multicultural and multilingual education may also have been prompted by economic motives, since it is cheaper to give limited aid to ethnic part-time schools, or even to the still relatively small number of full-time ethnic schools, than to embark upon the wide-ranging application of a national language policy for all students in all schools. The implicit motives for the privatisation of ethnic education may also involve a hope that, in isolation, with limited funds, and operating in institutions with little prestige, ethnic cultures (and languages in particular) are more likely to suffer a greater wastage and gradual extinction. The ethnocentric desire to keep one's own culture pure, and avoid its exposure to other cultures, may also have played some part, in the tacit effort to keep ethnicity in its place.

Such a policy of ethnic separatism (if continued) is bound to exert a negative effect on the evolution, as well as upon acceptability of the existing overarching framework of values by all sections of the community. It may also have the effect of reinforcing any incipient tendency among some of the minority groups towards ethnic exclusiveness within their narrow ranks. An important consequence of the simultaneous operation of such diverse forces as economic parsimony, fears of ethnic cultural contamination of the overarching framework, or simply a misunderstanding of the benefits of bilingualism and multiculturalism for all Australian children, might be the development in Australia of at least partial ethnic educational separatism. This would be reinforced by the growth of fully fledged ethnic *day* schools, such as the Jewish group already displays (Klarberg, 1982). In fact there are early warning signals that 'separatism for survival' may be virtually inflicted upon what has been described as the 'isolated and beleaguered' Vietnamese community in Australia which numbered 53,000 in 1981, but was expected to grow to 126,000 (or 0.87 of the population) by 1986 (Duncan, 1983, p. 31). The same phenomenon towards privatisation of ethnicity, and of education in particular, may affect other groups, such as the Lebanese, Turkish, and Latin American, as well as some sections of the much larger and better established Greek and Italian minorities.

CONCLUSION

If the majority group wishes to avoid fragmentation of education along ethnic lines, then it must recognise that a policy of residual multiculturalism in the mainstream schools, combined with the encouragement of separatism through the support of part-time or full-time ethnic schools, must be subjected to a fundamental revision. A full-scale multicultural education programme, involving the application of a national language policy to all levels of education, appears as the only realistic solution for a plural society. This represents the most effective way to achieve a state of stable multiculturalism in which overarching values are given an opportunity to develop in harmony with the ethnic values of the constituent groups.

REFERENCES

Bullivant, M. B. (1980). The STEPS Case against multicultural education: some cross-national findings, *Proceedings*, (Annual Conference of the Australian Association for Research in Education), pp. 393–404.

Bullivant, B. M. (1981). *The Pluralist Dilemma in Education* (Sydney, Allen & Unwin).

Bullivant, B. M. (1982). *Politics of Multiculturalism Versus Multi-cultural Butterfly Collecting in Australian Education* (paper circulated at the Alf Sampson Leadership Institutes on Multicultural & Intercultural Education, Ballarat).

Clyne, M. (1982). *Multilingual Australia* (Melbourne, River Seine Publications).

Duncan, T. (1983). Our isolated Vietnamese, *The Bulletin*, 103, No. 5356, pp. 31–33.

Harris, T. K. (1982). Reasons for the decline of Judeo-Spanish, *International Journal of the Sociology of Language*, No. 37, pp. 71–98.

Hodges, J. (1982). Opening address, National Language Policy Conference organized by the Federation of Ethnic Communities' Council, Canberra, October 22, p. 7.

Klarberg, M. (1982). Unpublished paper presented to language seminar for E. Haugen (Monash University); see also Diglossic education: the Jewish tradition, some Australian manifestations and their implications, *Journal of Intercultural Studies*, 4 (2), 1983, pp. 55–66.

Majoribanks, K. (1979). *Families and their Learning Environments* (London, Routledge & Kegan Paul).

Marjoribanks, K. (1980). *Ethnic Families and Children's Achievements* (Sydney, Allen & Unwin).

Menadue, T. (1981). Multilingualism and multiculturalism, *Babel*, 17 (5), pp. 4–12.

Ramirez, M., & Castaneda, A. (1975). *Cultural Democracy, Biocognitive Development and Education* (New York, Academic Press).

Selleck, R. J. W. (1980). The trouble with my looking glass: a study of the attitude of Australians to Germans during the Great War, *Journal of Australian Studies*, 6, pp. 2–25.

Smolicz, J. J. (1979). *Culture and Education in a Plural Society* (Canberra, Curriculum Development Centre).

Smolicz, J. J. (1981a). Core values and cultural identity, *Ethnic and Racial Studies*, 4, pp. 75–90.

Smolicz, J. J. (1981b). Culture, ethnicity and education: multiculturalism in a plural society, in: Megarry, J., Nisbet, S. & Hoyle, E. (Eds) *World Year Book of Education 1981: Education of Minorities* (New York, Nichols Publishing Co.).

Smolicz, J. J. (1981c). Cultural pluralism and educational policy: in search of stable multiculturalism, *Australian Journal of Education*, 25 (2), pp. 121–145.

Smolicz, J. J. (1983). Meaning and values in cross-cultural contacts, *Ethnic and Racial Studies*, 6, pp. 33–49.

Smolicz, J. J. (1984a). Social systems in multicultural societies, *International Journal of Sociology and Social Policy* (in press).

Smolicz, J. J. (1984b). Minority Languages and the Core Values of Culture: Changing Policies and Ethnic Response in Australia, *Journal of Multilingual and Multicultural Development* (in press).

Smolicz, J. J. & Piesiewicz, J. (1983). Greek-Australians and Anglo-Australians: a comparative study of attitudes to family and other primary social relationships (unpublished study).

Smolicz, J. J. & Secombe, M. J. (1977). A study of attitudes to the introduction of ethnic languages and cultures in Australian schools, *Australian Journal of Education*, 21, pp. 1–24.

Smolicz, J. J. & Secombe, M. J. (1981). *The Australian School Through Children's Eyes* (Melbourne University Press).

Smolicz, J. J. & Secombe, M. J. (1983). Future teachers' attitudes to community languages in Australia, *Unicorn: Bulletin of the Australian College of Education*, 9, pp. 63–66.

Smolicz, J. J. & Secombe, M. J. (1984). Multicultural television for all Australians, *International Journal of the Sociology of Language* (in press).

Szacki, J. (1969). Three concepts of tradition, *Polish Sociological Bulletin*, 2, pp. 27–29.

CHAPTER FOUR

Multicultural Education: For Freedom's Sake

James A. Banks

If we are to remain a free and pluralistic society, we can neither do away with the Western canon nor exclude the contributions of people of color. The traditionalists and multiculturalists must come together.

In *The Dialectic of Freedom*, Maxine Greene (1988) asks, "What does it mean to be a citizen of the free world?" It means, she concludes, having the capacity to choose, the power to act to attain one's purposes, and the ability to help transform a world lived in common with others. An important factor that limits human freedom in a pluralistic society is the cultural encapsulation into which all individuals are socialized. People learn the values, beliefs, and stereotypes of their community cultures. Although these community cultures enable individuals to survive, they also restrict their freedom and ability to make critical choices and to take actions to help reform society.

Education within a pluralistic society should affirm and help students understand their home and community cultures. However, it should also help free them from their cultural boundaries. To create and maintain a civic community that works for the common good, education in a democratic society should help students acquire the knowledge, attitudes, and skills they will need to participate in civic action to make society more equitable and just.

Multicultural education is an education for freedom (Parekh, 1986) that is essential in today's ethnically polarized and troubled world. It has evoked a divisive national debate in part because of the divergent views that citizens hold about what constitutes an American identity and about the roots and nature of American civilization. The debate in turn has sparked a power struggle over who should participate in formulating the canon used to shape the curriculum in the nation's schools, colleges, and universities.

THE DEBATE OVER THE CANON

A chorus of strident voices has launched an orchestrated and widely publicized attack on the movement to infuse content about ethnic groups and women into the school and university curriculum. Much of the current debate over multicultural education has taken place in mass media publications such as *Time* (Gray, 1991), *The Wall Street Journal* (Sirkin, 1990), and *The New Republic* (Howe, 1991), rather than in scholarly journals and forums. The Western traditionalists (writers who defend the canon now within the schools and universities) and the multiculturalists rarely engage in reflective dialogue. Rather, scholars on each side of the debate marshal data to support their briefs and ignore facts, interpretations, and perspectives that are inconsistent with their positions and visions of the present and future.

In his recent book, *Illiberal Education*, D'Souza (1991) defends the existing curriculum and structures in higher education while presenting an alarming picture of where multiculturalism is taking the nation. When multiculturalists respond to such criticism, they often fail to describe the important ways in which the multicultural vision is consistent with the democratic ideals of the West and with the heritage of Western civilization. The multicultural literature pays too little attention to the fact that the multicultural education movement emerged out of Western democratic ideals. One of its major aims is to close the gap between the Western democratic ideals of equality and justice and societal practices that contradict those ideals, such as discrimination based on race, gender, and social class.

Because so much of the debate over the canon has taken place in the popular media, which encourages simplistic, sound-byte explanations, the issues related to the curriculum canon have been overdrawn and oversimplified by advocates on both sides. The result is that the debate often generates more heat than light. Various interest groups have been polarized rather than encouraged to exchange ideas that might help us find creative solutions to the problems related to race, ethnicity, gender, and schooling.

As the ethnic texture of the nation deepens, problems related to diversity will intensify rather than diminish. Consequently, we need leaders and educators of good will, from all political and ideological persuasions, to participate in genuine discussions, dialogue, and debates that will help us formulate visionary and workable solutions and enable us to deal creatively with the challenges posed by the increasing diversity in the United States and the world. We must learn how to transform the problems related to racial and ethnic diversity into opportunities and strengths.

SHARING POWER

Western traditionalists and multiculturalists must realize that they are entering into debate from different power positions. Western traditionalists hold the balance of power, financial resources, and the top positions in the mass media, in schools, colleges and universities, government, and in the publishing industry. Genuine discussion between the traditionalists and the multiculturalists can take place only when power is placed on the table, negotiated, and shared.

Despite all of the rhetoric about the extent to which Chaucer, Shakespeare, Milton, and other Western writers are threatened by the onslaught of women and writers of color into the curriculum, the reality is that the curriculum in the nation's schools and universities is largely Western in its concepts, paradigms, and content. Concepts such as the Middle Ages and the Renaissance are still used to organize most units in history, literature, and the arts. When content about African and Asian cultures is incorporated into the curriculum, it is usually viewed within the context of European concepts and paradigms. For example, Asian, African, and American histories are often studied under the topic, "The Age of Discovery," which means the time when Europeans first arrived in these continents.

FACING REALITIES

If they are to achieve a productive dialogue rather than a polarizing debate, both Western traditionalists and the multiculturalists must face some facts. The growing number of people of color in our society and schools constitutes a demographic imperative educators must hear and respond to. The 1990 Census indicated that one of every four Americans is a person of color. By the turn of the century, one of every three will be of color (The Commission, 1988). Nearly half of the nation's students will be of color by 2020 (Pallas et al., 1989). Although the school and university curriculums remain Western-oriented, this growing number of people of color will increasingly demand to share power in curriculum decision making and in shaping a curriculum canon that reflects their experiences, histories, struggles, and victories.

People of color, women, and other marginalized groups are demanding that their voices, visions, and perspectives be included in the curriculum. They ask that the debt Western civilization owes to Africa, Asia, and indigenous America be acknowledged (Allen, 1986; Bernal, 1987). The advocates of the Afrocentric curriculum, in sometimes passionate language that reflects a dream long deferred, are merely asking that the cultures of Africa and African-American people be legitimized in the curriculum and that the African contributions to European civilization be acknowledged. People of color and women are also demanding that the facts about their victimization be told, for truth's sake, but also because they need to better understand their conditions so that they and others can work to reform society.

However, these groups must acknowledge that they do not want to eliminate Aristotle and Shakespeare, or Western civilization, from the school curriculum. To reject the West would be to reject important aspects of their own cultural heritages, experiences, and identities. The most important scholarly and literary works written by African-Americans, such as works by W. E. B. DuBois, Carter G. Woodson, and Zora Neale Hurston, are expressions of Western cultural experiences. African-American culture resulted from a blending of African cultural characteristics with those of African peoples in the United States.

REINTERPRETING WESTERN CIVILIZATION

Rather than excluding Western civilization from the curriculum, multiculturalists want a more truthful, complex, and diverse version of the West taught in the schools. They want the curriculum to describe the ways in which African, Asian, and indigenous American cultures have influenced and interacted with Western civilization. They also want schools to discuss not only the diversity and democratic ideals of Western civilization, but also its failures, tensions, dilemmas, and the struggles by various groups in Western societies to realize their dreams against great odds.

We need to deconstruct the myth that the West is homogeneous, that it owes few debts to other world civilizations, and that only privileged and upper-status Europeans and European-American males have been its key actors. Weatherford (1988) describes the debt the West owes to the first Americans. Bernal (1987), Drake (1987), Sertima (1984), and Clarke (1990) marshal considerable amounts of historical and cultural data that describe the ways in which African and Afroasiatic cultures influenced the development of Western civilization. Bernal, for example, presents linguistic and archaeological evidence to substantiate his claim that important parts of Greek civilization (technologies, language, deities, and architecture) originated in ancient Africa.

We should teach students that knowledge is a social construction, that it reflects the perspectives, experiences, and the values of the people and cultures that construct it, and that it is dynamic, changing, and debated among knowledge creators and users (Banks, 1991). Rather than keep such knowledge debates as the extent to which African civilizations contributed to Western civilization out of the classroom, teachers should make them an integral part of teaching. The classroom should become a forum in which multicultural debates concerning the construction of knowledge take place. The voices of the Western traditionalists, the multiculturalists, textbook authors, and radical writers should be heard and legitimized in the classroom.

TOWARD THE DEMOCRATIC IDEAL

The fact that multiculturalists want to reformulate and transform the Western canon, not to purge the curriculum of the West, is absent from most of the writings of the Western traditionalists. It doesn't support their argument that Shakespeare, Milton, and Aristotle are endangered. By the same token, the multiculturalists have written little about the intersections of multicultural content and a Western-centric canon, perhaps because they have focused on ways in which the established Western canon should be reconstructed and transformed.

Multicultural education itself is a product of the West. It grew out of a struggle guided by Western ideals for human dignity, equality, and freedom (Parker, 1991). Multicultural education is a child of the civil rights movement led by African Americans that was designed to eliminate discrimination in housing, public accommodation, and other areas. The leaders of the civil rights movement, such as Fannie Lou Hamer, Rosa Parks, and Daisy Bates, internalized the American democratic ideal stated in such important United States documents as the Declaration of Independence, the Constitution, and the Bill of Rights. The civil rights leaders of the 1960s and 1970s used the Western ideals of freedom and democracy to justify and legitimize their push for structural inclusion and the end of institutionalized discrimination and racism.

The civil rights movement of the 1960s echoed throughout the United States and the world. Other groups, such as Native Americans and Hispanics, women, and people with disabilities, initiated their own freedom movements. These cultural revitalization movements made demands on a number of institutions. The nation's schools and universities became primary targets for reform, in part because they were important symbols of the structural exclusion that victimized groups experienced, and in part because they were easily accessible.

It would be a serious mistake to interpret these cultural revitalization movements and the educational reforms they gave birth to as a repudiation of the West and Western civilization. The major goals of these movements are full inclusion of the victimized groups into Western institutions and a reform of these institutions so that their practices are more consistent with their democratic ideals. Multicultural education not only arose out of Western traditions and ideals, its major goal is to create a nation-state that actualizes the democratic ideals for all that the Founding Fathers intended for an elite few. Rather than being divisive as some critics contend, multicultural education is designed to reduce race, class, and gender divisions in the United States and the world.

Given the tremendous social class and racial cleavages in United States society, it is inaccurate to claim that the study of ethnic diversity will threaten national cohesion. The real threats to national unity—which in an economic, sociological, and psychological sense we have not fully attained but are working toward—are the deepening racial and social-class schisms within United States society. As Wilson (1987) points out in *The Truly Disadvantaged*, the gap between the rich and the poor has grown tremendously in recent years. The social-class schism has occurred not only across racial and ethnic groups, but within these groups. Hence, the rush to the suburbs has not just been a white flight, but has been a flight by the middle class of many hues. As a consequence, low-income African Americans and Hispanics have been left in inner-city communities without the middle-class members of their groups to provide needed leadership and role models. They are more excluded than ever from mainstream American society.

EDUCATING FOR FREEDOM

Each of us becomes culturally encapsulated during our socialization in childhood. We accept the assumptions of our own community culture, internalize its values, views of the universe, misconceptions, and stereotypes. Although this is as true for the child socialized within a mainstream culture as it is for the minority child, minority children are usually forced to examine, confront, and question their cultural assumptions when they enter school.

Students who are born and socialized within the mainstream culture of a society rarely have an opportunity to identify, question, and challenge their cultural assumptions, beliefs, values, and perspectives because the school culture usually reinforces those that they learn at home and in their communities. Consequently, mainstream Americans have few opportunities to become free of cultural assumptions and perspectives that are monocultural, that devalue African and Asian cultures, and that stereotype people of color and people who are poor, or who are victimized in other ways. These mainstream Americans often have an inability to function effectively within other American cultures, and lack the ability and motivation to experience and benefit from cross-cultural participation and relationships.

To fully participate in our democratic society, these students and all students need the skills a multicultural education can give them to understand others and to thrive in a rapidly changing, diverse world. Thus, the debate between the Western traditionalists and the multiculturalists fits well within the tradition of a pluralistic democratic society. Its final result will most likely be not exactly what either side wants, but a synthesized and compromised perspective that will provide a new vision for the nation as we enter the 21st century.

REFERENCES

Allen, P. G. (1986). *The Sacred Hoop: Recovering the Feminine in American Indian Traditions.* Beacon Press.

Banks, J. A. (1991). *Teaching Strategies for Ethnic Studies,* 5th ed. Boston: Allyn and Bacon.

Bernal, M. (1987). *The Afroasiatic Roots of Classical Civilization,* Vol. 1: *The Fabrication of Ancient Greece 1785–1985.* London: Free Association Books.

Clarke, J. H. (1990). "African People on My Mind." In *Infusion of African and African American Content in the School Curriculum: Proceedings of the First National Conference,* edited by A. G. Hilliard III, L. Payton-Stewart, and L. O. Williams. Morristown, N.J.: Aaron Press.

The Commission on Minority Participation in Education and American Life. (May 1988). *One-Third of a Nation.* Washington, D.C.: The American Council on Education.

D'Souza, D. (1991). *Illiberal Education: The Politics of Race and Sex on Campus.* New York: The Free Press.

Drake, St. C. (1987). *Black Folk Here and There.* Vol. 1. Los Angeles: Center for Afro-American Studies, University of California.

Gray, P. (July 8, 1991). "Whose America?" *Time* 138: 13–17.

Greene, M. (1988). *The Dialectic of Freedom.* New York: Teachers College Press.

Howe, I. (February 18, 1991). "The Value of the Canon." *The New Republic*: 40–44.

Pallas, A. M., G. Natriello, E. L. McDill. (June–July 1989). "The Changing Nature of the Disadvantaged Population: Current Dimensions and Future Trends." *Educational Researcher* 18, 2: 2.

Parekh, B. (1986). "The Concept of Multi-Cultural Education." *In Multicultural Education: The Interminable Debate,* edited by S. Modgil, G. K. Verma, K. Mallick, and C. Modgil. Philadelphia: The Falmer Press, pp. 19–31.

Parker, W. P. (1991). "Multicultural Education in Democratic Societies." Paper presented at the annual meeting of the American Educational Research Association, Chicago.

Sirkin, G. (January 18, 1990). "The Multiculturalists Strike Again." *The Wall Street Journal,* p. A14.

Sertima, I. V., ed. (1984). (Ed). *Black Women in Antiquity.* New Brunswick, N.J.: Transaction Books.

Weatherford, J. (1988). *Indian Givers: How the Indians of the Americas Transformed the World.* New York: Fawcett Columbine.

Wilson, W. J. (1987). *The Truly Disadvantaged: The Inner City, the Underclass, and Public Policy.* Chicago: the University of Chicago Press.

SUGGESTED LEARNING EXPERIENCES

1. Review two or three curriculum guides from local school districts and at least one curriculum document developed by a state department of education. Compare the statement of the philosophy, purpose, or mission of

schools with the purpose of schooling for Native Americans at the turn of the century as described by David Adams; Jerzy Smolicz' description of assimilation, separatism, and various categories of multiculturalism; and James Banks' description of positions held by multiculturalists and traditionalists.

2. Working with a small group of colleagues, develop a written description of current ideology supporting the purpose and process of schooling in the United States. Compare and contrast this with the ideology supporting the purpose and process of schooling for Native Americans at the turn of the century.

3. Working with a small group of colleagues, develop a one-paragraph statement of what you believe should be the purpose of schooling in a culturally diverse society. Identify key elements of the ideology supporting this statement of purpose.

PART TWO

CURRICULUM PLANNING

CRITICAL QUESTIONS

1. Who is best prepared to participate in curriculum planning and what insights are essential?
2. To what extent should local values and specific cultural, ethnic, and social class groups be considered and/or included in curriculum planning efforts?
3. Which approaches to curriculum planning are most likely to be productive?
4. What should be the relationship between the curriculum product, its construction, curriculum policymaking, and the purpose of schooling in a culturally diverse society?

OVERVIEW

Curriculum is what is successfully conveyed to differing degrees to different students, by committed teachers using appropriate materials and actions, of legitimated bodies of knowledge, skill, taste, and propensity to act and react, which are chosen for instruction after serious reflection and communal decision by representatives of those involved in the teaching of a specified group of students who are known to the decisionmakers. (Schwab, 1983)

> Curriculum is not a tangible product but the actual, day-to-day interaction of students, teachers, knowledge, and the milieu. (Cornbleth, 1988)

The way curriculum is conceptualized influences the practice of curriculum planning including who participates, what insights are considered essential, which internal and external influences are to be considered, the purpose and function to be served, and how the effort and its impact will be evaluated. The three authors in this part agree that curriculum is what happens in classrooms between teachers and their students. This conceptualization of the curriculum precludes the transportation and replication of curriculum developed external to the situation in which it will be implemented. This suggests that the curriculum planning process should be a school-community effort with at least representative participation of all parties who have an interest or who will be affected.

In Part I the authors address the purpose and ideologies undergirding schooling in a culturally diverse society. In Part II the reader is invited to consider the relationship between the purpose of schooling in a culturally diverse society and the practice of curriculum planning.

Joseph Schwab, the first author in Part II, brings attention to the importance of addressing issues of diversity in his discussion of local considerations in curriculum planning. He points out that there is variation among different groups in their values, needs, and expectations of schools and that curriculum planning must address this diversity.

Schwab describes in great detail the roles and attributes of those who should participate in curriculum planning. He identifies four commonplaces in curriculum planning that include the subject matter, teachers, learners, and the milieu and describes how and by whom each is to be represented in the planning process. Schwab meticulously delineates the knowledge, experience, and insight each committee member needs to have in order to make the most meaningful contribution to the curriculum planning effort. He suggests that teachers should be the first committee members selected because of the critical role they play in curriculum implementation. He also points out the importance of involving school principals because they are responsible for the financial resources of the school, have immediate knowledge of the school environment, influence teachers' attitudes toward acceptable school practices, have direct contact with the school board and district level administration, and usually interact regularly with parents and local community members.

An apparent shortcoming in Schwab's discussion of who should participate in curriculum planning is his failure to include roles that represent the issues of diversity addressed at the beginning of the chapter. This omission raises critical questions about the composition of the curriculum group. To what extent should members of the curriculum group represent the diversity found in the school for which the curriculum planning is to be done? Given the growing discrepancy between the cultural and experiential backgrounds of teachers and their students, to what extent are teachers actually knowledgeable about the students they teach? Does Schwab's emphasis on teacher participation in curriculum planning in the absence of representatives from diverse cultural and experiential backgrounds pose a potential risk for implementing a curriculum that is valued more by teachers than students or their parents and other adults from the local community? Is it possible to identify and utilize a planning process that will overcome the absence of representation for diversity?

In an earlier work, "The Practical 3," Schwab presents the planning process as equally important to that of participation. He identifies three operations as basic tools for curriculum planning, which are collaboration among those representing the four commonplaces, coalescence of what is discovered through collaboration, and utilization of the coalesced body of concerns. Schwab describes these operations as occurring simultaneously rather than serially. He anticipated the outcome of this collaboration to be a balance of insights in relationship to child-centered, social change-centered, subject matter-centered, and teacher-centered perspectives.

In Schwab's characterization of the curriculum planning process the chair of the committee is the pivotal role. He describes in detail the competency, knowledge, skill, and training necessary for this role. Again, in this discussion Schwab does not mention knowledge of diversity or skill in cross-cultural interaction. What Schwab presents is a practical model for curriculum planning that has identifiable flaws that can be overcome.

Henrietta Schwartz, the second author in Part II, extends the discussion of curriculum planning by introducing examples of approaches employing aspects of Schwab's practical model. She proposes a two-way analysis of curriculum employing Schwab's four commonplaces and Herskovitz's nine universal cultural patterns. This two-way analysis provides a framework for data gathering as preparation for identifying aspects of the curriculum in need of change. Schwartz illustrates what information can be gathered using the two-way analysis to examine a literature curriculum at an urban high school serving a culturally diverse population. The illustration using Schwartz's matrix clearly reveals the potential for discrepancies between the four commonplaces in relationship to the cultural universals.

Schwartz presents three examples of curriculum planning efforts that generated varying degrees of success while employing aspects of the collaborative structure Schwab recommends. Each effort involved a core group and a chair, similar responsibilities for curriculum change and a comparable process involving participatory deliberation and decision making. While the curriculum planning efforts Schwartz describes are located in culturally diverse or ethnic minority communities, she does not describe how individuals from diverse backgrounds participated in the planning process.

Schwartz brings attention to the fact that Schwab has intentionally omitted discussion of external factors that directly influence curriculum planning and implementation such as university program requirements, changes in the economy, changes in the teacher population, legislated changes in school practices, technological changes, the impact of teachers' unions, and pressure from special interest groups. She does not explain how these factors might be addressed by the curriculum group or in the curriculum planning process. Schwartz does, however, introduce a broader context of influence on curriculum planning. This discussion is expanded by Catherine Cornbleth, the final author in Part II.

Cornbleth distinguishes between the *nominal context*, which is anything that might influence curriculum planning and implementation, and the *relevant context*, which refers to aspects of the nominal context that have a more direct and immediate influence on curriculum in a particular instance. The relevant context includes the structural context and the sociocultural context. The *structural context* is defined as "the established roles and relationships, including operating procedures, shared beliefs, and norms (i.e., tradition, culture) . . . The *relevant sociocultural context of curriculum* consists of extrasystemic demographic, social, political, and economic conditions; traditions and ideologies; and events that influence curriculum and curriculum change" (p. 156, this volume). Cornbleth's categorization helps clarify the contextual influences on curriculum change.

Cornbleth describes curriculum as a contextualized social process, rather than a tangible product. She contends that "if curriculum is contextualized social process, then curriculum change is a function of contextual change. Curriculum is unlikely to change in the absence of supportive structural changes, which are unlikely to be initiated in the absence of external pressures. This line of reasoning indicates the futility of trying to bring about curriculum reform by substituting one curriculum document for another" (p. 159, this volume). Instead, she poses a series of questions that can be used to inform curriculum change efforts. The questions Cornbleth raises are intended to place curriculum planning in a relevant context.

It is important to point out that while each of the authors in this part describes curriculum as the day-to-day occurrences in classrooms, this does not preclude the development of curriculum documents to inform classroom practice. These authors are more specifically concerned with issues related to who should participate in curriculum planning, under what conditions, and with what outcomes; the relationship between curriculum policymaking, curriculum planning and implementation; and the sociocultural and structural context of curriculum planning. These issues are critically important in curriculum planning for a culturally diverse society.

REFERENCES

Cornbleth, C. (1988). Curriculum in and out of context. *Journal of Curriculum and Supervision, 3*(2), 85–96.

Schwab, J. J. (1983). The Practical 4: Something for Curriculum Professors to do. *Curriculum Inquiry, 13*(3), 239–265.

CHAPTER FIVE

The Practical 4: Something for Curriculum Professors to Do

Joseph J. Schwab

This paper, by contrast to the three papers which precede it (See Appendix, Note 2) is a practical paper on the practical. Such a practical paper must necessarily exemplify arts of the practical insofar as this is possible in expository prose as against the natural language of the practical which is deliberative exchange and consideration among several persons or differing selves about concrete alternatives in relation to particular times and places.

The process of exemplification gives rise to certain stylistic qualities, some of which may annoy the reader. First, the structural elements of its syntax are not premises, argument, and conclusion but circumstances and alternative ways of changing them. In consequence, there are numerous examples. Second, some of these exemplify the same point as it might present itself under a variety of circumstances (an emphasis on the particularity of the practical). Third, there is extended consideration of details of many of these circumstances. Fourth, the quality of deliberative discourse is maintained by raising doubts to matters suggested. Finally, there are passages which would be digressions in normal expository discourse. Most are set within parentheses or brackets. Here, they exist as instances of the elastic boundaries characteristic of practical problems and of the need to pursue possible effects of considered solutions to practical problems into areas beyond the scope of the problem as formulated.

I should add that this paper stands on its own, despite its origin in predecessors. It does this by virtue of summaries, where necessary, of points made in the earlier papers.

CURRICULUM

I stipulate the following conception of curriculum: Curriculum is what is successfully conveyed to differing degrees to different students, by committed teachers using appropriate materials and actions, of legitimated bodies of knowledge, skill, taste, and propensity to act and react, which are chosen for instruction after serious reflection and communal decision by representatives of those involved in the teaching of a specified group of students who are known to the decisionmakers.

I repeat: What is successfully conveyed. By committed teachers. Using appropriate materials and methods. Of legitimated matters. Which are chosen *via* serious reflection on alternatives. By those involved in the teaching of a specifiable and known group of students. Who will differ from time to time and place to place.

I add: Curriculum is not an endless collection of objectives. It is not decided in Moscow and telegraphed to the provinces whether Moscow be conceived as the specialist in biology, or the specialist in curriculum, or the teacher claiming academic freedom, or the legislator or parents, or students. All of these are involved. No one of them moreover, is the fountainhead of decision and choice except as particular circumstance convinces a majority of them that one be treated for a particular occasion or problem as the fountainhead. Curriculum is not necessarily the same for all students of a given age and standing. Nor does it differ necessarily in all respects for each and every student or school. Finally., curriculum is not something about which decisions can be certified in advance of trial as the best decisions. Some of these matters require further elucidation.

OBJECTIVES

Stricture on endless strings of objectives is a matter on which very much has been well-written. Here, then, I shall be content to emphasise two curricular objections to such strings. In the first place, but not of first importance, such strings often, even usually, anatomize matters which may be of great importance into bits and pieces which, taken separately, are trivial or pointless. Lists of objectives often so trivialize because they anatomize, not only a subject-matter, but teachers' thoughts about it, the pattern of instruction used to convey it, the organization of textbooks, and the analysis and construction of tests.

In the second place, and of first importance, ends or objectives can be defensibly selected only in the light of consideration of available or obtainable means, materials, and teaching skills; nor can ends chosen lead to means and materials which yield only the ends for which they were chosen.

There are side effects to teaching devices as there are to pharmaceuticals and the side effects of teaching may be as dangerous, or as useful and suggestive of alternative uses, as pharmaceutical side effects. Therefore reflection on curriculum must take account of what teachers are ready to teach or ready to learn to teach; what materials are available or can be devised; what effects actually ensue from materials and methods chosen, not merely how well they yield intended purposes but what else ensues. But none of these can be identified except as some ends or objectives are tentatively selected and pursued. Hence, curriculum reflection must take place in a back-and-forth manner between ends and means. A linear movement from ends to means is absurd.

EQUALITY OF THE COMMONPLACES

I remarked above that, although no one contributor to curriculum decision is by nature the fountainhead of decision, any one of them may, under some circumstances, be adjudged the fountainhead for that occasion or problem. This point about occasional fountainheads is of personal as well as general importance since it bears on a carelessness of mine. I have said, perhaps too often, that the four commonplaces of education (teacher, student, what is taught and milieux of teaching–learning) which the contributors to curriculum decision represent, are of intrinsically equal importance. I have put such emphasis on this matter because curriculum decision has been so commonly based on subject-matter considerations alone, or political-communal considerations alone, or the individual child's want or need alone and so on. My repeated insistence on the *theoretically* equal importance of the several commonplaces has been repeatedly taken to mean that in all and every curricular debate, each of the commonplaces should be given equal weight.

This is not the case. There are times and places when the welfare of the state is of paramount importance (during threat of war for example) and what contributes most to the future happiness of individual students, or justice to a subject-matter, or the bents of teachers, must take subordinate positions. There are times when the state's welfare can be relegated to secondary importance in deference to what education might confer on individual lives. And both may be subordinated at times to the desirability of recruiting some of the best students to the service of a subject-matter.

Nevertheless, it is only by consideration of the present state of the curriculum, the present condition of students and surrounding circumstances, all in the light of all the commonplaces equally, that a decision to favor one or another is justified. Without such consideration, curricular planning results in errors which later require corrections which turn out to be another misemphasis requiring another correction, and so on indefinitely. Consider recent pressures for a large-scale core curriculum in the high schools to "correct" the indefinite electivism which arose from unconsidered primacy of student "wants and needs," an unexamined emphasis on subject-matter which will almost certainly require (if successful) a further "correction" to meet national and personal economic needs. The current concern about subject-matters (math and science) is another case in point: a "correction" of the "correction" generated by the massive Moscovian curricular pressures of the early sixties. The now-dying press for "career" education and "basics," arising from heavy emphasis on supposed social needs for labor orientation and enough of the three R's to permit understanding of orders and instructions, is another case in point.

MOSCOW, THE PROVINCES AND FEDERALISM

The plaint of my earlier papers on the practical is that professors of curriculum almost invariably seek to fight the revolution in Moscow and telegraph it to the provinces. They seek the right curriculum by consulting and constructing theories which they hope will be theories of curriculum. They conceive theory as being immediately applicable to every instance of its subject-matter. Hence, most act as if an adequate theory of curriculum, were it to be found, would tell us once and for all what to do in every grade and every stage of every school in every place.

I, on the other hand, assert that a diversity of needs, resources, and recipients of education characterize American times and places, and, hence, call for a diversity of curricula. The differences from curriculum to curriculum will often be small (though crucial), and may sometimes be of a substantial order. The construction of needed diversities entails attention by planners of curriculum to the *local*.

The locality I have in mind is exemplified by the locality of the students of a school, district, or town. They often are of a prevailing social class, ethnic or religious background which has its own view of what should be taught and learned and its own view of the value of education in general. They are often of a prevailing band of economic standings which determine what pressures are on them, what time and privacies they have for study. The place may be urban, suburban, or rural; Southern, Texan, or any other region of special characteristic; prevailingly industrial, managerial, or agricultural. These features will determine the exemplifications of adulthood and of a desirable life which students encounter and which determine, in some part, what they will expect from schooling and upon what they are most willing to devote their energies.

Such matters are crucial factors in decisions about curriculum. For example, to ignore socio-ethnic views of what is worth learning is to fail to teach well what a larger view determines to be desirable or is to put resources in the service of an aspect of instruction which is unnecessary. To be innocent of the constrictions on time and privacy which students enjoy at home may well mean to impose burdens of learning which the students of that place cannot bear. In similar fashion, to ignore the exemplifications of adulthood and a good life which characterize the place is to fail to utilize student energies which press for fuller expression in some direction or is, by complement, to fail to see the need for special mobilization of student energies for the pursuit of other goals. Similar localisms affect the teacher of a school or district, the resources in the community for instruction and for examples of matters taught, and the availability of financial support for one or another aspect of education.

It is this very locality of instances of the subject-matter of a theory which theorists necessarily ignore in order to make theories theoretical, that is, to confer on them a required universality by taking account only of the elements common to all members of their universe. There is a second weakness of such theories: they are almost always psychological theories of one kind of psychology or another, *or* political-economic theories, *or* sociological *or* epistemological. Each such theory usually takes account of only one of the commonplaces that together constitute education, hence such theories are incomplete.

As a corrective alternative to such theoreticism, I have proposed cultivation and use of two sets of arts which treat, respectively, the need for localism of curriculum and the need for adaptation of theories to one another and to the educational problems on which they are brought to bear. I call these arts, employing an ancient tradition, arts of the practical i.e. prudence and deliberation, *and* arts of eclectic.

These theses about the practical and the arguments supporting them have generated a certain amount of discussion, both by way of approval and condemnation. Ironically, even some highly theoretic discussion has been evoked (e.g., "What is the true [*sic*] nature of theory and practice?"). The theses and arguments have not, however, conspicuously transformed curricular theorists into practitioners. Discussants, including myself, have suggested three reasons for this failure: that curricularists are unfamiliar with the arts of deliberation and eclectic and unprepared to master them; that the practical is not particularly respectable academically and professors of education desperately pursue academic respectability; that the bureaucratic structure of American education provides no pathway for exercise of the arts of practice by professors of education.

The first of these, unfamiliarity with the practical and eclectic arts, is being dealt with by groups of involved friends and colleagues.[1] The second reason,

[1]I have in mind especially Thomas Roby, Professor of Humanities, Kennedy-King College, Chicago; Peter Pereira, Professor of Education, Chicago; and William Reid, professor of Education, University of Birmingham, England.

pursuit of academic respectability must, it appears to me, be dealt with only indirectly. In this paper, I deal with the third, a path for professorial involvement in the practical. I shall do so by first describing the character and usefulness of a new role or office to be installed in individual schools or small school systems. I shall then indicate the initial higher education which would prepare men and women to fill this office, and the professorial scholarly activity which would continuously refresh those who fill this office. Such preparation and refreshment would be practical functions of professors of curriculum. So much for starting points. Let us proceed.

THE OFFICE—ITS FORERUNNER

Let us suppose that School X has decided to institute a continuing watch and correction of its curriculum. Who shall take on the task? The first answer, the principal, will not fly, at least not in the United States. At a graduation party of teacher candidates a year or so ago, one young man, allowed to speak for five minutes as a reward for excellence of record, said, in effect, "I'm going into teaching because that is the route to becoming a principal and a principal is what I want to be. He runs things and gives orders and is obeyed." It would be unfair to suppose that the young man was representative of the bents of principals generally, as far as his expressed wish for getting and exercising power is concerned. With respect, however, to his emphasis on a managerial function, he may not be far wrong. I know of no data on principals' wishes in this respect nor even of a reliable way to discover them. I do know that managing is what most principals mostly do.

One review of research, emanating from The Ontario Institute for Studies in Education, suggests that only half of elementary school principals actually attempt to improve instructional programs and this half, I suspect, do only a little toward this end and rarely sustain an effort until it has been successful. This need not be because of psychological bents but because there is so much managing to be done. There is, first, the work of the school to do, that is, watching over the attendance and work of teachers, the attendance and behavior of students, the availability of supplies and materials, the selection of new teachers as needed, the distribution of times and places of teachers, courses, and programs. Then there are money sources to be located and exploited: community relations to be maintained; and communication lines with School Boards and Superintendents to be kept open and useful to the school. For sustained and continuing watch over curriculum, another agency is required.

Once we set aside the traditional assignment of the task to the principal, it becomes obvious that the nature of curriculum change, that is, identification of the places where change is wanting, the borrowing or invention of alternative ways of fulfilling identified wants, deliberation on the costs and benefits of these alternatives, and, at last, their initiation with convinced and ready teachers, requires, not one person, but a group. A group is required, first of all, by the dependence of warranted decision on all the commonplaces, that is, the considerations they remind us to take into account in making decisions and the need to examine circumstances for the relative weighting of the commonplaces which is appropriate to this time and place. The commonplaces demand a group because no one person adequately commands the concrete particularities of all the commonplaces. What should be taught, how teaching should run, who is available to do it, which students most need the change in question, are each matters requiring their own expertise or experience.

A group is further required in order to make likely the invention of some diversity of appropriate alternatives. Again, a group is required to deliberate on these alternatives, for, though inner deliberation on an extensive matter is possible, it is extremely difficult, especially because it requires a state of nonbias with respect to emphasis on one commonplace or another. There is still another need for a group which will be raised at a more appropriate moment. Hence, the question has changed. It is no longer who shall do it, but who shall constitute the group who shall do it.

The first answer to the question of who should be a member of the group is the teacher. Again, and louder: THE TEACHER. There are two major reasons for this emphasis. First, the children of the school as learners: their behavior and misbehavior in classrooms: what they take as "fair" or "unfair" in the course of teaching-learning: what rouses hopes, fears, and despairs with respect to learning: what the children are inclined to learn: what they disdain and what they see as relevant to their present or future lives, are better known by no one than the teacher. It is he who tries to teach them. It is she who lives with them for the better part of the day and the better part of the year.

There are important generalities about learning which can be proferred by some kinds of psychologists. There are some desirable and undesirable tendencies on the part of teachers which are best known by certain other social scientists. But the generalities of psychology require particularization to these teachers here and now. And what social scientists may know about the behavior of teachers in the classroom (a) will not be invariant from teacher to teacher and (b) is unlikely to be accompanied by knowledge of effective ways to alter undesirable and encourage wanted behaviors.

The second reason for insisting that the teacher be first-named member of the curricular group is a matter it has taken decades for us to learn or, at least, to realize we must take into account. Some scholarly specialists very likely would correct this to read, ". . . to which to capitulate." It is simply this: teachers will not and cannot be merely told what to do. Subject specialists have tried it. Their attempts and failures I know at first hand. Administrators have tried it. Legislators have tried it. Teachers are not, however, assembly line operators, and will not so behave. Further, they have no need, except in rare instances, to fall back on defiance as a way of not heeding. There are a thousand ingenious ways in which commands on what and how to teach can, will, and must be modified or circumvented in the actual moments of teaching. Teachers practice an art. Moments of choice of what to do, how to do it, with whom and at what pace, arise hundreds of times a school day, and arise differently every day and with every group of students. No command or instruction can be so formulated as to control that kind of artistic judgment and behavior, with its demand for frequent, instant choices of ways to meet an ever varying situation. (The personal practical knowing in back of this kind of teacher judgment is currently under study at the Ontario Institute for Studies in Education with early results which are extremely interesting.) Therefore, teachers *must* be involved in debate, deliberation, and decision about what and how to teach. Such involvement constitutes the only language in which knowledge adequate to an art can arise. Without such a language, teachers not only feel decisions as impositions, they find that intelligence cannot traverse the gap between the generalities of merely expounded instructions and the particularities of teaching moments. Participation in debate-deliberation-choice is required for learning what is needed as well as for willingness to do it.[2] There is an obvious moral here for teacher-training. Persons involved in teacher-training might well puzzle over it.

What teachers do we need? A few schools are fortunate in having some teachers who are especially ingenious at thinking up ways of solving problems of what and how to teach. We need representatives of those teachers. There are, second, the teachers who will, if they are persuaded of its worth, undertake the altered teaching which arises as a solution to the problems in hand. They must be represented.

In addition to ingenious teachers and teachers who represent the area of schooling under discussion, there should also be at least one teacher-representative of an area remote from that under discussion. She could be a teacher of literature when the problem under discussion concerns science. She could be a teacher of the social studies when the problem concerns literature. This representation is desirable because a curricular change in

---

[2]What I have said above applies to every art, whether it be teaching, stone-carving or judicial control of a court of law. Every art has rules but knowledge of the rules does not make an artist. Art arises as the knower of the rules learns to *apply* them appropriately to the particular case. Application, in turn, requires acute awareness of the particularities of that case and ways in which the rule can be modified to fit the case without complete abrogation of the rule. In art, the form must be adapted to the matter. Hence the form must be communicated in ways which illuminate its possibilities for modification.

any area of schooling which leaves the rest of the curriculum unaffected is rare indeed. At the least, a change in one area of the curriculum adds or subtracts from the money, student time and student interest addressed to other aspects of the curriculum. More specifically, a change in substance or emphasis in the teaching of literature may directly affect, say, the teaching of history and the social sciences. The converse also holds. Consider, for example, the close connection between the moral-social import of a George Eliot novel and the content of social studies texts or a history of the 19th Century. Scientific materials will exhibit similar connections with literature and the social studies. The heredity-environment issue is one case in point. Biological studies of population growth and legislative considerations of contraception and abortion is another. The role and nature of emotion seen in novels and short-stories have intimate ties to what psychologists may affirm, deny, or leave unmentioned.

How many teachers? Two of the ingenious would be helpful indeed, especially because such people stimulate one another. Two (or three if the school is on the biggish side) of the possible users of the change is a necessity if the recommendations of the curriculum group are to have weight with remaining teachers affected by the proposed change. Of course, if only a few teachers will be involved in use of the change, all of them should be in the curriculum group or in one of its subcommittees. At least one, possibly two, representative(s) of remote subject areas will be needed.

The other members of the curriculum group can be discussed more briefly.

The principal is an indispensable member of the group, not only for the sake of the group's curricular work but for the sake of the school as a whole. He contributes to the success of the curricular work in four ways. In the first place, his knowledge and approval of the curricular change which may be proferred is critical to effective installation of the change, i.e., its adoption by willing and understanding teachers. This holds especially for teachers not involved in the group's work and for new teachers arriving after the work is done. This arises from the hierarchical administrative structure of most schools and the mythos of authority.

Second, the principal, if long in his post, will have fullest knowledge of the smallest but most potent social milieu which affects teaching and learning, that is, the milieu of the school itself. He will know the tradition, the taboos, and requirements passed on from established to younger teachers of the school. He will know better than others in the school what status the school labors under or enjoys vis-à-vis the school board and those who influence its decisions. He will know what funds are available or whether it is wise to divert funds from present activities to a newly proposed one. He is likely to be aware of wants and attitudes among parents and neighbors of which the teachers are unaware. All of these are germane to curricular decision.

Third, the absence of the principal from the curricular group would elevate the Curriculum Chairmanship, the new school office for which we are at this moment preparing the background, to that of an administrative office. This would be fatal to its holder's pursuit of his task, as we shall describe it. He must be, and be seen by teachers, as one of theirs.

Fourth, involvement of the principal in group membership will, in many cases, serve both as a way for him to participate in curriculum decision *and* as a persuasive way. It will be a way, pure and simple, in the many cases where principals have felt that the pressure of time imposed by other duties forbade concern in curriculum structure. It will be so because membership in a group as against leadership, permits the principal some flexibility in apportioning the time devoted to the curricular tasks. Others share in the thinking; he can absent himself on occasion. It will be a persuasive way to involve him in curriculum since the typical administrator will be reluctant to have an important undertaking proceed without some cognizance and contribution by him.

Finally, it is obvious that establishment of a Curriculum Chairman as head of a group which can alter curriculum without participation of the Principal is to establish a dual, competitive administration of the school. Such a state of affairs would not be tolerated by principals, would complicate the maneuvers of teachers vis-à-vis the administration, including the temptation to set Chairman and principal at odds with one another, and would confuse the efforts of parents and citizens concerned with the school.

A curriculum ought to be known by the persons it produces, as well as by other signs and standards. In schools generally, an approximation to such knowledge is supplied by the results of standardized achievement tests of various kinds. These would most certainly be consulted by our group. In many consolidated schools and schools of small towns and cities, an additional and broader source of information is available; that is, persons who employ the school's graduates, work with them, and see their behavior in the neighborhood and at public functions. Such persons should be represented on our curricular group. (Obviously, what is seen of young persons at work and play cannot be blamed or credited only to the schools. This must be a matter for discussion in the group and possibly for research.)

For this role, a superb choice would be a member of the local school board. He is peculiarly appropriate because of several functions and qualities combined in him. First, he is a non-school member of the community, hence he has a set of biases which differ from those of school men and women. He is elected or appointed to the school board because he represents powerful or numerous members of the community with whom, presumably, he remains in communication. He is not only, however, a peculiarly apt representative of the community, he is also a member of the school board. As such, his service on the curriculum group should generate knowledge of what the schools do and why they do it, knowledge which school boards do not, as a rule, possess in plenitude. He would inevitably carry back to the board meetings some of this knowledge and attitudes altered by its possession. This would, I think, convey to school boards a degree of the same sort of commitment which participation in curriculum decision making confers on teachers.

In many instances, it will not be possible to coopt a member of the school board. They are full time workers elsewhere in most cases, and the desirable ones for our purposes are frequent attendants at board meetings. Their time is further consumed by letters and phone calls of parents and others and by the labors engendered by these communications. In such cases, it might be possible to coopt two board members who would attend a few early meetings of the curriculum group together, then alternate in attendance at the group's meetings. If board members are unavailable, the function under consideration might well be served by an active, recent retiree with similar recent immersion in the school community, a newspaper editor or publisher, or someone whose work, such as banking, insurance, or housing, has brought him into touch with a wide variety of the citizenry. There is little more to be said at this level of the hypothetical.

Thus far, five sorts of persons constitute the regular members of our curricular group: three sorts of teachers, the principal, and a school board or business community member. There is one other: a representation of students. My suggestion of such a representation is no mere hangover from the fury of the rebellious sixties. It is made for two good educational reasons. First, students can tell us some things about the effects of what and how we teach which no others can. Second, their participation in curricular decision can provide a sense of proprietorship in their school lives, a realization that learning is something more than an arbitrary imposition, and that what they are asked to learn is more than the product of mere adult whim. (Such changes in attitude touch on two of the most frequently voiced reasons or excuses for minimal participation in schooling.)

Student representation would, of course, vary from level to level and from place to place. It would vary in number of representatives, in kind, that is, those with vote, with voice but not vote, etc., and in manner of selection (by administrative appointment, by teacher nomination followed by teacher election or administrative appointment, by student nomination and faculty selection, etc.). We must beware, however, lest we be guilty of a fault common at the college level, that is, choice of students for their incapacity to participate or for their responsiveness to the blandishments of the powerful, "company men." Such "representatives" are quickly seen to be fraudulent by the remainder of students, and consequently create alienation instead of closer ties.

The roster, so far, of those who constitute the regularly attending members of the curriculum group are these: four to six teachers representing faculty members of three interests; the principal; a school board member or substitute; one or two representatives of students; a total of circa nine.

A brief glance at the commonplaces will show us what we have taken into account in shaping this group and what remains to be considered. Obviously, we have dealt with some of the particularities which represent student and teacher. We have dealt with the closest encircling mileux. We have yet to consider, then, what is taught, that is, the "subject-matter" in the usual but misleading language *and* the larger milieux. To anticipate, we shall find that additional group members suggested by consideration of these factors need be only occasional attendants.

What is taught in a school falls, for our present purposes, into two categories. One consists of skimmings or thoughtful selections from the outcomes of customary fields of academic enquiry, such as physics, literary criticism, history and arts used in, or derived from, such fields, for instance, reading, writing, measurement, careful observation, and calculation. The other category consists of nonintellective propensities to act or respond to things, persons, and events. Examples in this second category would be honest reporting, collaboration, charity toward less effective others, interest and welcome toward differing others, readiness to deal with the unexpected and the repetitive, and deferral of gratification. These two categories will each require its own kind of specialist.

For the first category, the specialist will obviously be a professorial academic. It is worth noting, however, that academics are of different kinds, not all of them equally desirable as counsellors to our curriculum group. One kind consists of those whose forte is thorough knowledge of the content of upper-level textbooks and whose limitation consists in restriction of their involvement in the academic to this knowledge and to that which they learned in the course of doctoral candidacy. A second kind adds to such thorough knowledge a participation, to one degree or another, in contributing to this knowledge, of engaging in research. The third and rarest sort is one who has not only participated in research but has also reflected on the modes of enquiry or creation in his field. Such a person differs from the second kind by knowing enough of the past of his field of enquiry to know that the modes of enquiry currently practised are but one or a few among more numerous alternatives. Knowing this, he knows also that unqualified truth and falsehood are not properties of the fruits of enquiry, whether they be in the hard sciences, the soft, or in fields of enquiry which do not claim to be sciences. He knows that conclusions are not only based on evidence which is rarely entirely sufficient but also upon decisions as to what shall constitute the problems of enquiry, what shall pass for data, and what principles are currently used to interpret data.

When an academic matter is under consideration by our curricular group, a member of the third class of academic, though somewhat frightening as seen through my description, is by far the best advisor. This follows from what is probably the most durable, widespread and self-destructive fallacy of American school men and women: the belief that there is an eternally true, ineluctable content of school subjects, such as mathematics, biology, physics, and an almost equally fixed basis of social studies and history. Consequently, "teaching" in these subjects is largely "telling," written or oral, with little thoughtful attention to argument and evidence; even less concern with alternatives and their different strengths and weaknesses; still less with consideration by students of what is yet to be known and how it might be sought through enquiry.

This mistaking of the habitually taught for the durable truth stands as one of the great barriers to any curricular change and as the greatest of barriers to change which will not, in its turn, become virtually religious dogma.

The academic whom we have described as of the third kind is, by reason of his critical grasp of his field, best qualified to insure that the curricular group will consider a range of legitimated bodies of knowledge and skills (recall our stipulated definition of curriculum). He is also an advisor who can and will be aware of evidences and arguments, experiments and discoveries, weaknesses and omissions in what is known. These matters, argument, evidence, and so on, may themselves be legitimate and highly useful matters for curricular inclusion.

Specialists of the third kind are rare. They tend, however, to be much more willing to contribute some of their time to secondary-primary school efforts at improvement than are those of the second kind. Persons of the second kind usually consider themselves much too busy. Members of the third kind may, consequently, be hard to find in nearby universities. In that case, I do NOT suggest entire substitution of a member of the first or second kind. Rather, I suggest that a member of the first kind be a source of first suggestions and largest participation and that a member of the third kind be sought from afar if necessary, despite the costs, and brought to the curricular group, if only for one extended meeting, to comment on the suggestions of the first advisor. Without, of course, embarrassment of the first advisor by naming him, if he chooses to be absent from such a meeting.

I add that it will be extremely helpful to the success of the curriculum group effort if the first advisor be asked for titles and authors of advanced texts which contain exposition of the matters he expounds and suggests. Scrutiny of such texts often reveal qualifications and doubts which are omitted in oral discourse. Their availability and use will also profitably reduce the frequency of attendance required from the advisor.

Where the curricular problem in hand concerns what we have called nonintellective propensities, the relevant specialist will be of another kind entirely. He may be an artist, a former convict or alcoholic, a man of wealth, a mother on relief, a widow or widower, a professional marriage counsellor, arbitrator or parole officer. Who he is will be determined by the propensities under consideration. A good advisor may be found in one who has suffered and mastered a problem, such as grief, alteration of habitual behavior, control of power, deprivation. One who regularly advises or assists persons who have such problems may be the helpful person for the curricular group. Again, whether the potential counsellor be one who has mastered a kind of problem or one who helps such sufferers, there will be some who have only mastered the problem or given their advice and others who have reflected on what they have done. The latter is worth looking for.

There is one further group of persons from whom consultations may be sought, social scientists. There can be need to consult one or another kind of psychologist: psychiatric, emotional, cognitive, or "learning." A few sociologists can provide useful advice on likely group behavior. Ethnographers have begun to seek and discover much useful information about teacher behavior and schoolroom behavior of both teachers and students. With such persons, with the possible exception of ethnographers, it is, however, important to remember their penchant for generalization, a penchant on which we have earlier remarked at greater length.

A last word about the makeup of our curricular group. We are fortunate, indeed, that the functions of those named in the last several paragraphs can be served by only occasional attendance. There are the obvious reasons for being pleased: the business elsewhere of these persons and the cost of obtaining their services. There is a third reason: the need for regular members of our curricular group to discover one another and to create from the diversity of members a coherent and effective group. This process requires that the group be and remain of a reasonable size, eight to ten members. It is also much aided in its work by remaining the same group from meeting to meeting. The latter condition dictates that the occasional attendant be seen as such, as an advisor or commentator, and not as a pro tem member of the group. It may even be desirable in the interest of coherence that some of the occasionals be consulted on their own home grounds rather than in the meeting place of the curricular group. It may be desirable that they be consulted on occasion, not by the group as a whole, but by a subcommittee which will report back to the group.

[The alert reader may well have noted that in the beginning of our discussion of nonregular participants in the group (some ten paragraphs back, concerning subject-matter specialists) we referred to them as additional group members. The name given them then progressively changed: from group members to non-regular attendants, to advisors, to counselors, to consultants. This gradual shift of title illustrates a classic difference between the theoretic and the practical and the incomplete usefulness of each. The persons represented by these several titles were brought to our attention by consultation of the commonplaces, which constitute a highly general, "theoretic" treatment of education as a whole. Only as we moved away from the commonplaces to consider these persons as persons of a certain character affecting the behavior of a particular group and its particular members, a matter of practicality, did the importance of these persons in their relations to the group and suggestions for control of these relations become matters of concern.]

To return to our subject, we now have a curriculum group of eight to ten members composed of teachers, students, the principal, and a school-board or community member. These persons constitute an explosive mixture and one not particularly competent to solve curricular problems, which brings us to our next step.

THE GROUP: ITS CHAIRMAN

It is the chairman's task to move the group to effectiveness. Let us see what that will involve but let us move more briskly than we have, since, after all, our concern for the curriculum group and its chairman is preliminary to consideration of new teaching and new scholarly roles for Professors of Curriculum.

The Chairman's contributions to the effectiveness of the group are of two kinds: the performance of tasks which complement those of the group; activities with the group or with specific members of it designed to enhance their competence. The contributions to enhanced competence will consist mainly of reducing or removing barriers to collaboration among members of the group, barriers arising from biases, stereotypical responses toward one another, and omissions in the earlier education of members of the group. Let us consider these first.

The student members of the group constitute one problem for the Chairman. They must see themselves as genuine members of the group and see that others see them so. This poses a problem for obvious reasons: students are habitually treated in school as patients, not as agents, undergoers rather than actors, and will suspect that such a relation will continue. Teachers and principal may find it awkward to communicate with students as genuinely fellow-members of the curricular group. The Chairman of the group can meet this problem by functioning simultaneously as a model for teachers and the principal and as an example for the students. He will do so by raising at the earliest possible moment of the first meeting of the group, perhaps as the initial move of that meeting, a point addressed first to students because it is one they are best able to corroborate, question or deny: for example, his moot interpretation of some student attitudes or behaviors. His action, his manner in raising the question, the direction of his eyes and attention to students will constitute the modeling-example to teachers, principal, and students alike. To soothe possible ruffled feelings, he may then turn to teachers with the same invitation to comment. Such an early action also reinforces the status of the Chairman as one who must seek comfort and collaboration in order to proceed. There will also be need to teach teachers (and, perhaps, the principal) that the principal, in his service as member of the group, is a peer. This could be done by conspiracy, an arrangement with the principal that he voice a view that the Chairman can and will question and on which he can ask teachers to comment, affirm, deny.

There may be other matters of stereotype to be dealt with but these suffice to indicate the quality of one sort of tact and rhetoric which the Chairman must have learned in order to do his job.

With respect to biases, one of the commonest of those which constitute a barrier to collaboration among members of the group lies between teachers on the one hand, and specialist-scholars, whether of subject-matters or of educational behavioral sciences, on the other. The barrier consists, on the side of scholars, of snobbery toward nonspecialists, often expressed as a benign and irritating patronage of teachers, coupled with demand for thoroughgoing evidence when opinions are set forth by teachers. It consists, on the teacher's side, of subservience to specialist status or habitual use of a quite different kind of convincing "evidence." The former is seen in acceptance of specialists' views as authoritative, whether relations of the views to the viewer's specialism make the views authoritative or not. It also takes a form on which I shall remark in a moment. The difference in the two groups' view of evidence is shaped by the great confidence of many teachers in the personally experienced incident or the vivid anecdote conveyed by a peer, whether these be adequate samples of the matter in question or not. The conflict between teacher view and specialist view of evidence is further complicated by a usual inexperience of teachers with what passes for scholarly evidence and scholarly questioning of evidence. This arises, not only from inexperience with formal enquiry but also from unfamiliarity with their report in scholarly journals. The latter is an unfamiliarity which can be laid at the door of their teacher-training.

This biased barrier to collaboration cannot be overcome by simple and quickly used devices. It requires frequent and tactful direction of specialists' attention to their own lay views based on vivid experience or personal anecdote; on the perennial uncertainty of scholarly evidence, instances of past reversal of scholarly views and modes of enquiry (e.g., on the lifelong stability or ability of aptitudes; and the recent passage from overwhelming Skinnerism to weedlike growth of cognitive psychology). These commentaries may often be carried on in private between Chairman and specialist, with appeal for cognizance of teachers' inexperience of scholarly views of evidence. On the teachers' side, the situation requires from the Chairman equally tactful, and, again, perhaps, with teachers apart from other members of the committee, illustrations of the limited background of personal experience and the possible weaknesses back of personal anecdote together with positive comment on the usefulness of anecdote and experience as bases for particularization of the inevitably general character of scholarly conclusions, and hence, of the need for teacher modification of specialists' views.

Teachers' unwarranted confidence in the personally experienced can also be shaken by locating other teachers who can relate contrary instances. The specialist's notion that his generalities are immediately applicable to the schoolroom situation can be treated by pointing out to him, perhaps, again, in private and certainly with tact, the many instances in a day and the serious moments in a life in which action must be taken though evidence for one or another alternative cannot be sufficient by scholarly standards; e.g., the choice of a wife or an investment or whether to choose this moment to cross the street.

As remarked above, a further consequence often ensues from teacher subservience to specialist status. It consists of teacher imitation during curricular debate of what they take to be the marks of scholarly procedure. One of these is insistence on elaborate experiment where classroom trial may suffice. The other consists of demand for precise definition of all "key" terms, a demand which serves to postpone curricular modification indefinitely.[3]

The demand for elaborate experiment can be met by pointing out that such experiment is the province of specialists and can be suggested to some of them, while indicating at the same time the usefulness of classroom trial to the formulation of problems for scholarly research which is germane to education, that is, schoolroom problems, and the further usefulness of classroom trial as a necessary complement to bring home to teachers that their trial of curricular modifications is as much a contribution to knowledge as it is to educational practice, that is, a blunting of the unnecessarily sharp distinction between knowing and doing.

So much for the Chairman's treatment of biases. The instances are sufficient to indicate additional matters which should be conferred by his education: once again, tact, and command of small-group rhetoric; a reasonable familiarity with the outcomes of current and recent research in the education-directed aspects of the behavioral sciences, and a good grounding in philosophical summaries of scientific investigation, of the truth-status of its outcomes, and of the characteristics of common experience.

In addition to removing barriers to communication among members of the group, the Chairman will need to evoke and maintain an appropriately deliberative mode of discussion. The problem of evocation arises from the near-universal inexperience of most of us with deliberation. We are flooded

[3]I am indebted to Margret Buchmann of the Institute for Research in Teaching, Michigan State University for comment on the latter.

with news of a quite different mode of treatment of an issue, that of debate. The adversary structure of our law courts, the adversary pattern of legislative sessions and the drama of attack-defense-counter-attack of most newspaper-radio-television commentators constitute a ubiquitous model. That legislative committees, corporate boards, group decisions of managers of all sorts, carry on discussion in a quite different manner is unknown to most of us, since these groups usually carry on their work without an audience.

The problem of maintenance of deliberation consists mainly of seeing to it that once the relative importance of the four commonplaces has been dealt with deliberatively and agreed upon, the subsequent deliberations adhere to this agreed-on ratio. This problem arises because groups of all sorts, including those which are habitually deliberative, are prone to persevere on one or another commonplace whose consideration is initiated by chance or by the assertiveness of some particular member of the group.

Means for dealing with the problem of evocation of deliberation are best conveyed by illustration. Hence, let us suppose that a well-understood and agreed-upon problem confronts the group. The Chairman asks for suggested solutions. After a pause (one of our absurd conventions is that no one speaks first) a teacher responds, persuaded perhaps by the Chairman's lifted eyebrow: "Well, I think that what we should do is . . ." Another teacher, acting according to the well-worn pattern of debate, replies, "I don't agree. I think we should . . ." The Chairman then reenters the discussion: "There may be other suggestions but let us deal a bit with these two, first." He turns to a third member of the group, chosen on the basis of prior knowledge of the members, and asks, "Mr. Jones, what do you see as the strengths of the first position?"

Mr. Jones may say that he prefers the second. Directly to Mr. Jones, the Chairman remarks that in fairness and to make his own record-keeping comprehensible (he clearly is making notes on what is going on) the first-stated option deserves first attention, and remarks, "Go ahead." If Mr. Jones had immediately addressed the first option, the Chairman would have asked him to do a similar job on the second. Mr. Jones represses his impulse to take the other side and tries to address the question. He may even have to ask the first speaker to repeat her initial proposal.

The Chairman then asks another member to identify strengths seen in the second proposal. When these are on the table, he invites other members in general to add or subtract or comment otherwise. When these begin to run down, the Chairman turns to weaknesses, especially possible-probable unwanted consequences, of the two proposals on the table.

Thus the Chairman affords the group an alternative to the pattern of debate, a deliberative process in which all pool their ingenuities, insights, and perceptions in the interest of discovering the most promising possibilities for trial, rather than forming sides, each of which look only to the strengths of a selected one alternative, hence discarding any means of coming to decision except eloquence and nose-counting. It might be noted that the Chairman affords the example out of the group's own mouths and not by setting himself up as the model.

It need hardly be added that this initial example will do no more than afford an example to be tried by the group. They will fall back again and again into debate and the Chairman, again and again, will have to find means for bringing them back to deliberation. As meeting follows meeting, however, the group will not only be slowly habituated to deliberation but the best and brightest of them will early begin to discern its advantages over debate as means for their purpose, and hence becomes allies of the Chairman in turning combative moments back toward deliberation. My implied praises of deliberation here are not to be taken as condemning adversary methods in the solution of other kinds of problems. Debate has its own virtues.

The problem of maintenance as against evocation is, as noted, mainly a problem of ensuring appropriate emphasis among the commonplaces. There are at least three devices which the Chairman can bring to bear on the problem. In the course of participation in the deliberation, he can watch for moments when one or another alternative receives overwhelming support or condemnation from considerations which represent but one commonplace. At such moments he can raise a point against the favored or for the condemned, a point which clearly arises from consideration of a matter representing another commonplace. Second, he can explicitly but informally bring the company's attention to a perseveration on one or a few commonplaces and remind them of what remains on the agenda of commonplaces. Third, he can and will record his minutes of each meeting in a way that makes conspicuous the time spent or not spent on this or that consideration and present such minutes for perusal and approval at the beginning of each subsequent meeting.[4]

It is clear that these duties as Chairman require that his education have contained an extensive exposure to deliberative committee work, both as a member of a committee and as its Chairman. We shall return to this and other needs when we discuss his education as a whole.

All the above is, in one respect, premature. It is a discussion of the treatment of a curricular problem, though we have yet to say anything about the means by which problems of curriculum are discovered. We deal with this matter forthwith, though only briefly, since it suggests but one matter of importance about the needed education of the Chairman.

Curricular problems will be sought both at home and abroad. The search at home will use most of the usual procedures. For instance, there will be

---

[4] I am indebted to Professor Seymour Fox of the Hebrew University, Jerusalem, for developing and testing this procedure.

continuing visitation of classrooms. These will not begin, however, until teachers have been assured that the purpose of visitation is only to educate the Chairman concerning the scope and variety of teaching-learning which takes place in the school, and only after enough time has elapsed since the Chairman's appearance at the school for him to have been seen as a regular habitué of teachers' tables or cafeterias and their commonroom, as not dignified by a private secretary or a spacious office and as seen by teachers as one of theirs and not as an extension of the administration. There will be comparative study of standardized achievement and aptitude tests where they exist, of textbooks used and of obligations imposed by law or administrative fiat.

The search at home will also take place by means which are usually possible only when the searcher is a curriculum Chairman, charged with responsibility for such a search and with the time to do it. These unusual places of search will include streets and playgrounds of the school and community where the behaviors and propensities of students can be noted, and, when the Chairman has become a familiar figure to students, where informal talks with them about school affairs and students' lives in general can take place. The search will also take place through talks and visits to the homes of parents and similar talks and visits with employers of the school's graduates, again, after appropriate introduction. He will also learn much through immersion in teacher-talk in lunch and commonroom and by explicit conference with teachers about satisfactions and dissatisfactions with what they do and do not do. These discussions may also include, from the Chairman's side, remarks on student failures, satisfactions and concerns as he has discovered them.

The search abroad will take place via two quite disparate activities. One consists of interschool visitation. The Chairman himself will visit schools of neighboring communities. He will identify schools to which he will arrange visitation by teachers of his school. With teachers of his own school he will identify teachers in other schools whose undertakings are sufficiently promising possibilities for the Chairman's school to warrant invitations to such "foreign" teachers to visit for discussion of his or her undertaking.

The other search abroad will take place through educational journals which are concerned with development in the national political economy and ethos, developments in subject-matters taught in schools, and developments in the behavioral sciences bearing on curriculum. There are at least four journals in North America of the requisite generality. *Teachers College Record, The Harvard Review, The American Journal of Education,* and *Curriculum Inquiry* come to mind. These would serve the Chairman and many of the teachers. Meanwhile, teachers might welcome access to journals which concern special subject-matters or particular segments of schooling, e.g., the biology teacher. I have in mind that schools might well maintain a small library of journals for use by their staff-members and the Chairman might well arrange for regular staff discussions of papers selected from such journals.

In earlier papers on the practical I have remarked on a peculiar characteristic of practical problems, that they are not given but taken. That is, in the words of John Dewey, one encounters problematic situations, conditions which are discomforting or disconcerting, but the concrete formulation of the problem requires delicate consideration of alternative formulations. This is to say that practical problems are well-realized only by application of arts of problemation. Needless to say, I expect that our Chairman's education will have included practice in application of these arts.

With the curricular problems defensibly formulated, solutions must be devised or discovered. Discovery can mean the Chairman's consultation of his own memory of curricular devices learned in his graduate education. It can mean his consultation of journals concerned with teaching in the subject-matter field under question, this in collaboration with appropriate teachers. It can mean consultation of the practices and experiments in schools of neighboring districts, again with teacher help. This collaboration with teacher plays three practical roles. It not only serves as aid in discovery of solutions to the curricular problem in hand but in cementing the collaborative relations of Chairman and teachers. Of greatest importance, perhaps, it brings to the classroom teacher an executive and creative contribution to the role of "teacher," a sadly needed contribution of self-determination, variety and challenge. Beyond solutions discovered, others may be devised, again, through contributions of ingenious teachers, with or without collaboration of the Chairman.

We have, then, discovery and formulation of curricular problems, construction of alternative solutions, deliberation on and deliberative modification of these alternatives. There remains the task of instituting and testing the changes decided on. Institution of change, in the absence of such a role as that of curriculum Chairman, has had, as earlier mentioned, a long history of frustration of what has been called, significantly, "dissemination." "Dissemination" signifies the Moscovian revolution telegraphed to the provinces, precisely the procedure which the role of Chairman is intended to displace.

With a curricular Chairman, we have a mode of curricular change which arises at home, seeded, watered, and cultivated by some or all of the teachers who might be involved in its institution. Clearly, the question of trial has become a matter totally different from that of "dissemination," not withstanding the help which may have come from abroad by way of journals, consultants, and neighboring schools. I suggest that institution of such changes will pose no problem. Only trial will prove me right or mistaken.

As to trial of the curricular change, there is little to be said which is new. The teachers who try it will test the effect of its use on them and shape a view of its effectiveness. Tests (oral and written) some made at home, some standardized, will contribute their kind of evidence. Other teachers, not yet involved in the change, will visit the arenas of its trial. So will the curricular Chairman and, if possible, some of the others involved in its choice. And the Chairman will pursue consequences of the change, unintended as well as intended, into the highways and byways where students as students and as graduates show themselves for what they are. And so we come at last to the matter of education of a curricular Chairman, something for curriculum professors to do.

THE CHAIRMAN: HIS EDUCATION AND REFRESHMENT

Let us first summarize the competences and knowledge which an ideal curricular Chairman requires. (What justifies appearance of an "ideal" in a practical paper on the practical? The answer is that it is the best available guide under the circumstances, for our problem bears on the character of schools and departments of education and these vary so significantly that a hypothetical, typical case cannot be constructed. Among the significant variations: the quality of their faculties and of the number of relatively good students who come to them; the resources afforded by the surrounding college or university; and above all, the risk-taking competence of the Deans or Chairmen involved, their readiness to rock the boat of faculty-members when the Dean's own reappointment is at stake.)

To return, the curricular chairman must be capable of skillful use of rhetorics of persuasion and elicitation. These rhetorics are needed, not as orator to audience, but as Chairman and member of a small group and in person-to-person dealings with individuals. Moreover, his use of these rhetorics must be skilled with respect to a diversity of conversants. He must do well with his peers: teachers and parents. He must deal with administrative and social elders: the school principal, professors of subject-matters and behavioral sciences, school board members and employers in the community. He must deal with juniors: students as encountered on street, playground and workplace.

He must be experienced in deliberation, its antecedent arts of problemation and its coordinate arts of eclectic (of the latter, an explanatory word in a moment). These arise in a context of teaching and learning, a context which involves bodies of theoretic knowledge applicable to understanding teaching and learning. Hence his need for what I have called arts of eclectic: arts by which useful parts of diverse bodies of theoretic knowledge are put together in relation to a practical problem of curriculum. The need for these arts is patent in all the Chairman's various dealings with his curricular group and its consultants.

He must be an able and habitual reader of "learned" journals which bear upon his professional function. These include journals which treat curriculum in various fields and levels of schooling. They include journals which convey an idea of the change and progress of fields of learning represented in school curricula. They must also include journals which convey an idea of changing patterns of social scientific enquiry bearing on teaching-learning. This habit, brought to bear on these journals, is necessary if our Chairman is not to be obsolescent five to ten years after taking on his function.

He needs ability to guide his teacher-colleagues to use of some journals. Through consulting journals which publish materials stemming from the behavioral sciences, teachers will learn something of scholarly standards of evidence, hence enhance somewhat their ability to overcome barriers to communication between specialists and teachers. It is by consulting and reporting on matters appearing in such journals that teachers will enhance the professional standing of their work and their recognizance of its professional character. It is by reading journals whose content is contributed by teachers for an audience of teachers that they will note that school curriculum vary from place to place and change from time to time. So much for the skills required by the Chairman. What of the knowledge he requires?

He will need to know curricular practices in his country, both current and past, insofar as such information is available. The question of current practice poses a problem since no one knows very much about what currently goes on in the diverse schools of the nations.[5] Knowledge of past practice, which is available, is required because of the tendency of the young to suppose that the world as they discover it between the ages of 5 and 25 is the way the world has always been. In the case of schooling, this means profound ignorance of numerous curricular practices and purposes, including the many which bear and have borne on non-academic purposes by way of shaping taste, character, habits, and expectations, social-political attitudes and ways of earning a living. Knowledge which would come of a union of materials and points of view of L. Cremin and David Tyack would be appropriate. To these, we would need to add example and comment on changes and efforts at change of recent decades: the long controversy on the teaching of reading; the current hegemony of the notion that "reading" consists mainly of decoding visible marks into audible sounds, most else being "thinking"; the stultification of learning by restricting textbooks to a vocabulary accessible to all; the costly efforts of the '60s to reform science curricula, and the recent Rand study of their effects; the "new" math and its fate; the self-interested efforts to teach "values clarification." (I should apolo-

[5]Perhaps in the not too distant future, however, Theodore Sizer, John Goodlad and the project reported as taking shape at Stanford University will begin to fill this conspicuous gap in our knowledge.

gize for pointing the "self-interested" finger only at backers of "value clarification." Most efforts by college-university specialists to import their specialty into the schools are tainted in some degree by the wish to make jobs for their graduates, hence to keep their own.)

The potential Chairman will also require knowledge about the numerous behavioral sciences which contribute to guidance of educational practice: various psychologies, sociology, ethnography and so on. He needs this knowledge, not only for guidance of his own invention and judgment of curricular devices but in order to know on whom to call as consultant in curricular deliberations and what questions to ask such consultants.

In view of the uses to which he will put such knowledge, it must be a liberal knowledge in the most traditional sense of that adjective. The usual smattering of fact and allegedly verified dogma which constitute undergraduate survey courses is wholly beside the point. The similarly dogmatic skimmings which often constitute the courses designed by behavioral scientists for "outsiders" are also inadequate. These courses convey only a sample of what passes for knowledge in the field. What our curriculum Chairman needs, in addition, is sound knowledge of what the field investigates, what kinds of questions it asks of its subject in the course of enquiry, and what restrictions it places on the acceptability of answers. In brief, he needs to know about the problems, principles and methods of the field. He also needs to know something of the history of changes in these matters, since the behavioral sciences are notorious for the plurality of their principles and the frequency with which they change.

Our Chairman will need a similarly liberal nodding acquaintance with some of the academic fields from which school curricula are drawn. He will need this acquaintance in order to recognize some of the various corruptions and selections which are made of these fields as they pass from their own communities of enquiry through the hands of textbook writers and curriculum makers into the versions which represent them in the schools; this to alert him to the ubiquity of such modifications, and to help him to judge their usefulness and cost when they touch his school.

These bodies of knowledge and skills constitute a substantial and challenging graduate curriculum, much of it beyond the purview of conventional curriculum programs. How shall they be conveyed? A few suggestions follow. (I have not forgotten the Chairman's need for knowledge of non-intellective aspects of growing up, of ways in which circumstance inhibits their growth, and of ways in which their sustenance can be aided in the schools. However, the state of well-verified knowledge of such matters and the prevalence of passionately held doctrines concerning them are such that I am intimidated. I leave the problem to others or to the future.)

Consider, first, conveyance of knowledge and practice with respect to small-group and person-to-person rhetorical skills. I put this item first because it appears to be the most alien to existing graduate programs in curriculum of all my suggestions. It is also the locus of the most radical proposal I shall make with respect to alteration of such programs.

Conveyance of these rhetorical skills should begin, I think, in a formal course taught by a capable professor of rhetoric. Such persons are usually not and need not be members of an Education faculty. Their services would be borrowed from the Department of Rhetoric or Department of English Language and Literature in the institution of which our school of education is neighbor or part. The course would consist of demonstration and guidance in the identification, analysis and imitation of the rhetorical devices which form parts of current debate, in speeches, television programs, magazines, editorial pages, on current problems of politics, ethics, economics, education, and other social institutions and problems. Such a course would afford an introduction to the nature and practice of rhetoric, though not small-group rhetoric. Second, it would afford a valuable sampling of social forces and tensions which constitute one root of school curriculum, and introduce our students to the sources from which samplings of future debate on such matters can be obtained.

Since such a course is only an introduction and does not touch on small-group rhetoric and deliberation, a substantial additional experience must follow. It would consist of an extended practicum in deliberation and use of the rhetorics which will be the bread-and-butter of our Chairman's work. This practicum would begin in a semester-long participation in a curriculum deliberation chaired by a member of the Education faculty with experience in management of schools or collegiate-graduate departments or other office involving a substantial body of committee work. The deliberation would concern a simulated problem in a simulated school and body of circumstances with each student-member of the deliberative practicum taking on the role of one or another member of a curriculum group as earlier described. First establishment of a simulation of this kind is onerous but, once done, the modifications required to refresh it for succeeding waves of students is relatively easy. I have described construction and operation of such a simulation. (See Appendix.)

Participation in such a deliberative group would carry our candidate a second step, disclosing to him the modifications in large group rhetoric required by the vastly different structure of audience–speaker relations in a small committee group. In addition, it would introduce him to some of the problems involved in curricula, their alteration, and to the sorts of persons involved in them. It would not convey sufficient facility in the use of small-group rhetoric nor any experience of chairing such a group. It is here that my most radical proposal arises.

I suggest that the doctoral dissertation of a candidate for curricular Chairman consist of a report, analysis and assessment of an internship, an internship which would place him, during his last year of graduate studies, in the office of curriculum Chairman in a real school with real problems and consisting of real people. This will, of course, require that some schools, neighboring the training institution or not, must be persuaded to collaborate in such an enterprise and pay the intern a stipend on the ground of its contribution to the on-going improvement of education, its own improvement with regard to teacher morale as well as curriculum, and the glory it would reap as a pioneer in such an undertaking. It would also require some supervision by the principal and probably some handholding by members of the candidate's graduate department.

The dissertation proper would derive from records of this internship: tape-recordings of deliberative sessions, diaries of the Chairman's activities apart from deliberative meetings, and assessments of the experience of working with him by the school Principal, the teachers and the others involved. The written dissertation and its tangible sources would be evaluated by the candidate's doctoral committee, and the candidate and his dissertation would submit to the same kind of oral defense required for any doctoral degree. So much for rhetorical skill and its conveyance.

I turn now to a triply useful device, one which will instill the skill and habit of consulting "learned" journals, provide means for repairing the commonly dogmatic skimmings of graduate courses, and make a substantial contribution to arts of eclectic. The device consists simply of replacing at least half of the lecture-listening and textbook reading which usually constitute graduate courses by a bibliography of scholarly papers which report researches in the behavioral sciences and criticisms of such researches. The researches treated and the papers which treat them would be selected jointly by a practitioner of a behavioral science and a professor of curriculum, and the two of them would jointly "teach" the seminar which follows.

Responsibility for conveying the substance of these papers to the group would be distributed among pairs of students. The members of a pair would individually read the paper or papers on which they are to report at a meeting of the group. They would then compare and discuss what they understood of the papers' conclusions, its experiments or other starting points, and intervening interpretations. They would agree on the strengths and weaknesses of the papers or agree to disagree. They would then write a precis of the paper and their assessment of it, a precis not to exceed, say, a close-packed, single-spaced typewritten page. The page would be duplicated and copies provided all participants in the seminar before it is to meet. At the meeting, one or both members of the pair will expand orally on the precis, respond to questions put by professors and fellow students, and conduct a discussion of the papers. The joint leaders of the seminar would see to it that their respective interests are involved in the discussion, the behavioral scientist steering questions toward the research or criticism *per se*, the professor of curriculum steering questions toward application of the research to a curricular procedure, or toward joining results of the research to that of other papers read in other behavioral seminars in which the curriculum professor has accompanied the candidates.

A similar joining of forces by the professor of curriculum and a historian would develop and jointly chair a similar seminar on past, recent and present curricular practices and changes, again using a body of primary sources as at least half the resource material of the seminar. This seminar would, as the behavioral science seminars probably would not, invite practitioners of schooling, that is, principals, heads of departments, supervisors, experienced teachers, to speak to the seminar and respond to questions. Again, we have an eye on more than one educational purpose: not only contribution to liberal knowledge of curriculum but practice in person-to-person rhetoric, as seminarians question practitioners and respond to their replies.

A brief word, finally, about the scholarship which professors of curriculum would carry on under this regimen. To their present concerns, they would add enquiries which would inform, advise and refresh their former students working in the schools.

First, curricularists would revive a practice which characterized them in the first quarter of this century but has long been dropped. They would attend to what they perceive as evils and vicissitudes of our government and society. They would try to convince readers that these troubles exist, show the threats they pose, and suggest ways in which alteration of school practice might help ameliorate the conditions discussed. Such publications would, of course, depart markedly from the mores of "objective" scholarship. There might not be a correlation coefficient for page after page. The curricularists would, instead, take positions in debate, concern themselves with a variety of evils and problems, be founded on differing views of what constitutes the politically beautiful and good. As such, they would rouse thought and debate, among themselves and among their graduates. They would thus inject into the lives of educators an element of active intellectualism which is sadly wanting.

Some curricularists would perform a similar task with respect to the tastes, mores, and attitudes of our fellow citizens in their daily lives. They might question the ubiquity and intensity of competition in our way of life and ask how the schools might contribute to the lessening of it, or concern themselves with the inanities of television entertainment, or face the question of means by which schools could go beyond mere propinquity in lessening the xenophobias and racisms which afflict us. Some papers from curricularists might be addressed, not to colleagues and former students but to the public at large, thus assisting their graduates in more ways than one.

Chairmen at work in the schools would also learn to expect from their former professor periodic critical reviews of proposed and actual changes and pressures for change in school curricula: analysis and judgment on, say, the uncritical insistence of legislators and some school boards on "equality" in the treatment of normals and the handicapped; the use of early childhood education merely for language correction; emphases on melting pot and contrary emphases on preservation of minority cultures; new views of the nature of high quality in literature and the arts; in brief, changes in knowledge and attitude which might be important in consideration of curriculum changes. And, of course, our Chairman would expect reports on advances in knowledge of learning processes and modes of teaching, as these might modulate efforts to improve school curricula.

Finally, he might expect publication by curricularists of thoughtful consideration of the role of the public schools vis-à-vis the many other agencies of education which characterize our time.

APPENDIX

(1) A brief version of this paper was delivered to professors of Curriculum, March 9, 1982.

(2) The antecedent papers which this one concludes are:
The Practical: A Language for Curriculum (1970).
The Practical: Arts of Eclectic (1971).
The Practical 3: Translation into Curriculum (1973).
All may be found in Joseph J. Schwab, *Science, Curriculum and Liberal Education*, Edited by Ian Westbury and Neil J. Wilkof, Chicago: University of Chicago Press, 1978.

(3) Construction and operation of a simulation for decision-making may be found on pages 148–181 of Joseph J. Schwab, *College Curriculum*.

(4) I am indebted to Elizabeth Vallance for an invitation (declined) which moved me to write this paper.

(5) A most idiot side-effect of emphasis on "behavioral objectives" is its tendency to induce manufacture of a separate means for each "objective" in view. Consequently, one of the more useful characteristics of the practical exemplified here is the multi-purposed role of its one proposed bureaucratic change. This change is labelled "something for Curriculum Professors to do" but it might properly be named for one of its several other functions. It is designed:
   (a) To put the special knowledge and special mode of knowing of teachers into greater service to schooling and to provide recognition of such contributions.
   (b) To enhance the possibility of attracting a greater number of daring experimental and intellectually active persons to the function of teaching.

(c) To establish challenging, decision making, and collaborative functions as part of the role of teachers.
(d) To provide a basis for teachers' recognition of themselves as masters of a special lore and competence, and constituting, in short, a profession by providing them, via journals, meetings, and visitations, with a sense of intellectual community *and* by providing them with occasions on which they utilize representatives of other scholarly communities as resources to be judged, used, or not used as may seem appropriate.

(6) It is a way to enhance the occasions for the Principals to participate in their schools as *schools*.

(7) It is a way to enhance students' understanding of the roles of schooling by making students party to the planning of the school.

(8) Most of all, perhaps, it is a way to transform the impossible task of mere "dissemination" of curriculum to one of stimulating schools to devise and institute their own curricular ways of meeting a changing world.

CHAPTER SIX

Dialogue: Schwab's "Practical 4" and Its Corroboration in Recent History

Henrietta Schwartz

It is always a pleasure to read and listen to Joe Schwab. In his unique and sometimes piquant way, Schwab has done much to influence how educators think about curriculum and how we approach the complex problems of changing curriculum and revising instructional strategies. In his fourth article on the theoretical and practical elements of curriculum, he emphasizes the practical aspects of local school curriculum development, suggesting that even university professors of curriculum might be able to contribute to the process. The article is titled: "The Practical 4: Something for Curriculum Professors to Do."

Schwab examines both the theoretical and the practical sides of the curriculum profession in recommending the creation of a new role at the local school level. The curriculum change structure and membership are familiar under other names, including cross-role cadres, Teacher Corps coordinating committees, urban school task forces. It is in his explication of the *processes* by which the Curriculum Chairman (a new role) would function with the group, and his description of the *content* and scope of the training needed to function in the role, that Schwab, in "The Practical 4," contributes to our understanding of what is necessary to foster curriculum change. His synthesis of the current research on schools, the role of the teacher, and the nature of change is unobtrusively coupled with clear conceptions of how organizations and people behave when challenged with dissatisfaction and the need to change.

Although Schwab disregards the organizational pitfalls of school change (staff turnover, declining enrollments, unions etc.), his practical suggestion for a curriculum group chaired by a knowledgeable and committed scholar/practitioner from the university is compelling. It should be tested, but it should be tested in full, without compromise in the ingredients and procedures he proposes; anything short of the full experiment risks producing yet another bit of cosmetic surgery. We have witnessed some examples of similar efforts in the past; we have learned, in bits and pieces, what the strengths and limitations of cooperative curriculum change models are. Schwab now offers us an unusually clear conception of a fruitfully practical role for university-based and theoretically trained curriculists. Whether this model can prove more productive and more enduring than those of the past cannot be determined without a full test.

This essay looks at Schwab's prescription for a university-based Curriculum Chairman working on site in schools, and assesses its feasibility in the context of three similar efforts in the past two decades.

SCHWAB'S PROPOSAL AND THE UNIVERSALS OF SCHOOLING

Schwab conceives of the curriculum as follows:

> Curriculum is *what is successfully conveyed* to differing degrees to different students, *by committed teachers using appropriate materials and actions*, of *legitimated bodies of knowledge*, skill, taste, and propensity to act and react, *which are chosen* for instruction *after serious reflection* and communal decision by representatives *of those involved in the teaching of a specified group of students* who are known to the decision makers. [Schwab's emphasis]

The above statement captures the situational nature of curriculum and instruction. It reflects what Goodlad (1983), Brophy (1982), and others are saying based on extensive studies of schooling and classrooms: There is no "American public school system," no uniform curriculum. Each school is a unique culture sharing only some common elements with all other schools. "Curriculum is not necessarily the same for all students of a given age and standing. Nor does it differ necessarily in all respects for each and every student or school" (Schwab, 1983, p. 240).

From an anthropologist's perspective, schools and classrooms, like other systems of human behavior, build cultures which are complex, probabilistic, and self-regulating. Also, like cultures, most schools and classrooms can be observed to have purposes and some degree of coherence. One can view schools and classrooms in terms of the anthropologist's "nine universal patterns." These systems, as described by Herkovitz, have become commonly accepted by anthropologists as being universal to all cultural units, including the individual school as a cultural microcosm. The universals develop as systems within the classrooms of a school as the teacher transmits knowledge to the students, and as teacher and student interact with the values, skills, knowledge, and attitudes to be learned from the curriculum materials. The whole process is called education, a special form of the general cultural universal known as socialization.

Each classroom, school, community, and culture has some way of handling these universal aspects of behavior, though each of these cultures, or subcultures, has a unique way of doing so. For example, all cultures and subcultures have a *value system* which indicates the preferred ways of doing things or specifying what is good and what is bad. All have a cosmology or *world view* which specifies the beliefs concerning the position of man in the cosmos, and the limits individuals must adhere to in the school, the community, the church, or the classroom. Each cultural unit has some form of *social organization* which governs individual and group relationships even to the point of determining forms of verbal address. Each system has a *technology*, a body of knowledge and skills used to perform the tasks necessary for the system to function and survive. There is an *economic system* which regulates the allocation of goods and services in the school and the classroom. Furthermore, there is a form of governance or a *political system* regulating individual and institutional behavior which specifies how decisions are made, how power, authority, and influence are acquired and used, and who participates in what decision. Typically, there is a special *language* uniquely suited to the educational process or the subject matter of the classroom. There is an *aesthetic system* which defines what is beautiful, creative, and artistic. Finally, there is a *socialization process* or educational process which regularizes the transmission of knowledge to the neophytes, the unlearned ones in the group. The cultural universals model is only one of many conceptual frameworks which anthropologists used to look at the world, but it serves a useful purpose here as an analytical tool, particularly when considered in the context of Schwab's four "commonplaces."

In Schwab's view of the school as an organization, curriculum delivery is a negotiated process between the four commonplaces or universals of education: the teacher, the student, what is taught, and the milieux of teaching–learning. While each of the four commonplaces is theoretically important, at any given time one may become more important than the others, as in the case of the current emphasis by the federal government on the need to correct the high school curriculum. The emphasis today is on *what is taught*, with a hue and cry to eliminate the electives introduced in response to the demands of the 1960s and 1970s to meet the students' individual needs; we are urged now to go "back to basics" with one basic curriculum for all. Schwab, by contrast, calls for a "diversity of curricula." He would have schools attend to Herskovitz's universals, while also accommodating the uniqueness of local needs, attending to the practical and fulfilling the need for localism in curricula; he would have curriculists attend to the theoretical—as well as to the specifics of a curriculum. Most of all, he would have university professors be involved with the practical aspects of curriculum change, and he outlines the path by which curriculum professors can contribute to their *real* subject matter, the schools.

Schwab calls for the formation of a curricular group in which the principal actors are the teachers, including the principal and selected others. The curriculum professor would function as a chairman, guiding the group through the identification, planning, and implementing of a successful curriculum project. As Schwab correctly points out, teachers know the most about the school and students. The Curriculum Chairman, and other specialists from the university, would know the content of the curriculum and the process of curriculum development well. Sometimes, teachers need analytical tools to make their knowledge and intuitions work for them. The combining of Schwab's four "commonplaces" and Herskovitz's nine "universals" is such a tool, for in the hands of a skillful Curriculum Chairman, the model taps teachers' store of knowledge, reinforces teachers' status in the school, and allows for checking perceptions with peers and superiors about the place whose task is to educate children.

Let us assume that Herskovitz's nine universal patterns will accurately describe most of the group behavior found in schools and classrooms, communities, and cultures and that these universal patterns constitute one set of variables in an analytical matrix. If these cultural universals are combined with Schwab's basic concepts of the curriculum, the two perspectives can provide the framework necessary to any curriculum change project and function as a prelude to the specific fact-finding necessary to establishing entry points for curriculum change. Combining the two conceptual schemes (Schwab and Herskovitz) allows us to use them as a way of codifying data, identifying what additional facts must be gathered, and synthesizing commonalities and uniqueness—discrepancies and similarities—among the variables. The use of this format, or any other scheme, establishes *enquiry* as a basic process in all curriculum development and meets Schwab's "need for regular members of our curricular group to discover one another, and to create from the diversity of members a coherent and effective group" (Schwab, 1983, p. 251).

Looking at Table 1, the curricular group attempts to fill in the table through discussion, deliberation, debate and inquiry, and fact-finding, where necessary, with the understanding that there are tasks to be done within a limited time frame. Curricular options and system entry points are identified in this "deliberative process in which all pool their ingenuities, insights and per-

TABLE 6.1
Matrix Analysis Using Schwab's Four Commonplaces and Nine Cultural Universals

School or Classroom Cultural Universals	*The Four Commonplaces of Curriculum*			
	The Teacher	*The Student*	*What is Taught*	*The Milieu*
	How Instruction is Delivered	*Who is Being Taught*	*The Content*	*Of Teaching-Learning*
Value system of the school	Mainstream values, teacher talks, lecture-discussion, reading-homework	Subcultural street-peer values; diverse; learns via 7 hours of TV and stereo a day	Mainstream values; delayed gratification; individual achievement; love nature or conquer nature	Superior adult teacher; instructs many unlearned youth in isolation 5 hours a day
Cosmology	Adult human being is center of the universe; nature must be subdued	Peers/parents/self is center of universe; nature is there	Judaeo-Christian world view with adults at center; man subduing nature	Adults control universe of school; nature is kept outside
Social organization	Superior-subordinate relationship with administrators and students; peer relations with other teachers	Student is told what to do by teacher; student seeks status among peers by doing what they wish	Role models are "good" adults or "superkids"; e.g., young Hiawatha acquiesces to adult advice	Peer norms govern youth behavior; more youths than adults in school
Technology	Tried-and-ture processes and tools are best; e.g., texts, lecture, chalkboards	New is better than old; audio and visual tools are good	Mixed messages; computers are valued as are classics	*Avant garde* is technologically "with it," respected and feared at once

(Continued)

TABLE 6.1
(Continued)

School or Classroom Cultural Universals	*The Four Commonplaces of Curriculum*			
	The Teacher	*The Student*	*What is Taught*	*The Milieu*
	How Instruction is Delivered	*Who is Being Taught*	*The Content*	*Of Teaching-Learning*
Economic system	Instruction is offered in time; bound periods; senior faculty are valued resources	Learning is continuous tracking	"Important subjects" get more time and resources	Goods and services go to con-forming teachers and students
Political system	Limited input into decisions; too-down	No input into governance of school	Democratic principles	Principal/teachers make decisions
Language	Teacher talk-standard American English with localisms; rarely bilingual	Peer street talk; English is second language	Formal English prose and poetry	Students use school talk in class, peer talk in halls; teachers use standard English
Aesthetic system	Neat & Clean are Beautiful. Messy is ugly. Bright is Creative	Peer play is beautiful; work along is punishment and ugly	Mainstream-looking; people are beautiful	Well-groomed is better than functional casual
Socialization Process	First observation successfully completed marks rite of passage; Robinson Crusoe in the classroom	by peers to lead a group effort; easy participation with peers	Learn norms of group majority; abide by them	Little tolerance for deviant behavior; little patience for "different drummer"

ceptions in the interest of discovering the most promising possibilities for trial, rather than forming sides, each of which look only to the strengths of a selected one alternative, hence discarding any means of coming to decision except eloquence and nose-counting" (Schwab, 1983, p. 255).

Let me illustrate how the two-way analysis can assist the efforts of building a group, organizing information about the school culture about to receive the curriculum change, and forecasting potential problems. Table 1 illustrates what might be some of the information gathered by a Curriculum Chairman in the initial discussion of members of curriculum group in an urban high school with a multicultural population who wish to revise and update the ninth-grade literature unit.

The current curriculum includes the study of Shakespeare's *Julius Caesar*, selected short stories by American and British authors written before World War I, works by American poets such as Longfellow, Whitman, and Poe, and some social protest essays written in the early 1930s. Students are issued an anthology with the above works and most teachers supplement the literature unit with required book reports aimed at more contemporary literature. There is an adequate school library and sufficient funds to purchase class sets of pocketbooks. Teachers find it difficult to get students to read the material, much less understand and appreciate it. In the first few meetings of the curriculum group, the Curriculum Chairman has begun deliberation about the nature of the students, the culture of the school, the values of the adults, and the values of the students. The core comments are encapsulated in Table 1. (It should be noted that this technique, like any other that attempts to categorize human behavior, is reductionistic and must be supplemented by careful listening, questioning, clarifying, and selecting what to write down.)

A comparison of the information on the first line of Table 1 concerning the values system in the school reveals discrepancies between teachers' and students' values, between "mainstream" school cultural values and those of the student, and the value-laden content of much of the curriculum material. Given this information, the group's first set of deliberations needs to address the set of values to be featured in the changed curriculum, or—if diverse values schemes are to be presented—how teachers help students, through the vehicle of literature, think through value conflicts and acquire knowledge, skills, and coping strategies.

I have filled in the areas in Table 1 in terms of the hypothetical urban school—social organization and language. Again, the discrepancies and commonalities are clear. If we seek to start from the familiar and move to the unknown, then some entry points for successful curriculum change, by which Schwab means what is successfully conveyed in differing degrees to different students, might be to look at curriculum materials and instructional strategies that examines:

(1) the diversity and commonalities of value schemes in the world through Asian, Native American, or Eastern literature;
(2) the essential elements of peer relationships, whether they are adult or youth or other than those of the human animal;
(3) the nature of effective communication and the thousands of ways humans send and understand messages, including movies of the classics, videotape, sign language, etc.;
(4) the ingredients of effective superior–subordinate relationships throughout human history and the nature of power, strength, friendship, organizations, and individual will.

This last item—the explication of superior and subordinate relationships, as portrayed in the literature—might also allow teachers to review their expectations for administrators in curricular areas. The active presence of the principal in the curricular group's deliberations is an essential element in any change project.

Schwab rightly points out that the principal of a school is too busy managing the enterprise to engage in sustained and continuing watch over curriculum; another agency is required. He proposes that that agency be a curriculum group which will address the question of what should be taught, how, to whom, by whom, and for how long. To be responsible and effective, the group needs certain standard elements. The teachers are the most important members of such a group; for they know the students and the classrooms best. In forming the group the principal needs to understand that the *political system* of the school will change as teachers are involved in real decision-making about curriculum.

Teachers will not and cannot be merely told what to do. Subject specialists have tried it. Their attempts and failures I know first hand. Administrators have tried it. Legislators have tried it. Teachers are not, however, assembly line operators and will not behave so. Furthermore, they have no need, except in rare instances, to fall back on defiance as a way of not heeding. There are a thousand ingenious ways in which commands on what and how to teach can, will and *must* be modified or circumvented in the actual moments of teaching.

Teachers practice an art:

> Teachers must be involved in *debate*, *deliberation* and *decision* about what and how to teach. Such involvement constitutes the only language in which knowledge adequate to an art can arise. Without such a language, teachers not only feel decisions as impositions, they find that intelligence cannot traverse the gap between the generalities of merely expounded instructions and the particularities of teaching moments. Participation in debate–deliberation–choice is required for learning what is needed as well as for willingness to do it. There is an obvious moral here for teacher-training. (Schwab, 1983, p. 245)

Schwab's emphasis on willing participation by teachers is supported by a three-year study some colleagues and I have just completed on dysfunctional stress (burnout) among teachers in urban schools. We tried to identify the working conditions related to absenteeism, nonparticipation, and apathy. We identified the contributors to negativism about the job, the school, the children, and, most of all, one's self. They tended to be characteristic of highly stressed faculties in schools with poor achievement scores, or in schools with low productivity. The cosmology of high-stress schools revealed that the adults—the teachers—no longer believed anything they did would make a difference in students' learning. More specifically, the three major factors which were related to high-stress situations were teachers' feelings of lack of:

(1) *status* (feelings of being a worthwhile professional, consulted on curriculum decisions, being "put down" by the principal, the media and the central office, etc.),
(2) *security* (fiscal and physical safety and job security), and
(3) *sociability* (the time and opportunity to interact with other adults and discuss personal and professional issues in an atmosphere of trust and respect).

Teachers also cite barriers to teaching as a factor in "burnout"; and by this they mean anything which interferes with what they see as their proper role and behavior in the classroom, and anything they are asked to do without consultation, discussion and choice (Schwartz, 1983). A typical comment is, "The lack of power to change the situation for the better makes the job stressful." Teachers perceive that directives forced upon them from above clearly affect the performance of their job. At the same time, they see that they have little input into the decision-making process, that little opportunity is given to them to express ideas to policymakers, and that administrators manipulate them and can be either too authoritarian or nondirective. In addition, principals expect teachers to do a variety of nonteaching functions—patrolling halls, lunchroom duty, taking attendance in a homeroom—and teachers resent having to function as security personnel to bolster safety inside schools. Boards of education commonly demand copious, and often repetitive, paperwork, whether it be new forms or daily lesson plans.

Without positive feelings of status, security, and sociability, teachers "burnt-out," "dropped-out," or were "carried-out." The survivors were certainly not interested in curriculum-change projects ordered from above without consulting them. The social organization and political systems in highly stressed schools robbed teachers of their opportunities for collegiality, innovation, and the creativity of peer interaction: Significant here is that these systems also robbed teachers of a voice in the curriculum decisions, which was at the core of their professional identity.

The cornerstone of the participatory structure Schwab recommends is the Curriculum Group with specified roles, and it would address precisely the problems identified above. Teachers would be central to the change process, their status and opportunities for collegiality and sociability would be enhanced, and change would come as a function of consultation and choice. Other members of the group would include the principal, persons from the local school board or the local community council who are also members of the business community, and students. This regular core group is supplemented by other visiting members such as a group facilitator and curriculum or subject-matter experts, preferably those who have done research and reflected on the field—scholar practitioners, in other words. This Curriculum Group of eight to ten members with occasional consultants would be chaired by a professor of curriculum with experience in both research and practice.

The structure is familiar, and there are records of programs over the last decade which tried a very similar arrangement, with varying degrees of success. Perhaps we should recall the important lessons of these other efforts before implementing the process Schwab proposes. I will describe here three such examples with which I have had first-hand experience. The three are programs that incorporated some of the same collaborative structure as Schwab proposes, with a core group and a chair; they had similar responsibilities for curriculum change and comparable processes involving participatory debate, discussion, and decision-making.

EXAMPLES OF EARLIER SIMILAR EFFORTS

The Ford Training and Placement Program

The Ford Training and Placement Program, funded by the foundation of the same name, operated from 1967 through 1973 as a collaborative effort housed in the Department and Graduate School of Education at the University of Chicago and in conjunction with the Chicago public schools. The Ford program model was based on the view of the school as a social system described by J. W. Getzels (1967). The operational program was based on two assumptions: First, each school, while culturally similar to all other schools, is a unique social system characterized by institutional role sets and filled by personalities with individual needs. The chief implication of this assumption is that the persons who will be filling the roles in a specific school should be trained together as a group before they enter the school. Second, universities cannot prepare teachers for the inner-city (or any other) school without the active participation of professionals in the field and members of the communities to be served by the school. Therefore, an effective training must be collaborative, involving the trainer (the university), the user (the public schools), and the client (the community and students).

The basic training and socialization mechanism of the Ford program was called a *cadre*—a group of about 20 persons for each target school. Each cadre included anywhere from four to six new teachers or interns, second-year Master of Arts in Teaching students from the university representing various subject matter areas or grade levels. They were matched by six to eight experienced teachers in like areas from the target school. The principal agreed to be a member of the group along with community members and others in the school such as a counselor or teacher–nurse.

Two staff assistants were assigned to each cadre by the university, a cadre liaison and a group-process consultant. Other university faculty participated as requested by the cadre and/or staff. The group was organized during the summer and given intensive training for six weeks at the university in three areas: The Learner and the Community, Curriculum Development and Instructional Strategies, and Group Process or Human Relations. The interns were then placed in part-time teaching roles in the school. The group continued to meet, weekly after school for two or three hours, to continue the training of cadre members in school-specific issues related to teaching. The cadre's tasks were to provide personal and professional support for new interns, to structure socialization experiences in the school and community, to renew the enthusiasm as well as the curriculum and instructional skills of the experienced teachers, to assist in solving school-wide problems, and to bridge the gap between the university, the school, and the community. The program's directors hoped that increased understandings and better communications would improve the instructional program of the school.

Over the five years of operation, 13 cadres were established and the program research and evaluation reports estimated that about nine cadres survived and contributed to the school over a three-year period (Schwartz, 1974; Doyle, 1973). A number of programs influencing and changing curriculum in several schools were successful due to the integral involvement of teachers in "debate," "deliberation," and "choice" concerning the curriculum proposals. Most notable among these projects was the program at DuSable High School in Chicago, where a mathematics project began in 1968 and was still in place in 1974 when the Ford program ended. The DuSable program built, with the aid of the university consultant, from pure inservice education through debate and deliberation to a cooperative effort involving interns, regular department faculty, and the consultant. Teachers were involved in decision-making about what was to be taught and how. Mini-projects involving teaching plans developed into a cohesive approach to mathematics instruction. Many new supplies such as Cuisinare rods, desk calculators, and geoboards were purchased on request of the teachers and used in the instructional program. In other schools that were part of the

Ford program, curriculum changes occurred as beneficial by-products of the preservice teacher-training of the interns. For example, faculty members at the DuSable High School and the Kenwood High School developed a four-year Black literature component that was inserted into the regular Language Arts curriculum. This grew out of the efforts of the preservice interns who were working with a professor of English at the University on Black literature. Several of the inservice teachers from the two schools became interested in the project. These experienced teachers worked with the interns and created a teacher-collated anthology of Black poets in 1968. The English Curriculum Committee composed of staff from both schools expanded in 1969 to include other faculty and high school students to continue deliberation about the curriculum. Technical assistance was provided by the Ford program. "In the process of shaping the curriculum the student played an equal role with faculty in making these decisions" (Schwartz, 1972, pp. 375–380). The committee developed a comprehensive plan for all levels of English instruction, and presented this plan to the DuSable principal, who approved the plan and succeeded in obtaining $500 from the Board of Education for books. The Ford Training program matched the funds. As a consequence of this focus on Black literature, several curriculum-related field trips were made, each attended by hundreds of students, including a viewing of the film adaptation of *The Learning Tree* by Gordon Parks, *Dutchman* by LeRoi Jones and *Amen Corner* by James Baldwin. The student reception to the program was so enthusiastic that many pupils agreed to purchase their own books for class when the delivery of texts was delayed.

The number of successful curricular projects is too numerous to describe here, but a partial list includes:

Gikuyu anthropology unit—Kenwood High School
Art curriculum development—Forrestville High School
The use of movies in guidance—Kenwood High School
Reading through film-making—Forrestville High School
Reading project—Hyde Park High School
The science of photography: a unit for ninth-grade students taking General Science in an inner-city school, DuSable High School
Multicultural approach to the improvement of reading abilities—Horace Mann Elementary School
An evaluation of the instrumental music program of summer 1971 and proposal for summer 1972—Simeon Vocational High School
Cross-cadre student tutoring project—Hirsch High School and Tanner Elementary School cadres
Cross-cadre adult reading project—Hirsch cadre
Critical thinking unit—Kenwood High School
Tanner School enrichment program—Tanner Elementary School

Jobs for teens—Dunbar Vocational High School
Sub-Saharan Africa: an interdisciplinary approach to the slow learner—Forrestville High School

Teacher involvement in curriculum change was essential in all projects.

It should be noted that beneficial effects accrued to the university as well as to the target schools. The university graduate program benefited through the year-long school placements, allowing interns to receive practical training in the field. This resulted in well-trained new professionals capable of carrying out the traditional tasks required of teachers, and who also were accessible to future cadres. Their knowledge and skills in correcting teacher training efforts in the MAT programs could be built upon. Feedback to the university from the cadre meetings became important in re-forming concepts concerning teaching, and teacher training, as ideas were floated by the university specialists to be considered by the target school faculty. The experienced teachers in the cadres did not hesitate to criticize ideas for their practicality or impracticality in the culture of the school and classroom.

Four cadres actually accomplished significant curriculum changes in their buildings, and their success rate improved over time. These four groups, who continued to meet and work together after the initial year, and who socialized their interns to the school culture, were sufficiently well organized to capture university resources for the second and third years of operation, or they had university-based contact who functioned as an advocate and facilitator for procuring resources from the school system or university. The single most successful group (Martin Luther King High School, formerly Forrestville High School) worked together for six years; this group made significant changes in the math curriculum and established an effective remedial reading program in an inner-city high school. The group persuaded the university to assemble a cadre of all-experienced teachers as the MAT students in 1972 when vacancies to accommodate new interns were no longer available.

In turn, the advent of the experienced teachers in classes caused changes in the programs at the university. University faculty felt compelled to get into city schools to understand what these mature teachers were reporting in class. But the Ford program's university-based Curriculum Chairman's involvement in this project was finite. Continued participation in the field by university faculty for more than three years was nearly impossible without the external fiscal support or rewards built into the institutional tenure and promotion process. The economic system of the university never did recognize field experiences in public schools as currency for tenure and promotion for faculty. At the university, participation in a "practical program" meant reallocation of faculty resources and time. One could not engage in theoretical research while conducting workshops for cadres. A few persons did both: They were much like the Curriculum Chairman described by Schwab in their skills, scope of knowledge, and academic background. While the reward structure of the university did not include tenure and promotion credit for participation in "practical programs," some talented faculty members did find ways to combine their research interests with their participation in the program and, typically, they could be linked to the productive cadres.

In retrospect, the roles of cadre liaison and group process consultant should have been filled by those few faculty members who possessed the technology Schwab wants his Curriculum Chairman to have. That technology requires a "command of small-group rhetoric; a reasonable familiarity with the outcomes of current and recent research in the education-directed aspects of the behavioral sciences, and a good grounding in philosophical summaries of scientific investigation, of the truth-status of its outcomes, and of the characteristics of common experiences . . ." and the ability to "evoke and maintain an appropriately deliberate mode of discussion" (Schwab, 1983, p. 254).

These successful curriculum projects grew out of curriculum groups similar to Schwab's interdisciplinary core group. Not all curriculum efforts were successful, for problems arose due to a lack of focus. The cadre at Kenwood High School failed to come up with an integrated, refined anthropology unit on the Gikuyu due to a lack of a systematic approach to planning for task competition. The cadre gathered materials together but failed to organize these materials into a truly unified interdisciplinary unit. Consequently, the material was merely made available to the faculty; the option of incorporating the material into the classroom was left up to individuals. Those teachers who actually used the Gikuyu materials found the unit very useful, according to the FTPP report. The monograph concludes that "A more overriding and articulated concern with the question of task orientation of the cadres would have been much more beneficial" (Schwartz, 1979, p. 50). The Ford Program was primarily a teacher-training and placement project, and any curriculum reforms that resulted were beneficial by-products of a process not concerned directly with curricular reform. As a result, acquiring funds from the university for curriculum projects became difficult at times. Since the university's chief concern was with preservice training for its graduate interns, the provision of resources tended to be spotty and on a "somewhat ad hoc basis" (Schwartz, 1979, p. 51). By contrast, Schwab focuses his core group on curriculum and on what is to be taught and how. Schwab actually scripts the scenario for the Curriculum Chairman to guide deliberation and debate and focus on task orientation in his curriculum group. The liaisons and consultants in the Ford program were not Curriculum Chairmen. The Ford program selected its liaisons and consultants with a less precise set of criteria than Schwab proposes.

The Ford program staff expended most of its energy on the cultural universals of socialization of interns and on managing the political system of the school structure. Staff spent time helping the preservice interns learn the norms of the institution and assisting them to successfully accomplish the rites of passage from student teacher to teacher. Much staff and cadre time was devoted to opening up the decision-making structure and governance system so that the cadre members could exercise some control over the political system and (ultimately) the economic processes of allocation of resources and working conditions. Although time was built into the summer training program and the weekly meetings to consider curriculum issues, rather than concentrating equally on each of Schwab's four commonplaces in deliberating curricular needs, during the first year, in cadres with large numbers of preservice interns, attention was invariably focused on who was being taught—the inner-city student. Those cadres with more experienced teachers and preservice interns who had some informal teaching experiences in Peace Corps, Vista, summer camp, etc., could accomplish more quickly the tasks of understanding the school culture and move on to curriculum development projects.

During the course of a year, Ford program staff worked with many schools and attempted to achieve multiple goals. By contrast, Schwab's proposal focuses on one school at a time, on a single overriding goal in curriculum change: It clearly specifies the content of the role of the Curriculum Chairman, limits the membership of the core group to full-fledged members of the school culture, and thereby avoids the problems of entry into a system faced by any newcomer. He details the process for the operation of the group never allowing it to postpone consideration of problems and curriculum modification by demanding "precise definitions of all 'key terms' . . ." and for "elaborate experiments" (Schwab, 1983, p. 250).

Schwab's proposal encourages the Curriculum Chairman to assist the curriculum group in developing a common language descriptive of the cultural system of the school as a way of facilitating change and saving time. In a sense, the Ford Program was able to accomplish this linguistic coherence by the third year of the program; use of this common professional language seemed to be a hallmark of the "successful" cadres.

The Ford program did not produce national models of new curriculum. What the Ford Training and Placement Program did do was to produce a body of research and commentary, and some staff members who could specify the details of tested patterns of successful collaborative efforts between university and schools. There were certain conditions of the Ford Program that have, over the years, become more important than the program goals or the cadre training mechanism, because they reflected a basic shift in the relationships between universities and the public schools—shifts which teacher-training programs must heed. A curriculum professor and a teacher educator, in addition to searching for interesting curriculum problems in education journals, must be in schools and talking to teachers, students, parents, and administrators. The university professor must be around often enough so that he or she is viewed "as a regular habitué of teachers' tables, or cafeterias and classrooms, and has become a familiar figure to students as well as a respected peer of the principal and community members" (Schwartz, 1979, p. 43).

The Ford program also demonstrated the importance of collaboration at all levels of the involved organizations. The program literature defined collaboration as *parity* among the cooperating parties in decision-making, with specified *liaison* roles at the important points of interaction between school, university, and community; and identified *negotiation* as the chief cadre and program process. Ultimately, the program required a willingness to share decision-making about time-honored university and public school policies, often requiring changes in the economic system of each institution, resulting in a reallocation of resources. For the public school, participation in the joint effort meant changes in selection, certification, and placement practices of new teachers. For the university, participation meant accommodation of a new kind of faculty member—one who operated more like an applied anthropologist, always going out into the field and participating in the lifeway of a culture. Participation in the Ford Program limited faculty members' normal scope of decision-making and made demands on time and energy which could not be dismissed. The role analogous to Schwab's Curriculum Chairman created difficulties not found by faculty in their regular responsibilities, and in so doing it provided a preview of the demands Schwab's proposal would make on traditional faculty.

The faculty and staff members who were successful in working with the productive cadres were those willing to spend two days a week in the schools observing in classrooms; doing demonstration lessons; working with interns and experienced teachers; attending cadre and subcommittee meetings; keeping the principal, the department chair, and significant others informed of the cadre's activities; and winning allies to the program by providing service (usually in the form of expertise from the university). These faculty members listened to experienced teachers and treated them as colleagues, respecting their sphere of expertise and, in turn, winning their respect by demonstrating their area of expertise and how it could be helpful in the school. The relationships had to be authentic, based on an understanding of the value system, and expectations of the school culture, as well as useful transferable skills and knowledge which the teacher could apply immediately in the classroom. Furthermore, beneficial results should be apparent rather quickly as an outcome of the application of the new procedure.

Faculty members or project staff who patronized interns and other faculty, who came to the schools and cadres with missionary zeal and an inflexible belief in "the right way" to do things, and who were unwilling to listen, were soon ignored. In the long run, the cadres burdened with this kind of guidance were immobilized.

Federal Programs

In the early 1960s, as a kind of domestic Peace Corps, the federal Teacher Corps program emerged as a response to a national teacher shortage in the U.S. It was an attempt to improve the schools in poor urban and some rural settings, by providing better trained teachers who were responsive to poverty and minority community needs and had some sense of missionary zeal. Typically, an experienced teacher was hired by a university (usually at a junior faculty level) to supervise a corps of interns in the advanced stages of their teacher preparation programs. Interns went as teams to schools and taught under the supervision of a master teacher for part of a day for a full year's internship. During the time the interns were supported by the Teacher Corps program grant, they finished their university work and teacher credential program, met with their team leader, other interns, and community persons while they attempted to implement reforms in the schools. From the first 12 two-year funding cycles the goals of the program were focused on preservice preparation multicultural education, equity in terms of minority representation on the teams, community involvement in the schools, improving and introducing field-based learnings into university teacher education programs, enhancing public school programs, and curriculum reform. For the most part, the first decade of Teacher Corps programs were add-on and peripheral to the mainstream of the university-based, teacher-preparation programs. In 1975, the federal program changed its guidelines to require that the universities make an institutional commitment to incorporate some of the Teacher Corps goals into their regular teacher-preparation programs, and further required that the programs have a powerful policy board with equal representation from the university, the cooperating public schools, and the community. The new guidelines required that the number of schools be limited to one, preferably a secondary school, although occasionally the federal program allowed the project to work with two feeder schools. The 12th Cycle Teacher Corps program (1976–1978), rather than concentrating on preservice education, concentrated on staff development, inservice education, and *curriculum reform* in those areas referred to as basic skills. However, the funding cycle was still only two years—hardly enough time to achieve entry and credibility in a school building.

After more than a decade of evaluations and expert advice, the Teacher Corps program again changed its approach in 1978 as a result of amended federal regulations. Rather than attempting to change the cultures of school, the university, and the community in two years, the new guidelines emphasized improving instruction in a single school, developing diagnostic/prescriptive teaching, and recasting curriculum to reflect education that was suited to a multicultural population. Prior to 1978, the Teacher Corps contained no formal curriculum mandates. The new guidelines required a curriculum component, required programs to focus on one school for five years, and required the universities to develop plans for incorporating the best elements of the funded program into their preservice teacher and administrator preparation programs. The five-year programs had a strong curriculum component—in the emphasis upon basic skills and multicultural education. Unfortunately, federal funding cuts interrupted this experiment in the third year of the first five-year cycle, disrupting a number of planned curriculum changes. For example, the comprehensive differentiated achievement program planned by San Francisco State University had to be cancelled, although research produced by the project prior to funding cuts allowed Williard High School in Berkeley to initiate a skill program for low-achieving students. By 1982, the national Teacher Corps program was out of business (Moore, 1982).

Like the Ford program, for the first ten years of its operation the Teacher Corps program was a social action and equity effort. Interns studied the culture of the school community, the technology of teaching, manipulation of the political system of the school, and socialization for purposes of job placement. Little formal attention was paid to the content of the curriculum, although some concern was paid to the culture of poverty from which most students came. If consideration was paid to the teacher and administrator it was typically from the perspective of Teacher Corps interns and team leaders from the "new frontier" criticizing the beliefs and behavior of the "fossilized old guard" and viewing the children and communities as victims in need of rescue. The school personnel and the tenured university faculty tended to view the Teacher Corps group as wild-eyed militants who would do violence to their cultures. Certainly not all Teacher Corps projects fit this stereotype, but the national reputation of the program did not include the many isolated provocative and productive curriculum efforts. Typically, useful curriculum efforts emerged in the early days where a mutuality of effort existed among schools, communities, and universities.

According to a massive but aborted SRI evaluation effort, those programs which had the benefit of a two-year cycle plus three years of the new five-year funding did accomplish some permanent reforms in individual schools. The documentation is difficult to find, as the national evaluations are incomplete, but some individual reports are available and some tentative conclusions can be drawn from them.

One example of a Teacher Corps program that succeeded involved Roosevelt University in Chicago and Hinton Elementary School (Ginsberg & Melnick, 1981). Data concerning teachers' needs and the metric system were collected by the school principal and the Teacher Corps staff at a workshop held in the summer of 1976. The following fall, inservice training began at Hinton for the school faculty and the interns. In the spring of 1977, the program shifted its attention to in-class activities; the shift was in response to an evaluation done in November and to declining interest and attendance at schoolwide workshops manifested by Hinton faculty reacting to the original, purely theoretical program approach. The Teacher Corps staff, in collaboration with a group of teachers and several interns, prepared self-instruction packets for all teachers in the school in January. Between four and six classes were held each week during February and March in a classroom set aside for the purpose of demonstrations by the staff, teachers, interns, and outside experts. These were observed by members of the faculty in a schedule alternating with discussion of suggested class activities, evaluations of materials, or other related concerns. As a result of the program, metrics were adopted as a normal component of the mathematics curriculum at Hinton (Olson, 1977, pp. 18–20). This example, together with other successful Teacher Corps programs, such as the Valley Park LOFTS program near St. Louis (Nemec, 1980), and the dozens of other curriculum projects under Teacher Corps sponsorship, demonstrates that even before the change in focus in the Teacher Corps program, groups similar to Schwab's interdisciplinary group were being successful—albeit in a rather haphazard fashion.

The new five-year Teacher Corps program instituted in 1978 had six conditions: the grantee could work in only one school, had to present a plan designed to improve school climate or morale, deliver a participatory staff development program at the site, influence the preservice education program for teachers and others at the university, work with preservice interns (two per year), identify and work on one or two curriculum problems (of which reading and language skills was a requirement), interact with the community, and participate in a national evaluation effort (SRI Executive Summaries, 1982, pp. i–vi). By 1978, this program, had refocused its social action and equity goals to emphasize improving the curriculum and instructional program of a school, attending to the cultural universals only as they influence what was taught, to whom, and how.

The Teacher Corps staff had to be at the schools at least half-time to provide support and service. Tenured university faculty had to demonstrate involvement in and commitment to the program. Individual case studies of over 50 programs consistently demonstrated a positive impact on the schools when the active group (faculty, administration, interns, and university faculty) was involved in discussion and decision-making around specific curriculum problems (Bush & Fox, 1981). The SRI Executive Summaries concluded that this involvement of university staff benefited the participating institutions of higher education (IHE) as well as the target schools. The report states, "In some IHE's, Teacher Corps contributed to the revamping of courses and entire degree programs. Typically, the content of courses was reconstructed around the practical problems of the school or contemporary issues in education. In a substantial number of IHE's, degree programs were developed or revised to accommodate the requirements of inservice teachers in field-based settings" (p. 70). Feedback to the universities from interns and participating school faculty was an important source of information to the universities for modifying degree programs.

In all, almost one-third of all American teacher education institutions participated in the Teacher Corps program over its 20-year history. Given that one of the program's constant goals was teacher education, what can be said about the efficacy of the program in curriculum reform? In the area of teacher education, the Teacher Corps did change curriculum at IHEs through the required extensive interaction between interns and inservice teachers, between university faculty and public school personnel. This was the most visible contribution of the national program. At the local level designing and putting into practice curriculum reforms remained an option until 1978, and the changes were less consistent.

As a national effort, the Teacher Corps probably had more impact on universities than on the targeted elementary or secondary schools they served. In those instances where aspects of the school curriculum were changed, certain program characteristics were to be found again and again. In all of the curriculum projects, the need for change was established by the Teacher Corps group first by giving needs assessment instruments to teachers in the target school. The teachers were then involved with debate on the assessed needs and deliberation on proposed changes. Expert counsel and training was given by the university staff to participating teachers and interns; this training always had an immediate applicability in the classroom. The acquisition of knowledge through this training was rewarded by increases in status, and sometimes salary, for the participating teacher. Finally, a feeling of collegiality was established between the teachers and the university trainers; the trainer received valuable feedback data for his or her efforts. It is easy to see that these beneficial processes have something in common with the group procedures described by Schwab.

A recent follow-up study of the impact of the national Teacher Corps program, which surveyed 130 institutions of higher education who had Teacher Corps programs in 1981, documents the impact of the program at the university level (Anglin, Grady, & Stephenson, 1984, pp. 3–4). Table 2 summarizes the responses. The most frequent program contribution cited (34%) was that Teacher Corps strengthened IHEs' collaborative working arrangements with school districts, particularly in the area of field-based teacher education and staff development.

A similar study needs to be undertaken asking the principals and faculty of participating schools what the major contributions of the program were.

Once more, an unfinished effort with noble purposes might have been more effective with a conceptual model of curriculum and an analytical tool to learn the territory and the paths of least resistance through the territory.

TABLE 6.2
Major Contributions of the Teacher Corps Program to SFSU

Number	*Percent*	*Category*
31	34	Strengthened field-based teacher education and staff development programs and developed closer (collaborative) working relations with schools.
21	23	University staff development (provided professors as opportunity to work in school classrooms)
14	15	Served as a model for teaching training (special mention of multicultural and bilingual education)
8	9	Restructured graduate programs (M.A. and MAT
5	6	Developed closer ties between the university and community groups
5	6	Developed a research base for the university
3	3	Opportunities to explore, try, and reflect from both a local and national perspective
2	2	No contribution
1	1	Hired personnel who made substantial contribution
1	1	No response
91*	100 totals	

*Nine respondants identified two major contributions.

Single School Efforts

The third and final example of coordinated group process for curricular change is to be found in San Francisco's Bayview–Hunters Point, the low-income, black area of the city.

The Bayview–Hunters Point Educational Complex was formed in 1978 by a faculty member at San Francisco State University, Fannie W. Preston, and funded for three years by the San Francisco Foundation. The Bayview–Hunters Point Educational Complex was part of Superintendent Robert Alioto's Redesign Plan for the San Francisco Unified School District and part of the Urban Mission program of the university. The overriding goal of the Complex was to upgrade the quality of the curriculum and the instructional program in three geographically and racially isolated elementary schools. The curricular efforts sought chiefly to establish a program that would have a long-term continuing effect on these black schools, such that the program would appeal to others—whites, Hispanics, Asians, and others. In the words of the proposal, the revised curriculum was to "lead to a voluntary balanced enrollment." Second, the project was to involve the professional preparation programs and faculty at the university in field-based curriculum development and inservice training programs. Finally, the program was to provide enrichment opportunities for students.

While some faculty from the university did place teams of student teachers at one or more of the three schools, it was understood that faculty were to work with the existing staff on curriculum problems which they identified together. When the funding ended, the university adopted one of the Complex elementary schools as a laboratory school and continued to support faculty involvement in curriculum projects; these included the development of a children's literature curriculum with the primary teachers, an oral language program, a global education curriculum, and an English proficiency program (Preston, 1982).

Although external funding ceased in 1981, both the university and the district continue to support curriculum development and change activities at the laboratory school; test scores in reading at the school have gone up significantly during the course of the program. This single school project featured tenured university faculty in the field, interacting with classroom teachers involved as colleagues in shared decision-making. The project director was able to function as a Curriculum Chairman and had credibility in the school, the district, and the community, as well as at the university. The focus was on curriculum development, by individuals who were members in good standing of their respective school cultures and by university faculty members who understood and were accepted by the school culture, and who knew the points of entry into the system.

The pattern seen in the other two examples held true here as well: Productive and appropriate curriculum changes, in public school or university teacher preparation programs, were successful when one particular individual functioned as an on-site facilitator of the process. That individual was important, and his or her credibility had to come from several sources. The three case studies cited above together suggest some common characteristics of the setting in which Schwab's Curriculum Chairman can work effectively in cooperative projects involving school and university. They are summarized in a recent Carnegie Foundation Report (Maeroff, 1983). When planning for a successful program, one should expect that:

(1) a common agenda must be acknowledged,
(2) a true spirit of collaboration must emerge (collaboration as defined earlier in the description of the Ford program),
(3) a single project must be identified,
(4) those involved must be adequately rewarded,
(5) the focus must be on activities, not machinery (Maeroff, 1983, p. 5).

And most important, from the perspective of this discussion, there must be an intelligent, scholarly, dynamic, facilitative, and likable Curriculum Chairman. Assuming one has all of the above, is curriculum reform guaranteed? Let us turn now to the political realities of schools, and universities and human resistance to change, to the cultural aspects of the analytical matrix.

THE REALITIES OF SCHOOLING

The public schools are society's socialization agents outside the home and the local community. As such, they are subject to the vagaries of private agendas and public pressure. Both the Ford program and the Teacher Corps fell victim to the bureaucracy, with schools unable to place the new interns and continue to work with experienced teachers: Changes in the economic system, the declining need for teachers, the seniority system, the legislated equity value requiring involuntary transferring of experienced teachers to achieve racial integration, budget cuts, school closings, revolving-door principals, the incoming technology requiring skills in areas like metrics education, mastery learning, and the impact of unionization on the socialization of new teachers and the lifeway of older teachers and other factors interfered. Initially, the programs tried to do battle with the devil, but the constant bombardment of minutiae, the shifting and contradictory norms, dampened the zeal of program staff. These nontraditional efforts, involving grass roots participation in curriculum decisions rather than top-down efforts, were hard work and required high levels of energy and selfless devotion; they were probably too ambitious from the start. It was only when efforts were focused and decisions were followed by hard sustained work that the programs in individual schools made a difference. With some regularity, university faculty members left the field when under siege; rightly arguing that working in the public schools was not their job. While some university faculty functioned well in what Schwab would call the Curriculum Chairman role, none had been specifically trained for it. All had come through the traditional ranks of graduate programs, trained as scholars.

Schwab, of course, envisions a very different training for the Curriculum Chairman, one whose "education and refreshment" result in a true Renaissance man (or woman): ". . . the curricular chairman must be capable of skillful use of rhetorics of persuasion and elicitation. These rhetorics are needed, not as orator to audience, but as Chairman and member of a small group and in person-to-person dealings with individuals. Moreover, his use of these rhetorics must be skilled with respect to a diversity of conversants. He must do well with his peers: teachers and parents. He must deal with administrators and social elders: the school principal, professors of subject-matters and behavioral sciences, school board members and employers in the community. He must deal with juniors: students as encountered on street, playground and workplace" (Schwab, 1983, p. 259). He or she must further be a reader of scholarly journals, a teacher, a learner, an applied researcher, have a knowledge of past practices in curriculum and current advances, in addition to the philosophy, psychology, sociology, and anthropology of the field. The Curriculum Chairman must know something about each of the curricular content areas offered in the school's program, plus something of "nonintellective aspects of growing up, of ways in which circumstance inhibits their growth, and of ways in which their sustenance can be aided in the schools" (Schwab, 1983, p. 261).

Schwab is aware that most traditional graduate programs do not prepare graduate students in the skill areas he has specified. Neither do the traditional programs give graduate students the analytical tools to describe and analyze the cultural systems in which they will work. It is clear that practicing curriculum directors as well as school administrators, teachers, and university professors with responsibilities in the field, are not educated along the lines Schwab proposes. Asked how useful their graduate work was in preparing them for their current roles, their responses can be codified as follows (Pitner, 1982):

(1) The teacher/supervisor's workday is characterized by brief, disjointed, verbal encounters with a wide range of people seeking immediate solutions to problems, while academic programs ask graduate students to spend long hours reading, writing, and weighing alternative solutions to problems.

(2) The supervisor's role requires skill in conflict resolution, and the graduate student typically learns to avoid conflict and to accept the authority of expertise.

(3) Supervisors, like Schwab's Curriculum Chairman, depend on their skills in face-to-face communications to accomplish their work, while graduate students function in an atmosphere that emphasizes written communication.

(4) The final area of discrepancy deals with the emotional content of the work place, highly charged with eruptions and rare periods of calm in the schools but with the expectation that supervisors will be calm and rational. University training programs particularly at the graduate level, value ideas and reasoning, downplaying the practical use of feelings.

Schwab would change the programs and he makes some excellent suggestions for the fulfillment of the dissertation requirement and for the addition of courses more in tune with the realities of schooling. Indeed, the relevance of university graduate programs to practical curriculum responsibilities can be seen through some important similarities between the university graduate school, and the public school as workplace. Among these similarities are:

(1) Both institutions evidence high levels of ambiguity and environments over which the actors have little control.

(2) University and school are replete with tasks which are initiated by others, but which the actor (the Curriculum Chairman, in this case) must implement.

(3) Graduate students, public school personnel, and university faculty receive little systematic feedback on their work except at transition periods or crisis times, and then they are told when they do wrong, but rarely are they told when they are doing right.

(4) Both the graduate student and the supervisor are subjected to feelings of isolation.

For a long time the difficulty in talking about the kind of individual and role needed to assist with curriculum revision programs in schools was that of insufficient knowledge: The ordinary organizational life and tasks of people in schools were not described adequately. Empirical and ethnographic studies over the last decade with their "thick" descriptions (Wolcott, 1978; Bridges, 1978; Goodlad, 1983; Berliner, 1982; Schwartz, 1983) have partially remedied this situation and we now have some answers to the questions: What knowledge, skills, and abilities do the curriculum change agents require? What structures must support individual efforts to install curriculum change? How long will it take? Who must be involved? Every documented experimental effort over the last two decades has contributed some bit of information to the answers.

In each of the three examples cited above, curricularists, program developers, and teacher educators were groping for and working toward essentially a Schwabian model. Each of these three programs displayed one or more elements of the model. The Ford program of the early 1970s featured the holistic vision of the school as a unique social system; it supported the notion of training those who would work in a given school with those already familiar with the patterns of culture in the building. In this collaborative training, the new teachers would quickly learn something about the "four commonplaces" as a prelude to curriculum efforts. But the Ford program lacked focus; for although it had a stated curriculum development goal, it began as a university-based MAT format. For the most part, the university faculty who participated in the program were interested in the theory of curriculum and research. Involvement in practical field-based curriculum projects was not regarded by the university as serious scholarly activity and therefore was not rewarded. Furthermore the social upheaval prevalent in urban school/communities at that time lacked appeal for university professors and distracted teachers in the schools from engaging in curricular issues.

The post-1978 Teacher Corps program made the same assumptions about the school as a social system as did the Ford program, and it also had a curriculum focus. The federal guidelines legislated the content of certain curriculum efforts and even required a particular instructional strategy called "diagnostic-prescriptive teaching." It specified the milieu (a single school) and required the participation of schools whose students were poor and/or minority.

This national program focus dealt with all four of the commonplaces, specifying what would be taught in certain areas, who would be taught, how instruction would be delivered, and in what context. By 1978, things had settled down sufficiently in the schools to permit teachers to focus on curriculum and instruction, and cooperating universities recognized the benefits of collaborative programs with schools in training practitioners. Inservice efforts were well received in those Teacher Corps schools which were fortunate enough to have an effective team leader, the role closest to Schwab's Curriculum Chairman. Then the money ran out. What is left is the spirit of collaboration and randomly documented curriculum projects, thus making generalizations about this federal initiative very difficult.

Of the three examples described here, the Bayview–Hunters Point program was most Schwabian in its approach to experienced teachers, eliciting their participation in the identification of curriculum issues, and in effective delivery of instruction, in its attention to student characteristics and the content of the curriculum, in the single-school focus, and in the utilization of an expert university-based Curriculum Chairperson. But the program personnel could not control the external variables of transfer of key school personnel.

Although each of the three programs was flawed, each contributed something to our knowledge of how to accomplish curriculum reform. Each also points up the elegance and comprehensiveness of Schwab's theoretical model and practical structures and processes.

Joe Schwab's unique contribution to the dialogue is that he is able to take this body of information and, without a single correlation coefficient, or literature review, or annotated bibliography, synthesize the best of the data and reshape it into a functional and detailed set of roles, structures, expectations, and processes. Additionally, he anticipates the problems and presents detailed dialogues of solutions to address the problem. Finally, he uses the theoretical to outline a practical professional preparation program for the professor of curriculum, who would, from time to time, function as a Curriculum Chair with the Curriculum Group. He then suggests the kind of scholarship which these professionals would carry out under his plan. "To their present concerns, they would add inquiries which would inform, advise, and refresh their former students working in the schools" (p. 263).

The evidence presented in each of these case studies and in many others over the last two decades suggests that Schwab's model does work—and has worked. When attention is given to the four commonplaces, when teachers are intensively and meaningfully involved in the curriculum reform effort from its inception, when the principal is included as an active participant and when the Curriculum Chairman is a skilled knowledgeable practitioner/scholar, curriculum change can be effective.

But there are pitfalls, which can be anticipated by knowing what to look for in the local school culture and in the centralized school district. Schwab says he does not wish to deal with the political realities of teachers and principals who are transferred from one school to another, irrespective of their crucial participation in a curricular effort at a particular school. He says he does not wish to address the realities of the impact of the unions on the values and social organization of a school and the economic consequences for the allocation of faculty time and other instructional resources. But someone must address these issues.

Certainly, the deliberations among teachers and others in the curriculum group can address the tensions related to conflicting values at the school-building level, but how does one work through the problem of a top-down mandated curriculum unit with world views discrepant from those of the students and the teachers.

Perhaps the best that can be done by the theorist is to urge awareness, analysis, and ongoing monitoring of these variations in the patterns of the cultural universals at the classroom, building, district, and community levels. The Curriculum Chairman should have access to the knowledge and insights provided by the analytical matrix which combines Schwab's four commonplaces and the nine cultural universals or some similar framework. The added cultural dimension will assist the theorist and the practitioners to anticipate disruptions and suggest strategies for coping with them while preserving the curriculum reform effort.

To ignore or not acquire this contextual information, to assume others will do it, or to count on immunity will turn the ordinary pitfalls of change in the schools into snakepits, unbridgeable chasms which discourage the intelligent, the faithful, and the brave. So, in addition to the functions and skills Schwab has specified for the Curriculum Chairman, I would add that he or she must also be a bit of an ethnographer, mapping, describing, and analyzing the cultures of the systems affected by, and affecting, the curriculum effort. In this way, the fragile craft can maintain its delicate balance and can be guided into running before the wind, tacking, or staying in port and out of dangerous waters.

The external constraints on the collaborative attempts by university and school people to implement new programs and practices are those which an "intimidated" Schwab "leaves to others or to the future." The constraints embodied in the prejudice against the practical at the university require "the risk-taking competence of the Deans or Chairman involved, their readiness to rock the boat of faculty members when the Dean's own reappointment is at stake . . ." (Schwab, 1983, p. 258). Schwab's clarity of mind and language informs, advises, and refreshes all of us as we seek to overcome the constraints of the practical.

REFERENCES

Algin, L., Grady, M., & Stephenson, J. "Federally Funded Programs: A Follow-Up Case Study." Paper presented at the American Association of Colleges of Teacher Education, San Antonio, Texas, February 1, 1984.

Asser, E., Laffey, J., Melnick, C., Olson, G., & Schwartz, H. "A Description and Evaluation of the 1979 Summer Workshop for Preservice and Inservice Teachers and Community Council Members," Roosevelt University and the Chicago Board of Education, Spring, 1980.

Bautista-Myers, L., Ed. *Issues and Perspectives: The Teacher Corps Experience*, The Teacher Corps Plains Network, University of Nebraska at Omaha, June 30, 1980.

Berliner, D. "Introduction" to *Schools as a Workplace: The Realities of Stress*, by H. Schwartz et al., a project paper for Roosevelt University; Chicago, Illinois, 1980.

Bridges, E. M. "Job Satisfaction and Teacher Absenteeism" Education Administration Quarterly, 16 (Spring 1980): 41–56.

Brophy, J. "Advances in Teacher Effectiveness Research." Paper presented at the annual meeting of the American Association of Colleges of Teacher Education, Detroit, 1983.

Bush, R. "Perspectives on 11th and 12th Cycle Teacher Corps Projects." *Teacher Corps Evaluation*, University of Nebraska, Omaha, 1978, pp. 119–169.

Doyle, W. "Transactional Evaluational in Program Development." In *Transactional Evaluation*, edited by Robert Rippey, Berkeley, CA: McCutchan Publishing, 1973, pp. 195–222.

Getzels, J. W. "Education for the Inner City: A Practical Proposal by an Impractical Theorist." *The School Review* 75, no. 3 (Autumn 1967): 283–299.

Ginsberg, R., & Melnick, C. C., Eds. Resource Papers Monograph, Roosevelt University with Chicago Board of Education, Spring, 1981.

Goodlad, J. I. *A Place Called School.* New York, McGraw-Hill, 1983.

Herskovitz, M. J. *Man and His Work.* New York: Alfred Knopf, 1949.

Maeroff, G. I. *School and College: Partnership in Education.* The Carnegie Foundation for the Advancement of Teaching, New York, 1983.

Moore, R., et al. Final Report of the San Francisco State University and the Berkeley Unified School District Teacher Corps Project, May 1982.

Nemac, J. "The Valley Park-Loft Process." In: *Plains Network Issues and Perspectives: The Teacher Corps Experience*, Lilian Bautista-Meyers, University of Nebraska at Omaha, June 30, 1980, p. 165–183.

Olson, G. "The Curriculum Development Model and Metric Education." In *Resource Papers for the Successful Teaching Models Conference*, Chicago: Roosevelt University and Chicago Board of Education, May 18–20, 1977.

Pitner, N. "Training of the School Administrator: State of the Art." Paper presented at the American Educational Research Association Meeting, New York, 1982.

Preston, F. W. Final Report of the Bayview–Hunters Point Educational Complex, San Francisco Foundation, January 1980–June 1981.

Schwab, J. "The Practical 4: Something for Curriculum Professors To Do" in *Curriculum Inquiry* (Fall 1983): 239–265.

Schwartz, H. "When University and Schools Relate." *Educational Leadership* (February, 1973): 397–380.

Schwartz, H. "An Experiment in Training Teachers for Inner City Schools: A Social Systems Approach in the Ford Training and Placement Program." *North Central Association Quarterly* XLVI, no. 4. (Spring, 1972): 375–380.

Schwartz, H. Ford Training and Placement Program Monograph, Roosevelt University, 1979.

Bennet, A., Olson, G., & Ginsberg, R. "Schools as a Workplace: The Realities of Stress." NIE publication, 1983 (in press) (NIE-G-80-0011).

SRI Executive Summaries.

Wolcott, H. *Teachers vs. Technocrats: An Educational Innovation in Anthropological Perspectives.* Eugene, Oregon; Center for Educational Policy and Management, University of Oregon, 1977.

CHAPTER SEVEN

Curriculum In and Out of Context

Catherine Cornbleth

The disappointments of curriculum theory in practice mostly come from treating curriculum out of context—both conceptually and operationally. Conceptual decontextualization has meant separating curriculum as product (e.g., a document such as a syllabus or course of study, a package of materials accompanied by directions for their use) from curriculum policy-making, design, and use. Operational decontextualization has meant treating curriculum, however defined, apart from its structural and sociocultural contexts as if it were independent of its location in an educational system, society, and history. When confronted, the isolation of curriculum from its multiple, interacting contexts is an absurdity, yet isolation remains another commonplace in curriculum discourse and practice.

In this essay, I briefly examine the decontextualization of curriculum—curriculum out of context—and then consider the possibilities of an alternative—curriculum in context. My purpose is to sketch an alternative theoretical framework that might inform empirical studies and reform efforts as well as more general analysis and understanding of curriculum phenomena.

CURRICULUM OUT OF CONTEXT

Conceptual Separation

How we conceive of curriculum is important because our conceptions and ways of reasoning about curriculum reflect and shape how we think and talk about, study, and act on the education made available to students.

Concern with conceptions is not "merely theoretical." Conceptions grow out of and enter into practice.

The prevailing technocratic conception views curriculum as a tangible product, usually a document or plan for instruction in a particular subject. The detail of the curriculum product ranges from a brief outline of topics to be taught and learned to an elaborate outline accompanied by teacher and student materials (e.g., readings, worksheets, transparencies) and a teacher guide including directions for teaching and testing.

In the technocratic view, curriculum construction is a presumably objective development project separate from policy-making and implementation. A set of procedures or steps to be followed guides the project—for example, specifying learning objectives to be obtained by students; selecting or creating and arranging the subject-matter content, activities, and materials; devising means of assessing students' attainment of the specified objectives; and providing directions for the intended use of the curriculum product. This development task typically is undertaken by curriculum specialists outside the schools or by teacher committees guided by specialists. The curriculum product produced is then disseminated for teachers to implement.[1]

The procedural steps of curriculum development suggest that curriculum is composed of discrete components (e.g., objectives, subject matter, materials) that can be constructed separately, often in a linear sequence, and then assembled to make a coherent curriculum. The procedures are intended to efficiently manage and control development resources and activities once others have made curriculum policy decisions (e.g., legislatures, school boards). Thus, the procedures are assumed to be value-neutral, and the curriculum developers are assumed to be disinterested specialists.[2]

Additional assumptions underlying a technocratic conception of curriculum and its construction concern change and rationality. If curriculum is a tangible product, then changing the curriculum means constructing and

---

[1]To make the presentation manageable, I have synthesized particular instances to present a composite that reflects the spirit and substance if not the particulars of individual cases. Also, while acknowledging differences in the form and substance of curriculum activities (e.g., at national, state or province, and local district, school, and classroom levels), I do not believe that considering these differences is germane to exploring the broader question of curriculum meanings and implications; conceptions span organizational levels.

[2]The mechanization of curriculum construction and the separation of curriculum policy-making and development inherent in the technocratic view contrast with a craft view of curriculum construction. A craft view implies a holistic conception of curriculum products as well as an appreciation of creativity in their construction. Craftmanship acknowledges both technical skill and personal preference in curriculum construction. The values and particular aims of the curriculum developer as artisan guide the imaginative use of procedure and technique. Procedure is thus subordinated to purpose, and the curriculum artisan is personally involved in determining both. From a craft perspective, curriculum construction as technical project is not unlike painting by number. The craft view, however, still views curriculum as a tangible product.

implementing a different document or package. Change is a function of the curriculum product. Rationality, of the means-end variety, assumes that ends are set, that means are known or knowable, and that the path between them is direct. We therefore follow step-by-step procedures to obtain the predetermined end state (i.e., finished curriculum product). This rational approach provides precision and control over the otherwise disorderly nature of curriculum and teaching.[3] Curriculum construction, thus conceived as a technocratic project of efficiently managing resources to produce a tangible product, gives the appearance of being scientific, which tends to enhance its appeal to administrators, funding agencies, and the general public as well as specialists. It conveys images of scientific efficiency, effectiveness, and benevolence.[4]

Although substantial questions remain about the viability of the technocratic conception of curriculum and its construction,[5] more serious concerns are that it tends to obscure critical questions of responsibility, value, and interest. With respect to value and interest, a technocratic approach seems to be apolitical and non-ideological. Curriculum is developed according to presumably neutral procedures or decision steps. In effect, we are offered a curious form of problem solving with predetermined problems and solutions. The problem is usually taken to be that not enough students are learning enough of whatever is considered desirable for them to learn (e.g., calculus, computer programming, commitment to national principles and policies). The solution is to change the curriculum to include or emphasize whatever students are to learn. The technocratic model simply specifies the procedures to use to obtain this solution. Major curriculum decisions fall to others.[6]

Attention to the values that a curriculum conveys (e.g., in its selection, organization, and treatment of knowledge) and the social groups and interests those values serve allows a critical evaluation of curricular appropriateness and an examination of alternatives and their implications.[7] By ignoring questions of value as well as the conservative values inherent in the techno-

---

[3]Michael W. Apple, "Curricular Form and the Logic of Technical Control," in *Cultural and Economic Reproduction in Education*, ed. Michael W. Apple (London: Routledge and Kegan Paul, 1982), pp. 247–274; William A. Reid, *Thinking about the Curriculum* (London: Routledge and Kegan Paul, 1978).

[4]Thomas S. Popkewitz, "Educational Reform as the Organization of Ritual: Stability as Change," *Journal of Education* 164 (Winter 1982): 5–29.

[5]Catherine Cornbleth, "Reconsidering Social Studies Curriculum," *Theory and Research in Social Education* 13 (Summer 1985): 31–45.

[6]Herbert M. Kliebard, "Systemic Curriculum Development, 1890–1959," in *Value Conflicts and Curriculum Issues*, ed. Jon Schaffarzick and Gary Sykes (Berkeley, Calif.: McCutcheon, 1979); William A. Reid, *Thinking about the Curriculum* (London: Routledge and Kegan Paul, 1978).

[7]Herbert M. Kliebard and Barry M. Franklin, "The Course of the Course of Study: History of Curriculum," in *Historical Inquiry in Education*, ed. John H. Best (Washington, D.C.: American Educational Research Association, 1983), pp. 138–157.

cratic model itself, the technocratic conception of curriculum and its construction tends to perpetuate myths of curriculum neutrality and benevolence.[8]

Denial of responsibility is evident not only in the technocratic emphasis on procedure but also in the separation of curriculum policy-making, construction, and implementation. Curriculum developers do not see themselves (nor are they usually seen by others) as responsible for curriculum policy or implementation. Someone else decides curricular goals and uses. The curriculum developer is thus absolved from responsibility for curriculum purposes and practices.

Therefore, technocratic models conceptually decontextualize curriculum in at least two related ways. Curriculum as product and its construction are arbitrarily separated from curriculum policy-making and use. Also, curriculum and its construction are seen as apolitical or neutral, apart from or above competing social values and interests. Ironically, curriculum developers are not responsible for the education made available to students, and the curriculum document rather than the curriculum use in classroom practice receives attention.

Structural and Sociocultural Isolation

Isolating curriculum and curriculum construction processes from their structural (i.e., systemic) and sociocultural (i.e., extrasystemic, societal) contexts is especially evident in national curriculum projects.[9] Curriculums produced in national centers, such as the new math and social studies projects of the 1960s, were assumed to be appropriate for students and teachers, schools, and school systems across the country. Curriculum developers largely ignored the features of the U.S. education system and local variations, while sociocultural influences on the shape and substance of the new curriculums remained unexamined at least until others raised critical questions.

Structural and sociocultural decontextualization follows from the technocratic conception of curriculum and its construction. The predetermination of curricular problems and solutions limits sensitivity and responsiveness to context, as does the presumed nature of curriculum change. Separating curriculum products and their development from policy-making and implementation discourages attention to structural conditions, and assuming value neutrality deflects attention from sociocultural influences. The curriculum

---

[8]Other models of curriculum and its construction, such as a craft model (see note 2) or Walker's naturalistic model, address normative assumptions and implications. But they still view curriculum construction largely as a product-development task. See Decker F. Walker, "A Naturalistic Model for Curriculum Development," *School Review* 80 (November 1971): 51–65.

[9]Even more dramatic examples are found in cases of international transfer of curriculum products. See, for example, Jong J. Lee, Don Adams, and Catherine Cornbleth, "Transnational Transfer of Curriculum Knowledge: A Korean Case Study," *Journal of Curriculum Studies* (in press).

developer's role is to question neither the curriculum product's feasibility nor its desirability.

A technocratic curriculum model could address the contexts in which its products are formed and used. Decisions about objectives and subject matter could be made with explicit reference to structural constraints and sociocultural pressures. But these considerations would complicate matters and compromise rationality. In response to criticism and resistance to top-down models, some have advocated local, bottom-up models of curriculum construction. Here, the technocratic procedures are largely unchanged, except that local actors make the decisions. Although local actors might be expected to be more sensitive and responsive to immediate structural conditions and sociocultural influences, their sensitivity and responsiveness are likely to remain limited, tacit, and unexamined. Curriculum still is conceived as a tangible product.

Because of the widespread decontextualization of curriculum both conceptually and operationally, continuing discrepancies between curriculum documents and curriculum practice or repeated disappointments with the effects of curriculum change efforts should not surprise us. Neither the promised efficiency nor the benefits have been obtained. Rather than attempt to refurbish unworkable and inappropriate models, we might well consider alternatives. One such alternative would contextualize and thus redefine curriculum. It would treat curriculum critically rather than technically, as a contextualized social process.

CURRICULUM IN CONTEXT

Conceptual Integration

Here, curriculum construction is an ongoing social activity shaped by various contextual influences within and beyond the classroom and accomplished interactively, primarily by teachers and students. Curriculum is not a tangible product but the actual, day-to-day interactions of students, teachers, knowledge, and milieu. The curriculum is what others have called the curriculum-in-use. Curriculum as product or object, the conventional view, is seen as one aspect of the context that shapes curriculum-in-use.[10] This alternative conception shifts attention from intention to realization, from plan to practice. The focus is on what knowledge and learning opportunities actually are made available to students, how they are created, and what values they reflect and sustain. Viewing curriculum as a contextualized social process explicitly

[10] I do not mean to discount planning and product development but to suggest modifications of their purpose and perceived relation to curriculum. Planning involves crucial choices about the nature, selection and organization, distribution, treatment, and evaluation of knowledge made available to students. But prior planning, regardless of how it is undertaken, at best provides an inert curriculum skeleton. Curriculum comes to life as it is enacted.

recognizes critical philosophical, social, and political questions about what is taught, how, and to whom. This view does not merely celebrate practice.[11]

Curriculum as contextualized social process encompasses both subject matter and social organization and their interrelations. Social organization, including teacher and student roles (and their rights and obligations) and patterns of interaction, provides a setting for academic activities that can extend or constrain students' learning opportunities. Recitation activities, for example, reflect the super- and subordinate roles of teachers and students and the limited communication patterns found in many classrooms. The recitation organization constrains the learning opportunities because students are discouraged from pursuing ideas, raising questions, or offering personal observations. Social organization and academic activities also communicate normative messages, including the meaning of knowledge, authority, responsibility, work, and success.[12]

Where the technocratic model is analytic, the contextualized social process conception of curriculum and its construction is synthetic. It does not separate curriculum policy-making, construction, and implementation as a linear sequence of events. Instead, it posits dynamic interaction among policy, planning, enactment, and their structural and sociocultural contexts.[13] Curriculum is constructed and reconstructed in situated practice. In a technocratic view, curriculum is instrumental to classroom practice; in a social view, curriculum exists in practice and is not independent of it. A technocratic view tends to be prescriptive of practice; a social view is interpretive and critical.

From a contextualized social process perspective, curriculum causality and change are complex and problematic. Causality and change (or stability) involve the interplay of biographical (personal and professional), structural, and sociocultural factors over time. Curriculum construction and reconstruction reflect and respond to their immediate more distant contexts.[14]

---

[11]A contextualized social process view of curriculum and its construction reflects a critical rather than a technical rationality. Critical rationality is characterized by wide-ranging skepticism as well as a grounding in logical argument and empirical data. It entails probing beneath surface appearances and questioning claims, evidence, and proposals, such as those for technocratic models of curriculum. Technical concerns do not become ends in themselves; instead, they serve both debunking and generative purposes, for example, in questioning data on curriculum change.

[12]See, for example, Catherine Cornbleth and Willard Korth, "Doing the Work: Teacher Perspectives and Meanings of Responsibility," *Educational Forum* 48 (Summer 1984): 413–420.

[13]Compare William A. Reid, "The Changing Curriculum: Theory and Practice," in *Case Studies in Curriculum Change*, ed. William A. Reid and Decker F. Walker (London: Routledge and Kegan Paul, 1975), pp. 240–259.

[14]Catherine Cornbleth, "Socioecology of Critical Thinking" (Paper presented at the American Educational Research Association, Chicago, April 1985); Catherine Cornbleth, Willard Korth, and Ernest B. Dorow, "Creating the Curriculum: Beginning the Year at a Middle School" (Paper presented at the American Educational Research Association, Montreal, 1983); Linda M. McNeil, *Contradictions of Control: School Structure and School Knowledge* (New York: Routledge and Kegan Paul, 1986); Thomas S. Popkewitz, B. Robert Tabachnick, and Gary Wehlage, *The Myth of Educational Reform* (Madison: University of Wisconsin Press, 1982).

Structural and Sociocultural Contextualization[15]

Contextualization is inherent in the alternative conception of curriculum and its construction just offered. Context situates and shapes curriculum; thus, changing a curriculum involves changing its context. We still need to elaborate the nature of relevant contextual settings and influences. Recognizing that context is widely acknowledged but largely uncharted territory—not unlike the "new world" of fifteenth-century European maps and perhaps for good reason—I proceed with caution. The complexity and elusiveness of context make pinning it down and linking it empirically to a particular curriculum difficult. What follows, then, is a tentative sketch; these outlines are yet to be worked out theoretically and empirically.

First, the nominal context is not necessarily the relevant context of curriculum. Nominal context refers to what is "out there" that might influence curriculum, in other words, the environment at large. That environment includes social, political, economic, and demographic conditions that are translated into constraints, demands, and priorities by groups with diverse and often conflicting interests. Also, events within and outside the schools are potential contexts for subsequent curricular activity, and within the education system, each organizational layer (e.g., state department of education, school) is a potential context for curricular activity nested within it. Relevant context, in contrast, refers to aspects of the nominal context that can be shown to influence curriculum in a particular instance, directly or indirectly. Compared to other education sectors such as teacher education, the relevant context of school curriculums is extensive.

Distinguishing between structural or systemic and sociocultural or societal contexts is in part an attempt to make context more manageable. Also, the distinction calls attention to the education system context of curriculum, which we tend to overlook in curriculum discourse and take for granted in curriculum practice. Critical theoretical work, for example, typically treats curriculum in relation to larger sociocultural dynamics, such as economic and gender relations, but neglects its more immediate setting, in effect leapfrogging the intervening structural context of curriculums. Education systems are not simply conduits that reflect and thus reproduce larger societal patterns. The structural context is important because it both mediates extrasystemic sociocultural influences and generates curriculum experience.

[15]This and the following sections draw from prior work on the contexts of U.S. teacher education policy change and of educational planning. See Catherine Cornbleth and Don Adams, "The Drunkard's Streetlamp? Contexts of Policy Change in U.S. Teacher Education," in Higher Education Group, Governments and Higher Education: The Legitimacy of Intervention (Toronto: OISE-Higher Education Group, 1987); Don Adams and Catherine Cornbleth, "Contexts of Educational Planning" (Pittsburgh: University of Pittsburgh, International and Development Education Program, February 1987).

Another feature of the relevant curriculum context is its variability or fluidity. It varies over time and with the curriculum of interest and the local situation within the national milieu. Variability can be seen in the presence of particular context factors, their relative strength or intensity, and their interaction (e.g., aggregation, conflict). For example, recent decades have witnessed alternating demands for "basic skills" and "higher order thinking." Differences in the numerical strength and activism of extremist religious groups from one community to the next provides another example.[16]

Therefore, the relevant structural and sociocultural contexts of curriculum are multifaceted and fluid. While nested one within another, they also overlap and interact. So no generic curriculum context, no fixed set of parameters or invariant grid, exists that can be imposed on any curriculum. Instead, potential aspects of curriculum context can be identified, and their relevance to a particular curriculum can be illustrated.

The System as Structural Context

Social (as distinguished from natural, e.g., biological) systems are typically described in terms of their form and their process or mode of operation. I treat the form and mode of operation as structure, defined as the established roles and relationships, including operating procedures, shared beliefs, and norms (i.e., tradition, culture). The structure of an education system conditions outsiders' interaction with it and participants' interaction within it.[17]

---

[16]How context is identified is another source of its variation. For example, are relevant contextual factors those perceived and reported by curriculum participants or those that appear to an observer to have influenced curriculum activity? Empirically linking curriculum and context is neither simple nor straightforward.

[17]Margaret S. Archer, *Social Origins of Educational Systems* (London: Sage, 1984). Although the literature on systems and systems analysis is extensive, little theoretical or empirical work exists on education systems as systems. The conventional distinction in organizational and systems theory between formal structure and process obscures the dynamic nature of structure in action. Like Katz and Kahn, among others, I believe that "a social system is a structure of events or happenings rather than of physical parts and it therefore has no structure apart from its functioning"; see Daniel Katz and Robert L. Kahn, *The Social Psychology of Organizations* (New York: Wiley, 1966), p. 31. Also, see Anthony Giddens, *Central Problems in Social Theory* (Berkeley: University of California Press, 1979). The conceptualization of systems presented here is compatible with Gouldner's portrayal of natural (non-organic) as opposed to a rational systems and Scott and Meyer's "societal sectors." See Alvin W. Gouldner, "Organizational Tensions," in *Sociology Today*, ed. R. K. Merton, L. Bloom, and L. S. Cottrell, Jr. (New York: Basic Books, 1959); W. Richard Scott and John W. Meyer, "The Organization of Societal Sectors," in *Organizational Environments*, ed. John W. Meyer and W. Richard Scott (Beverly Hills, Calif.: Sage, 1983), pp. 129–153.

Also, the conception of education system offered here is non-organismic. That is, while education systems are treated as real (i.e., having an independent existence that is observable, analyzable, and perhaps measurable), I do not endow them with purpose or action apart from the people who occupy roles in the system or influence it from outside. Individuals and groups

A system consists of two or more interrelated components (e.g., legislature and judiciary in political system, school and state department of education in education system) and associated roles and patterns of interaction, which can be simple or complex; complex components often constitute subsystems. For example, classrooms and the elementary and secondary schools that house them constitute subsystems of most national education systems. As subsystems of a national education system, elementary and secondary education and their curriculums are subject to the structural conditioning and social interaction of the larger system as well as their own internal dynamics. Viewing the education system as the structural context of curriculum thus directs attention to the roles, relationships, patterns of activity, and culture of interacting system components.[18]

The historical experience of national systems of formal, mass education is one of (1) expansion and extension to serve more people for longer periods of time and (2) more specialized and differentiated educational provisions, accompanied by (3) increasing complexity, bureaucratization, and standardization. Another historically rooted feature of education systems with major consequences for curriculum is conservatism. Because of the purposes of national education systems, it is not surprising that their structure fosters cultural transmission and societal continuity. Once a national identity and tradition have been established, with the help of the education system, a major function of the education system is to perpetuate that way of life.

Education systems also tend toward self-perpetuation. System participants and beneficiaries have a stake in its maintenance and perhaps also its expansion. Curriculum change efforts that are seen as strengthening or extending the education system (or one of its subsystems) are more likely to

---

have purposes and take action; systems do not. Social systems do not have lives of their own. See Michael Keeley, "Realism in Organizational Theory: A Reassessment," *Symbolic Interaction* 6 (No. 2, 1983): 279–290. Thus, I reject, as overly deterministic, conceptions of structure as external, controlling " 'objective' features of social organization that exist apart from culture and the consciousness of participating actors" or apart from the intentions and actions of participants; see David Rubenstein, "The Concept of Structure in Sociology," in *Sociological Theory in Transition*, ed. Mark L. Wardell and Stephen P. Turner (Boston: Allen and Unwin, 1986), pp. 80–94. At the same time that structural factors are recognized and respected, so too is human agency. I am assuming a dynamic interaction between structure and agency in time and place that is compatible with Mills's macro conceptualization of the interaction of history, biography, and social structure; see C. Wright Mills, *The Sociological Imagination* (New York: Oxford University Press, 1959).

[18]My focus here is on the national rather than classroom, school, or other level of the education system. For illustrations of the nature and influence of school-level structural context, see Linda M. McNeil, *Contradictions of Control: School Structure and School Knowledge* (New York: Routledge and Kegan Paul, 1986); on the classroom and school district levels, see Catherine Cornbleth, "The Social Nature of Social Studies," in *Locating Learning across the Curriculum*, ed. Catherine Emihovich (Norwood, N.J.: Ablex, in press).

be embraced than those that appear to weaken or reduce it or that otherwise challenge its operation or underlying values.

Curriculum-relevant differences across education systems include the nature and extent of bureaucratic coordination and control, decentralization, and boundary clarity and permeability. These and other features of education systems are made reasonable by their cultural traditions. Culture means operating procedures, shared meanings and beliefs, and norms, including goals and priorities. It is not uncommon to find shifting priorities or simultaneous pursuit of a multiplicity of seemingly conflicting goals within an education system or subsystem (e.g., efficiency, equity, quality), especially within large systems in heterogeneous societies.

Understanding a curriculum and how it might be changed requires understanding the culture of the education system, which may involve several subcultures associated with occupational groups (e.g., teachers, administrators), subsystems (e.g., elementary education, teacher education), or regions (e.g., urban, rural). As several studies have documented, change efforts that "do not consider the underlying patterns of school belief and conduct . . . may only rearrange the technological surface."[19]

Because education systems tend to be open rather than closed, the context of curriculum is not solely structural. Unlike self-sufficient or closed systems, education systems depend on their environment and thus are sensitive to environmental influences. Dependence on government funding, for example, usually means government influence, if not control of how its funds are used. The U.S. education system is highly permeable, providing relatively easy access to interested groups. The tradition if not the practice of local, public control of elementary and secondary education encourages efforts of external groups to influence the contours and course of schooling, including and often especially curriculum. The permeable character of the U.S. education system makes it highly susceptible to external influences (i.e., sociocultural context).

Sociocultural Context

The relevant sociocultural context of curriculum consists of extrasystemic demographic, social, political, and economic conditions; traditions and ideologies; and events that influence curriculum and curriculum change. Influence can be direct or indirect, and indirect influence may involve the education system as mediator.

The sociocultural context often provides the impetus for curriculum change (e.g., computer literacy). At times, education systems seem more responsive

[19]Thomas S. Popkewitz, "Educational Reform and the Problem of Institutional Life," *Educational Researcher* 8 (May 1979): 8.

to sociocultural expectations and demands than to those of their clients or participants (e.g., students, teachers). This response may be a function of "the external legitimation, definition, and control of their internal processes,"[20] stemming from what Meyer and Rowan describe as widespread acceptance of "the schooling rule," which defines education as "a certified teacher teaching a standardized curricular topic to a registered student in an accredited school." Referring primarily to the U.S. experience, they conclude:

> Schooling is thus socially defined by reference to a set of standardized categories, the legitimacy of which is publicly shared. As the categories and credentials of schooling gain importance in allocation and membership processes, the public comes to expect that they will be controlled and standardized. The large-scale public bureaucracy created to achieve this standardization is now normatively constrained by the expectations of the schooling rule. To a large degree, then, education is coordinated by shared social understandings. . . . The legitimacy of schools and their ability to mobilize resources depend on maintaining congruence between their structure and these socially shared categorical understandings of education.[21]

With a few notable exceptions, the sociocultural context is less conservative (or at least more heterogeneous and turbulent) than the structural context.[22] External demands for change are often moderated within the system. Acknowledged problems or desirable but difficult to attain goals are likely to be redefined and acted on in ways that maintain the education system rather than reform it.

CURRICULUM CHANGE AS CONTEXTUAL CHANGE

If curriculum is a contextualized social process, then curriculum change is a function of contextual change. Curriculum is unlikely to change in the absence of supportive structural changes, which are unlikely to be initiated in the absence of external pressures. This line of reasoning indicates the futility of trying to bring about curriculum reform by substituting one cur-

---

[20]John W. Meyer, "Conclusion: Institutionalization, and the Rationality of Formal Organizational Structure," in *Organizational Environments*, ed. John W. Meyer and W. Richard Scott (Beverly Hills, Calif.: Sage, 1983), p. 269.

[21]John W. Meyer and Brian Rowan, "The Structure of Educational Organizations," in *Organizational Environments*, ed. John W. Meyer and W. Richard Scott (Beverly Hills, Calif.: Sage, 1983), p. 84.

[22]See, for example, Ronald G. Corwin, "Models of Educational Organizations," in *Review of Research in Education* (Vol. 2), ed. Fred N. Kerlinger and John B. Carroll (Itasca, Ill.: Peacock, 1974), pp. 249–295.

riculum document for another. Instead, we should answer questions such as the following to inform curriculum change efforts:

- What are the demographic, social, political, and economic conditions and trends that seem to shape the existing curriculum and seem likely to affect the desired changes? How is the desired curriculum change compatible or at odds with cultural traditions and prevailing ideologies? What influential groups are affected? (What are the potential sources of support and opposition?) What historical, recent, or continuing events are apt to influence the curriculum change effort?
- Which education system components or subsystems could mediate (supporting or oppositional) sociocultural influences? How are past experiences with curriculum change likely to influence the present effort?
- What system components are affected? (What roles, relationships, and patterns of activity? At which levels?) How is the desired curriculum change compatible or at odds with the prevailing culture of the education system? What are the bureaucratic operating procedures and the channels of formal and informal control of the affected system components? (Who controls what, to what extent, and how?) What and where are the tensions or contradictions within the system that might become loci for curriculum change?

To put curriculum in context, we must reformulate curriculum conceptions and reconstruct curriculum practice, including the practice of curriculum theorizing, research, design, and change. Contextualization avoids the reductionism and impotence of technocratic models of curriculum and curriculum construction. But contextualization has problems, such as complexity and situational contingency. These human, social-structural problems are not amenable to technical solutions. We may not be able to resolve them. Coping with complexity and contingency requires tolerance of ambiguity, flexibility and responsiveness, imagination and persistence, as well as further understanding of the interaction of curriculum and context.

SUGGESTED LEARNING EXPERIENCES

1. Extend Schwab's discussion of who should participate in curriculum planning to include the competencies, skills, knowledge, and disposition needed by those who are to represent the values, perspectives, and voices of diversity including culture, ethnicity, social class, and different intellectual and physical attributes. Discuss the cross-cultural skills needed by the chair of the curriculum group.
2. Based on the readings in Part II and your own ideas, revise one of the curriculum planning efforts described by Schwartz.

3. Identify external factors that influence curriculum planning and implementation, research and describe approaches to overcoming these factors.

4. Invite a curriculum coordinator or director from a local school district to describe local curriculum development practices. The following questions can be used to inform the presenter:

   (a) Who participated in the curriculum planning effort and how were they selected?
   (b) Describe the curriculum planning process.
   (c) To what extent were local values and specific cultural, ethnic, and social class groups considered and/or included in the curriculum planning effort?
   (d) How were the curriculum and the curriculum planning effort evaluated?
   (e) What is the relationship between the curriculum product, its construction, curriculum policymaking, and the purpose of schooling?

5. Interview school personnel who have participated in curriculum planning efforts or who have responsibilities for curriculum decision making. These individuals may be identified by a curriculum coordinator or an administrator responsible for directing elementary or secondary education. The following questions may be used to guide the interview:

   (a) What role/responsibility did the person interviewed assume in the curriculum planning effort? What were the roles/responsibilities of others who were participating in the effort?
   (b) What was the purpose of the curriculum planning effort? Who should benefit and how?
   (c) Describe the curriculum planning process.
   (d) How was the curriculum/curriculum effort evaluated?
   (e) So far, what has resulted from the curriculum planning effort?

6. Compare and contrast the curriculum planning practices described by presenters and interviewees with the recommendations found in the readings for this section. Describe the strengths, weaknesses, and potential impact of these efforts on school practices.

PART THREE

CURRICULUM PERSPECTIVES

CRITICAL QUESTIONS

1. To what extent and under what conditions does a teacher's knowledge of the learners' social class, racial, or ethnic background have either a positive or negative effect on how the curriculum is presented in a particular situation? Are there ways to influence such potential effects?
2. To what extent does a teacher's own cultural and experiential background influence curriculum perspectives?
3. How should the curriculum be related to the learners' cultural and experiential background? To what extent and under what conditions should the heritage, values, and practices of ethnic minority cultures be part of the regular curriculum in a culturally diverse society? What should be the relationship between the curriculum and personal and group identity?
4. To what extent should the school curriculum support replication of the existing social structure?

OVERVIEW

The three authors in Part II view curriculum as what happens in the daily occurrences in classrooms in the interactions between teachers and their students. This view of curriculum makes clear the central role of the teacher in curriculum translation and implementation. Consequently, Schwab stresses the importance of teachers being the first members selected for the curriculum group. He describes in detail what knowledge and skills teachers should possess. Schwab contends that teachers have the most immediate knowledge of learners and that this knowledge is essential to planning a meaningful curriculum.

The chapters in Part III take the reader inside classrooms to examine variations in how the teacher's perception of the students influence curriculum implementation. It is important to point out that several factors influence how teachers perceive their students, among which are (a) the students' social status and future adult role in the society, (b) school culture, (c) external validation and personal experiences, and (d) personal commitment.

The first author in Part III, Curtis Branch, presents a discussion of the *competing curriculum*, which he describes as "unwritten influences that intrude on the parameters of the classroom" (p. 172, this volume). The competing curriculum, which is difficult to document, is projected through the attitudes and behaviors of educators. Branch uses ecological systems theory to describe educator's background experiences and early socialization as sources in the development of the competing curriculum. Branch's discussion of the competing curriculum provides a framework for better understanding the research reports presented by the other authors in this section.

The second author in Part III, Jean Anyon, presents a study of schools serving students from four different social class groups, which she describes as working class, middle class, affluent professional, and executive elite. She describes how teachers translate the curriculum differently in each situation despite the fact that they use the same text and share similar routines. Anyon concluded from her study that the presentation of the curriculum is influenced by the teacher's perception of the learners' status and future adult roles in the society. For example, in the working-class schools, learning experiences consist of following the steps of a procedure, rote behavior, and little decision making or choice. This is appropriate training for work that is mechanical and routine. In the middle-class schools, learning experiences consist of getting the right answer. Students learn to follow directions in order to get the right answer, which requires decision making and choice. These students are learning to function within a bureaucracy in white-collar mid-management roles. In the affluent professional schools, learning experiences are made up of creative activity carried out independently. These students move about freely in the classroom and exercise more choice than those in the previous two categories of schools and develop skills in negotiation. These students are developing the linguistic, artistic, and scientific skills associated with professional and cultural roles. The students in the executive elite schools develop their analytical intellectual powers. They are the only students who learn to analyze systems. These students learn the socially prestigious academic content as well. They are prepared to manage people and to run the society.

Anyon does not mention school culture, external validation and personal experiences, or personal commitment as factors influencing teachers' presentation of the school curriculum. However, Page (1987) describes a similar study involving two comprehensive high schools in the same school district with similar student populations and, supposedly, the same curriculum where the students are perceived as being from different social class backgrounds. In this study, Page describes the school culture and external validation from the central office as reinforcing the teachers' presentation of the curriculum and treatment of the students.

In the studies by Anyon and Page, social class is a reference point for students' status in the society. Curriculum implementation is influenced by their social status.

Race is another example of social status to which teachers respond in curriculum implementation, however, this factor may be confounded by social class status as well. In a study of teachers' responses to inner-city students (the majority of whom were African American), Linda Winfield (1986) used four metaphors as labels to categorize teachers' responses. The categories are (a) *tutors*, teachers who believe the students can improve their performance and who assume personal responsibility for making and monitoring individual learning plans for each student and for maintaining discipline and keeping students on task; (b) *general contractors*, teachers who believe the students can improve their academic performance, but rely on other persons or programs; (c) *custodians*, teachers who are not concerned with improving the students' academic performance, but rather, provide learning experiences and materials that maintain their present condition; and (d) *referral agents*, teachers who do not believe the students can improve their academic performance, but shift responsibility for teaching to other persons and programs.

The skills-based remedial curriculum Winfield describes does not reach the academic preparation level of the working-class schools described in Anyon's study. It seems reasonable to conclude that students in Winfield's study are being prepared for minimum wage service roles or for public welfare. Many students in Winfield's study will be unemployable in any role requiring a minimal level of literacy.

The third author in this part, Jerry Lipka, provides a view of culture in school learning. Lipka documents an approach used by a Yup'ik Indian teacher to teach Yup'ik children in an elementary school located in rural Alaska. The Yup'ik culture is clearly visible in the classroom routines, the framing of the curriculum, and the social interaction among the students and between the students and the teacher. Lipka contrasts the introduction of a lesson using the Yup'ik cultural traditions and one using European-

American cultural traditions. He points out the difference in the children's responses to the Yup'ik teacher in comparison to European-American teachers. When taught by European-American teachers the children remain silent and their participation is passive. In the Yup'ik teacher's classroom the children are gregarious and actively involved in the lesson. Lipka's characterization of the Yup'ik teacher's commitment, knowledge, and use of culture in the classroom might raise questions about classrooms with more than one cultural group and how teachers might go about learning to teach children from cultures other than their own.

The significance of culture in curriculum implementation is supported by Michaels' (1981) study of differences in narrative styles used by African-American children and their European-American teacher. In Michaels' study, a European-American teacher did not make explicit the literate narrative style employed in school learning and, thus, African-American children did not acquire a prerequisite skill for reading acquisition. Narrative styles are culturally acquired. The narrative style employed in school is based on the European-American culture and does not need to be made explicit to most members of that culture. Schools and the curriculum are often portrayed as culturally neutral and, because the practice of schooling has become traditional, it is difficult to identify the specific aspects of culture that are present. A more specific example of teachers' response to students' cultural or ethnic background is found in a research study reported by Perry Gilmore (1985) in which African-American children's access to advanced literacy is denied on the basis of their level of acculturation rather than acquisition of prerequisite skills.

The fourth chapter in Part III is a case study of a European-American high school teacher who reframes the traditional English curriculum to include African-American literature. Spears-Bunton, the author, contends that the inclusion of African-American literature (a) clearly reveals the conflicts and contradictions of class, race, and gender bias in a democratic society, (b) puts students in touch with their own bias and that of their peers, and (c) helps students learn to challenge bias in themselves, their peers, and the larger society, and in the literature they read. The educational background of the teacher in this study did not include African-American literature, therefore, she was left to self-education in this area. This teacher's personal commitment allowed her to overcome aspects of the school culture and resistance and racial conflict among her students to reach a point of shared understanding and experience for her students. The racial conflict described in this case study clearly raises the issue of personal and group identity, however, its significance is not explained.

The authors in Part III support teachers' participation in curriculum planning as important in producing useful results, however, factors that influence the variation in teacher's perception and its potential impact on curriculum implementation is evident in the research presented. Curriculum planners must take into account this variation in teachers' perception and practice in curriculum implementation and the multiple factors that influence both.

REFERENCES

Gilmore, P. (1985). "Gimme room": School resistance, attitude, and access to literacy. *Journal of Education, 167*(1), 111–128.

Michaels, S. (1981). "Sharing time": Children's narrative styles and differential access to literacy. *Language in Society, 10*, 423–442.

Page, R. (1987). Teachers' perceptions of students: A link between classrooms, school cultures, and the social order. *Anthropology and Education Quarterly, 18*, 77–99.

Winfield, L. (1986). Teacher beliefs toward academically at risk students in inner urban schools. *The Urban Review, 18*(4), 253–267.

CHAPTER EIGHT

Lessons (in Identity) Learned From the Competing Curriculum: Some Thoughts

Curtis Branch

Since the great migrations of immigrants to the United States after the 1860s, education has been regarded as a method whereby people who are "different" are homogenized and made into good Americans. This process of shaping children and adolescents results from facts and values that are taught through concrete structured activities, the educational curriculum. However, other valuable lessons are also taught in school without the benefit of structured activities. These lessons are powerful messages about self-worth, intergroup relations, and the development of identities. Knefelkamp (1992) referred to the social messages taught as a result of the dynamics in school classrooms as the *competing curriculum.*

This chapter examines the ways the competing curriculum is introduced into the standard curriculum and its impact on the learning and social behaviors of African-American children and adolescents. Specifically, the issue of development of identities is addressed. An ecological systems theory approach is used to explain the sources of the competing curriculum (i.e., messages given to African-American students) and how they help shape identity concepts that African-American children internalize. Finally, examples from the pedagogical and psychological literature concerning teaching strategies that are evidences of the competing curriculum will be offered.

Knefelkamp's original use of the phrase *competing curriculum* referred to social aspects of the life of students. She was particularly interested in the contributions of clubs, community organizations, the media and institutions external to the education enterprise and their impact on the learning, and social development of students. The phrase, as used here, refers to similar conditions but limits the explorations to teachers and other adults who have an impact on the lives of children. This is not to negate the overwhelming contributions from peers and other community agencies consistent with Kneflekamp's original meaning for the phrase *competing curriculums.* In light of the preliminary articulations of microsystemic and mesosystemic contributions to the identity formation and conceptualization of African-American children, it is clear that competing curriculums exist also at the exosystemic and mesosystemic levels. Those issues are not explored here, but are certainly recognized as major contributors.

Knefelkamp explained that the standard curriculum is only a small part of the learning process. Its contents are easily articulated, as are its goals and objectives; it is fairly easy to determine what it is educators want children to internalize as feats and skills. Methods for determining the mastery of material include standard procedures such as examinations and experimental exercises. By contrast, the impact of the competing curriculum is rarely directly measured. Rather, the lessons are taught, internalized by children, and the long-term effects of the lessons significantly alter the internal psychological life of its recipients. How well children respond to the standard curriculum and its contents is determined partially by the power of the strength and quality of messages from the competing curriculum.

Despite their striking differences, the standard and the competing curriculums are created by very similar processes, individuals translating their idiosyncratic values and life experiences into a product that has powerful consequences for others. In the case of the competing curriculum, how the product gets dispensed to consumers is a very abstract entity that is difficult to measure. It is problematic to predict the outcome(s) with any degree of certainty. Both curriculums are the result of multiple social factors and forces converging at one point, curriculum development. The multiple social factors and forces that shape the curriculum developers' thinking have been described by Bronfenbrenner (1979) as ecological systems. The systematic approach to understanding the competing curriculum's contribution to the formation of identity among African-American children and adolescents is potentially a useful way of organizing and thinking about the multiple and sometimes conflicting messages young African-American children receive about themselves.

ECOLOGICAL SYSTEMS THEORY

The conceptual framework recognized today as ecological systems theory has its origin in the works of Lewin (1935) and Barker and Gump (1964). These researchers noted that individuals have connections to different segments of their life space and, as a result, get different messages about who they are and who they can become from these varied sources. More specifically, Barker and Gump (1964) noted that adolescents, because of their high level of mobility, participate in multiple settings simultaneously and are likely to get very different, perhaps even conflicting, messages about their quest to resolve their developmental issues, particularly identity resolutions. More recently, Bronfenbrenner (1979) refined this mode of thinking by developing a system of taxonomy for the multiple systems by which one individual is influenced. He termed his layer of systems an *ecological network*; it is composed of four layers.

Microsystems are those that are composed of face-to-face contacts between the child and others. In the course of establishing and maintaining relationships with others in microsystems, the children receive very direct messages of how they are perceived by others. It would not be unreasonable to assume that a child's first externally driven messages about self come from microsystemic relationships. Settings in which these relationships are likely to occur include home and school. Other individuals, who may be directly involved in a systemic exchange, include adults (i.e., parents, extended family members, teachers, siblings, and peers).

Mesosystems refer to the relationship between two or more microsystems simultaneously interacting or sharing the child. Each system is giving the child a message about his or her worth and how he or she is viewed by others. As in the case of the microsystem, when conflicting messages are sent to the child the potential for a dynamic tension is dramatically increased. Other examples of mesosystem dyads include home–church, home–peer group, school–church, and peer group–church. Of course, each institution involved in a mesosystem relationship provides a child with messages of self-definition or values/behaviors that are consistent with the philosophy and domain of that institution. Religious communities concern themselves with spirituality, morality, and one's relationship with a deity. Schools concern themselves with formal learning and intellectual growth and development.

Exosystems affect children by secondary impacts. By definition, children are excluded from exosystems, but nevertheless they are affected by what happens within the institutions composing the system. Parents' place of employment and their circle of friends and associates are classic examples of exosystems. Children are very much affected by the psychological ambience of their parents' job (i.e., status that parents have at work, conditions of employment, and salary). Also, they are continuously affected by the values and behavioral changes that parents acquire through social interactions with their own friends. Other examples of exosystems include local school boards who set policies governing children, government officials who make laws concerning after-school employment, and neighborhood merchants who control the availability of jobs for youth.

Macrosystems refers to the larger social blueprint that encompasses the aforementioned systems. An example of a macrosystem is a larger geographical or political unit, such as a country or continent.

THE CURRICULUMS (STANDARD, COMPETING) AND ECOLOGICAL SYSTEMS

Creators of the standard curriculum as members, of the society, function in multiple settings (e.g., systems) and, as a result, are socialized by many agents. In response to these socializers their attitudes about what children should be taught and how they should be taught are shaped. Likewise, attitudes about social issues such as race and ethnicity are also influenced heavily by multiple systems-giving messages, sometimes conflicting messages, about the importance of these factors. Branch (1993) suggested that the ethnicity and race of the teachers/educators and learners figure prominently in the learning equation. He posits that the attribution of characteristics to learners influences how they perform in the classroom, perhaps as much as their abilities. Frequently, teachers view African-American children's academic performance as a function of their race and ethnicity and the children themselves may develop limiting self-perceptions as a consequence of their interactions within the ecosystem. For example, Fordham and Ogbu (1986) reported that some African-American high school students perceive academic excellence as an instance of "acting White."

In deliberating the standard curriculum, its creators directly project their own values in the form of statements that guide the educational experiences of children. Such projections are overt and easily observed in the standard curriculum. The relationship between the competing curriculum and the authors' values is less easily documented. The *competing curriculum* refers to unwritten influences that intrude on the parameters of the classroom. It makes its presence felt in the form of teacher/educator attitudes and behaviors, which often defy documentation but which nevertheless significantly impact the learning environment of children in school.

The competing curriculum develops as an amalgam of influences from micro-, meso-, exo-, and macrosystem contributions. Purveyors of the competing curriculum are often unaware of its long-term impact on developing children. Take, for example, teachers who oppose the recitation of the pledge of allegiance in school because of the reference to God. On one hand, it introduces the idea of teachers dictating the culture of the school community based on their own value system. Conversely, teachers censoring the concept of God from the classroom because it does not fit their religious belief system may be eliminating a powerful concept that the children bring to school from home. Eliminating the God concept from the classroom may also create a significant conflict of values between two powerful mesosystemic institutions, school and home. Such a position could be potentially disruptive in traditional African-American communities where participation in church and Christian religious communities are a given. Even segments of communities that have moved away from the Christian church toward Islam or other nationalistic religious expressions accept the concept of God, submission to a higher authority, and the hope of redemption through the power of that God figure. Teachers who exorcise God and religious concepts from the classroom introduce values of their own. In so doing they run the risk of extinguishing well established ideologies and beliefs that children may bring with them to school. Even in this day of increased emphasis on multiculturalism, such censorship deprives children of learning about what others believe about a supreme being. This is only one example of how teachers/educators may operate with an alternative value system, different from that which is articulated in the standard curriculum and different from the a priori knowledge children bring to school.

The competing and standard curriculums are borne out of social conditions that are interpreted by educators. Claims of all inclusiveness in the standard curriculum are really bogus. The curriculum is really simply a distillation of its creators' social values and political positions. Unfortunately, little or no energy has gone into studying the competing curriculum. Many researchers have recognized the existence of such a curriculum evidenced by the large body of literature on teacher expectation, teacher behaviors in the classroom, and even differential behaviors teachers emit toward children when race and gender are considered. The competing curriculum has rarely been identified as such. Rather, it is often downplayed and viewed as a variation in implementing the standard curriculum, which is a function of teacher competence. It is suggested here that the origins of the competing curriculum should be examined from an ecological system framework. Such an exploration would undoubtedly confirm that teachers, as members of the society at large, are the products of multiple systems at work. A compelling issue meriting scholarly investigation is the relationship between the two curriculums and ecological systems.

One of the striking features of the competing curriculum is that it is a political and social voice that finds expression within the confines of the classroom in opposition to the standard curriculum and/or in conjunction with it. What is not clear, however, is the primary source of the competing curriculum. A microsystemic relationship? A mesosystem? An exosystem? The macrosystem? All of the preceding? It appears that the bearer of the competing curriculum may knowingly participate in the implementation of the standard curriculum where the execution of the task may inadvertently introduce the competing curriculum. That is to say, how a teacher presents ideas may create a dynamic that is the source of incidental learning for students. With such an interaction between both curriculums it is hard to know which ecological system is primarily responsible for the teacher's behavior or the students' incidental learning.

THE SCHOOL AS A MICROSYSTEM

Within the structure of a school community, students and teachers have the opportunity to participate in many and varied microsystems. These face-to-face dyads are critical for the development of a sense of self-empowerment. Children learn very quickly that they can get others to respond to them by emitting positive or negative behaviors. Other children get to observe this in a way that is not likely to happen in a home environment. Teachers responding to the emitted behaviors reinforce some behaviors and not others. It is suggested that the behaviors that are reinforced and those that are not provide clues about the teacher's value system (e.g., competing curriculum). Perhaps the greater issue lies in determining the factors that gave rise to the teachers' values. From the values come the behaviors that the teacher exhibits in the classroom.

It has been documented rather extensively that teachers selectively reinforce boys and girls for identical behaviors in the classroom. The cause of such differentials in handling of similar behaviors is again the preconceived ideas that teachers, through their own socialization, bring to the classroom the competing curriculum at work in the context of the standard curriculum. Over time students internalize powerful messages about who is to behave, how, and what the consequences are for changing the routine. The lesson learned in such a pattern is that some behaviors are acceptable for some people but those same behaviors are unacceptable when emitted by others. Obvious class categories, along which these separations are made, include race/ethnicity and gender. Behavioral patterns that have been identified in this area include things such as assertiveness, intellectual curiosity, instrumental versus nurturing behavior, and leadership among peers.

Teacher attitudes are also major determinants in creating the atmosphere in which young children are expected to learn. The level and type of socialization that teachers have had with respect to African-American children and their culture will drive their behavior in the classroom. Here, the idea that social values and attitudes are crystallized before entering a teacher-education program will have a primary effect. The result is that all of the college and university pedagogical training will be filtered through the teacher's a priori socialization. A recent example of this can be found in the debate about cultural learning styles and the value of African-American culture in influencing the school performance of children from that reference context. The work of Frisby (1993) has created something of a heated debate in the literature.

Frisby contends that African-American cultural learning styles are more myth than reality. He criticizes proponents of African-American cultural learning styles who insist that the long history of academic achievement problems of African-American children can be attributed to a mismatch between their culturally derived learning styles and what is required in most public schools. Specifically, the mismatch refers to schools teaching from a perspective that favors ethnocentric approaches to learning and mastery (i.e., linear thinking). African-American children, by contrast, according to Afro-centric theorists, rely more on African-based learning styles (i.e., holistic thinking). Frisby also contends that African-American cultural learning styles are merely a throw-back to early theories. His ideas are primarily in response to empirical and conceptual ideas in the theoretical tradition of Willis (1989).

According to Willis' review of theories, research, and models of learning styles, African-American children learn in ways qualitatively different from their White counterparts. Specifically, Willis asserted that African-American children's learning is characterized by "factors of social/affective emphases, harmony, holistic perspectives, expressive creativity, and non-verbal communication" (p. 47). She further asserted that the underlying conceptual assumption of all of these dimensions is the idea that African-Americans have been strongly influenced by their African heritage and culture, reminiscent of Wade Noble's characterization of African-American lifestyles and behaviors, which are reflective of "African roots that produce African fruits." Willis restated that her analysis of the literature confirms that African-American children's learning styles are different, not deficient. In critiquing Willis' suggestions, and others that have attempted to demonstrate the differences between African-American and other learners as differences and not deficiencies, some scholars have been quick to question the applicability and generalizability of the theory. Willis (1989) defended her position by noting that:

> Not all Black children demonstrate all of the characteristics described in Boykin's (1983), Hale-Benson's (1986) or Hilliard's (1976) typologies and models. What is characterized here are the ends of the continuum of learning style. Placement along the continuum depends on factors such as variations in the types of socialization that occur in the family (i.e., how much parents identify with mainstream American versus African-American culture, what types of options they perceive they have in their lives, their ability to adapt to the requirements of various institutions, and numerous other complex factors) (McAdoo, 1981). The individual person's ability and desire to develop various behavior repertoires is another critical factor in where they fall along the continuum of learning styles. (p. 54)

The Frisby position, in response to theoretical positions like the one advanced by Willis, has been met with strong responses, most notably Hale (1993) and Richardson (1993). Hale argues that Frisby "seems to be discounting the work of Black scholars attempting to address the alarming statistics on the low achievement of Black youths" (p. 558). Beyond that, she attacks Frisby for what she sees as faulty logic filled with inferential leaps. She asserts that Afro-centric theorists are probing for new strategies to improve academic achievement levels of African-American children. Richardson also contends that historical factors, which have shaped the educational environments of African-American children, should not be ignored.

The central argument in this debate appears to be the relevance of history in explaining the repeated poor academic performance of African-American children. It seems that the debate about learning styles, real or imaginary, reveals what educators believe about African-American children. Those thoughts expressed by the teacher reflect the teacher's acquisitions from their own layers of micro-, meso-, and exosystems.

What is the implication of teachers devaluing or dismissing the contribution of history to the present day functioning of African-American children? The dismissing of African influence in the lives of African-Americans coupled with traditional portrayals in history serve to marginalize and devalue their existence. This message is conveyed to children and parents. If the effect of de-emphasizing African lifestyles and culture has the impact of devaluing, it seems that there are profound messages in the process concerning identity involved for children.

THE SCHOOL–HOME RELATIONSHIP AS A MESOSYSTEM

Mesosystems are relationships between microsystems in which the child experiences reality. There are many connections and there is mutual support between the two settings. For example, parents ask about school work, attend the school's parent functions, and perhaps, even volunteer their time for school activities (Garbarino, 1985).

The relationship between home life and school life for African-American children is clear and of major importance. When there are clashes between the values in these settings the child is given the awesome task of deciding which set of messages to hold in the highest regard. Garbarino and Asp (1981) describe how different cultures are reflective of the environments in which they exist. For example, school settings are referred to as academic cultures. School culture includes such factors as language codes and value codes (Getzels, 1974).

African-American homes have been depicted as being in conflict with academic culture. An early work by Boykin (1978) explores this issue at length. He asserted that the home environment of African-American children offers them a variety of complex and changing stimuli that fosters a highly adaptive style. He stated that "the absence of this vervistic dimension of the classroom, where quiet and passivity are the preferred behaviors, may be an unrecognized cause of the lack of intrinsic motivation for academic achievement shown by black children. The black child finds school less eventful and stimulating than life at home" (p. 343).

What are the lessons that can be learned from the competing curriculum? African Americans have recently made an attempt to re-affirm or establish linkages with the African legacy in their psychological and anthropological evolution. The African connection is the object of much suspicion, if not disdain and scorn, among many scholars. This type of response to African Americans in their attempts to self-define leads to a devaluation of the African influence. This has been illustrated in the aforegoing pages in the dialogue concerning African-American cultural learning styles and Frisby's contention that the historical contexts from which African Americans have evolved should not be considered a major explanation for the repeated failure of African-American children. It appears that one probable lesson in this sort of dynamic tension is the revelation of a process that disrupts African Americans' thrust toward self-definition and attempts to build a strong connection with their own heritage.

When teachers' values are at variance with African-American life and culture, the results may be the formation of a competing curriculum that has overwhelming potentials for the dynamics of the classroom. The fact that teachers may have a value system that differs from those of their students' is not surprising because many of the teachers in classrooms with African-American children may not share the experiences of African-American culture. Perhaps, even more important, there are variations in the African-American experience and these variations may also create situations where teachers who are of African-American culture may have had a very different experience than their students. It is suggested here that there should be increased recognition of teacher proclivities, teacher values, and individual developmental histories should be explored as a source of conflict within the classroom. Conflicts in this situation are not viewed as negative or with an avoidance valence attached to them, but rather, as the catalyst for some creative thinking about how to close the gap between service provider (i.e., the educator) and the consumer (i.e., the student).

The dynamic tension between multiple ecological systems is real. Frequently, the tensions are not overt but occur on a subtle level and find their way into classrooms in behavioral expressions that are counterproductive to the development of African-American children. The lesson to be learned from this is that avoidance of conflict, or even denial, that there are conflicts only serves to maintain the status quo. It is much more valuable, it seems, to reflect continuously on how each individual involved in the education of African-American children brings to the situation a vastly different set of historical experiences drawn from personal involvement in multiple ecological systems. Only when these kinds of differences, conflicts and variances in perceptions of outcome are constructively addressed, can there be a situation of dynamic tension which ultimately can be resolved in the creation of a pro-active, contemporary, positive curriculum and learning experience for children of African descent.

REFERENCES

Barker, R., & Gump, P. (1964). *Big school, small school.* Stanford, CA: Stanford University Press.

Boykin, A. W. (1978). Psychological/behavioral verve in academic task performance: Pretheoretical considerations. *Journal of Negro Education, 47,* 343–354.

Boykin, W. (1983). On academic task performance and Afro-American children. In J. R. Spencer (Ed.), *Achievement and achievement motives* (pp. 324–371). Boston: Freeman.

Branch, C. (1993). Ethnic identity as a variable in the learning equation. In E. Hollins, J. King, & W. Hayman (Eds.), *Teaching diverse populations* (pp. 207–224). Albany: State University of New York Press.

Bronfenbrenner, U. (1979). *The ecology of human development: Experiments by nature and design.* Cambridge, MA: Harvard University Press.

Fordham, S., & Ogbu, J. U. (1986). Black students' school success: Coping with the "burden of 'acting white'." *The Urban Review, 18*(3), 176–205.

Frisby, C. (1993). One giant step backward: Myths of Black cultural learning styles. *School Psychology Review, 22*(3), 535–557.

Garbarino, J. (1985). *Adolescent development: An ecological perspective.* Columbus, OH: C. E. Merrill.

Garbarino, J., & Asp, C. E. (1981). *Successful schools and competent students.* Lexington, MA: Lexington Books.

Getzels, J. W. (1974). Socialization and education. A note on discontinuities. *Teachers College Record, 76,* 218–225.

Hale, J. (1993). A rejoinder to ". . . myths of Black cultural learning styles" in defense of Afrocentric scholarship. *School Psychology Review, 22*(3), 558–561.

Hale-Benson, J. (1986). *Black children: Their roots, culture and learning styles* (2nd ed.). Baltimore: Johns Hopkins Press.

Hilliard, A. (1976). *Alternatives to IQ testing: An approach to the identification of gifted minority children* (Final report). San Francisco: San Francisco State University. (ERIC Document Reproduction Service No. EC 103067)

Knefelkamp, L. (1992, February). *The multicultural curriculum and communities of peace.* Speech presented at Roundtable on Cross-cultural council and psychotherapy, Teachers College, Columbia University, New York.

Lewin, K. (1935). *A dynamic theory of personality.* New York: McGraw-Hill.

Richardson, T. (1993). Black cultural learning styles: Is it reality or a myth? *School Psychology Review, 22*(3), 562–567.

Willis, M. (1989). Learning styles of African American children: A review of the literature and interventions. *Journal of Black Psychology, 16*(1), 47–65.

CHAPTER NINE

Social Class and the Hidden Curriculum of Work

Jean Anyon

This article discusses examples of work tasks and interaction in five elementary schools in contrasting social class communities. The examples illustrate differences in classroom experience and curriculum knowledge among the schools. The paper also assesses student work in each social setting in the light of a theoretical approach to social class analysis. It is suggested that there is a "hidden curriculum" in school work that has profound implication for theory—and practice—in education.

Scholars in political economy and the sociology of knowledge have recently argued that public schools in complex industrial societies like our own make available different types of educational experience and curriculum knowledge to students in different social classes. Bowles and Gintis (1976), for example, have argued that students from different social class backgrounds are rewarded for classroom behaviors that correspond to personality traits allegedly rewarded in the different occupational strata—the working classes for docility and obedience, the managerial classes for initiative and personal assertiveness. Basil Bernstein (1977), Pierre Bourdieu (Bourdieu and Passeron, 1977), and Michael W. Apple (1979), focusing on school knowledge, have argued that knowledge and skills leading to social power and reward (e.g., medical, legal, managerial) are made available to the advantaged social groups but are withheld from the working classes, to whom a more "practical" curriculum is offered (e.g., manual skills, clerical knowledge). While there has been considerable argumentation of these points regarding education in England, France, and North America, there has been little or no attempt to investigate these ideas empirically in elementary or secondary schools and classrooms in this country.[1]

This article offers tentative empirical support (and qualification) of the above arguments by providing illustrative examples of differences in student *work* in classrooms in contrasting social class communities. The examples were gathered as part of an ethnographical study of curricular, pedagogical and pupil evaluation practices in five elementary schools.* The article attempts a theoretical contribution as well, and assesses student work in the light of a theoretical approach to social class analysis. The organization is as follows: the methodology of the ethnographical study is briefly described; a theoretical approach to the definition of social class is offered; income and other characteristics of the parents in each school are provided, and examples from the study that illustrate work tasks and interaction in each school are presented; then the concepts used to define social class are applied to the examples in order to assess the theoretical meaning of classroom events. It will be suggested that there is a "hidden curriculum" in school work that has profound implication for the theory—and consequence—of everyday activity in education.

METHODOLOGY

The methods used to gather data were classroom observation; interviews of students, teachers, principals, and district administrative staff; and assessment of curriculum and other materials in each classroom and school. All classroom events to be discussed here involve the fifth grade in each school. All schools but one departmentalize at the fifth grade level. Except for that school where only one fifth grade teacher could be observed, all the fifth grade teachers (that is, two or three) were observed as the children moved from subject to subject. In all schools the art, music, and gym teachers were also observed and interviewed. All teachers in the study were described as "good" or "excellent" by their principals. All except one new teacher had taught for more than four years. The fifth grade in each school was observed by the investigator for ten three-hour periods between September 15, 1978 and June 20, 1979.

Before providing the occupations, incomes, and other relevant social characteristics of the parents of the children in each school, I will offer a theoretical approach to defining social class.

---

[1]But see, in a related vein, Apple and King (1977) and Rist (1973).

*The research was funded by Rutgers University Research Council and will be reported in detail elsewhere.

SOCIAL CLASS

One's occupation and income level contribute significantly to one's social class, but they do not define it. Rather, social class is a series of relationships. A person's social class is defined here by the way that person relates to the process in society by which goods, services, and culture are produced.[2] One relates to several aspects of the production process primarily through one's work. One has a relationship to the system of ownership, to other people (at work and in society) and to the content and process of one's own productive activity. One's relationship to all three of these aspects of production determines one's social class; that is, all three relationships are necessary and none is sufficient for determining a person's relation to the process of production in society.

Ownership Relations. In a capitalist society, a person has a relation to the system of private ownership of capital. Capital is usually thought of as being derived from physical property. In this sense capital is property which is used to produce profit, interest, or rent in sufficient quantity so that the result can be used to produce more profit, interest, or rent—that is, more capital. Physical capital may be derived from money, stocks, machines, land, or the labor of workers (whose labor, for instance, may produce products that are sold by others for profit). Capital, however, can also be symbolic. It can be the socially legitimated knowledge of how the production process works, its financial, managerial, technical, or other "secrets." Symbolic capital can also be socially legitimated skills—cognitive (e.g., analytical), linguistic, or technical skills that provide the ability to, say, produce the dominant scientific, artistic, and other culture, or to manage the systems of industrial and cultural production. Skillful application of symbolic capital may yield social and cultural power, and perhaps physical capital as well.

The ownership relation that is definitive for social class is one's relation to physical capital. The first such relationship is that of capitalist. To be a member of the capitalist class in the present-day United States, one must participate in the ownership of the apparatus of production in society. The number of such persons is relatively small: while one person in ten owns some stock, for example, a mere 1.6 percent of the population owns 82.2 percent of *all* stock, and the wealthiest one-fifth owns almost all the rest (see New York Stock Exchange, 1975; Smith and Franklin, 1974; Lampman, 1962).

At the opposite pole of this relationship is the worker. To be in the United States working class a person will not ordinarily own physical capital; to

[2]The definition of social class delineated here is the author's own, but it relies heavily on her interpretation of the work of Eric Olin Wright (1978), Pierre Bourdieu (Bourdieu and Passeron, 1977) and Raymond Williams (1977).

the contrary, his or her work will be wage or salaried labor that is either a *source* of profit (i.e., capital) to others, or that makes it possible for others to *realize* profit. Examples of the latter are white-collar clerical workers in industry and distribution (office and sales) as well as the wage and salaried workers in the institutions of social and economic legitimation and service (e.g., in state education and welfare institutions).[3] According to the criteria to be developed here, the number of persons who presently comprise the working class in the United States is between 50 percent and 60 percent of the population (see also Wright, 1978; Braverman, 1974; Levison, 1974).

In between the defining relationship of capitalist and worker are the middle classes, whose relationship to the process of production is less clear, and whose relationship may indeed exhibit contradictory characteristics. For example, social service employees have a somewhat contradictory relationship to the process of production because, although their income may be at middle-class levels, some characteristics of their work are working-class (e.g., they may have very little control over their work). Analogously, there are persons at the upper income end of the middle class, such as upper-middle-class professionals, who may own quantities of stocks and will therefore share characteristics of the capitalist class. As the next criterion to be discussed makes clear, however, to be a member of the present-day capitalist in the United States, one must also participate in the social *control* of this capital.

Relationships Between People. The second relationship which contributes to one's social class is the relation one has to authority and control at work and in society.[4] One characteristic of most working-class jobs is that there is no built-in mechanism by which the worker can control the content, process, or speed of work. Legitimate decision making is vested in personnel supervisors, in middle or upper management, or, as in an increasing number of white-collar working-class (and most middle-class) jobs, by bureaucratic rule and regulation. For upper-middle-class professional groups there is an increased amount of autonomy regarding work. Moreover, in middle- and upper-middle-class positions there is an increasing chance that one's work will also involve supervising the work of others. A capitalist is defined within

---

[3]For discussion of schools as agencies of social and economic legitimation see Althusser (1971); see also Anyon (1978; 1979).

[4]While relationships of control in society will not be discussed here, it can be said that they roughly parallel the relationships of control in the workplace, which will be the focus of this discussion. That is, working-class and many middle-class persons have less control than members of the upper-middle and capitalist classes do, not only over conditions and processes of their work, but over their nonwork lives as well. In addition, it is true that persons from the middle and capitalist classes, rather than workers, are most often those who fill the positions of state and other power in United States society.

these relations of control in an enterprise by having a position which participates in the direct control of the entire enterprise. Capitalists do not directly control workers in physical production and do not directly control ideas in the sphere of cultural production. However, more crucial to control, capitalists make the decisions over how resources are used (e.g., where money is invested) and how profit is allocated.

Relations Between People and Their Work. The third criterion which contributes to a person's social class is the relationship between that person and his or her own productive activity—the type of activity that constitutes his or her work. A working-class job is often characterized by work that is routine and mechanical and that is a small, fragmented part of a larger process with which workers are not usually acquainted. These working-class jobs are usually blue-collar, manual labor. A few skilled jobs such as plumbing and printing are not mechanical, however, and an increasing number of working-class jobs are *white*-collar. These white-collar jobs, such as clerical work, may involve work that necessitates a measure of planning and decision making, but one still has no built-in control over the content. The work of some middle- and most upper-middle-class managerial and professional groups is likely to involve the need for conceptualization and creativity, with many professional jobs demanding one's full creative capacities. Finally, the work that characterizes the capitalist position is that this work is almost entirely a matter of conceptualization (e.g., planning and laying-out) that has as its object management and control of the enterprise.

One's social class, then, is a result of the relationships one has, largely through one's work, to physical capital and its power, to other people at work and in society, and to one's own productive activity. Social class is a lived, developing process. It is not an abstract category, and it is not a fixed, inherited position (although one's family background is, of course, important). Social class is perceived as a complex of social relations that one develops as one grows up—as one acquires and develops certain bodies of knowledge, skills, abilities, and traits, and as one has contact and opportunity in the world.[5] In sum, social class describes relationships which we as adults have developed, may attempt to maintain, and in which we participate every working day. These relationships in a real sense define our material ties to the world. An important concern here is whether these relationships are developing in children in schools within particular social class contexts.

---

[5]Occupations may change their relation to the means of production over time, as the expenditure and ownership of capital change, as technology, skills, and the social relations of work change. For example, some jobs which were middle-class, managerial positions in 1900 and which necessitated conceptual laying-out and planning are now working-class and increasingly mechanical: e.g., quality control in industry, clerical work, and computer programming (see Braverman, 1974).

THE SAMPLE OF SCHOOLS

With the above discussion as a theoretical backdrop, the social class designation of each of the five schools will be identified, and the income, occupation, and other relevant available social characteristics of the students and their parents will be described. The first three schools are in a medium-sized city district in northern New Jersey, and the other two are in a nearby New Jersey suburb.

The first two schools I will call *Working-class Schools.* Most of the parents have blue-collar jobs. Less than a third of the fathers are skilled, while the majority are in unskilled or semiskilled jobs. During the period of the study (1978–1979) approximately 15 percent of the fathers were unemployed. The large majority (85 percent) of the families are white. The following occupations are typical: platform, storeroom, and stockroom workers; foundrymen, pipe welders, and boilermakers; semiskilled and unskilled assembly-line operatives; gas station attendants, auto mechanics, maintenance workers, and security guards. Less than 30 percent of the women work, some part-time and some full-time, on assembly lines, in storerooms and stockrooms, as waitresses, barmaids, or sales clerks. Of the fifth grade parents, none of the wives of the skilled workers had jobs. Approximately 15 percent of the families in each school are at or below the federal "poverty" level[6]; most of the rest of the family incomes are at or below $12,000, except some of the skilled workers whose incomes are higher. The incomes of the majority of the families in these two schools (i.e., at or below $12,000) are typical of 38.6 percent of the families in the United States (U.S. Bureau of the Census, 1979, p. 2, table A).

The third school is called the *Middle-class School,* although because of neighborhood residence patterns, the population is a mixture of several social classes. The parents' occupations can be divided into three groups: a small group of blue-collar "rich," who are skilled, well-paid workers such as printers, carpenters, plumbers, and construction workers. The second group is composed of parents in working-class and middle-class white-collar jobs: women in office jobs, technicians, supervisors in industry, and parents employed by the city (such as firemen, policemen, and several of the school's teachers). The third group is composed of occupations such as personnel directors in local firms, accountants, "middle management," and a few small capitalists (owners of shops in the area). The children of several local doctors attend this school. Most family incomes are between $13,000 and $25,000 with a few higher. This income range is typical of 38.9 percent of the families in the United States (U.S. Bureau of the Census, 1979, p. 2, table A).

---

[6]The U.S. Bureau of the Census defines "poverty" for a nonfarm family of four as a yearly income of $6,191 a year or less. U.S. Bureau of the Census, *Statistical Abstract of the United States: 1978* (Washington, D.C.: U.S. Government Printing Office, 1978, p. 465, table 754).

The fourth school has a parent population that is at the upper income level of the upper middle class, and is predominantly professional. This school will be called the *Affluent Professional School.* Typical jobs are: cardiologist, interior designer, corporate lawyer or engineer, executive in advertising or television. There are some families who are not as affluent as the majority (e.g., the family of the superintendent of the district's schools, and the one or two families in which the fathers are skilled workers). In addition, a few of the families are more affluent than the majority, and can be classified in the capitalist class (e.g., a partner in a prestigious Wall Street stock brokerage firm). Approximately 90 percent of the children in this school are white. Most family incomes are between $40,000 and $80,000. This income span represents approximately 7 percent of the families in the United States.[7]

In the fifth school the majority of the families belong to the capitalist class. This school will be called the *Executive Elite School* because most of the fathers are top executives (e.g., presidents and vice presidents) in major U.S.-based multinational corporations—for example, ATT, RCA, City Bank, American Express, U.S. Steel. A sizable group of fathers are top executives in financial firms on Wall Street. There are also a number of fathers who list their occupations as "general counsel" to a particular corporation, and these corporations are also among the large multinationals. Many of the mothers do volunteer work in the Junior League, Junior Fortnightly, or other service groups; some are intricately involved in town politics; and some are themselves in well-paid occupations. There are no minority children in the school. Almost all family incomes are over $100,000 with some in the $500,000 range. The incomes in this school represent less than 1 percent of the families in the United States (see Smith and Franklin, 1974).

Since each of the five schools is only one instance of elementary education in a particular social class context, I will not generalize beyond the sample. However, the examples of school work which follow will suggest characteristics of education in each social setting that appear to have theoretical and social significance and to be worth investigation in a larger number of schools.

SOCIAL CLASS AND SCHOOL WORK

There are obvious similarities among United States schools and classrooms. There are school and classroom rules, teachers who ask questions and attempt to exercise control and who give work and homework. There are

[7]This figure is an estimate. According to the Bureau of the Census, only 2.6 percent of families in the United States have money income of $50,000 or over. U.S. Bureau of the Census, *Current Population Reports*, series P–60, no. 118, "Money Income in 1977 of Families and Persons in the United States." (Washington, D.C.: U.S. Government Printing Office, 1979, p. 2, table A). For figures on income at these higher levels, see Smith and Franklin (1974).

textbooks and tests. All of these were found in the five schools. Indeed, there were other curricular similarities as well: all schools and fifth grades used the same math book and series (*Mathematics Around Us*, Scott Foresman, 1978); all fifth grades had at least one boxed set of an individualized reading program available in the room (although the variety and amounts of teaching materials in the classrooms increased as the social class of the school population increased); and, all fifth grade language arts curricula included aspects of grammar, punctuation and capitalization.[8]

This section provides examples of work and work-related activities in each school that bear on the categories used to define social class. Thus, examples will be provided concerning students' relation to capital (e.g., as manifest in any symbolic capital that might be acquired through school work); students' relation to persons and types of authority regarding school work; and students' relation to their own productive activity. The section first offers the investigator's interpretation of what school work *is* for children in each setting, and then presents events and interactions that illustrate that assessment.

The Working-Class Schools. In the two working-class schools, work is following the steps of a procedure. The procedure is usually mechanical, involving rote behavior and very little decision making or choice. The teachers rarely explain why the work is being assigned, how it might connect to other assignments, or what the idea is that lies behind the procedure or gives it coherence and perhaps meaning or significance. Available textbooks are not always used, and the teachers often prepare their own dittoes or put work examples on the board. Most of the rules regarding work are designations of what the children are to do; the rules are steps to follow. These steps are told to the children by the teachers and often written on the board. The children are usually told to copy the steps as notes. These notes are to be studied. Work is often evaluated not according to whether it is right or wrong, but according to whether the children followed the right steps.

The following examples illustrate these points. In math, when two-digit division was introduced, the teacher in one school gave a four-minute lecture on what the terms are called (i.e., which number is the divisor, dividend, quotient, and remainder). The children were told to copy these names in their notebooks. Then the teacher told them the steps to follow to do the problems, saying, "This is how you do them." The teacher listed the steps on the board, and they appeared several days later as a chart hung in the middle of the front wall: "Divide; Multiply; Subtract; Bring Down." The children often did examples of two-digit division. When the teacher went over the examples with them, he told them for each problem what the

[8]For other similarities alleged to characterize United States classrooms and schools, but which will not be discussed here, see Dreeben (1968), Jackson (1968), and Sarasan (1971).

procedure was, rarely asking them to conceptualize or explain it themselves: "3 into 22 is 7; do your subtraction and one is left over." During the week that two-digit division was introduced (or at any other time), the investigator did not observe any discussion of the idea of grouping involved in division, any use of manipulables, or any attempt to relate two-digit division to any other mathematical process. Nor was there any attempt to relate the steps to an actual or possible thought process of the children. The observer did not hear the terms dividend, quotient, etc., used again. The math teacher in the other working-class school followed similar procedures regarding two-digit division, and at one point her class seemed confused. She said, "You're confusing yourselves. You're tensing up. Remember, when you do this, it's the same steps over and over again—and that's the way division always is." Several weeks later, after a test, a group of her children "still didn't get it," and she made no attempt to explain the concept of dividing things into groups, or to give them manipulables for their own investigation. Rather, she went over the steps with them again and told them that they "needed more practice."

In other areas of math, work is also carrying out often unexplained, fragmented procedures. For example, one of the teachers led the children through a series of steps to make a one-inch grid on their paper *without* telling them that they were making a one-inch grid, or that it would be used to study scale. She said, "Take your ruler. Put it across the top. Make a mark at every number. Then move your ruler down to the bottom. No, put it across the bottom. Now make a mark on top of every number. Now draw a line from. . . ." At this point a girl said that she had a faster way to do it and the teacher said, "No, you don't; you don't even know what I'm making yet. Do it this way, or it's wrong." After they had made the lines up and down and across, the teacher told them she wanted them to make a figure by connecting some dots and to measure that, using the scale of one inch equals one mile. Then they were to cut it out. She said, "Don't cut until I check it."

In both working-class schools, work in language arts is mechanics of punctuation (commas, periods, question marks, exclamation points), capitalization, and the four kinds of sentences. One teacher explained to me, "Simple punctuation is all they'll ever use." Regarding punctuation, either a teacher or a ditto stated the rules for where, for example, to put commas. The investigator heard no classroom discussion of the aural context of punctuation (which, of course, is what gives each mark its meaning). Nor did the investigator hear any statement or inference that placing a punctuation mark could be a decision-making process, depending, for example, on one's intended meaning. Rather, the children were told to follow the rules. Language arts did not involve creative writing. There were several writing assignments throughout the year, but in each instance the children were given a ditto, and they wrote answers to questions on the sheet. For example, they wrote their "autobiography" by answering such questions as "Where were you born?" "What is your favorite animal?" on a sheet entitled, "All About Me."

In one of the working-class schools the class had a science period several times a week. On the three occasions observed, the children were not called upon to set up experiments or to give explanations for facts or concepts. Rather, on each occasion the teacher told them in his own words what the book said. The children copied the teacher's sentences from the board. Each day that preceded the day they were to do a science experiment, the teacher told them to copy the directions from the book for the procedure they would carry out the next day, and to study the list at home that night. The day after each experiment, the teacher went over what they had "found" (they did the experiments as a class, and each was actually a class demonstration led by the teacher). Then the teacher wrote what they "found" on the board, and the children copied that in their notebooks. Once or twice a year there are science projects. The project is chosen and assigned by the teacher from a box of three-by-five-inch cards. On the card the teacher has written the question to be answered, the books to use, and how much to write. Explaining the cards to the observer, the teacher said, "It tells them exactly what to do, or they couldn't do it."

Social studies in the working-class schools is also largely mechanical, rote work that was given little explanation or connection to larger contexts. In one school, for example, although there was a book available, social studies work was to copy the teacher's notes from the board. Several times a week for a period of several months, the children copied these notes. The fifth grades in the district were to study U.S. history. The teacher used a booklet she had purchased called "The Fabulous Fifty States." Each day she put information from the booklet in outline form on the board and the children copied it. The type of information did not vary: the name of the state, its abbreviation, state capital, nickname of the state, its main products, main business, and a "Fabulous Fact" (e.g., "Idaho grew 27 billion potatoes in one year. That's enough potatoes for each man, woman and . . ."). As the children finished copying the sentences, the teacher erased them and wrote more. Children would occasionally go to the front to pull down the wall map in order to locate the states they were copying, and the teacher did not dissuade them. But the observer never saw her refer to the map; nor did the observer ever hear her make other than perfunctory remarks concerning the information the children were copying. Occasionally the children colored in a ditto and cut it out to make a stand-up figure (representing, for example, a man roping a cow in the Southwest). These were referred to by the teacher as their social studies "projects."

Rote behavior was often called for in classroom oral work. When going over math and language arts skills sheets, for example, as the teacher asked for the answer to each problem, he fired the questions rapidly, staccato, and the scene reminded the observer of a sergeant drilling recruits: above all, the questions demanded that you stay at attention: "The next one? What do I put here? . . . Here? Give us the next." Or "How many commas in this sentence? Where do I put them . . . The next one?"

The (four) fifth grade teachers observed in the working-class schools attempted to control classroom time and space by making decisions without consulting the children and without explaining the basis for their decisions. The teacher's control thus often seemed capricious. Teachers, for instance, very often ignored the bells to switch classes—deciding among themselves to keep the children after the period was officially over, to continue with the work, or for disciplinary reasons, or so they (the teachers) could stand in the hall and talk. There were no clocks in the rooms in either school, and the children often asked, "What period is this?" "When do we go to gym?" The children had no access to materials. These were handed out by teachers and closely guarded. Things in the room "belonged" to the teacher: "Bob, bring me my garbage can." The teachers continually gave the children orders. Only three times did the investigator hear a teacher in either working-class school preface a directive with an unsarcastic "please," or "let's" or "would you." Instead, the teachers said, "Shut up," "Shut your mouth," "Open your books," "Throw your *gum* away—if you want to rot your teeth, do it on your *own* time." Teachers made every effort to control the movement of the children, and often shouted, "Why are you out of your *seat*??!!" If the children got permission to leave the room they had to take a written pass with the date and time.

The control that the teachers have is less than they would like. It is a result of constant struggle with the children. The children continually resist the teachers' orders and the work itself. They do not directly challenge the teachers' authority or legitimacy, but they make indirect attempts to sabotage and resist the flow of assignments:

Teacher:	I will put some problems on the board. You are to divide.
Child:	We got to divide?
Teacher:	Yes.
Several children:	(Groan) Not again. Mr. B, we done this yesterday.
Child:	Do we put the date?
Teacher:	Yes. I hope we remember we work in silence. You're supposed to do it on white paper. I'll explain it later.
Child:	Somebody broke my pencil. (Crash—a child falls out of his chair.)
Child:	(repeats) Mr. B., somebody broke my *pencil*!
Child:	Are we going to be here all morning?

(Teacher comes to the observer, shakes his head and grimaces, then smiles.)

The children are successful enough in their struggle against work that there are long periods where they are not asked to *do* any work, but just to sit and be quiet.[9] Very often the work that the teachers assign is "easy," that is, not demanding, and thus receives less resistance. Sometimes a compromise is reached where, although the teachers insist that the children continue to work, there is a constant murmur of talk. The children will be doing arithmetic examples, copying social studies notes, or doing punctuation or other dittoes, and all the while there is muted but spirited conversation—about somebody's broken arm, an afterschool disturbance of the day before, etc. Sometimes the teachers themselves join in the conversation because, as one teacher explained to me, "It's a relief from the routine."

Middle-Class School. In the middle-class school, work is getting the right answer. If one accumulates enough right answers one gets a good grade. One must follow the directions in order to get the right answers, but the directions often call for some figuring, some choice, some decision making. For example, the children must often figure out by themselves what the directions ask them to do, and how to get the answer: what do you do first, second, and perhaps third? Answers are usually found in books or by listening to the teacher. Answers are usually words, sentences, numbers, or facts and dates; one writes them on paper, and one should be neat. Answers must be in the right order, and one can not make them up.

The following activities are illustrative. Math involves some choice: one may do two-digit division the long way, or the short way, and there are some math problems that can be done "in your head." When the teacher explains how to do two-digit division, there is recognition that a cognitive process is involved; she gives several ways, and says, "I want to make sure you understand what you're doing—so you get it right"; and, when they go over the homework, she asks the *children* to tell how they did the problem and what answer they got.

In social studies the daily work is to read the assigned pages in the textbook and to answer the teacher's questions. The questions are almost always designed to check on whether the students have read the assignment and understood it: who did so-and-so; what happened after that; when did it happen, where, and sometimes, why did it happen? The answers are in the book and in one's understanding of the book; the teacher's hints when

---

[9]Indeed, strikingly little teaching occurred in either of the working-class schools; this curtailed the amount that the children were taught. Incidentally, it increased the amount of time that had to be spent by the researcher to collect data on teaching style and interaction.

one doesn't know the answer are to "read it again," or to look at the picture or at the rest of the paragraph. One is to search for the answer in the "context," in what is given.

Language arts is "simple grammar, what they need for everyday life." The language arts teacher says, "They should learn to speak properly, to write business letters and thank-you letters, and to understand what nouns and verbs and simple subjects are." Here, as well, the actual work is to choose the right answers, to understand what is given. The teacher often says, "Please read the next sentence and then I'll question you about it." One teacher said in some exasperation to a boy who was fooling around in class, "If you don't know the answers to the questions I ask, then you can't stay in this *class*! (pause) You *never* know the answers to the questions I ask, and it's not fair to me—and certainly not to you!"

Most lessons are based on the textbook. This does not involve a critical perspective on what is given there. For example, a critical perspective in social studies is perceived as dangerous by these teachers because it may lead to controversial topics; the parents might complain. The children, however, are often curious, especially in social studies. Their questions are tolerated, and usually answered perfunctorily. But after a few minutes the teacher will say, "All right, we're not going any farther. Please open your social studies workbook." While the teachers spend a lot of time explaining and expanding on what the textbooks say, there is little attempt to analyze how or why things happen, or to give thought to how pieces of a culture, or, say, a system of numbers or elements of a language fit together or can be analyzed. What has happened in the past, and what exists now may not be equitable or fair, but (shrug) that is the way things are, and one does not confront such matters in school. For example, in social studies after a child is called on to read a passage about the pilgrims, the teacher summarizes the paragraph and then says, "So you can see how strict they were about everything." A child asks, "Why?" "Well, because they felt that if you weren't busy you'd get into trouble." Another child asks, "Is it true that they burned women at the stake?" The teacher says, "Yes, if a woman did anything strange, they hanged them [*sic*]. What would a woman do, do you think, to make them burn them [*sic*]? See if you can come up with better answers than my other [social studies] class." Several children offer suggestions, to which the teacher nods but does not comment. Then she says, "OK, good," and calls on the next child to read.

Work tasks do not usually request creativity. Serious attention is rarely given in school work to *how* the children develop or express their own feelings and ideas, either linguistically or in graphic form. On the occasions when creativity or self-expression is requested, it is peripheral to the main activity, or it is "enrichment," or "for fun." During a lesson on what similes are, for example, the teacher explains what they are, puts several on the board, gives some other examples herself, and then asks the children if they can "make some up." She calls on three children who give similes, two of which are actually in the book they have open before them. The teacher does not comment on this, and then asks several others to choose similes from the list of phrases in the book. Several do so correctly, and she says, "Oh *good*! You're picking them out! See how *good* we are?" Their homework is to pick out the rest of the similes from the list.

Creativity is not often requested in social studies and science projects, either. Social studies projects, for example, are given with directions to "find information on your topic," and write it up. The children are not supposed to copy, but to "put it in your own words." Although a number of the projects subsequently went beyond the teacher's direction to find information and had quite expressive covers and inside illustrations, the teacher's evaluative comments had to do with the amount of information, whether they had "copied," and if their work was neat.

The style of control of the three fifth grade teachers observed in this school varied from somewhat easygoing to strict, but in contrast to the working-class schools, the teachers' decisions were usually based on external rules and regulations, for example, on criteria that were known or available to the children. Thus, the teachers always honor the bells for changing classes, and they usually evaluate children's work by what is in the textbooks and answer booklets.

There is little excitement in school work for the children, and the assignments are perceived as having little to do with their interests and feelings. As one child said, what you do is "store facts in your head like cold storage—until you need it later for a test, or your job." Thus, doing well is important because there are thought to be *other* likely rewards: a good job, or college.[10]

Affluent Professional School. In the affluent professional school, work is creative activity carried out independently. The students are continually asked to express and apply ideas and concepts. Work involves individual thought and expressiveness, expansion and illustration of ideas, and choice of appropriate method and material. (The class is not considered an open classroom, and the principal explained that because of the large number of discipline problems in the fifth grade this year they did not departmentalize. The teacher who agreed to take part in the study said she is "more structured" this year than she usually is.) The products of work in this class are often written stories, editorials and essays, or representations

[10]A dominant feeling, expressed directly and indirectly by teachers in this school, was boredom with their work. They did, however, in contrast to the working-class schools, almost always carry out lessons during class times.

of ideas in mural, graph, or craft form. The products of work should not be like everybody else's and should show individuality. They should exhibit good design, and (this is important), they must also fit empirical reality. Moreover, one's work should attempt to interpret or "make sense" of reality. The relatively few rules to be followed regarding work are usually criteria for, or limits on, individual activity. One's product is usually evaluated for the quality of its expression and for the appropriateness of its conception to the task. In many cases one's own satisfaction with the product is an important criterion for its evaluation. When right answers are called for, as in commercial materials like SRA (Science Research Associates) and math, it is important that the children decide on an answer as a result of thinking about the idea involved in what they're being asked to do. Teacher's hints are to "think about it some more."

The following activities are illustrative. The class takes home a sheet requesting each child's parents to fill in the number of cars they have, the number of television sets, refrigerators, games, or rooms in the house, etc. Each child is to figure the average number of a type of possession owned by the fifth grade. Each child must compile the "data" from all the sheets. A calculator is available in the classroom to do the mechanics of finding the average. Some children decide to send sheets to the fourth grade families for comparison. Their work should be "verified" by a classmate before it is handed in.

Each child and his or her family has made a geoboard. The teacher asks the class to get their geoboards from the side cabinet, to take a handful of rubber bands, and then to listen to what she would like them to do. She says, "I would like you to design a figure and then find the perimeter and area. When you have it, check with your neighbor. After you've done that, please transfer it to graph paper and tomorrow I'll ask you to make up a question about it for someone. When you hand it in, please let me know whose it is, and who verified it. Then I have something else for you to do that's really fun. (pause) Find the average number of chocolate chips in three cookies. I'll give you three cookies, and you'll have to *eat* your way through, I'm afraid!" Then she goes around the room and gives help, suggestions, praise, and admonitions that they are getting noisy. They work sitting, or standing up at their desks, at benches in the back, or on the floor. A child hands the teacher his paper and she comments, "I'm not accepting this paper. Do a better design." To another child she says, "That's fantastic! But you'll never find the area. Why don't you draw a figure inside [the big one] and subtract to get the area?"

The school district requires the fifth grades to study ancient civilizations (in particular, Egypt, Athens, and Sumer). In this classroom, the emphasis is on illustrating and re-creating the culture of the people of ancient times. The following are typical activities: The children made an 8mm film on

Egypt, which one of the parents edited. A girl in the class wrote the script, and the class acted it out. They put the sound on themselves. They read stories of those days. They wrote essays and stories depicting the lives of the people and the societal and occupational divisions. They chose from a list of projects, all of which involved graphic representations of ideas: for example, "Make a mural depicting the division of labor in Egyptian society."

Each child wrote and exchanged a letter in hieroglyphics with a fifth grader in another class, and they also exchanged stories they wrote in cuneiform. They made a scroll and singed the edges so it looked authentic. They each chose an occupation and made an Egyptian plaque representing that occupation, simulating the appropriate Egyptian design. They carved their design on a cylinder of wax, pressed the wax into clay, and then baked the clay. Although one girl did not choose an occupation, but carved instead a series of gods and slaves, the teacher said, "That's all right, Amber, it's beautiful." As they were working the teacher said, "Don't cut into your clay until you're satisfied with your design."

Social studies also involves almost daily presentation by the children of some event from the news. The teacher's questions ask the children to expand what they say, to give more details, and to be more specific. Occasionally she adds some remarks to help them see connections between events.

The emphasis on expressing and illustrating ideas in social studies is accompanied in language arts by an emphasis on creative writing. Each child wrote a rhebus story for a first grader whom they had interviewed to see what kind of story the child liked best. They wrote editorials on pending decisions by the school board, and radio plays, some of which were read over the school intercom from the office, and one of which was performed in the auditorium. There is no language arts textbook because, the teacher said, "The principal wants us to be creative." There is not much grammar, but there is punctuation. One morning when the observer arrived the class was doing a punctuation ditto. The teacher later apologized for using the ditto. "It's just for review," she said. "I don't teach punctuation that way. We use their language." The ditto had three unambiguous rules for where to put commas in a sentence. As the teacher was going around to help the children with the ditto, she repeated several times, "Where you put commas depends on how you say the sentence; it depends on the situation and what you want to say." Several weeks later the observer saw another punctuation activity. The teacher had printed a five-paragraph story on an oak tag and then cut it into phrases. She read the whole story to the class from the book, then passed out the phrases. The group had to decide how the phrases could best be put together again. (They arranged the phrases on the floor.) The point was not to replicate the story, although that was not irrelevant, but to "decide what you think the best way is." Punctuation marks on cardboard pieces were then handed out and the children discussed, and then decided, what mark was best at each place they thought one was needed. At the end of each paragraph the teacher asked, "Are you satisfied with the way the paragraphs are now? Read it to yourself and see how it sounds." Then she read the original story again, and they compared the two.

Describing her goals in science to the investigator, the teacher said, "We use ESS (Elementary Science Study). It's very good because it gives a hands-on experience—so they can make *sense* out of it. It doesn't matter whether it [what they find] is right or wrong. I bring them together and there's value in discussing their ideas."

The products of work in this class are often highly valued by the children and the teacher. In fact, this was the only school in which the investigator was not allowed to take original pieces of the children's work for her files. If the work was small enough, however, and was on paper, the investigator could duplicate it on the copying machine in the office.

The teacher's attempt to control the class involves constant negotiation. She does not give direct orders unless she is angry because the children have been too noisy. Normally, she tries to get them to foresee the consequences of their actions and to decide accordingly. For example, lining them up to go see a play written by the sixth graders, she says, "I presume you're lined up by someone with whom you want to sit. I hope you're lined up by someone you won't get in trouble with." The following two dialogues illustrate the process of negotiation between student and teacher.

Teacher: Tom, you're behind in your SRA this marking period.
Tom: So what!
Teacher: Well, last time you had a hard time catching up.
Tom: But I have my [music] lesson at 10:00.
Teacher: Well, that doesn't mean you're going to sit here for twenty minutes.
Tom: Twenty minutes! OK. (He goes to pick out a SRA booklet and chooses one, puts it back, then takes another, and brings it to her.)
Teacher: OK, this is the one you want, right?
Tom: Yes.
Teacher: OK, I'll put tomorrow's date on it so you can take it home tonight or finish it tomorrow if you want.

* * * *

Teacher: (to a child who is wandering around during reading) Kevin, why don't you do *Reading for Concepts*?
Kevin: No, I don't *like Reading for Concepts.*
Teacher: Well, what are you going to do?

Kevin: (pause) I'm going to work on my DAR. (The DAR had sponsored an essay competition on "Life in the American Colonies.")

One of the few rules governing the children's movement is that no more than three children may be out of the room at once. There is a school rule that anyone can go to the library at any time to get a book. In the fifth grade I observed, they sign their name on the chalkboard and leave. There are no passes. Finally, the children have a fair amount of officially sanctioned say over what happens in the class. For example, they often negotiate what work is to be done. If the teacher wants to move on to the next subject, but the children say they are not ready, they want to work on their present projects some more, she very often lets them do it.

Executive Elite School. In the executive elite school, work is developing one's analytical intellectual powers. Children are continually asked to reason through a problem, to produce intellectual products that are both logically sound and of top academic quality. A primary goal of thought is to conceptualize rules by which elements may fit together in systems, and then to apply these rules in solving a problem. School work helps one to achieve, to excel, to prepare for life.

The following are illustrative. The math teacher teaches area and perimeter by having the children derive formulae for each. First she helps them, through discussion at the board, to arrive at $A = W \times L$ as a formula (not *the* formula) for area. After discussing several, she says, "Can anyone make up a formula for perimeter? Can you figure that out yourselves? (pause) Knowing what we know, can we think of a formula?" She works out three children's suggestions at the board, saying to two, "Yes, that's a good one," and then asks the class if they can think of any more. No one volunteers. To prod them, she says, "If you use rules and good reasoning, you get many ways. Chris, can you think up a formula?"

She discusses two-digit division with the children as a decision-making process. Presenting a new type of problem to them, she asks, "What's the *first* decision you'd make if presented with this kind of example? What is the first thing you'd *think*? Craig?" Craig says, "To find my first partial quotient." She responds, "Yes, that would be your first decision. How would you do that?" Craig explains, and then the teacher says, "OK, we'll see how that works for you." The class tries his way. Subsequently, she comments on the merits and shortcomings of several other children's decisions. Later, she tells the investigator that her goals in math are to develop their reasoning and mathematical thinking and that, unfortunately, "there's no *time* for manipulables."

While right answers are important in math, they are not "given" by the book or by the teacher, but may be challenged by the children. Going over some problems in late September the teacher says, "Raise your hand if you do not agree." A child says, "I don't agree with 64." The teacher responds, "OK, there's a question about 64. (to class) Please check it. Owen, they're disagreeing with you. Kristen, they're checking yours." The teacher emphasized this repeatedly during September and October with statements like, "Don't be afraid to say if you disagree. In the last [math] class, somebody disagreed, and they were right. Before you disagree, check yours, and if you still think we're wrong, then we'll check it out." By Thanksgiving, the children did not often speak in terms of right and wrong math problems, but of whether they agreed with the answer that had been given.

There are complicated math mimeos with many word problems. Whenever they go over the examples, they discuss how each child has set up the problem. The children must explain it precisely. On one occasion the teacher said, "I'm more—just as interested in *how* you set up the problem as in what answer you find. If you set up a problem in a good way, the answer is *easy* to find."

Social studies work is most often reading and discussion of concepts and independent research. There are only occasional artistic, expressive, or illustrative projects. Ancient Athens and Sumer are, rather, societies to analyze. The following questions are typical of those which guide the children's independent research: "What mistakes did Pericles make after the war?" "What mistakes did the citizens of Athens make?" "What are the elements of a civilization?" "How did Greece build an economic empire?" "Compare the way Athens chose its leaders with the way we choose ours." Occasionally the children are asked to make up sample questions for their social studies tests. On an occasion when the investigator was present the social studies teacher rejected a child's question by saying, "That's just fact. If I asked you that question on a test, you'd complain it was just memory! Good questions ask for concepts."

In social studies—but also in reading, science, and health—the teachers initiate classroom discussions of current social issues and problems. These discussions occurred on every one of the investigator's visits, and a teacher told me, "These children's opinions are important—it's important that they learn to reason things through." The classroom discussions always struck the observer as quite realistic and analytical, dealing with concrete social issues like the following: "Why do workers strike?" "Is that right or wrong?" "Why do we have inflation, and what can be done to stop it?" "Why do companies put chemicals in food when the natural ingredients are available?" etc. Usually the children did not have to be prodded to give their opinions. In fact, their statements and the interchanges between them struck the observer as quite sophisticated conceptually and verbally, and well-informed. Occasionally the teachers would prod with statements such as, "Even if you don't know [the answers], if you think logically about it, you can figure it out." And "I'm asking you [these] questions to help you think this through."

Language arts emphasizes language as a complex system, one that should be mastered. The children are asked to diagram sentences of complex grammatical construction, to memorize irregular verb conjugations (he lay, he has lain, etc. . . .), and to use the proper participles, conjunctions, and interjections, in their speech. The teacher (the same one who teaches social studies) told them, "It is not enough to get these right on tests; you must use what you learn [in grammar classes] in your written and oral work. I will grade you on that."

Most writing assignments are either research reports and essays for social studies, or experiment analyses and write-ups for science. There is only an occasional story or other "creative writing" assignment. On the occasion observed by the investigator (the writing of a Halloween story), the points the teacher stressed in preparing the children to write involved the structural aspects of a story rather than the expression of feelings or other ideas. The teacher showed them a filmstrip, "The Seven Parts of a Story," and lectured them on plot development, mood setting, character development, consistency, and the use of a logical or appropriate ending. The stories they subsequently wrote were, in fact, well-structured, but many were also personal and expressive. The teacher's evaluative comments, however, did not refer to the expressiveness or artistry, but were all directed toward whether they had "developed" the story well.

Language arts work also involved a large amount of practice in presentation of the self and in managing situations where the child was expected to be in charge. For example, there was a series of assignments in which each child had to be a "student teacher." The child had to plan a lesson in grammar, outlining, punctuation, or other language arts topic and explain the concept to the class. Each child was to prepare a worksheet or game and a homework assignment as well. After each presentation, the teacher and other children gave a critical appraisal of the "student teacher's" performance. Their criteria were: whether the student spoke clearly; whether the lesson was interesting; whether the student made any mistakes; and whether he or she kept control of the class. On an occasion when a child did not maintain control, the teacher said, "When you're up there, you have authority, and you have to use it. I'll back you up."

The teacher of math and science explained to the observer that she likes the ESS program because "the children can manipulate variables. They generate hypotheses and devise experiments to solve the problem. Then they have to explain what they found."

The executive elite school is the only school where bells do not demarcate the periods of time. The two fifth grade teachers were very strict about changing classes on schedule, however, as specific plans for each session had been made. The teachers attempted to keep tight control over the children during lessons, and the children were sometimes flippant, boisterous, and occasionally rude. However, the children may be brought into line by reminding them that "it is up to you." "You must control yourself," "you are responsible for your work," you must "set your priorities." One teacher told a child, "You are the only driver of your car—and only you can regulate your speed." A new teacher complained to the observer that she had thought "these children" would have more control.

While strict attention to the lesson at hand is required, the teachers make relatively little attempt to regulate the movement of the children at other times. For example, except for the kindergartners, the children in this school do not have to wait for the bell to ring in the morning; they may go to their classroom when they arrive at school. Fifth graders often came early to read, to finish work, or to catch up. After the first two months of school the fifth grade teachers did not line the children up to change classes or to go to gym, etc., but, when the children were ready and quiet, they were told they could go—sometimes without the teachers.

In the classroom, the children could get materials when they needed them and took what they needed from closets and from the teacher's desk. They were in charge of the office at lunchtime. During class they did not have to sign out or ask permission to leave the room; they just got up and left. Because of the pressure to get work done, however, they did not leave the room very often. The teachers were very polite to the children, and the investigator heard no sarcasm, no nasty remarks, and few direct orders. The teachers never called the children "honey," or "dear," but always called them by name. The teachers were expected to be available before school, after school, and for part of their lunch time to provide extra help if needed.

DISCUSSION AND CONCLUSION

One could attempt to identify physical, educational, cultural, and interpersonal characteristics of the environment of each school that might contribute to an empirical explanation of the events and interactions. For example, the investigator could introduce evidence to show that the following *increased* as the social class of the community increased (with the most marked differences occurring between the two districts): increased variety and abundance of teaching materials in the classroom; increased time reported spent by the teachers on preparation; higher social class background and more prestigious educational institutions attended by teachers and administrators; more stringent board of education requirements regarding teaching methods; more frequent and demanding administrative evaluation of teachers; increased teacher support services such as in-service workshops; increased parent expenditure for school equipment over and above district or government funding; higher expectations of student ability on the part of parents, teachers, and administrators; higher expectations and demands regarding student achievement on the part of teachers, parents, and administrators; more positive attitudes on the part of the teachers as to the probable occupational futures of the children; an increase in the children's acceptance of classroom assignments; increased intersubjectivity between students and teachers; and increased cultural congruence between school and community.

All of these—and other—factors may contribute to the character and scope of classroom events. However, what is of primary concern here is not the immediate causes of classroom activity (although these are in themselves quite important). Rather, the concern is to reflect on the deeper social meaning, the wider theoretical significance, of what happens in each social setting. In an attempt to assess the theoretical meaning of the differences among the schools, the work tasks and milieu in each will be discussed in light of the concepts used to define social class.

What potential relationships to the system of ownership of symbolic and physical capital, to authority and control, and to their own productive activity are being developed in children in each school? What economically relevant knowledge, skills, and predispositions are being transmitted in each classroom, and for what future relationship to the system of production are they appropriate? It is of course true that a student's future relationship to the process of production in society is determined by the combined effects of circumstances beyond elementary schooling. However, by examining elementary school activity in its social class context in the light of our theoretical perspective on social class, we can see certain potential relationships already developing. Moreover, in this structure of developing relationships lies theoretical—and social—significance.

The *working-class* children are developing a potential *conflict* relationship with capital. Their present school work is appropriate preparation for future wage labor that is mechanical and routine. Such work, insofar as it denies the human capacities for creativity and planning, is degrading; moreover, when performed in industry, such work is a source of profit to others. This situation produces industrial conflict over wages, working conditions, and control. However, the children in the working-class schools are not learning to be docile and obedient in the face of present or future degrading conditions or financial exploitation. They are developing abilities and skills of resistance. These methods are highly similar to the "slowdown," subtle sabotage and other modes of indirect resistance carried out by adult workers in the shop, on the department store sales floor, and in some offices.[11] As these types of resistance develop in school, they are highly constrained and limited

[11] See, for example, discussions in Levison (1974), Aronowitz (1978), and Benson (1978).

in their ultimate effectiveness. Just as the children's resistance prevents them from learning socially legitimated knowledge and skills in school and is therefore ultimately debilitating, so is this type of resistance ultimately debilitating in industry. Such resistance in industry does not succeed in producing, nor is it intended to produce, fundamental changes in the relationships of exploitation or control. Thus, the methods of resistance that the working-class children are developing in school are only temporarily, and *potentially*, liberating.

In the *middle-class school* the children are developing somewhat different potential relationships to capital, authority, and work. In this school the work tasks and relationships are appropriate for a future relation to capital that is *bureaucratic*. Their school work is appropriate for white-collar working-class and middle-class jobs in the supportive institutions of United States society. In these jobs one does the paperwork, the technical work, the sales and the social service in the private and state bureaucracies. Such work does not usually demand that one be creative, and one is not often rewarded for critical analysis of the system. One is rewarded, rather, for knowing the answers to the questions one is asked, for knowing where or how to find the answers, and for knowing which form, regulation, technique, or procedure is correct. While such work does not usually satisfy human needs for engagement and self-expression, one's salary can be exchanged for objects or activities that attempt to meet these needs.

In the *affluent professional school* the children are developing a potential relationship to capital that is instrumental and expressive and involves substantial negotiation. In their schooling these children are acquiring *symbolic capital*: they are being given the opportunity to develop skills of linguistic, artistic, and scientific expression and creative elaboration of ideas into concrete form. These skills are those needed to produce, for example, culture (e.g., artistic, intellectual, and scientific ideas and other "products"). Their schooling is developing in these children skills necessary to become society's successful artists, intellectuals, legal, scientific, and technical experts and other professionals. The developing relation of the children in this school to their work is creative and relatively autonomous. Although they do not have control over which ideas they develop or express, the creative act in itself affirms and utilizes the human potential for conceptualization and design that is in many cases valued as intrinsically satisfying.

Professional persons in the cultural institutions of society (in, say, academe, publishing, the nonprint media, the arts, and the legal and state bureaucracies) are in an expressive relationship to the system of ownership in society because the ideas and other products of their work are often an important means by which material relationships of society are given ideological (e.g., artistic, intellectual, legal, and scientific) expression. Through the system of laws, for example, the ownership relations of private property are elaborated and legitimated in legal form; through individualistic and meritocratic theories in psychology and sociology, these individualistic economic relations are provided scientific "rationality" and "sense." The relationship to physical capital of those in society who create what counts as the dominant culture or ideology also involves substantial negotiation. The producers of symbolic capital often do not control the socially available physical capital nor the cultural uses to which it is put. They must therefore negotiate for money for their own projects. However, skillful application of one's cultural capital may ultimately lead to social (for example, state) power and to financial reward.

The *executive elite school* gives its children something that none of the other schools does: knowledge of and practice in manipulating the socially legitimated tools of analysis of systems. The children are given the opportunity to learn and to utilize the intellectually and socially prestigious grammatical, mathematical, and other vocabularies and rules by which elements are arranged. They are given the opportunity to use these skills in the analysis of society and in control situations. Such knowledge and skills are a most important kind of *symbolic capital*. They are necessary for control of a production system. The developing relationship of the children in this school to their work affirms and develops in them the human capacities for analysis and planning and helps to prepare them for work in society that would demand these skills. Their schooling is helping them to develop the abilities necessary for ownership and control of physical capital and the means of production in society.

The foregoing analysis of differences in school work in contrasting social class contexts suggests the following conclusion: the "hidden curriculum" of school work is tacit preparation for relating to the process of production in a particular way. Differing curricular, pedagogical, and pupil evaluation practices emphasize different cognitive and behavioral skills in each social setting and thus contribute to the development in the children of certain potential relationships to physical and symbolic capital, to authority, and to the process of work. School experience, in the sample of schools discussed here, differed qualitatively by social class. These differences may not only contribute to the development in the children in each social class of certain types of economically significant relationships and not others, but would thereby help to *reproduce* this system of relations in society. In the contribution to the reproduction of unequal social relations lies a theoretical meaning, and social consequence, of classroom practice.

The identification of different emphases in classrooms in a sample of contrasting social class contexts implies that further research should be conducted in a large number of schools to investigate the types of work tasks and interactions in each, to see if they differ in the ways discussed here, and to see if similar potential relationships are uncovered. Such research could have as a product the further elucidation of complex but not readily apparent connections between everyday activity in schools and classrooms and the unequal structure of economic relationships in which we work and live.

REFERENCES

Althusser, L. Ideology and ideological state apparatuses. In L. Althusser, *Lenin and philosophy and other essays*. Ben Brewster, Trans. New York: Monthly Review Press, 1971.

Anyon, J. Elementary social studies textbooks and legitimating knowledge. *Theory and Research in Social Education*, 1978, *6*, 40–55.

Anyon, J. Ideology and United States history textbooks. *Harvard Educational Review*, 1979, *49*, 361–386.

Apple, M. W. *Ideology and curriculum*. Boston: Routledge and Kegan Paul, 1979.

Apple, M. W., & King, N. What do schools teach? *Curriculum Inquiry*, 1977, *6*, 341–358.

Aronowitz, S. Marx, Braverman, and the logic of capital. *The Insurgent Sociologist*, 1978, *8*, 126–146.

Benson, S. The clerking sisterhood: rationalization and the work culture of saleswomen in American department stores, 1890–1960. *Radical America*, 1978, *12*, 41–55.

Bernstein, B. *Class, codes and control, Vol. 3. Towards a theory of educational transmission*. 2nd ed. London: Routledge and Kegan Paul, 1977.

Bourdieu, P., & Passeron, J. *Reproduction in education, society, and culture*. Beverly Hills, Calif.: Sage, 1977.

Bowles, S., & Gintis, H. *Schooling in capitalist America: educational reform and the contradictions of economic life*. New York: Basic Books, 1976.

Braverman, H. *Labor and monopoly capital: the degradation of work in the twentieth century*. New York: Monthly Review Press, 1974.

Dreeben, R. *On what is learned in school*. Reading, Mass.: Addison-Wesley, 1968.

Jackson, P. *Life in classrooms*. Holt, Rinehart & Winston, 1968.

Lampman, R. J. *The share of top wealth-holders in national wealth, 1922–1956*: A study of the National Bureau of Economic Research. Princeton, N.J.: Princeton University Press, 1962.

Levison, A. *The working class majority*. New York: Penguin Books, 1974.

New York Stock Exchange. *Census*. New York: New York Stock Exchange, 1975.

Rist, R. C. *The urban school: a factory for failure*. Cambridge, Mass.: MIT Press, 1973.

Sarasan, S. *The culture of school and the problem of change*. Boston: Allyn and Bacon, 1971.

Smith, J. D., & Franklin, S. The concentration of personal wealth, 1922–1969. *American Economic Review*, 1974, *64*, 162–167.

U.S. Bureau of the Census. *Current population reports*. Series P–60, no. 118. Money income in 1977 of families and persons in the United States. Washington, D.C.: U.S. Government Printing Office, 1979.

U.S. Bureau of the Census. *Statistical abstract of the United States: 1978*. Washington, D.C.: U.S. Government Printing Office, 1978.

Williams, R. *Marxism and literature*. New York: Oxford University Press, 1977.

Wright, E. O. *Class, crisis and the state*. London: New Left Books, 1978.

CHAPTER TEN

Toward a Culturally Based Pedagogy: A Case Study of One Yup'ik Eskimo Teacher

Jerry Lipka

This case study is part of an ongoing collaborative research project with Yup'ik teachers in southwest Alaska. On the surface, this lesson appears to be an art lesson, but a cultural interpretation suggests it is about subsistence and survival. Implicit in this case for minority education is the importance of adapting social interactions, knowledge, and values toward the minority culture as one possible means for improving schooling. ESKIMO EDUCATION, CLASSROOM ETHNOGRAPHY, CASE STUDY

THEORETICAL BACKGROUND

One of the problems with research on minority schooling and, in particular, schooling of Native Americans is that we have been looking, at times, in the wrong places (McDermott, 1987). Much of the research on and about the education of Native Americans from the Sixties to the present was done in classrooms with indigenous schoolchildren being taught by "outsiders," resulting in images of the "silent Indian" (Dumont, 1972), the "teacher as enemy" (Wolcott, 1974), and disharmony and lack of synchrony in the classroom (J. Collier, 1973). Not surprisingly, the cultural conflict or cultural discontinuity model gained saliency (Erickson, 1987). However, paying heed to Cazden's (1983) call to go beyond the status quo, some of the same research offers insights into classes where things were going right—active discourse was taking place between Indian children and their teacher (Dumont, 1972), and synchrony existed between an Anglo teacher and his students (M. Collier, 1979). Yet, these examples were reported as the exception to the rule—silence, resistance, and a lack of trust reigned.

There is a growing body of research that examines indigenous teachers teaching indigenous children and minority teachers teaching minority children. Modiano (1973) reports Indian teachers with less education and training than their mestizo counterparts perform better in Indian village schools. Research on Amish society and education (Hostetler & Huntington, 1971; Hostetler, 1980) reports equal or better standardized test scores for Amish children in Amish schools than Amish children in non-Amish schools. Similarly, in their film analyses of southwest Alaskan schools, J. Collier (1973) and M. Collier (1979) report that Yup'ik preschool teachers with less education and training than their counterparts seemed to have classrooms in which student intensity was high, and where there was a rhythm and flow between teacher and student, student and student, and class and content. Furthermore, research on Athabaskan teachers in Alaskan classrooms has reported different ways of organizing lessons (Barnhardt, 1982; Van Ness, 1981), while Mohatt and Erickson (1981) have shown that an Odawa teacher uses culturally compatible ways of organizing and instructing in her Odawa classroom. A sense of kinship in the classroom (Lubeck, 1984) is engendered, allowing for "civility" (Erickson, 1984, 1987) and cooperation instead of conflict and resistance (Ogbu, 1987). It appears that organizing and conducting schooling in a functionally similar way to community and cultural norms accounts for some of the trust and smoothness reported above.

Common sense and research suggest that indigenous teachers should be teaching indigenous students in indigenous communities. Yet the vast majority of the teachers in indigenous communities in Alaska, Australia, and Canada are typically novices from the majority culture, providing a model of teaching that is, unfortunately, oftentimes inappropriate for their indigenous counterparts who are preparing to become teachers. Very few role models exist for indigenous teachers. Nonindigenous teachers organize, conduct, and reward students in ways quite different from the community's prevailing indigenous values (Mohatt & Erickson, 1981; Philips, 1983). However, even more insidious is that these "outside" models of teaching have become the accepted norms, the standards upon which indigenous teachers are prepared and judged. In fact, there is evidence that when indigenous teachers emulate Western-oriented pedagogical practices, it sometimes results in the displacement of cultural norms for Western norms. For example, competition displaces cooperation (Graves & Graves, 1978), formal school discourse (initiation-response-evaluation) replaces overlapping speech and co-speakers, resulting in declined talk and empty bidding (Malcolm, 1979, 1980, 1982), and co-membership in ethnic identities is lost in formal role structures (Labov, 1972). Ethnicity does not appear to be the key classroom variable; it is the actual interactional style and relationship between the students and their teacher.

When Yup'ik teachers are teaching Yup'ik children and relating in culturally compatible ways in village settings, many of the so-called factors of minority school failure may be dismissed. For example, logically, there is none of the phonetic linguistic interference noted by Malcolm (1979) with Australian Aborigines, or of the sociolinguistic interference described in the literature on Native Americans and schooling (Philips, 1972, 1983; Greenbaum & Greenbaum, 1983); nor is there a lack of cultural knowledge, so cultural misunderstandings do not occur. In short, the cultural discontinuity between community and school is significantly reduced. Resistance theory (Dumont, 1972; Giroux, 1983) makes much less sense in a classroom where the teacher is your uncle or your aunt and where most of the school employees come from your community.

More recent research is beginning to extend our understanding of the importance of social relations beyond the notion of participant structures and the rules for speech events in the classroom to include the interrelationship between social relations and intrapsychic development. Work by Vygotsky, as analyzed in Cole (1985), suggests that social relations and the internalization of those relations are an essential part of cognitive development. Similarly, work by Lave (1988) demonstrates the contextual and interactive nature of everyday mathematics across cultures and situations.

Research on minority and indigenous school-aged students reveals a "relational" cognitive style, which has been noted with children from an extended family home environment that includes multiple caretakers. A relational cognitive style recognizes the importance of the whole and the context, as opposed to an "analytical" cognitive style, which is abstract and decontextualized (Cohen, 1969). Similarly, Denny's work on Inuit mathematics (1981, 1983) reports the contextualized socially and environmentally negotiated aspects of Inuit math as well as linguistic encoded concepts of mathematics that differ from mainstream approaches to mathematics. Stairs (1991) suggests that Intuit use a contextualized—relational—approach to cognition called *isumaqsayuq*, rather than a decontextualized—content disconnected from lived experience—approach.

Scollon and Scollon (1981) show how discourse patterns in Athabaskan communities are organized differently than in mainstream society. Cazden (1988) and Erickson (1984) note how Black American children, at times, use a different oral and written discourse pattern from mainstream society, which is oftentimes not recognized by their teachers. Heath (1982) has shown how paying attention to differing styles and ways of presenting questions to Black Appalachian schoolchildren resulted in more discourse between teachers and their students.

The case for indigenous teachers teaching indigenous students extends beyond the immediate classroom social relations and their concomitant cognitive dimensions to cultural survival (Harris, 1990), particularly for small, isolated indigenous groups. Therefore, it is the contention of this article that relationships—the "fourth R" (McDermott, 1977)—particularly cultural and social, are a key aspect of an emerging Yup'ik pedagogy. This case study demonstrates how one Yup'ik Eskimo teacher reinforces Yup'ik values, emphasizing the themes of subsistence and survival, and how he organizes his classroom along principles of individual autonomy and group harmony and solidarity. His classroom is a synthesis of Yup'ik and school culture.

This case study of one lesson of one experienced Yup'ik Eskimo teacher will illustrate that what appears on the surface to be an ordinary art lesson presented immediately before a holiday (which has been interpreted as "so much filler" by teacher educators involved in indigenous education in another culture [Lipka, 1990a]) is, in fact, a lesson about survival, respect, care, and patience. Such an interpretation is possible if the social environment created by this Yup'ik teacher is seen in relation to Yup'ik culture and community norms. Supportive data will be drawn from other lessons from this teacher, as well as from other Yup'ik and non-Yup'ik teachers. The possible significance of this lesson to the larger issues of minority school failure may well be that when minority teachers and their students have a degree of freedom to create classroom environments that are based upon a common respect for their cultural values, social organization, and discourse patterns, an ease and smoothness of in-classroom behavior will emerge, forming the basis upon which learning can develop.

This case study is drawn from a larger ongoing collaborative action-research project of the Yup'ik teachers (the group is called Ciulistet—leaders) of Southwest Region Schools and the author. For the past two and half years the Ciulistet group and I have been working together on:

1. understanding what Yup'ik teachers in the classroom have in common with each other;
2. identifying exemplary instances of Yup'ik pedagogy that simultaneously enhance Yup'ik identity; and
3. preparing a strategy for a systematic process of implementing, assessing, and evaluating classroom interventions that build upon culturally based pedagogy.

REGIONAL BACKGROUND

The Bristol Bay region of Alaska, located approximately 350 air miles southwest of Anchorage, is a roadless wilderness connected to the rest of the state and the surrounding villages by jet, bush planes, skiffs, and snow machines. The region's 26 villages are dispersed over 55,000 square miles, an area approximately the size of Ohio. This seemingly vast and unoccupied "wilderness" is used much of the time for subsistence hunting, fishing, and gathering by the area's major inhabitants, the Yup'ik Eskimo. In addition to the seasonal rounds of subsistence, cash is earned in this mixed economy through commercial fishing, trapping, and government sector jobs. Increasingly, the village and regional corporations, which are an outgrowth of the Alaska Native Claims Settlement Act (1971), are becoming an integral part of the socioeconomic climate of this region and the state of Alaska. Yet today, whole villages still move to their fish camps, where the year's supply of fish will be caught, dried, and smoked.

THE SCHOOLS

The region's villages range in size from approximately 60 to 600 people. Each village has its own primary school, and most of the larger villages have their own secondary schools, which range in size from one- to ten-teacher schools. Multigraded classrooms and teachers teaching outside of their area of expertise are a fact of life in rural Alaskan schools. Children in three of the villages start school speaking Yup'ik as their first language. However, the most recent testing of language dominance reveals that English is rapidly becoming dominant in two of these three schools. Approximately 90% of the teachers in the region are from outside the state of Alaska. There are few Yup'ik teachers teaching in Yup'ik classrooms, even in villages with 100% Yup'ik year-round residence. The vast majority of the Yup'ik teachers are graduates of the Cross-Cultural Education Development Program (X-CED) at the University of Alaska, Fairbanks

METHODOLOGY

The Yup'ik teachers (of Southwest Region Schools in the Bristol Bay region of Alaska) and I have collaborated with Stanford University's Teacher Assessment Project (Minority Consortium) to videotape and analyze classrooms of Yup'ik teachers and, occasionally, non-Yup'ik teachers. During the early phases of the research, our work was mostly exploratory, looking for ways in which the Yup'ik teachers were contributing to their schools and communities. Our research agenda has remained open and evolving. The Yup'ik teachers found it almost "cathartic" to see tape after tape of similar classroom patterns. Teachers anywhere often feel isolated from their colleagues, and in rural Alaska this is compounded by the great physical distance between schools and the small number of teachers. Moreover, Yup'ik teachers have not had the opportunity to observe other Yup'ik teachers.

The videotaping was done in a very straightforward manner. The camera was placed in a far corner of the classroom on a tripod, where it recorded all activity prior to, immediately following, and during the lessons. Following the procedures identified by Erickson and Shultz (1981), footage was selected for further analysis. In this particular study, one lesson was selected for its unusual, from a non-Yup'ik orientation, style and delivery. The teacher used a combination of demonstrating and modeling while speaking, and supported group cohesiveness and student self-reliance. The lesson was transcribed. In addition, lesson phases or lesson transitions were noted, nonverbal behaviors were recorded during some of the transitions, and an analysis of the discourse pattern was undertaken. A multidimensional analysis was achieved by analyzing the lesson along the following dimensions of social organization: how the lesson was started, the types of statements used to begin the lesson, the way the underlying Yup'ik values were brought to light, the relationship of the teacher to the students, and the way the content was delivered. In addition, the lesson was viewed and analyzed by the Yup'ik teachers, and an interview was conducted with the teacher while viewing the videotape. Specific sections of the tape that were of particular interest stimulated questions such as "Why did you do this?" and "Why didn't you do this?" In addition, during the viewing we would pause the tape and replay sections of mutual interest and analyze micro-events.

THE LESSON

The following lesson took place in March 1989 in a fifth-grade art class. Capenaq (his Yup'ik name) Sharp, an experienced teacher, is Yup'ik, and Yup'ik is his first language. However, all of his lessons that I observed, including this one, were delivered in English. The students speak primarily in Yup'ik to each other, as well as to the teacher. Occasionally, utterances are made in English. This lesson occurred at the end of the school day, right before the annual beaver round-up festival, held in the nearby regional center. At the close of the lesson, most of the students and their families were flying to the festival.

At this time of year, the trappers have finished trapping beavers and have already nailed their beaver pelts to wooden structures for drying. Fur buyers congregate in the regional center where the trappers walk around carrying their pelts to the different buyers. Beaver round-up also signifies the end of a long winter and the start of spring.

Direct excerpts from the transcription follow with brief remarks and then a more formal analysis.

1.	(sound of children laughing and talking)		
2.	T:	You need your pencils.	
3.	T:	Each of you will need a pencil.	(a student runs)
4.	T:	No running.	(students talking)
5.	T:	You need a pencil.	
6.	S_1:	All right a pencil.	
7.	T:	Good.	(students continue to file in)
8.	S_2:	Oh boy.	(students switch to Yup'ik)
9.	T:	You remember your story yesterday?	(teacher positions himself in front of his desk)

During the preparatory part of the lesson, the teacher's daughter enters the room and walks to his desk. She addresses her father head down, and the teacher does not make eye contact with his daughter, but looks down and to the side as they talk quietly. She leaves. In a few seconds, he issues directives to the students, "You need a pencil" (lines 2, 3, and 5). The first utterance occurs with only two students present (18% of the class). In total, only these six brief utterances were issued to the class to get them ready for the lesson. During this one minute and ten seconds, 91% of the teacher's time was spent in silence. The first introductory remarks are made in line 9: "You remember your story yesterday?" The teacher says this as he moves toward his desk, and students immediately switch from talking to one another to focusing their attention on him, although a few students have not entered the room yet. Within the next few seconds, all of the students are present, and no remarks are made to the late arrivals.

17.	T:	What did he tell?	
18.	S:	Beaver.	(choral response)
19.	T:	Yes, they catch some beaver.	
20.	T:	And, uh, what did Mr. Lobby say he and Nance did?	
21.			(three students respond in Yup'ik)
22.	S_2:	Shoot' em.	
23.	T:	Yes, we shoot' em.	
24.	T:	It was trapped, right?	(students are responding very quickly, coming right in on the teacher's closing words)
25.	S_3:	Snare.	
30.	T:	What do the trappers do after they skin it?	

Boys are animated, and in Yup'ik explain what the trappers do after they skin beavers. One boy demonstrates with his hands. The teacher laughs softly and continues the discourse that he had planned for this lesson.

31. T: Uh huh.
32. T: Okay.
33. T: What I want you to do is, I want you to hold this paper about like so in half and kinda of pinch it down there.

In lines 10 through 33, the boys in the class respond very quickly to these questions. There are no responses from the girls in this phase of the lesson. In line 21 three boys respond simultaneously. The question was not directed at any particular person. In line 24 the boys start talking over the teacher and respond to each other. In line 22 a student states, "Shoot 'em." The teacher's response is, "Yes, we shoot 'em." However, the teacher's next response is, "It was trapped, right?" First he acknowledges what the students have said and then he alters it to, "It was trapped." But, then he adds, "right?" The "right?" signifies respect for the students—for their agreement. In lines 30 through 33, the boys are answering in a very excited tone (all of the boys' responses are in Yup'ik). In this sequence, one boy says what the trappers do after they skin a beaver and is interrupted by another boy who demonstrates with his hands what trappers do while he is speaking. The teacher laughs softly and breaks eye contact with the student. The student picks up this nonverbal cue and ceases talking and refocuses his attention back to the teacher. Line 33 is a shift in the lesson. He is now simultaneously demonstrating and telling the students what he wants them to do.

A little further into the lesson the teacher's comments are as follows:

70. T: How many of you have ever watched your dad or somebody in your family make a beaver blanket?	
75. T: You could do this on the floor?	(students do not respond to his invitation to work on the floor)
82. T: We could do this on the floor. We could do this on the floor. . . . We could put this on the floor and you could tie your pencil like so and you'll make a compass.	(many voices speaking at once)

The first invitation, line 75, is not stated as a directive to the students. He is foreshadowing what will happen next. This sentence is said in the same tone of voice as the preceding sentences. However, in the next invitation there are multiple cues or markers for the students, to let them know that he wants them to sit on the floor. He puts more emphasis on "we could," and this invitation is coordinated with his sitting on the rug. As he starts to do his work on the floor, three students immediately begin to move onto the rug. Also, this phase of the lesson marks a shift in responsiveness by gender. Heretofore, the boys were actively participating, speaking and demonstrating with their hands how beavers are trapped, skinned, and hung to dry. At this juncture, it is the girls who are the first to sit on the rug.

The next section of the lesson is concerned with how to make a circle, how to hold your pencil, and where to place the pen. This occurs on the floor, as the teacher continues to work on his project. Students gather around, observe, and leave.

105. T: Did you see how I made the beaver blanket out in the hallway?
107. S: No.
108. T: Did you see me make little marks like this?
109. T: Okay.
110. T: You'll need to do the same thing.
111. T: Except yours will be smaller.
112. T: See.
113. T: Those are the nail marks.
119. T: We're making a *aqsatuyaaq*.
120. T: Beaver pelt.

Discourse Style

This whole section of the lesson is simulating how a beaver pelt should be properly made. Lines 70 and 119 are introductions to what the students will be doing today. They will be making a beaver pelt. However, when I interviewed the teacher, he said that the introduction was given by the student who showed the class, correctly, how the trappers skin a beaver. The teacher framed his lesson in a manner that appears unorthodox to a non-Yup'ik. He said he expected that the students understood the lesson's topic was beaver pelts.

Aqsatuyaaq (young beaver) is the only Yup'ik word used by the teacher in this lesson. Discussion continues about young beavers for a brief period.

136. T: You need to use your little marker and make the nail marks, see.

137.	T:	These are where the nails stretch the beaver to make a blanket.	
138.	T:	Right.	
139.	S:	Yup.	
140.	T:	Okay.	
144.	T:	And, when you are done you need scissors.	
145.	T:	So go ahead and cut your beaver blanket.	
155.	T:	You have to be patient.	
156.	T:	Just cut your, um, blanket out.	
158.	T:	This is what beaver round-up is all about.	

Careful attention is being paid to properly making a "beaver blanket" by cutting it out as if it were stretched.

166.	S:	*Assirtuq* (good) Cap (pronounced "chop").	
182.	T:	Okay, mine is all done.	
183.	T:	Cute, cute beaver blanket, huh.	
184.	T:	What do you think you are going to do when you are all done?	
185.	S:	Draw.	(choral response)
188.	T:	You are gonna make something about beaver round-up on the inside.	

This follows line 184 and is an elaboration of what the students will do in this section of the lesson. The teacher is at his desk doing the next piece of work, writing and drawing on his blanket. Some students have gathered around him. They leave and others come. The rest of the class is working at their desks and on the floor. There is much talking.

201.	T:	Who is our visitor?	(said very softly, almost inaudibly)
202.	S_1:	Qayaq.	(the boy's Yup'ik name)
202.	S_2:	Qayaq. Qayaq. Qayaq.	(said in a rising crescendo)
203.	S_3:	(responds in Yup'ik)	

A student from another class enters the room. He cautiously surveys the class and slowly moves into it, seating himself near his brother. The teacher makes no other remarks to this student.

205. T: Okay, we could write letters like beaver, and where would I put round-up?
209. T: What do you call this? (he is referring to the hyphen)
225. T: You could write anything you want to as long as it is about beaver round-up.
242. T: So for now, you could go ahead make your blanket, cut it out and if you want to you could write some letters on it and prepare for next week.
250. T: I wish we had more time, but we always only have fifteen or twenty minutes for art.

BRIEF DISCUSSION AND ANALYSIS

It is clear from the outset that a different sociolinguistic style than that used by mainstream Anglo teachers (Mohatt & Erickson, 1981) is being presented by the teacher in this case study. Notice, for example, the parsimonious use of words, the silences, and the considerable rights his students have to take responsibility for obtaining the resources and assistance they need to perform the task. This video has been shown to a number of different teacher educators (see Lipka, 1990a). Typically, Anglo viewers become impatient and want to know what he is going to do. However, the students show no sign of impatience and have no difficulty following his discourse. Quite to the contrary, the students are on task most of the time, are enthusiastic during certain discussions, and have no problem shifting from phase to phase, even when lesson phases shift abruptly.

If we reorganize the teacher's utterances that relate to what the students will do in today's lesson, then we begin to get a more familiar introductory pattern as follows:

> How many of you ever watched . . . somebody make a beaver pelt? What I want you to do is, I want you to hold this paper about like so in half and kinda of pinch it down there. We are finding where the center might be. We're making a *aqsatuyaaq* (young beaver). What do you think you are going to do when you are all done? You are gonna make something about beaver round-up on the inside.

If we compare these statements to one of the non-Yup'ik teacher's introductory remarks, differences in instructional discourse will emerge.

> Okay. Today we're—this morning, the first thing we're going to do is pick countries for what you're going to do your report on. And then we're going to talk about what requirements you have to fulfill for this unit. Okay? We're going to talk about the paper that you need to write and your map. . . .

The non-Yup'ik teacher states in a linear manner, first this and then this, prior to doing anything. The verbal messages are decontextualized from the content and the action in which the students are to engage. This procedure of introducing the lesson to students is common educational procedure (Good & Brophy, 1987) and is considered good pedagogy. These differences in ordering of introductory statements between Anglo and Yup'ik teachers are not mere happenstance; they are culturally grounded in Yup'ik and mainstream American culture. An analysis of lesson openings in several videotaped lessons with Yup'ik teachers indicates a similar parsimonious approach to introductions. Also, in Bristol Bay villages, introductory messages are not piled on top of one another. Activities begin without the customary lengthy verbal introduction Anglos expect. This suggests differences in cognitive ordering and structuring. The students seem quite comfortable following the modeled behavior. The teacher's instructional style also includes modeling (doing his "own work"), joining in with the students (seated on the floor with the students as he blends into the class), and reinforcing peer-group solidarity and deep respect for individuals.

There is intentionality in his style. For example, there are a few times during the lesson when students will say *nutmen* (where), and the teacher intentionally ignores the students. He does not want to reinforce dependence on verbal instruction during activities that call for observation. Instead, he is expecting them to visually follow the demonstration. He allows the students to move from their seats to get a closer look at his work or the work of one of their classmates. He is not necessarily the major focal point during this lesson; he shares the instructional load with the other group members. This is part of his strategy to build group solidarity.

Student Responses

The students are animated in this class. This is in contrast to the stereotypical image of the "silent Indian." There is evidence here that suggests a correlation between the culturally laden content and the social organization of the classroom with the students' enthusiasm. During the first phases of the lesson, the male students become very involved, possibly because it is a male role to trap beaver. We see the male students answering rapidly, talking to each other, and correcting each other about how trappers skin and dry a beaver. The students are allowed to respond in culturally comfortable ways, without the formalities of raising their hands, and are not required to speak in English. This shared intimate knowledge of specific cultural activities combined with culturally appropriate ways of responding gives students an opportunity to talk enthusiastically in class. In other videotapes made in a different village, similar response patterns were noted when the teacher localized the lesson, used her intimate knowledge of the students' use of the environment, and included it in her discussion (Lipka, 1990b). She also allowed students to alter the typical teacher to student discourse pattern. Again, with content of interest to the students and with familiar sociolinguistic rules, the students engage enthusiastically in class discussions. In the few instances where a direct remark such as "What are you doing?" was made, the student did not respond.

Cultural Values

The teacher in this case study is teaching cultural values related to how one skins a beaver—from its being trapped to its being dried and cut out, as well as how one is to act during such a process—with skill, care, and patience. Some teacher educators who have viewed this tape suggested that he may be killing time because this is an end-of-the-week lesson right before a holiday. Others said that the lesson is busywork and not creative. However, the contention of this analysis is that the students are learning the proper way, as defined by their culture, to act while doing such tasks. Indeed, this teacher is certainly not interested in busywork or killing time, when at the end of the lesson he says, "I wish we had more time, but we always only have fifteen or twenty minutes for art."

Other cultural values related to subsistence and survival are also being taught. In other analyzed tapes of this teacher, the cultural values of survival, knowledge of the land, and subsistence clearly emerge. These values are consistent with the story he told at the annual Bristol Bay Youth Conference a few years ago.

> How many of you had to survive away from the community? Here is the reason that I am standing here—because I survived this one incident. I made a mistake when I was just a little boy. In the old days when we were young, story-telling time was our entertainment. There was no television, no movies, but we listened to our elders tell stories to us and that was our entertainment. Anyway, I am going to share this with you, and this happened when I was about 4–5 years old. Way back then we got ready, got in our boat, and traveled 10–12 miles away from the place where I was born. We brought our tent, our food, and we went egg hunting. When we got to a place where we were going to have our lunch before we started hunting for eggs. So [what] I did, was I wrapped the [boat's] rope [around a tree] and it wasn't tight. We were not watching very closely, but as the tide went out, the boat went down and it pulled the boat down and out with the tide. And as the boat went down and out it sort of pulled the rope loose and my uncle started yelling. [Yup'ik]

> Which means "Our boat is drifting away, drifting away." So I ran to it, but too late it was already on the other side of the river, so it floated down the river. I was going to jump into the water, but I was too small, my uncle and aunt told me, "Don't do that." That was how scared I was. My uncle and aunt were very calm, my brother was really screaming, you know, I guess to him it was one of the scariest things that had ever happened to him, and also to me. But after the boat drifted down the river, my uncle did not say anything, he was calm and he told us to gather driftwood. So we looked around and gathered driftwood. He took every little piece that we found, cloth, old ropes and then he got maybe four/five logs and he put them together. He used the old ropes, the old clothing, and he made a raft. And after he made the raft, he made a paddle, and after he made the paddle he set the raft down on a creek and he put a pile of sticks on the raft where he would sit to keep him up out of the water. He also found an old five-gallon square can and I think he kept that in case that some wave might tip him over and he needed something to float on. Anyway, before he left to go search for the boat, he said a prayer, and the prayer was said to help him find the boat. So after he said his prayer, he drifted down the creek and he was on his way to look for his boat. And in the meantime, my aunt asked us to gather all the driftwood that we could and we piled them up and we made a little shelter, just in case my uncle did not return. So all day long, we kept listening for a boat and it was dark and the clouds were getting thicker and thicker and it was getting darker and the wind was blowing harder and harder. As the tide came up, I heard something—it was a really thin sound—it grew louder and louder and by golly, it was my uncle and that was the happiest time of my life, because I know my uncle came and here is what he told me: When he was searching for the boat, you know floating down the river, he had to make a decision because the stream split up into two branches. When he got there, he had to make the decision—which way did the boat drift? Did the boat drift this way or did it drift that way? Here is what he said: He put his hand on his tongue and checked the direction of the wind and the wind was blowing from the east so he knew he had to make this turn. What this lesson taught me is not to worry. Every time something happens to us we like to worry and we also have to make use of the natural resources that we have around if we are to survive. We have to use our brain.

This story underscores the significance of survival and knowledge of the land for the Yup'ik people. These critical values, survival and knowledge of the land, will be shown to be an integral part of the lesson, although they are hidden from casual observation.

Social Relations: Individual Autonomy and Group Cohesiveness

It is also interesting to note the social relations in this class. Students have a different set of "rights and responsibilities" than we would find in a mainstream classroom. The classroom has a relaxed, almost informal, manner.

The way students attend to his demonstrations and then observe peers is reminiscent of a lesson, taught by an elder during a cultural heritage week, I observed years ago in another Bristol Bay village. Similarly, the students in the elder's class moved in close to observe, then attended to peers, and then back to the elder according to their own judgment and timing. More recently, during another cultural heritage week, a teacher was giving a lesson on drying smelt, and these students, in a similar fashion, would choose who they attended to and when they attended (Lipka, 1990b). Students in all these situations began and finished the task at their own pace, within the confines of school. The teachers did not say, "Okay, let's all begin now," or, "Okay, it's three o'clock and it is time to leave, everybody hand in your work." The task itself partially determined time.

Students call the teacher Cap, a diminutive of his first name. They do not raise their hand to leave their seat. More important, students have the right not to comply with some procedural directives, even though the task is not negotiable. For example, when the teacher invites students to sit on the floor with him and begin this phase of the activity, some students choose to do so and some choose not to do so. However, there are no further statements, persuasions, coaxing, or any other form of control to get the students to the task. In fact, this manner of working with the students was not recognized as effective by Anglo-Australian teachers who viewed this segment. Rather, it was perceived as lacking in control. Yet, from a Yup'ik cultural perspective, what was done respected the individual and reinforced group harmony. He intentionally develops and fosters the group's cohesiveness and the students' attentiveness to other students. The fact that his very first remarks in the lesson, "You need a pencil," were stated to only two students becomes much more understandable when viewed from his perspective. He reported that he knew the other students would follow them and be ready to perform the task. I did not recognize this, after many viewings of the tape, until I interviewed him while viewing the tape.

The typical lesson pattern of elicitation, response, and evaluation (Mehan, 1979) is altered during this lesson. Even though the tripartite pattern of instruction is used within the lesson, the evaluative part has a different form here, as it entails, on occasion, "Yes" to an incorrect response. This pattern was also observed in lessons by an Odawa teacher (Mohatt & Erickson, 1981), and later reanalyzed by Malin (personal communication from Merridy Malin, 1990). Students, on occasion, offer clearly incorrect responses, as, for example, when they respond, "Shoot 'em," and the teacher says, "Yes, we shoot 'em [beaver]." Then in the next line he says, "It was trapped, right?" The boys respond with "Yup." I contend that this interaction is a compromise between the mainstream teacher discourse patterns and Yup'ik cultural norms, which typically avoid correcting someone or directly telling them that they are wrong. In addition, when he corrects the students in the next sentence by stating that the beaver was trapped, he ends the statement with a question, "right?" This is not a rhetorical statement. The boys respond. It is a cultural affirmation.

In line 201 the teacher asks, "Who is our visitor?" Of course, he knows who the visitor is. The student responds, "Qayaq [the boy's Yup'ik name]." Another student says, "Qayaq, Qayaq, Qayaq, Qayaq," in a rising crescendo. Another student says, "He is going to be one of us now." The teacher interprets this as "kind of a teasing statement against him," but not sufficiently strong enough to ask him to leave. He states,

> I don't mind the visitor as long as he is not interrupting. . . . I want the approval of the class. . . . I knew they knew him. . . . again I didn't want to be *direct*, cause, if I got started paying attention to Eric it would interrupt [the class]. If one of them didn't want him to be there, they would ask him to leave.

Capenaq (his Yup'ik name) again balanced his responsibility as a teacher against his knowledge of what is culturally appropriate and his idea of not being direct. He very subtly initiated a sequence that determined if the visitor would stay or not by asking (his class, not the visitor), "Who is our visitor?" The students responded by accepting the visitor into the classroom. At that point in the videotape the visitor repositions himself from facing sideways to facing the group. He visibly acknowledges the class's acceptance. This is another example of the blending of roles and cultural norms, signifying a different set of relations in this classroom than in a non-Yup'ik one.

Other Supporting Evidence

The underlying premise of this culturally based interpretation of the lesson is the importance of subsistence and survival. In addition to the survival story, other supporting evidence emerges from other classroom sessions as well as informal talks out of the classroom. Other video footage shows Capenaq presenting a unit on survival. The students must imagine that they are shipwrecked near Sitka. During the development of the unit, the students are asked to view a videotape and look for natural resources that would help them survive. At one point the teacher says, "Do you remember the story I told you about how we survived . . . how I survived? . . . We had to make a shelter out of driftwood. . . ." At another point in the lesson, one of the students tells him a story. The teacher says, "Did you hear Junior? He just told us a story. One little boy from the village hooked himself. In order to get help right away, he had to build a fire and cover it with grass and make a smoke signal; that's a good emergency story."

The importance of survival is further illustrated on another occasion. The teacher's daughter was involved in a caribou project. The essence of the project was to reintroduce caribou into a section of Bristol Bay where caribou have been extinct. Students flew from the region to the caribou release site.

At the release site, the students planned to assist the United States Department of Fish and Wildlife Service (USFWS) in releasing caribou. Shortly after the students arrived at the release site, the weather closed in, which made flying home impossible. The students and their chaperon were stuck in somewhat dangerous conditions. Fortunately, a number of villagers who also were at the release site assisting the USFWS decided that they would take the students back to the village by snow machine. A number of hours later, the snow machine party arrived safely back at the village. Because I was concerned about the students' safety, I telephoned Capenaq, not knowing if the students returned safely to the village. After the initial formalities, and once I knew of the students' safety, I asked if the students learned much from the experience of working with the caribou project. The response was, "They learned that they were not prepared to survive. . . . They were not dressed warm enough. . . . The next time they go out they will know better."

The underlying values and meaning of these classroom lessons relate to the larger cultural context from which this lesson emanates—Yup'ik values of survival and subsistence. On the surface, this lesson is about art and writing a story. However, the hidden curriculum in this lesson is about survival, patience, care, and doing things properly. Once this is realized, this lesson takes on a different meaning. This meaning is apparently not lost on the students, but it evades Anglo viewers of this tape who do not share the same context and underlying value structure of the lesson.

In this lesson, the teacher is using shared cognitive knowledge related to subsistence and survival and, at the same time, is conveying knowledge in a culturally appropriate manner through modeling and parallel work. The work of cross-cultural psychologists (Brenner, 1985; Cole, 1985; Lave, 1985, 1988) provides support for the importance of context, negotiation, and subsequent internalization of events into knowledge and psychological schema. It appears that the lesson being analyzed fits well into what Cohen (1969) calls "relational cognitive style."

Where Do We Go From Here? Further Research

Although we are interested in refining our understanding of how Yup'ik teachers teach, we are coming to the point where we can more systematically plan classroom intervention strategies based upon our research to date. We know that orienting school learning to the community and adapting the culture of the school toward the students' culture makes a difference in the students' comfort by using students' prior knowledge, and by engaging students in a familiar and known discourse style. To do this, we envision making curricula changes that take into account modes of instruction, cooperative learning, and the significance of Yup'ik cultural knowledge and activities. We will encourage using social organizations and discourse structures that support the Yup'ik values of group harmony and helping behavior while teaching academic content. We are planning to implement a series of curriculum units, which will be assessed both for unfolding classroom processes and for their relationship to cognitive and affective outcomes. Through such work, we hope to revise and refine our emerging pedagogical model. We hope to more clearly isolate those variables that allow students to perform in their "comfort zone," enhance Yup'ik identity, and support cognitive gains.

CONCLUSION

The importance of social relations, which imply shared context, knowledge, and values in the classroom, is underscored by this case study. The importance of cultural continuity and, concomitantly, cultural survival for small, isolated ethnic minority groups is also underscored in this lesson. The fourth "R," social relationships, is a critical factor in indigenous education. These social relations can create the conditions that make learning feasible and likely. However, the very nature of the Yup'ik style of teaching, with its lesson beginning without the customary teacher talk and its differing discourse patterns, increases the likelihood of this social and cognitive style being misinterpreted by supervisors and teaching colleagues from mainstream society. From analysis of lessons like these, the Yup'ik teachers themselves need to create alternative models of teaching, which can become accepted as equally effective means of teaching. The need for alternative models of evaluation is as great. Otherwise, the very differences that create the conditions for a Yup'ik-oriented classroom environment may be the same conditions that place Yup'ik teachers at odds with their non-Yup'ik colleagues.

Many of the Yup'ik characteristics of this lesson and others reported elsewhere (Lipka, 1990a) are not the ones being taught through the field-based teacher education program at the University of Alaska, Fairbanks. In fact, despite going through years of teacher preparation that emphasize mainstream teacher behaviors, this teacher and the others in the research project display patterns of teaching that are highly effective in their culture.

Some of what we are learning from the Yup'ik teachers can be effective elsewhere. For example, contextualizing schooling, making a meaningful relationship between school and community, certainly has a place in schooling anywhere. Recently, Stairs (1988), in her response to Resnick's (1987) concern about the importance of context in learning, suggested that we could all learn from the Inuit the importance of contextualizing learning. Similarly, exemplary cases of Yup'ik Eskimo teachers contribute further to our understanding of cooperative learning, as they integrate school learning into community interactional patterns and values (Lipka, 1990b).

The Ciulistet group's ongoing work of analyzing videotapes of their teaching is providing an exciting and important process for professional development and teacher preparation. The Yup'ik teachers themselves, through the support of the local school district and the University of Alaska, Fairbanks, are in a position to acknowledge their own teaching attributes and build upon them in the future. Curricular changes combined with increasing numbers of Yup'ik teachers able to build a culturally based pedagogy that recognizes and incorporates culturally compatible social relations and Yup'ik values of group cohesiveness, cooperation, and shared knowledge can have a positive effect upon schooling in rural Alaska and beyond.

ACKNOWLEDGMENTS

I wish to thank all the members of the Ciulistet group for their continued support and trust in me. In particular, I wish to thank Capenaq Sharp for his invaluable insights and interpretations of his classroom video footage. I wish to express my appreciation to Eleanor Bourke, Director, and Keith McConnochie, acting Director, Key Centre, the South Australian College of Advanced Education, for their support while working on this article during my sabbatical.

REFERENCES

Barnhardt, Carol (1982). Tuning In: Athabaskan Teachers and Athabaskan Students. *In* Cross-Cultural Issues in Alaskan Education, Volume 2. Ray Barnhardt, ed. Pp. 144–164. Fairbanks: Center for Cross-Cultural Studies, University of Alaska.

Brenner, Mary E. (1985). The Practice of Arithmetic in Liberian Schools. Anthropology and Education Quarterly 16(3):177–186.

Cazden, Courtney B. (1983). Can Ethnographic Research Go Beyond the Status Quo? Anthropology and Education Quarterly 14(1):33–41.

Cazden, Courtney B. (1988). Classroom Discourse: The Learning of Teaching and Learning. London: Heinmann Educational Books, Inc.

Cohen, Rosalie A. (1969). Conceptual Styles, Culture Conflict, and Nonverbal Tests of Intelligence. American Anthropologist 71(5):828–856.

Cole, Michael (1985). The Zone of Proximal Development: Where Culture and Cognition Create Each Other. *In* Culture, Communication, and Cognition: Vygotskian Perspectives. James Wertsch, ed. Pp. 146–161. Cambridge: Cambridge University Press.

Collier, John Jr. (1973). Alaskan Eskimo Education: A Film Analysis of Cultural Confrontation in the Schools. New York: Holt, Rinehart & Winston.

Collier, Malcolm (1979). A Film Study of Classrooms in Western Alaska. Fairbanks: Center for Cross-Cultural Studies, University of Alaska.

Denny, J. Peter (1981). Curriculum Development for Teaching Mathematics in Inuktitut: The Learning-from-Language Approach. Canadian Journal of Anthropology 1(2):199–204.

Denny, J. Peter (1983). Content in the Assessment of Mathematical Concepts from Hunting Societies. *In* Human Assessment and Cultural Factors. S. H. Irvine and John W. Berry, eds. Pp. 155–161. New York: Plenum Press.

Dumont, Robert V. Jr. (1972). Learning English and How to Be Silent: Studies in Sioux and Cherokee Classrooms. *In* Functions of Language in the Classroom. Courtney B. Cazden, Vera P. John, and Dell Hymes, eds. Pp. 344–369. New York: Teachers College Press.

Erickson, Frederick (1981). Some Approaches to Inquiry in School-Community Ethnography. *In* Culture and the Bilingual Classroom: Studies in Classroom Ethnography. H. Trueba, G. P. Guthrie, and K. Au, eds. Pp. 17–35. Rowley, Mass.: Newbury House Publishers.

Erickson, Frederick (1984). School Literacy, Reasoning, and Civility: An Anthropologist's Perspective. Review of Educational Research 54(4):525–546.

Erickson, Frederick (1987). Transformation and School Success: The Politics and Culture of Educational Achievement. Anthropology and Education Quarterly 18(4):335–355.

Erickson, Frederick, and Jeffrey Shultz (1981). When Is a Context? *In* Ethnography and Language in Educational Settings. J. Green and C. Wallet, eds. Pp. 147–161. Norwood, N.J.: Ablex.

Giroux, Henry (1983). Theories of Reproduction and Resistance in the New Sociology of Education: A Critical Analysis. Harvard Education Review 53(3):257–293.

Good, Thomas L., and Jere Brophy (1987). Looking in Classrooms. London: Harper & Row Publishers.

Graves, Nancy B., and Theodore Graves (1978). The Impact of Modernization on the Personality of a Polynesian People. Human Organization 37(2):115–135.

Greenbaum, P. E., and Susan B. Greenbaum (1983). Cultural Differences, Nonverbal Regulation, and Classroom Interaction: Sociolinguistic Interference in American Indian Education. Peabody Journal of Education 61(1):16–33.

Harris, Stephen (1990). Two-Way Aboriginal Schooling: Education and Cultural Survival. Canberra: Aboriginal Studies Press.

Heath, Shirley Brice (1982). Questioning at Home and at School: A Comparative Study. *In* Doing the Ethnography of Schooling: Educational Anthropology in Action. G. Spindler, ed. Pp. 105–131. New York: Holt, Rinehart & Winston.

Hostetler, John (1980). Amish Society, 3d edition. Pp. 183–185. Baltimore: Johns Hopkins University Press.

Hostetler, John, and Gertrude Huntington (1971). Children in Amish Society: Socialization and Education. Pp. 88–95. New York: Holt, Rinehart & Winston.

Labov, William (1972). Language in the City: Studies in the Black English Vernacular. Philadelphia: University of Pennsylvania Press.

Lave, Jean (1985). The Social Organization of Knowledge and Practice: A Symposium. Anthropology and Education Quarterly 16(3):171–176.

Lave, Jean (1988). Cognition in Practice: Mind, Mathematics and Culture in Everyday Life. Cambridge: Cambridge University Press.

Lipka, Jerry (1990a). Cross-Cultural Teacher Perceptions of Teaching Styles. Kaurna Higher Educational Journal 1:33–45.

Lipka, Jerry (1990b). Integrating Cultural Form and Content in One Yup'ik Eskimo Classroom—A Case Study. Canadian Journal of Native Education 17(2):18–32.

Lubeck, Sally (1984). Kinship and Classrooms: An Ethnographic Perspective on Education as Cultural Transmission. Sociology of Education 57 (October):219–232.

Malcolm, I. (1979). Classroom Communication and the Aboriginal Child: A Sociolinguistic Investigation in Western Australian Primary Schools. Unpublished Ph.D. dissertation, University of Western Australia, Perth.

Malcolm, I. (1980). The Discourse of the Reading Lesson: Sociolinguistic Observations in Aboriginal Classrooms. *In* Reading into the '80s. T. Bessell-Browne, R. Latham, N. Reeves, and E. Gardiner, eds. Pp. 81–97. Adelaide, Australia: Australian Reading Association, Inc.

Malcolm, I. (1982). Verbal Interactions in the Classroom. *In* English and the Aboriginal Child. R. Eagelson, S. Kaldor, and I. Malcolm, eds. Pp. 165–191. Canberra, Australia: Curriculum Development Centre.

McDermott, Ray (1977). Social Relations as Contexts for Learning. Harvard Educational Review 47(3):198–213.

McDermott, Ray (1987). The Explanation of Minority School Failure, Again. Anthropology and Education Quarterly 18(4):361–364.

Mehan, Hugh (1979). Learning Lessons: Social Organization in the Classroom. Cambridge: Harvard University Press.

Modiano, Nancy (1973). Indian Education in the Chiapas Highlands. Pp. 135–138. New York: Holt, Rinehart & Winston.

Mohatt, Gerald V., and Frederick Erickson (1981). Cultural Differences in Teaching Styles in an Odawa School. *In* Culture and the Bilingual Classroom: Studies in Classroom Ethnography. Henry T. Trueba, Grace Gutherie, and Kathryn Au, eds. Pp. 105–119. Cambridge, Mass.: Newbury House Publishers.

Ogbu, John U. (1987). Variability in Minority School Performance: A Problem in Search of an Explanation. Anthropology and Education Quarterly 18(4):312–334.

Philips, Susan U. (1972). Participant Structures and Communicative Competence: Warm Springs Children in Community and Classroom. *In* Functions of Language in the Classroom. Courtney Cazden, Vera John, and Dell Hymes, eds. Pp. 370–394. New York: Teachers College Press.

Philips, Susan U. (1983). The Invisible Culture: Communication in Classroom and Community on the Warm Springs Indian Reservation. New York: Longman Press.

Resnick, Lauren (1987). Learning In School and Out. Education Researcher 16(9):13–20.

Scollon, Ron, and Suzanne Scollon (1981). Narrative, Literacy, and Face in Interethnic Communication. Norwood, N.J.: Ablex.

Stairs, Arlene (1988). Native Models for Learning (A reply to Lauren Resnick). Educational Researcher 17(6):4, 6.

Stairs, Arlene (1991). Learning Processes and Teaching Roles in Native Education: Cultural Base and Cultural Brokerage. Canadian Modern Language Review 47(2):280–294.

Van Ness, Howard (1981). Social Control and Social Organization in an Alaskan Athabaskan Classroom: A Microethnography of "Getting Ready" for Reading. *In* Culture and the Bilingual Classroom: Studies in Classroom Ethnography. Henry T. Trueba, Grace Guthrie, and Kathryn Au, eds. Pp. 120–138. Cambridge, Mass.: Newbury House Publishers.

Wolcott, Harry (1974). The Teacher as an Enemy. *In* Education and Cultural Process: Toward an Anthropology of Education. George D. Spindler, ed. Pp. 411–427. New York: Holt, Rinehart & Winston.

CHAPTER ELEVEN

Welcome to My House: African American and European American Students' Responses to Virginia Hamilton's *House of Dies Drear*

Linda A. Spears-Bunton

BACKGROUND

The first section of this article addresses the relationship between reader response and culture. The second section consists of portraits of a teacher and her students as they navigated their way through a series of African American literary texts. Most of my remarks focus on Virginia Hamilton's *House of Dies Drear* (1968) because the reading of this text marked a turning point for the teacher and students I observed.

The portraits are drawn from a study which sought to explore the cultural dimensions of reader response among poor and working-class African American and European American high school students (Spears-Bunton, 1989). Ethnographic data including class observations and interviews were collected from a single eleventh grade honors English class of 28 students for six months. The school in which the data were collected serves two neighborhoods—one mostly African American, the other mostly European American—with a history of racially motivated animosity between them. All subject names used in this article are pseudonyms.

THE PROBLEM

The crisis of reading and school-related failures among African American students seems to persist without regard to the students' IQs or their facility with language and cognitive tasks outside of school (Labov, 1969; Rist, 1973;

Heath, 1983; Erickson, 1984). This seems to be true despite the development of sophisticated technology for reading instruction and new instructional methods based on comprehension research (Goodman, 1982). Moreover, instructional technology, special school programs, and the school curriculum seem to accentuate rather than alleviate the problems of African American students (Rist, 1973; Schofield, 1982; Erickson, 1984; Goodlad, 1984; Page, 1987).

Clearly, without an understanding of the cultural knowledge, attitudes and strategies African American students bring to a text, research will continue to document failure but do little to alter this phenomenon. These issues are particularly critical to our developing understanding of adolescent African American students because it is at this stage of cognitive, emotional, and social development that the crisis and failure of monocultural education may have the most chilling effects. As Gilligan (1988), in her discussion of the political and controversial nature of morality and gender research, asks: What is the cost of the omission of the voices of half the nation's population in research, academic disciplines, and education? A similar question respective to the voices of African Americans must be posed as we seek to uncover how those different voices inform perception and affect response to literature.

THE INTERPLAY BETWEEN CULTURE, LITERATURE, AND LITERACY

Given the scholarship which suggests that engagement with literature may pave the road to literacy (Britton, 1978; Hickman, 1983) and the historical prominence of the storyteller in African American communities (Smitherman, 1977; Stanford & Amin, 1978; Hemenway, 1978; Baker, 1984, 1988; Morrison, 1984), one must ask a different set of questions regarding why large numbers of African American children exhibit the behaviors typical of "disabled" readers. Cross-cultural studies of literature indicate that culture has a pronounced role in shaping the content and symbolic references in a literature text (Brewer, 1988; Rosenberg, 1988). Those studies indicate that one might anticipate differences in response to literary content depending upon one's cultural affiliation. For example, Steffenson et al. (1979) found that when an adult population matched by sex, age, level of education, academic specialty, and marital status read a letter describing a wedding in their own culture, they read faster with more recall and made culturally appropriate extensions of the text. Conversely, when readers read a letter about a wedding in a culture different from their own, they took longer to read, their recall decreased, and they made culturally inappropriate distortions of the text.

Several critical issues emerge from the Steffenson et al. study: (1) the cultural background of the reader may have a profound influence on reading comprehension, memory, and learning from a text; and (2) the reading problems of African American students may be related to a cultural mismatch between the student and the texts read for school. Their research supports the findings of both historical and contemporary reader response research in three important aspects: (1) engaging a text necessitates a dialogue—the willing participation in an exchange of ideas, opinions and perspectives (Purves, 1968, 1981; Freire & Macedo, 1987); (2) readers continuously attempt to link elements in a text with their own experience (Richards, 1929; Squire, 1964); and (3) sociocultural differences between readers, including prior knowledge of behavior of fictive characters, and readers' attitudes toward these behaviors affect their responses to literary illusions (Beach, 1983). Their findings further suggest that teachers and researchers need to consider the cultural content of the text as problematic rather than neutral. By locating the issue of culture as a source of conflict *at the level of the text*, scholars may be better able to reconceptualize research paradigms and drive a pragmatic marriage between theory and praxis.

AFRICAN AMERICAN LITERATURE: CONFLICT AND RECONCILIATION

African American literature in a secondary school classroom may serve a variety of purposes. These include the following: (1) the articulation of the African American voice may draw the conflicts and contradictions of class, race, and gender bias in a democratic society into sharp relief; (2) it may expose subtle and overt forms of bias among groups of readers; and (3) it may set the stage whereupon a community of readers may come to challenge the sociocultural assumptions within and outside their own group's cultural affiliations.

Engaging conflict and contradiction may also attend the development of critical literacy. However, such engagement, within the context of the lived culture of the secondary school English classroom, may be confounded by competing demands which include the following: (1) teachers' course-loads which may exceed 130 students; (2) district mandates to "cover" English subskills in specific amounts; and (3) limited material resources. Thus, the notion of teacher time and the corollaries of that time—how much material can be included, when, and how—are both critical and problematic to the inclusion of African American literature in high school. The following illustrates this point.

Miss Paula's Blues: So Much to Do—Too Little Time

Paula Reynolds, a veteran European American teacher of English, agreed to participate in the research project (Spears-Bunton, 1989) for professional and personal reasons. First, her students asked her to teach African American literature. Second, she was disenchanted with the version of American literature presented in the anthology; and third, she wanted to compensate for what she defined as her own "ignorance." Her self-assessment was based upon her determination that despite her master's degree in English she had little knowledge of the African American literary canon.

> All this time I've wondered where these people were for four hundred years. They were here all the time . . . I just wasn't taught. . . . I didn't even know until this summer that Timbuktu was a real place. . . . That's a shame, a doggone shame.

Paula avowed that neither she nor her students would be as ignorant by the end of the 1989–90 school year. By defining ignorance as the consequence of not being properly taught, Paula defined the curriculum as problematic and her classroom as the site for individuals to act as agents for social change (Weiler, 1988). As the first and only individual to broach a subject that had never been taught in her school before, she opened herself to criticism from administrators and colleagues. As a European American female teaching both African American and European American students, she was exposed to challenges from students as well. According to Paula, she fortified herself by reading everything she could get her hands on about the subject, by sharing her personal excitement about new learning with colleagues and students, and by drawing upon her belief that "literature is about understanding how other people feel and how they see the world."

Paula's struggle to decide how much African American literature to include in her curriculum and how to offer these materials to her students derived from her two-pronged question: "What happens to Black kids who never get to read a book written by a Black author, and how do White students feel about the emphasis on Black literature?" Thus, the allocation of class time and teacher-directed emphasis on African American literature posed compelling questions for Paula. Her queries underscored her search for ways to establish symmetry in her honors literature curriculum while giving equal attention to the traditional curriculum.

Adding Some Things On

To resolve the conflict Paula juxtaposed an African American perspective onto her historical literary framework. For example, she supplemented the "planters and puritans" material in the traditional course anthology by adding African American historical documents and literature to the reading of *The Scarlet Letter* (1981). The supporting materials included Harriet Jacobs's (1988) "The Perils of a Slave Woman's Life," Julius Lester's "Louis" and "Ben" (1972), and Charles Johnson's "The Education of Mingo" (1987). In addition to reading in class and reading several chapters of these texts nightly as homework, students and teacher attended to weekly vocabulary lists, composition lessons, and a term paper. Trying to serve triple masters—the canon, district mandates, and African American literature—required Paula and her students to read constantly. Both African and European American students met Paula's enthusiasm and assignments with cacophonous protestations against teacher-imposed work. The African American students leveled their most vocal criticisms at *The Scarlet Letter* and the traditional anthology materials. Importantly, student resistance to teacher-imposed work set the stage for the emergence of cultural and racial conflicts.

The Storm Before the Calm

Class "discussion" of *The Scarlet Letter* frequently was interrupted by requests for Paula to read Lester's (1969) "Stagolee." Whenever Paula complied, students laughed uproariously, calmed themselves, and then resumed their composure. They were able to convince Paula to read that story five times in as many weeks. Jacobs's "Narrative of a Slave Girl" also provoked a lively but digressive debate. Latoya, a "mixed-race" student, asked if Harriet had "good" hair. Smiling, Paula responded to the girl with questions of her own: "Why did you ask that? What is 'good' hair? What in the narrative made you think of that?" Before Latoya could answer, Burt, a European American student, made a comment to an African American male student about "buckwheat, peas, and naps," whereupon a European American female student intervened, telling Burt: "Shut up, this is interesting." Paula then managed to redirect the students' attention back to the text.

On the surface, most of the students seemed to enjoy the African American literature Paula offered them; however, below the surface, tension brewed. The African American students were active participants in class discussions while the European American students were relatively quiet. Paula viewed the latter group's silence as problematic. "I hate silence," she remarked. "I like to know what they are thinking." Inadvertently the class had separated into small groups along racial lines, with a single exception: "the fellas," four of Paula's male students (two African Americans and two European Americans), typically joked and failed harmoniously. However, she noted subtle changes as the class progressed: Troy, the leader of the African American "fellas," abandoned the group when he wanted to read or complete an assignment, but he only read the African American literature components of the class assignments.

It was Burt who brought the tension to the surface when Paula expelled him from the room for popping balloons during class. Shouting at Paula, he explained his behavior and his failing grades by saying, "I hate Black literature." When I talked to Paula about this apparent contradiction, she responded directly and with a sense of relief:

> See, I knew it. There is racism in this school and in my class. I think he is basically a very confused boy. He is probably a racist but doesn't know it, and neither do his buddies. Well, better that it comes out so I can deal with it.

This public display of cultural tension mirrored the more private and subtle cultural tensions in African American and European American students. When I met Paula's students in August 1989 none of them had read any African American literature; however, their expressed attitudes toward such texts were drawn upon obvious ethnic and racial lines. The African American students articulated the view that there were differences between African Americans and other people and that African American literature was tied to their personal survival. The European American students were cautious and contradictory in discussing cultural differences. In their statements they seemed to distance themselves from the issue of culture. Two examples excerpted from transcripts of interviews with an African American and a European American student, respectively, illustrate this point:

> . . . I would read about struggle—how long it took to fight for what we have now . . . because this is where our heritage comes from. . . . It'll [African American literature] be different in language and the way people live or the customs they live by . . . (Tasha)

> . . . I think that slavery and everything—it seems like such an old issue. I think there's no sense in talking about the past. I don't like to be in a position where you have to pick from side to side what you are. We should all be just equal Americans not African Americans . . . they're the same as us. (Courtney)

Although both students make distinctions between the past and the more immediate present, their association with the past is strikingly different. Tasha affirms that the past is connected to her present situation and concerns; Courtney articulates ambivalence, some which may be related to the presence of an African American adult (the interviewer). Even so, Courtney distances her present and her cultural group from "them" and from a past that lacks personal relevance for her.

Reconciliation: Miss Paula's Song

When Paula informed her students that they would be getting another novel to read, they were less than enthusiastic. Most of them had managed to fail the final exam on "that book [*The Scarlet Letter*] Miss P. gave us." On the appointed day, the students strolled up to Paula's desk to receive their new book, *The House of Dies Drear*. Some of them held the book away from their bodies as if it had a very foul smell. A few peered surreptitiously at the back cover.

The next day, however, one of the students, a vocal, self-proclaimed "White male chauvinist superior being" and erstwhile critic of all literature as "stupid lies," bounced into class and asked her excitedly: "Who was behind the mirror? Was it Mr. Pluto? Who was Mr. Pluto? How did he get into the house?" Another student exclaimed: "I've read more of this already than all of that other one." Before students and teacher could exchange "good mornings"—even before roll could be taken—discussion about the book was initiated and sustained by the students for the first half hour of class.

Paula then instructed the class to read silently for 30 minutes and complete a grammar assignment. For the first time in six weeks, the classroom took on a library-like quietness. Paula eased into the chair at her desk and picked up her copy of the book as her students sat engrossed before her, elbows and novels settled on their own desks. The big clock ticked away the reading time, yet no one seemed to notice. One minute before the bell, Paula spoke up to alert her students.

When they were gone, Paula virtually jumped out of her chair, whooping joyously. "Did you see them?" she asked me. "They were reading! They were actually reading their little hearts out! I was afraid to stop them, afraid to break the spell! It's a miracle! Even the fellas, who never do *anything*, were reading!"

From that day, the vocabulary lists disappeared from the side board. The revolution in Room 161 gave way to questions, negotiations, interpretations—to "book talk" (Chambers, 1985). At last, the students had a text they were reading, feeling, and thinking about. Every one completed the reading before Paula's deadline and they each passed all the written assignments. Paula directed her time away from making students read to teaching them how to write formal, structured paragraphs using *House* and its characters as focal points. The writing lessons provided them with a way of transforming and transferring thought and feeling into text.

Reading in the Spirit

In taped interviews Tasha and Courtney revealed two more miracles. For the five weeks prior to the introduction of the *House* reading assignment Tasha's response to my questions about her reading was, "Unless the spirit hits me, Tasha don't do no reading." She maintained this posture despite her acknowledgment that being a good student with a positive and determined attitude were important to her, that college and law school were part of her plans for the future, and that English and journalism were her favorite subjects. Equally contradictory was her attitude about writing and her reputation as an astute school newspaper journalist:

> I love to write about anything . . . sometimes I can express my thoughts better on paper. When I write my stories, mostly about what happened, you really have to listen—pay attention so that when other people read they can say, "Well, it did happen like that." Then, I figure out some way to put my comments in—the way I feel.

Tasha's attitude toward reading and her strategy for coping with canonical texts impacted negatively on her grades. She acknowledged that whatever reading of *The Scarlet Letter* she had done was done "quick, real quick to get it over with." She had participated in small group discussions and writing activities by closing the book and putting her head down. Both Tasha and Paula had begun to doubt whether honors-level coursework was suitable for her, and Tasha expressed the view that "maybe college isn't for me after all."

At the end of six weeks, however, Tasha bounced into our interview session and responded to my request to "tell me about your reading of *The House of Dies Drear*" with a deluge of words. She said she liked the book and identified with (its main character) Thomas, and she was enjoying the book's mystery, its language, and the vivid pictures it conjured in her head. She reported that this reading experience reminded her of the enjoyment she derived from reading to little children: "You can really get into it, you can put in motion and little voices." As she mused:

> Do you remember those doors? One [in *The Scarlet Letter*] was a prison door; you know, a place for keeping people in like a slave. The other door [in *The House of Dies Drear*] made you free. Do you think Miss P. will let me write a paper about that—about the doors?

Passing the open door of Room 161 after school that day, I observed Paula and Tasha sitting with their heads tilted together absorbed by the word images they were constructing on the computer screen. They looked like two navigators charting new ground.

Courtney's Revision

When asked to talk about her reading of *House*, Courtney smiled, settled back in her chair, and wrapped her arms snugly about herself. Then she began to speak:

> Oh, I could just see those caves. I can imagine running across that river there and getting to that house. I would have explored every one of those caves and I would have been so glad to be there and to be safe. . . . You know, maybe Black literature should be set aside, special like, so I can see it better for myself.

Courtney's response to *House*, her choice of language about the text, suggests that she engaged the text in a personal and affective manner. She visualized herself in the novel's dark caves. So close was her identification with Thomas, her favorite character, that when he dropped a flashlight in one cave scene, Courtney reported that she "grabbed his hand and ran." Identifying with the plight of a runaway slave, Courtney found wonder and security under the house of Dies Drear. Moreover, she revised her thinking about the cultural differences between people and among literary texts. Her references to African American literary texts changed from comments about what "they [teachers] wanted [students] to read and understand" to observations on how she felt about her reading. Her references to "them" (African Americans) were replaced with "*I* would have run, *I* would have felt glad and safe." As we closed our interview, she indicated that she would "love to visit a house" like the one described in the novel and that she planned to buy its sequel.

During the lessons on *House*, Courtney's grades did not change significantly; she had always been a good student. What began to change was her attitude toward African American people. Although she claimed to have a few African American friends, and despite school integration, Courtney's vision of cultural distinctiveness was limited to the superficial—to noting differences in hairstyles and food preferences. The reading she did in Paula's class, the new information and new understanding she gained, seemed to foster in her a desire to question old assumptions. For Courtney, a visit to the house of Dies Drear was an opportunity to analyze the biases of her racial/cultural group. In later interviews she began to speak passionately and critically about family members and friends who belonged to racist organizations:

> . . . these gangs like the KKK and everything—I mean, they're not necessary. There are people who had a hard life, like my brother-in-law, and they just take it out on Black people.

SUMMARY AND IMPLICATIONS

The educational applications of cultural inclusion are far reaching and specific yet problematic. On an individual level the reading of culturally conscious African American literary texts may introduce turned-off readers to the world of literacy. Moreover, the reading of culturally conscious texts may provide a bridge upon which both African American and European American adolescent readers may build and ultimately expand their literacy experiences (Sims, 1982). The development of higher or deeper literacy moves students toward questioning, reflecting, and participating in an evolving dialogue about traditions and ideas (Langer, 1988; Wolf, 1988). This kind of literacy is critically different from acquiescence to received interpretations, and it is essential to the achievement of success in school subjects as well as to fuller participation in the larger society.

Research further reminds us that students typically learn what is consciously and unconsciously taught. Students, including teachers who have been students, attend to both the manifest and the hidden curriculum (Purves, 1981; Sola & Bennett, 1985; Marshall, 1986). Research and universities can support teachers like Paula by welcoming the voices of African Americans in their research agendas and curricula because neither her willingness to re-examine her own priorities, particularly the use of teacher time and resources, nor her courage to do so is typical. Such battles with "ignorance" are often isolated ones.

Paula's introduction of African American literature into her curriculum invited individual and group confrontation on difficult issues of race, sex, and class; yet, importantly, students crossed perceptual, gender, and cultural lines as they engaged the world of the text. Following the reading experience of *The House of Dies Drear*, the differences in Paula's students' scholarship, school work, and test performance tended to converge; both the successful students and those less successful performed equally well on classroom tasks. By giving Tasha a perceptual space and a cultural lens through which she could view the world of literature, *House* opened a door through which an African American student could explore the symbolic referents in both African American and European American fiction. The experiences of both Tasha and Courtney remind us that response to literature is a cumulative, recursive, and evolutionary process in which readers transact with a text, reflect upon their own experiences of it, and then participate in discussions as part of a larger community such as the classroom (Rosenblatt, 1976, 1978; Fish, 1980; Langer & Smith-Burke, 1982; Langer, 1988; Wolf, 1988). Moreover, the experiences of Paula and her students serve to remind us that response to literature occurs within a triad—reader, text, and context (Hickman, 1983; Langer, 1982)—and that facilitating active response takes time and multiple and diverse literary experiences.

REFERENCES

Baker, H. A., Jr. (1988). *Afro-American poetics: Revisions of Harlem and the Black aesthetic.* Wisconsin: University of Wisconsin Press.

Baker, H. A., Jr. (1984). *Blues ideology and Afro-American literature: A vernacular theory.* Chicago: University of Chicago Press.

Beach, R. (1983). Attitudes, social conventions and response to literature. *Journal of Research and Development in Education, 16*(3), 47–51.

Brewer, W. F. (1988). Story structure, characterization, just world organization, and reader affect in American and Hungarian short stories. *Poetics, 17,* 395–415.

Britton, J. (1977). The nature of the reader's satisfaction. In M. Meeks, A. Warlow, & G. G. Barton (Eds.), *The cool web: The pattern of children's reading* (pp. 106–111). London: The Bodley Head.

Chambers, A. (1985). *Book-Talk: Occasional writing on literature and children.* New York: Harper and Row.

Erickson, R. B. (1984). School literacy, reasoning and civility: An anthropologist's perspective. *Review of Educational Research, 54*(4), 525–546.

Fish, S. (1980). *Is there a text in this class?: The authority of interpretive communities.* Cambridge, MA: Harvard University Press.

Freire, P., & Macedo, D. (1987). *Literacy: Reading the word and the world.* South Hadley, MA: Bergin and Garvey.

Gilligan, C., Ward, J. V., Taylor, J. (Eds.). (1988). *Mapping the moral domain: A contribution of women's thinking to psychological theory and education.* Cambridge, MA: Harvard University Press.

Goodlad, J. I. (1984). *A place called school.* New York: McGraw-Hill.

Goodman, Y. M. (1982). Retellings of literature and the comprehension process. *Theory in Practice, 21*(4), 301–307.

Hamilton, V. (1968). *The house of Dies Drear.* New York: Collier.

Hawthorne, N. (1981). *The scarlet letter.* New York: Signet.

Heath, S. B. (1983). Everything considered: Response to literature in an elementary school setting. *Journal of Research and Development in Education, 16*(3), 8–13.

Hemenway, R. (1982). In J. C. Harris, *Uncle Remus: His songs and sayings* (pp. 7–47). New York: Penguin.

Hickman, J. (1983). Everything considered: Literature in an elementary school setting. *Journal of Research and Development in Education, 16*(3), 8–13.

Jacobs, H. (1988). The perils of a slave woman's life from incidents in the life of a slave girl. In M. H. Washington (Ed.), *Invented lives: Narratives of Black women,* 1860–1960 (pp. 16–69). New York: Anchor Books.

Johnson, C. (1987). *The sorcerer's apprentice: Tales and conjurations,* pp. 3–23. New York: Penguin.

Labov, W. (1969). *The study of nonstandard English.* Urbana, IL: National Council of Teachers of English.

Langer, J. A. (1988). The role of literature in cognitive development. From the Law and Citizenship Unit, St. Louis Public Schools, Missouri and the School of Education, State University of New York–Albany, *Reading, writing and civic literacy: A conference report* (pp. 19–24). Albany, NY: State University of New York Press.

Langer, J. A., & Smith-Burke, M. T. (Eds.). (1982). *Reader meets author: Bridging the gap.* Newark, DE: International Reading Association.

Lester, J. (1969). *Black folktales.* New York: Grove Press.

Lester, J. (1972). *The long journey home.* New York: Dell.

Marshall, J. (1986). Classroom discourse and literary response. In B. F. Nelms (Ed.), *The 1987 yearbook of the National Council of Teachers of English* (pp. 2–21). Urbana, IL: NCTE.

Morrison, T. (1984). Rootedness: The ancestor as foundation. In M. Evans (Ed.), *Black women writers (1950–1980): A critical evaluation* (pp. 339–369). New York: New American Library.

Page, R. (1987). Teachers' perceptions of students: A link between classrooms, school cultures, and the social order. *Anthropology and Education Quarterly, 18*(2), 77–99.

Purves, A. C. (1981). *Reading and literature: American achievement in international perspective.* Urbana, IL: NCTE.

Richards, I. A. (1929). *Practical criticism: A study of literary judgment.* New York: Harcourt, Brace.

Rist, R. C. (1973). *The urban school: A factory for failure.* Cambridge, MA: The MIT Press.

Rosenberg, S. (1988). Personality and affect in Hungarian and American short stories: A replication and extension. *Poetics, 17,* 385–394.

Rosenblatt, L. (1976). *Literature as exploration.* New York: Modern Language Association.

Rosenblatt, L. (1978). *The reader, the text, the poem: The transactional theory of the literary work.* Carbondale, IL: Southern Illinois University Press.

Schofield, J. W. (1982). *Black and White in school.* Washington, D.C.: Praeger.

Sims, R. (1982). *Shadow and substance: Afro-American experience in contemporary children's fiction.* Urbana, IL: NCTE.

Smitherman, G. (1977). *Talkin & testifying: The language of Black America.* Boston: Houghton Mifflin.

Sola, M., & Bennett, A. T. (1985). The struggle for voice: Narrative, literacy and consciousness in an East Harlem school. *Journal of Education, 167*(1), 88–110.

Spears-Bunton, L. A. (1989). *Cultural Consciousness and Response to literary texts: A study of texts, classroom contexts, and the responses of African and Euro-American readers.* Unpublished manuscript, University of Kentucky, School of Education.

Stanford, B. D., & Amin, K. (1978). *Black literature for high school students.* Urbana, IL: NCTE.

Steffensen, M. S., Joag-Dev, C., & Anderson, R. C. (1979). A cross-cultural perspective in reading comprehension. *Reading Research Quarterly, 15*(1), 10–29.

Weiler, K. (1988). *Women teaching for change: Gender, class and power.* South Hadley, MA: Bergin and Garvey.

Wolf, D. P. (1988). *Reading reconsidered: Literature and literacy in high school.* New York: College Entrance Examination Board.

SUGGESTED LEARNING EXPERIENCES

1. Collaborate with a peer in conducting several hour-long observations in the same classroom. Use the format in Lipka's paper to document interactions in the classroom. Interview several students from the class to get their views of the classroom, what students like and what they would like to change. Interview the teacher about the intent of the lesson, the students' responses, and the teacher's perception of the students' backgrounds and academic and social needs. Collaborate in writing an analysis of your findings that includes (a) a description of the classroom setting, the type of learning experiences provided, and the subject matter presented; (b) a discussion of the relationship between the teacher's perception of the students and the framing of learning experiences and subject matter; (c) a comparison of the teacher's and the students' perception of the value and intent of the lesson; (d) implications of your findings for curriculum planning.

2. Interview several high school students from different ethnic and cultural backgrounds concerning their responses to the literature presently being studied in their English class. Examples of questions to ask include: What literature are you presently reading for your English classes? What do you like or dislike about this piece of literature? What other types of literature would you like included in your English class? Examine the responses and suggestions based on culture or ethnicity. Compare findings with several

peers. Discuss the potential of this approach as a strategy to inform curriculum planning efforts.

3. Invite a local psychologist to discuss the significance of personal and group identity with the class. This individual should be knowledgeable about research on cultural and racial aspects of personal and group identity.

PART FOUR

ASSESSMENT AND EVALUATION

CRITICAL QUESTIONS

1. How should the relationship between school practices, their social function, the structure of the society, other social institutions, cultural and societal ideologies, and the outcomes of schooling be assessed?
2. What specific aspects of school practices should be assessed in a culturally diverse society? What criteria and processes should be employed in assessing school practices?
3. To what extent should equitable outcomes based on culture or ethnicity, social class, and gender be addressed in assessing school practices?
4. Who or what should determine which aspects of school practices should be assessed?

OVERVIEW

Historically, there has been a preoccupation with the type of educational measurement that reveals the quality of the nation's schools and provides information on individual student achievement in comparison to others. This preoccupation with individual achievement has supported the parcelling out of the best educational and occupational opportunities to the most talented students.

Darling-Hammond (1994), the first author in Part IV, provides a brief historical review of the practice of educational measurement that is useful for understanding how and why the process came to be as it is today. She examines the beliefs and purposes supporting practices in educational measurement.

In summary, the tradition in educational measurement is derived from 19th-century European psychology and is based on belief in scientific regularity, rationality, quantification, theoretical explanations, and prediction and control over outcomes. These factors were to translate into schools being accountable for educational outcomes. The test and measurement movement in the United States was given impetus by Yerke's (1929) work on the Alpha and Beta tests commissioned by the army to determine levels of literacy among enlisted men during World War I and to identify those most suitable for leadership roles (Eisner, 1993).

According to Eisner, the curriculum reform movement of the 1960s brought about a rethinking of what was being taught in schools and how it was being evaluated. Evaluation became the new focus and was much broader than testing. It included examining the quality of curriculum content, the nature of learning experiences, availability of curriculum materials, curriculum format, and multiple outcomes. During this time the practice of qualitative study of what goes on in classrooms emerged. This 1960s movement did not take hold for a variety of social and political reasons. Test and measurement prevailed.

Darling-Hammond describes the motivations for assessment reform as (a) attempts to bring consistency between "the kinds of learning desired and the approaches to curriculum and instruction that will support such learning," (b) "the belief that if assessment can exert powerful influences on behavior, it can be used to change school organizational behavior as well as classroom work," and (c) "concerns about equity and access to educational opportunity" (p. 248, this volume). She points out that not all proposals for assessment reform are the same. They vary in the way participant roles are defined; the intended relationship between teaching, learning, and testing; the type of curriculum advocated; and the intended relationship between assessment and the national agenda to equalize educational opportunity.

Darling-Hammond contends that performance-based assessment is not necessarily more equitable than traditional standardized testing. She proposes policy changes to build a more equitable system. The proposed policy changes include improving teacher capacity, "top–down support for bottom–up reform," and relating assessment reform to school restructuring. These changes are aimed at eliminating negative consequences such as those commonly found in standardized testing. She introduces the term *consequential validity*, which refers to "the extent to which an assessment tool and the ways in which it is used to produce positive consequences both for the teaching and learning process and for students who may experience different educational opportunities as a result of test-based placements" (p. 252, this volume). Darling-Hammond's discussion of assessing the societal impact of assessment is limited to issues of access and equity.

In contrast, the final chapter in Part IV by Apple and Beyer (1983) returns to issues introduced by Adams in Part I in examining the following questions: What social purpose should education serve in a culturally diverse society? What ideology and values presently support school practices? What ideology and values should support school practices in a culturally diverse society? They argue that such questions are essential in the evaluation of the outcomes of schooling. These questions suggest that the unit of analysis for evaluating the outcomes of schooling must be broadened to include what goes on within and outside of schools. The evaluation must address the curriculum presented, the ideologies and values evident in the daily practices of school, the social interactions that occur in school, and the relationship of these factors to external societal structures.

Apple and Beyer advocate ethnographic techniques for collecting data to evaluate school practices. This allows for a broad-based evaluation of school practices that extends beyond academic achievement for individuals and groups. Ethnographic techniques have weaknesses, as do other approaches. For example, these authors refer to findings from a study conducted by Willis (1977) in which it was inferred that working-class high school boys rejected school learning in favor of the physical labor that had become a tradition in their community. Similarly, Fordham and Ogbu (1986) concluded that African-American high school students rejected school success as "acting White." Such inferences should be viewed with some skepticism in the face of other studies showing the influence of the teacher's perception of the students on the nature and quality of the curriculum presented (Anyon, 1980; Gilmore, 1985, Page, 1987; Winfield, 1986). These latter studies clearly reveal the relationship between schooling and social status. The students in these studies are aware of the inferior quality of the schooling they received and some either actively or passively rejected it. Such inferior schooling often leaves students with inadequate literacy skills. This is a serious impediment to academic success beyond elementary school and can itself generate psychological responses.

Conflicting findings in ethnographic studies may suggest bias in the nature of the questions asked, the data collected, or the inferences drawn. This potential pitfall does not negate the need for assessment to address the societal impact of schooling. Certainly, there is a critical need to understand the extent to which school practices support desirable ideologies and values, social structures, and institutions. Thoughtfully designed assessment practices, including ethnography, can provide meaningful information.

REFERENCES

Anyon, J. (1980). Social class and the hidden curriculum of work. *Journal of Education, 162,* 67–92.

Apple, M. W., & Beyer, L. F. (1983). Social evaluation of curriculum. *Educational Evaluation and Policy Analysis, 5*(4), 425–434.

Darling-Hammond, L. (1994). Performance-based assessment and educational equity. *Harvard Educational Review, 64*(1), 5–30.

Eisner, E. W. (1993). Reshaping assessment in education. Some criteria in search of practice. *Journal of Curriculum Studies, 25*(3), 219–233.

Fordham, S., & Ogbu, J. U. (1986). Black students' school success: Coping with the "burden of 'acting white'." *The Urban Review, 18*(3), 176–205.

Gilmore, P. (1985). "Gimme room": School resistance, attitudes, and access to literacy. *Journal of Education, 167,* 111–128.

Page, R. (1987). Teachers' perceptions of students: A link between classrooms, school cultures, and the social order. *Anthropology and Education Quarterly, 18,* 77–99.

Willis, P. (1977). *Learning to labour: How working class kids get working class jobs.* Lexington, MA: D. C. Heath.

Winfield, L. (1986). Teacher beliefs toward academically at risk students in inner urban schools. *The Urban Review, 18*(4), 253–267.

Yerkes, R. (1929). *Army Mental Tests.* New York: Henry Holdt.

CHAPTER TWELVE

Performance-Based Assessment and Educational Equity

Linda Darling-Hammond

The use of educational testing in the United States has been criticized for its inequitable effects on different populations of students. Many assume that new forms of assessment will lead to more equitable outcomes. Linda Darling-Hammond argues in this article, however, that alternative assessment methods, such as performance-based assessment, are not inherently equitable, and that educators must pay careful attention to the ways that the assessments are used. Some school reform strategies, for example, use assessment reform as a lever for external control of schools. These strategies, Darling-Hammond argues, are unlikely to be successful and the assessments are unlikely to be equitable because they stem from a distrust of teachers and fail to involve teachers in the reform processes.

Darling-Hammond argues instead for policies that ensure "top-down support for bottom-up reform," where assessment is used to give teachers practical information on student learning and to provide opportunities for school communities to engage in "a recursive process of self-reflection, self-critique, self-correction, and self-renewal." Ultimately, then, the equitable use of performance assessments depends not only on the design of the assessments themselves, but also on how well the assessment practices are interwoven with the goals of authentic school reform and effective teaching.

In recent years, the school reform movement has engendered widespread efforts to transform the ways in which students' work and learning are assessed in schools. These alternatives are frequently called performance-based or "authentic" assessments because they engage students in "real-world" tasks rather than multiple-choice tests, and evaluate them according to criteria that are important for actual performance in a field of work (Wiggins, 1989). Such assessments include oral presentations, debates, or exhibitions, along with collections of students' written products, videotapes of performances and other learning occasions, constructions and models, and their solutions to problems, experiments, or results of scientific and other inquiries (Archbald & Newman, 1988). They also include teacher observations and inventories of individual students' work and behavior, as well as of cooperative group work (National Association for the Education of Young Children [NAEYC], 1988).

Much of the rationale for these initiatives is based on growing evidence that traditional norm-referenced, multiple-choice tests fail to measure complex cognitive and performance abilities. Furthermore, when used for decisionmaking, they encourage instruction that tends to emphasize decontextualized, rote-oriented tasks imposing low cognitive demands rather than meaningful learning. Thus, efforts to raise standards of learning and performance must rest in part on strategies to transform assessment practices.

In addition, efforts to ensure that *all* students learn in meaningful ways resulting in high levels of performance require that teachers know as much about students and their learning as they do about subject matter. However, teachers' understandings of students' strengths, needs, and approaches to learning are not well supported by external testing programs that send secret, secured tests into the school and whisk them out again for machine scoring that produces numerical quotients many months later. Authentic assessment strategies can provide teachers with much more useful classroom information as they engage teachers in evaluating how and what students know and can do in real-life performance situations. These kinds of assessment strategies create the possibility that teachers will not only develop curricula aimed at challenging performance skills, but that they will also be able to use the resulting rich information about student learning and performance to shape their teaching in ways that can prove more effective for individual students.

Recently, interest in alternative forms of student assessment has expanded from the classroom-based efforts of individual teachers to district and statewide initiatives to overhaul entire testing programs so that they become more performance-based. Major national testing programs, such as the National Assessment of Educational Progress and the College Board's Scholastic Assessment Tests (formerly the Scholastic Aptitude Tests), are also undergoing important changes. These programs are being redesigned so that they will increasingly engage students in performance tasks requiring written and oral responses in lieu of multiple-choice questions focused on discrete facts or decontextualized bits of knowledge.

However, proposals for assessment reform differ in several important ways: 1) in the extent to which they aim to broaden the roles of educators, students, parents, and other community members in assessment; 2) in the extent to which they aim to make assessment part of the teaching and learning process, and use it to serve developmental and educational purposes rather than sorting and screening purposes; 3) in the extent to which they anticipate a problem-based interdisciplinary curriculum or a coverage-oriented curriculum that maintains traditional subject area compartments for learning; and 4) in the extent to which they see assessment reform as part of a broader national agenda to improve and equalize educational opportunities in schools. Some see assessment reform as part of a broader agenda to strengthen the national educational infrastructure (the availability of high-quality teachers, curriculum, and resources) and to equalize access so that all students start from an equal platform for learning. Others, however, view performance-based assessment as a single sledgehammer for change, without acknowledging other structural realities of schooling, such as vast inequalities in educational opportunities.

These differences in approaches to assessment reform predict very different consequences for the educational system, and dramatically different consequences for those who have been traditionally underserved in U.S. schools—students in poor communities, "minorities," immigrants, and students with distinctive learning needs. In this article, I argue in particular that *changes in the forms of assessment are unlikely to enhance equity unless we change the ways in which assessments are used as well*: from sorting mechanisms to diagnostic supports; from external monitors of performance to locally generated tools for inquiring deeply into teaching and learning; and from purveyors of sanctions for those already underserved to levers for equalizing resources and enhancing learning opportunities.

The extent to which educational testing serves to enhance teaching and learning and to support greater equality or to undermine educational opportunity depends on how a variety of issues are resolved. Among these are issues associated with the nature of assessment tools themselves:

- whether and how they avoid bias;
- how they resolve concerns about subjectivity versus objectivity in evaluating student work;
- how they influence curriculum and teaching.

A second set of issues has to do with whether and how assessment results are used to determine student placements and promotions, to reinforce differential curriculum tracking, or to allocate rewards and sanctions to teachers, programs, or schools.

A final set of issues concerns the policies and practices that surround the assessment system and determine the educational opportunities available to students to support their learning. A fundamental question is whether assessment systems will support better teaching and transform schooling for traditionally underserved students or whether they will merely reify existing inequities. This depends on the extent to which they promote equity in the allocation of resources for providing education, supports for effective teaching practices, and supports for more widespread school restructuring.

MOTIVATIONS FOR ASSESSMENT REFORM

The current movement to change U.S. traditions of student assessment in large-scale and systemic ways has several motivations. One is based on the recognition that assessment, especially when it is used for decisionmaking purposes, exerts powerful influences on curriculum and instruction. It can "drive" instruction in ways that mimic not only the content, but also the format and cognitive demands of tests (Darling-Hammond & Wise, 1985; Madaus, West, Harmon, Lomax, & Viator, 1992). If assessment exerts these influences, many argue, it should be carefully shaped to send signals that are consistent with the kinds of learning desired and the approaches to curriculum and instruction that will support such learning (Cohen & Spillane, 1992; O'Day & Smith, 1993).

A second and somewhat related motive for systemic approaches to assessment reform stems from the belief that if assessment can exert powerful influences on behavior, it can be used to change school organizational behavior as well as classroom work. The idea of using assessment as a lever for school change is not a new one: many accountability tools in the 1970s and 1980s tried to link policy decisions to test scores (Linn, 1987; Madaus, 1985; Wise, 1979). Unfortunately, these efforts frequently had unhappy results for teaching and learning generally, and for schools' treatment of low-scoring students in particular. Research on these initiatives has found that test-based decisionmaking has driven instruction toward lower order cognitive skills. This shift has created incentives for pushing low scorers into special education, consigning them to educationally unproductive remedial classes, holding them back in the grades, and encouraging them to drop out (Allington & McGill-Franzen, 1992; Darling-Hammond, 1991, 1993; Koretz, 1988; Shepard & Smith, 1988; Smith, 1986). In addition, school incentives tied to test scores have undermined efforts to create and sustain more inclusive and integrated student populations, as schools are punished for accepting and keeping students with special needs and are rewarded for keeping such students out of their programs through selective admissions and transfer policies. Those with clout and means "improve" education by manipulating the population of students they serve (Smith, 1986). Schools serving disadvantaged students find it increasingly hard to recruit and retain experienced and highly qualified staff when the threat of punishments for low scores hangs over them. Thus, such policies exacerbate rather than ameliorate the unequal distribution of educational opportunity.

Nonetheless, a variety of proposals have recently been put forth that involve the use of mandated performance-based assessments as external levers for school change (Commission on Chapter I, 1992; Hornbeck, 1992; O'Day & Smith, 1993). Even those who do not endorse such proposals share the view that assessments can promote change. Other proposals, raised from a different philosophical vantage point and envisioning different uses of assessment, suggest the use of alternative classroom-embedded assessments as internal supports for school-based inquiry (Darling-Hammond & Ascher, 1990; Wolf & Baron, in press).

A third reason for assessment reform addresses concerns about equity and access to educational opportunity. Over many decades, assessment results have frequently been used to define not only teaching, but also students' opportunities to learn. As a tool for tracking students into different courses, levels, and kinds of instructional programs, testing has been a primary means for limiting or expanding students' life choices and their avenues for demonstrating competence. Increasingly, these uses of tests are recognized as having the unintended consequence of limiting students' access to further learning opportunities (Darling-Hammond, 1991; Glaser, 1990; Oakes, 1985).

Some current proposals for performance-based assessment view these new kinds of tests as serving the same screening and tracking purposes as more traditional tests (Commission on the Skills of the American Workforce, 1990; Educate America, 1991; National Center on Education and the Economy, 1989). The presumption is that more "authentic" assessments will both motivate and sort students more effectively. Others see a primary goal of assessment reform as transforming the purposes and uses of testing as well as its form and content. They argue for shifting from the use of assessment as a sorting device to its use as a tool for identifying student strengths and needs so that teachers can adapt instruction more successfully (Darling-Hammond, Ancess, & Falk, in press; Glaser, 1981, 1990; Kornhaber & Gardner, 1993). Given the knowledge now available for addressing diverse learning needs and the needs of today's society for a broadly educated populace, the goals of education—and assessment—are being transformed from deciding who will be permitted to become well-educated to helping ensure that everyone will learn successfully.

Clearly, the current press to reform assessment entails many motivations and many possible consequences, depending on decisions that are made about 1) the nature of the "new" assessments; 2) the ways in which they are used; and 3) the companion efforts (if any) that accompany them to actually improve education in the schools.

In this article I outline the range of equity issues that arise with respect to testing generally, and with respect to proposals for the development of new "authentic" assessments specifically. I argue that the outcomes of the current wave of assessment reforms will depend in large measure on the extent to which assessment developers and users:

- focus on both the quality and fairness of assessment strategies;
- use assessments in ways that serve teaching and learning, rather than sorting and selecting;
- develop policies that are congruent with (and respectful of) these assessment goals, as well as with assessment strategies and limitations;
- embed assessment reform in broader reforms to improve and equalize access to educational resources and opportunities;
- support the professional development of teachers along with the organizational development of schools, so that assessment is embedded in teaching and learning, and is used to inform more skillful and adaptive teaching that enables more successful learning for all students.

USES AND CONSEQUENCES OF TESTING

Historical Perspectives

For over one hundred years, standardized testing has been a tool used to exert control over the schooling process and to make decisions about educational entitlements for students. Testing proved a convenient instrument of social control for those superintendents in the late nineteenth century who sought to use tests as a means for creating the "one best system" of education (Tyack, 1974). It also proved enormously useful as a means of determining how to slot students for more and less rigorous (and costly) curricula when public funding of education and compulsory attendance vastly increased access to schools in the early twentieth century.

Given the massive increase in students, the limits of public budgets, and the relatively meager training of teachers, strategies were sought to codify curriculum and to group students for differential instruction. IQ tests were widely used as a measure of educational input (with intelligence viewed as the "raw material" for schooling) to sort pupils so they could be efficiently educated according to their future roles in society (Cremin, 1961; Cubberly, 1919; Watson, in press). Frequently, they were used to exclude students from schooling opportunities altogether (Glaser, 1981).

Though many proponents argued that the use of these tests as a tool for tracking students would enhance social justice, the rationales for tracking—

like those for using scores to set immigration quotas into the United States—were often frankly motivated by racial and ethnic politics. Just as Goddard's 1912 data—"proving" that 83 percent of Jews, 80 percent of Hungarians, 79 percent of Italians, and 87 percent of Russians were "feebleminded"—were used to justify low immigration quota for those groups (Kamin, 1974), so did Terman's test data "prove" that "[Indians, Mexicans, and Negroes] should be segregated in special classes. . . . They cannot master abstractions, but they can often be made efficient workers" (Terman, cited in Oakes, 1985, p. 36). Presumptions like these reinforced racial segregation and differential learning opportunities.

Terman found many inequalities in performance among groups on his IQ test, which was adapted from Binet's work in France. Most, but not all of them, seemed to confirm what he, and presumably every "intelligent" person, already knew: that various groups were inherently unequal in their mental capacities. However, when girls scored higher than boys on his 1916 version of the Stanford-Binet, he revised the test to correct for this apparent flaw by selecting items to create parity among genders in the scores (Mercer, 1989). Other inequalities—between urban and rural students, students of higher and lower socioeconomic status, native English speakers and immigrants, Whites and Blacks—did not occasion such revisions, since their validity seemed patently obvious to the test-makers.

The role of testing in reinforcing and extending social inequalities in educational opportunities has by now been extensively researched (Gould, 1981; Kamin, 1974; Mercer, 1989; Oakes, 1985; Watson, in press) and widely acknowledged. It began with the two fallacies Gould describes: the fallacy of reification, which allowed testers to develop and sell the abstract concept of intelligence as an innate, unitary, measurable commodity, and the fallacy of ranking, which supported the development of strategies for quantifying intelligence in ways that would allow people to be arrayed in a single series against each other (Gould, 1981). These two fallacies—recently debunked (though not yet dismantled) by understandings that intelligence has many dimensions (Gardner, 1983; Sternberg, 1985)—were made more dangerous by the social uses of testing as a tool for allocating educational and employment benefits rather than as a means for informing teaching and developing talents.

Negative Consequences of Standardized Testing

Current standardized tests are widely criticized for placing test-takers in a passive, reactive role (Wigdor & Garner, 1982), rather than one that engages their capacities to structure tasks, produce ideas, and solve problems. Based on outmoded views of learning, intelligence, and performance, they fail to measure students' higher order cognitive abilities or to support their capacities to perform real-world tasks (Resnick, 1987a; Sternberg, 1985).

In a seminal paper on the past, present, and future of testing, Glaser (1990) makes an important distinction between testing and assessment. These two kinds of measurement have different purposes and different social and technical histories. Glaser describes testing as aimed at selection and placement: it attempts to predict success at learning by "measur[ing] human ability prior to a course of instruction so that individuals can be appropriately placed, diagnosed, included or excluded" (p. 2). Assessment, on the other hand, is aimed at gauging educational outcomes: it measures the results of a course of learning. What is important for testing is the instrument's predictive power rather than its content. What is important for assessment is the content validity of an approach—its ability to describe the nature of performance that results from learning.

Recently, another validity construct has emerged: *consequential validity*, which describes the extent to which an assessment tool *and the ways in which it is used* produce positive consequences both for the teaching and learning process and for students who may experience different educational opportunities as a result of test-based placements (Glaser, 1990; Shepard, 1993). This emerging validity standard places a much heavier burden on assessment developers and users to demonstrate that what they are doing works to the benefit of those who are assessed and to the society at large. The emergence of this standard has led many educators and researchers to question test-based program placements for students and to press for forms of assessment that can support more challenging and authentic forms of teaching and learning. Some test developers are just beginning to understand that the criteria against which their products are being evaluated are changing.

For most of this century, much of the energy of U.S. measurement experts has been invested in developing tests aimed at ranking students for sorting and selecting them into and out of particular placements. Standardized test developers have devoted much less energy to worrying about the properties of these instruments as reflections of—or influences on—instruction (Wigdor & Garner, 1982). As a consequence, the tests generally do not reflect the actual tasks educators and citizens expect students to be able to perform, nor do they stimulate forms of instruction that are closely connected to development of performance abilities. Similarly, to date, though awareness levels are heightened, virtually no attention has yet been paid to the consequences of test-based decisions in policy discussions about developing new assessment systems.

These shortcomings of U.S. tests were less problematic when they were used as only one source of information among many other kinds of information about student learning, and when they were not directly tied to decisions about students and programs. However, as test scores have been used to make important educational decisions, their flaws have become more damaging. As schools have begun to "teach to the tests," the scores have become ever poorer assessments of students' overall abilities, because class work oriented toward recognizing the answers to multiple-choice questions does not heighten students' proficiency in aspects of the subjects that are not tested, such as analysis, complex problem-solving, and written and oral expression (Darling-Hammond & Wise, 1985; Haney & Madaus, 1986; Koretz, 1988).

As the National Assessment of Educational Progress (NAEP) found: "Only 5 to 10 percent of students can move beyond initial readings of a text; most seem genuinely puzzled at requests to explain or defend their points of view." The NAEP assessors explained that current methods of testing reading require short responses and lower level cognitive thinking, resulting in "an emphasis on shallow and superficial opinions at the expense of reasoned and disciplined thought, . . . [thus] it is not surprising that students fail to develop more comprehensive thinking and analytic skills" (NAEP, 1981, p. 5).

During the 1970s, when test-oriented accountability measures were instituted in U.S. schools, there was a decline in public schools' use of teaching methods appropriate to the teaching of higher order skills, such as research projects and laboratory work, student-centered discussions, and the writing of essays or themes (National Center for Education Statistics [NCES], 1982, p. 83). Major studies by Boyer (1983), Goodlad (1984), and Sizer (1985) documented the negative effects of standardized testing on teaching and learning in high schools, while the disadvantage created for U.S. students by the rote learning stressed in U.S. standardized tests has been documented in international studies of achievement (McKnight et al., 1987).

The effects of basic skills test misuse have been most unfortunate for the students they were most intended to help. Many studies have found that students placed in the lowest tracks or in remedial programs—disproportionately low-income and minority students—are most apt to experience instruction geared only to multiple choice tests, working at a low cognitive level on test-oriented tasks that are profoundly disconnected from the skills they need to learn. Rarely are they given the opportunity to talk about what they know, to read real books, to write, or to construct and solve problems in mathematics, science, or other subjects (Cooper & Sherk, 1989; Davis, 1986; Oakes, 1985; Trimble & Sinclair, 1986). In short, they have been denied the opportunity to develop the capacities they will need for the future, in large part because commonly used tests are so firmly pointed at educational goals of the past.

Thus, the quality of education made available to many students has been undermined by the nature of the testing programs used to monitor and shape their learning. If new performance-based assessments point at more challenging learning goals for all students, they may ameliorate some of this source of inequality. However, this will be true only to the extent that teachers who serve these students are able to teach in the ways demanded by the assessments—that is, in ways that support the development of higher order thinking and performance skills and in ways that diagnose and build upon individual learners' strengths and needs.

The Uses of Assessment Tools in Decisionmaking

As noted earlier, testing policies affect students' opportunities to learn in other important ways. In addition to determining whether students graduate, tests are increasingly used to track students and to determine whether they can be promoted from one grade to the next. Research suggests that both practices have had harmful consequences for individual students and for U.S. achievement generally. If performance-based assessments are used for the same purposes as traditional tests have been, the outcomes for under-served students are likely to be unchanged.

Tracking. In the United States, the process of tracking begins in elementary schools with the designation of instructional groups and programs based on test scores, and becomes highly formalized by junior high school. The result of this practice is that challenging curricula are rationed to a very small proportion of students. Consequently, few U.S. students ever encounter the kinds of curricula that most students in other countries typically experience (McKnight et al., 1987). As Oakes (1986) notes, these assignments are predictable:

> One finding about placements is undisputed. . . . Disproportionate percentages of poor and minority youngsters (principally black and Hispanic) are placed in tracks for low-ability or non-college-bound students (NCES, 1985; Rosenbaum, 1980); further, minority students are consistently underrepresented in programs for the gifted and talented. (College Board, 1985, p. 129)

Students placed in lower tracks are exposed to a limited, rote-oriented curriculum and ultimately achieve less than students of similar aptitude who are placed in academic programs or untracked classes. Furthermore, these curricular differences explain much of the disparity between the achievement of White and minority students and between those of higher and lower income levels (Lee & Bryk, 1988; Oakes, 1985). In this way, the uses of tests have impeded rather than supported the pursuit of high and rigorous educational goals for all students.

Grade Retention. In addition, some U.S. states and local districts have enacted policies requiring that test scores be used as the sole criterion for decisions about student promotion from one grade to the next. Since the student promotion policies were enacted, a substantial body of research has demonstrated that the effects of this kind of test-based decisionmaking are much more negative than positive. When students who were retained in grade are compared to students of equal achievement levels who were promoted, the retained students are consistently behind on both achievement and social-emotional measures (Holmes & Matthews, 1984; Shephard & Smith, 1986). As Shephard and Smith put it, "Contrary to popular beliefs, repeating a grade does *not* help students gain ground academically and has a negative impact on social adjustment and self-esteem" (1986, p. 86).

Furthermore, the practice of retaining students is a major contributor to increased dropout rates. Research suggests that being retained increases the odds of dropping out by 40 to 50 percent. A second retention nearly doubles the risk (Mann, 1987; see also Carnegie Council on Adolescent Development, 1989; Massachusetts Advocacy Center, 1988; Wehlage, Rutter, Smith, Lesko, & Fernández, 1990). Thus, the policy of automatically retaining students based on their test-score performance has actually produced lower achievement for these students, lower self-esteem, and higher dropout rates for them and for the nation.

Graduation. Perhaps the ultimate test-related sanction for students is denying a diploma based on a test score. The rationale for this practice is that students should show they have mastered the "minimum skills" needed for employment or future education in order to graduate. The assumption is that tests can adequately capture whatever those skills are. While this appears plausible in theory, it is unlikely in reality, given the disjunction between multiple-choice tests of decontextualized bits of information and the demands of real jobs and adult tasks (Bailey, 1989; Carnevale, Gainer, & Meltzer, 1989; Resnick, 1987b). In fact, research indicates that neither employability nor earnings are significantly affected by students' scores on basic skills tests, while chances of employment and welfare dependency are tightly linked to graduation from high school (Eckland, 1980; Gordon & Sum, 1988; Jaeger, 1991). Thus, the use of tests as a sole determinant of graduation imposes heavy personal and societal costs, without obvious social benefits.

Rewards and Sanctions. Finally, a few states and districts have also tried to use student test scores to allocate rewards or sanctions to schools or teachers. President Bush's proposal for a National Test included a suggestion to allocate some federal funds based on schools' scores on the "American Achievement Tests" (U.S. Department of Education, 1991). An independent commission on Chapter I has recently proposed, over the formal dissent of a number of its members, a rewards and sanctions system for Chapter I programs based on aggregate "performance-based" test scores (Commission on Chapter I, 1992). An analogous policy proposal has been enacted, though not yet implemented, for use with performance-based tests in the state of Kentucky. There, all schools that do not show specified percentage increases in student achievement scores each year will automatically suffer sanctions, which may include actions against staff. Those that meet the standards will be financially rewarded (Legislative Research Commission, 1990, p. 21).

Oblivious to the fact that schools' scores on any measure are sensitive to changes in the population of students taking the test, and that such changes can be induced by manipulating admission, dropouts, and pupil classifications, the policy will create and sustain a wide variety of perverse incentives, regardless of whether the tests are multiple-choice or performance-oriented. Because schools' aggregate scores on any measure are sensitive to the population of students taking the test, the policy creates incentives for schools to keep out students whom they fear may lower their scores—children who are handicapped, limited English speaking, or from educationally disadvantaged environments. Schools where average test scores are used for making decisions about rewards and sanctions have found a number of ways to manipulate their test-taking population in order to inflate artificially the school's average test scores. These strategies include labelling large numbers of low-scoring students for special education placements so that their scores won't "count" in school reports, retaining students in grade so that their relative standing will look better on "grade-equivalent" scores, excluding low-scoring students from admission to "open enrollment" schools, and encouraging such students to leave schools or drop out (Allington & McGill-Franzen, 1992; Darling-Hammond, 1991, 1993; Koretz, 1988; Shepard & Smith, 1988; Smith, 1986).

Smith explains the widespread engineering of student populations that he found in his study of a large urban school district that used performance standards as a basis for school level sanctions:

> Student selection provides the greatest leverage in the short-term accountability game. . . . The easiest way to improve one's chances of winning is (1) to add some highly likely students and (2) to drop some unlikely students, while simply hanging on to those in the middle. School admissions is a central thread in the accountability fabric. (1986, pp. 30–31)

Needless to say, this kind of policy that rewards or punishes schools for aggregate test scores creates a distorted view of accountability, in which beating the numbers by playing shell games with student placements overwhelms efforts to serve students' educational needs well. Equally important, these policies further exacerbate existing incentives for talented staff to opt for school placements where students are easy to teach, and school stability is high. Capable staff are less likely to risk losing rewards or incurring sanctions by volunteering to teach where many students have special needs and performance standards will be more difficult to attain. This compromises even further the educational chances of disadvantaged students, who are already served by a disproportionate share of those teachers who are inexperienced, unprepared, and under qualified.

Applying sanctions to schools with lower test score performance penalizes already disadvantaged students twice over: having given them inadequate schools to begin with, society will now punish them again for failing to perform as well as other students attending schools with greater resources and more capable teachers. This kind of reward system confuses the quality of education offered by schools with the needs of the students they enroll; it works against equity and integration, and against any possibilities for fair and open school choice, by discouraging good schools from opening their doors to educationally needy students. Such a reward structure places more emphasis on score manipulations and student assignments or exclusions than on school improvement and the development of more effective teaching practices.

POLICIES FOR BUILDING AN EQUITABLE SYSTEM

Improving Teacher Capacity

Because this nation has not invested heavily in teacher education and professional development, the capacity for a more complex, student-centered approach to teaching is not prevalent throughout the current teaching force. Furthermore, because teacher salaries and working conditions are inadequate to ensure a steady supply of qualified teachers in poor districts, low-income and minority students are routinely taught by the least experienced and least prepared teachers (Darling-Hammond, 1991; Oakes, 1990). Differences in achievement between White and minority students can be substantially explained by unequal access to high-quality curriculum and instruction (Barr & Dreeben, 1983; College Board, 1985; Darling-Hammond & Snyder, 1992a; Dreeben, 1987; Dreeben & Barr, 1987; Dreeben & Gamoran, 1986; Oakes, 1990).

From a policy perspective, perhaps the single greatest source of educational inequity is this disparity in the availability and distribution of highly qualified teachers (Darling-Hammond, 1990). Providing equity in the distribution of teacher quality will be required before changes in assessment strategies result in more challenging and effective instruction for currently underserved students. This, in turn, requires changing policies and long-standing incentive structures in education so that shortages of well-prepared teachers are overcome, and schools serving poor and minority students are not disadvantaged by lower salaries and poorer working conditions in the bidding war for good teachers. Fundamental changes in school funding are essential to this task. Since revenues in poor districts are often half as great as those in wealthy districts, state aid changes that equalize district resources are the first step toward ensuring access to qualified teachers (Darling-Hammond, in press).

This crucial equity concern is finally gaining some attention in the rush to improve schools by testing. The recent report of the National Council on Education Standards and Testing (NCEST), while arguing for national performance standards for students, acknowledged the importance of "school delivery standards" for educational improvements to occur. The Council's Standards Task Force noted:

> If not accompanied by measures to ensure equal opportunity to learn, national content and performance standards could help widen the achievement gap between the advantaged and the disadvantaged in our society. If national content and performance standards and assessment are not accompanied by clear school delivery standards and policy measures designed to afford all students an equal opportunity to learn, the concerns about diminished equity could easily be realized. Standards and assessments must be accompanied by policies that provide access for all students to high quality resources, including appropriate instructional materials and well-prepared teachers. High content and performance standards can be used to challenge all students with the same expectations, but high expectations will only result in common high performance if all schools provide high quality instruction designed to meet the expectations. (NCEST, 1992, pp. E12–E13)

Delivery standards make clear that the governmental agencies that are imposing standards upon students are simultaneously accepting responsibility for ensuring that students will encounter the opportunities necessary for their success (Darling-Hammond, 1993). Though this may seem a straightforward prerequisite for making judgments about students or schools, it marks an entirely different approach to accountability in U.S. education than the one that has predominated for most of the last two decades and is widespread today. Earlier approaches to outcomes-based accountability legislated minimum competency tests and sometimes punished schools or students with low scores without attempting to correct the resource disparities that contributed to poor performance in the first place.

Ensuring that all students have adequate opportunities to learn requires enhancing the capacity of all teachers—their knowledge of students and subjects, and their ability to use that knowledge—by professionalizing teaching. This means that teacher education policies must ensure that *all* teachers have a stronger understanding of how children learn and develop, how assessment can be used to evaluate what they know and how they learn, how a variety of curricular and instructional strategies can address their needs, and how changes in school and classroom organization can support their growth and achievement.

Such teacher capacities are also important for supporting the promise of authentic assessment to enable richer, more instructionally useful forms of evaluation that are also fair and informative. A major reason for the advent of externally controlled highly standardized testing systems has been the belief that teachers could not be trusted to make sound decisions about what students know and are able to do. The presumed "objectivity" of current tests derives both from the lack of reliance upon individual teacher judgment in scoring and from the fact that test-takers are anonymous to test-scorers (hence, extraneous views about the student do not bias scoring).

Of course, many forms of bias remain, as the choice of items, responses deemed appropriate, and content deemed important are the product of culturally and contextually determined judgments, as well as the privileging of certain ways of knowing and modes of performance over others (García & Pearson, in press; Gardner, 1983; Sternberg, 1985; Wigdor & Garner, 1982). And these forms of bias are equally likely to plague performance-based assessments, as the selection of tasks will rest on cultural and other referents, such as experiences, terms, and exposures to types of music, art, literature, and social experiences that are differentially accessible to test-takers of different backgrounds.

If assessment is to be used to open up as many opportunities as possible to as many students as possible, it must address a wide range of talents, a variety of life experiences, and multiple ways of knowing. Diverse and wide-ranging tasks that use many different performance modes and that involve students in choosing ways to demonstrate their competence become important for this goal (Gordon, no date; Kornhaber & Gardner, 1993). Substantial teacher and student involvement in and control over assessment strategies and uses are critical if assessment is to support the most challenging education possible for every student, taking full account of his or her special talents and ways of knowing. As Gordon puts it:

> The task is to find assessment probes which measure the same criterion from contexts and perspectives which reflect the life space and values of the learner. . . . Thus options and choices become a critical feature in any assessment system created to be responsive to equity, just as processual description and diagnosis become central purposes. (no date, pp. 8–9)

The objective of maintaining high standards with less standardization will demand teachers who are able to evaluate and eliminate sources of unfair bias in their development and scoring of instructionally embedded assessments, and who can balance subjectivity and objectivity, using their subjective knowledge of students appropriately in selecting tasks and assessment options while adhering to common, collective standards of evaluation. These same abilities will be crucial for other assessment developers. In many respects, even greater sensitivity to the sources of bias that can pervade assessment will be needed with forms that frequently eliminate the anonymity of test-takers, drawing more heavily on interpersonal interaction in tasks and on observations on the part of teachers.

"Top-Down Support for Bottom-Up Reform"

The need for greater teacher knowledge and sensitivity in developing and using authentic assessments in schools will cause some to argue that they should not be attempted; that externally developed and scored "objective" tests are safer for making decisions because local judgement is avoided. However, the argument for authentic assessments rests as much on a changed conception of the *uses* of assessment as on the *form* in which assessment occurs. Rather than being used largely to determine how students rank against one another on a single, limited dimension of performance so as to determine curriculum or school placements of various kinds, many reformers hope that assessment can be used to *inform and improve* teaching and learning.

In this view, assessment should be integrally connected to the teaching and learning process so that students' strengths and needs are identified, built upon, and addressed. School-wide assessments should continually inform teachers' collective review of their practice so that improvements in curriculum, instruction, and school organization are ongoing. Thus, students should actually *learn* more as a result of assessment, rather than being more precisely classified, and schools should be able to inquire into and improve their practices more intelligently, rather than being more rigidly ranked. Assessment should increase the overall amount of learning and good practice across all schools, rather than merely measuring how much of a nonexpanding pool of knowledge is claimed by different students and schools.

If authentic assessment is to realize its potential as a tool for school change, however, policies must enable assessments to be used as a vehicle for student, teacher, and school development. Like students, teachers also learn by constructing knowledge based on their experiences, conceptions, and opportunities for first-hand inquiry. They must be deeply engaged in hands-on developmental work if they are to construct new understandings of the teaching-learning process and new possibilities for their own practices in the classroom and in the school. They must come to understand the kinds of higher order learning and integrated performance goals of current school reforms from the inside out if they are to successfully develop practices that will support these goals. They must create partnerships with parents and students toward the achievement of jointly held goals if the will to change is to overcome the inertia of familiar patterns.

This suggests a policy paradigm that provides "top-down support for bottom-up reform," rather than top-down directives for school-level implementation. Different policy proposals envision different uses for performance-based assessments. State and local district initiatives vary in their views of the uses of assessment results, and of the role of school and teacher participation in assessment development and use. At one end of the continuum is a state like Kentucky, where performance-based assessments are to be developed externally and used at every grade level above grade three, not only to rate children but also to allocate rewards and sanctions to schools. Because the planned system intends to continue the tradition of development and management of most testing by agencies external to the school—and the uses of such tests for individual and organizational decisionmaking—the costs of developing Kentucky's state assessment system are now estimated at over $100 million, excluding implementation costs (Wheelock, 1992).

Some state programs plan to change the nature of existing standardized tests, but not the locus of control of test items, scoring, and uses of results. Tests will still be used primarily for ranking students and schools and controlling instruction from outside the school. Similarly, some proposals for national testing envision NAEP-like instruments used to rank schools, districts, and states on measures that use more performance-oriented tasks, but these would enter and leave schools on "testing days" just as current assessments do.

Due to their intended uses, such tests will need to be carefully controlled and managed to ensure scoring reliability and security. This means local teachers, parents, and students can have little voice in choices of tasks and assessment opportunities or the means of configuring them; that those assessments that count will still be occasional and threatening rather than continuous and developmental; that the strategies for assessment will be limited to what can be managed with external development and reliable scoring at "reasonable" costs; and that the learning available to school people will be limited to that which can occur at several removes from hands-on participation.

If performance-based assessments are used in the same fashion as current externally developed and mandated tests are used, they are likely to highlight differences in students' learning even more keenly, but they will be unlikely to help teachers revamp their teaching or schools rethink their ways of operating. If they arrive in secured packets and leave in parcels for external scoring, teachers will have only a superficial understanding of what the assessments are trying to measure or achieve. If assessments are occasional externally controlled events used primarily for aggregated measures of student achievement levels, they are unlikely to be constructed in ways that provide rich information about the processes of student learning and their individual, idiosyncratic approaches to different kinds of tasks and opportunities. Consequently, teachers will have little opportunity to use the results to understand the complex nuances of student learning in ways that support more successful instruction, and little information on which to act in trying to rethink their daily practices. They will have no new grist for ongoing conversations with parents and with their peers about the insights and dilemmas raised through an ongoing, integrated, collaborative process of teaching, learning, and assessment.

Furthermore, if the results are used to allocate rewards and sanctions for students, teachers, and/or schools, the assessments will inspire fear and continual game playing to manipulate student populations, but they will be unlikely to open up the kinds of honest inquiry and serious innovation needed to stimulate new learning and transform practices in fundamental ways.

Another approach is exemplified in states such as New York, Vermont, Connecticut, and California. These states envision carefully targeted state assessments at a few key developmental points that will provide data for informing policymakers about program successes and needs, areas where assistance and investment are needed, and assessment models for local schools. Meanwhile, locally implemented assessment systems—including portfolios, projects, performance tasks, and structured teacher observations of learning—will provide the multiple forms of evidence about student learning needed to make sound judgments about instruction. In these models, assessment is used as a learning tool for schools and teachers rather than as a sledgehammer for sorting and sanctioning.

In the New York Plan, state assessments will provide comparable data on student performances on a periodic sampling basis, including data from longer term projects and portfolios as well as controlled performance tasks. In addition, investments in the development of local assessment systems will support schools in developing continuous, multifaceted records of achievement and information about students in authentic performance situations. Supports for school learning and equalization of resources are also included through a newly proposed equalizing formula for school funding (including an add-on factor for rates of poverty) and a school quality review process to support teacher and school learning (New York Council, 1992). Both California and New York are currently piloting such practitioner-led school review processes modeled, in part, after long-standing practices of Her Majesty's Inspectorate in Great Britain.

Reformers hope that these initiatives will use assessment as a vehicle for student development and adaptive teaching, rather than as a tool for sorting, screening, and selecting students out of educational opportunities. They also intend for assessment to inform teacher and school learning so that the possibilities of multiple pathways to student success are enhanced. These kinds of initiatives acknowledge the need to experiment with diverse methods for assessment that can support Gardner's (1991) conception of "individually configured excellence"—efforts that will tap the multiple intelligences and potentials of students obscured by traditional testing practices.

Many schools, reform networks, and professional organizations have already made inroads in the development of such assessments and their use for supporting teaching and learning. Strategies for assessing learning through exhibitions, portfolios, projects, and careful observations of children have been invented and shared among grassroots school reform initiatives stimulated by such organizations as the Coalition of Essential Schools, Project Zero, the Foxfire Teacher Outreach Network, the North Dakota Study Group, the Prospect Center, and other networks of progressive schools, along with organizations such as the National Association for Education of Young Children, the National Council of Teachers of Mathematics, and other professional associations.

These approaches to assessment development aim at strengthening teaching and learning at the school level by engaging students in more meaningful, integrative, and challenging work, and by helping teachers to look carefully at performance, to understand how students are learning and thinking, to reflect upon student strengths and needs, and to support them with adaptive teaching strategies.

Where these efforts are underway, changes in teaching and schooling practices occur—especially for students who are not as often successful at schoolwork. Kornhaber and Gardner (1993) illustrate how students whose strengths, interests, and talents are not visible on standardized tests can be understood and better taught. They describe how varied classroom opportunities for performance and assessments can illuminate productive "entry points" that build on children's developed intelligences and extend them into new areas of learning. Case studies of the use of such instruments as the Primary Language Record (Barrs, Ellis, Hester, & Thomas, 1988; Centre for Language in Primary Education [CLPE], 1990), an observational tool for teachers to document student language and literacy development in diverse performance contexts, also demonstrate how developing teachers' capacities to look closely at students' work and learning strategies helps them to provide more supportive experiences, especially for students who have previously had difficulties in learning or whose first language is not English (Falk & Darling-Hammond, 1993).

Teacher learning about how to support student learning has also occurred as teams of teachers have developed authentic assessment strategies at New York's International High School, whose population is 100 percent limited English proficient immigrants. Portfolios, projects, and oral debriefings on the work of cooperative learning groups have become the primary instruments for judging the effectiveness of both students' progress and teachers' own instruction. Students' portfolios and products are evaluated by the students themselves, their peers, and their teachers. These multiple perspectives on student work along with student evaluations of courses provide teachers with a steady stream of feedback about their curriculum and insights about individual students. This system of assessment makes the act of teaching itself an act of professional development, because teachers analyze student responses and use them in the development of their pedagogy. The press to cover content has been supplanted by the press to support students in successful learning, with extraordinary results for student success (Ancess & Darling-Hammond, in press).

At International, Central Park East Secondary School, the Urban Academy, and other urban high schools engaged in portfolio assessment for graduation, students who would normally fail in central city schools succeed—graduating and going on to college at rates comparable to affluent suburban schools (Darling-Hammond, Ancess, & Falk, in press; Darling-Hammond et al., 1993). As teachers learn about how students approach tasks, what helps them learn most effectively, and what assessment tasks challenge and support the kinds of learning desired, they find themselves transforming both their teaching and their assessment strategies. The more information teachers obtain about what students know and think as well as how they learn, the more capacity they have to reform their pedagogy, and the more opportunities they create for student success.

These and other assessment initiatives that embed authentic assessment in the ongoing processes of teaching and curriculum development share Glaser's (1990) view that schools must move from a selective mode "characterized by minimal variation in the conditions for learning" in which "a narrow range of instructional options and a limited number of paths to success are available" (p. 16), to an adaptive mode in which "conceptions of learning and modes of teaching are adjusted to individuals—their backgrounds, talents, interests, and the nature of their past performances and experiences" (p. 17). Fundamental agreement with this view leads to a rejection of the traditional uses of testing, even performance-based testing, as an externally controlled tool for the allocation of educational opportunities, rewards, or sanctions. As students are offered wider opportunities for learning and the assessment of their achievement becomes an integral part of learning and teaching, tests are required that provide multi-dimensional views of performance.

As an alternative to past uses of standardized testing, Glaser (1990) proposes the following criteria for evaluating how new assessments should be designed and used:

1. *Access to Educational Opportunity:* Assessments should be designed to survey possibilities for student growth, rather than to designate students as ready or not ready to profit from standard instruction.
2. *Consequential Validity:* Assessments should be interpreted and evaluated on the basis of their instructional effects; that is, their effectiveness in leading teachers to spend time on classroom activities conducive

to valuable learning goals and responsive to individual student learning styles and needs.

3. *Transparency and Openness:* Knowledge and skills should be measured so that the processes and products of learning are openly displayed. The criteria of performance must be transparent rather than secret so that they can motivate and direct learning.
4. *Self-Assessment:* Because assessment and instruction will be integrally related, instructional situations should provide coaching and practice in ways that help students to set incremental standards by which they can judge their own achievement, and develop self-direction for attaining higher performance levels.
5. *Socially Situated Assessment:* Assessment situations in which the student participates in group activity should increase. In this context, not only performance, but also the facility with which a student adapts to help and guidance can be assessed.
6. *Extended Tasks and Contextualized Skills:* Assessment should be more representative of meaningful tasks and subject matter goals. Assessment opportunities will themselves provide worthwhile learning experiences that illustrate the relevance and utility of the knowledge and skills that are being acquired.
7. *Scope and Comprehensiveness:* Assessment will attend to a greater range of learning and performance processes, stimulating analysis of what students can do in terms of the cognitive demands and performance skills tasks entail, as well as their content.

These guidelines suggest strategies for creating assessment systems that serve the daily, intimate processes of teaching and learning. Though a continuing role for external assessments that provide information for policymakers and guideposts for district and school analysis is legitimate, the broader vision of school restructuring demands a much more prominent and highly developed role for school-based assessment initiatives as well.

The Relationship of Assessment Reform to School Restructuring

At the policy level, the different approaches to developing and using performance-based assessments reflect different theories of organizational change and different views of educational purposes. One view seeks to induce change through extrinsic rewards and sanctions for both schools and students, on the assumption that the fundamental problem is a lack of will to change on the part of educators. The other view seeks to induce change by building knowledge among school practitioners and parents about alternative methods and by stimulating organizational rethinking through opportunities to work together on the design of teaching and schooling and to experiment with new approaches. This view assumes that the fundamental problem is a lack of knowledge about the possibilities for teaching and learning, combined with lack of organizational capacity for change.

The developmental view of assessment seeks to create the conditions that enable responsible and responsive practice, including teacher knowledge, school capacity for improvement and problem-solving, flexibility in meeting the actual needs of real people, shared ethical commitments among staff, and appropriate policy structures that encourage rather than punish inclusive education (Darling-Hammond & Snyder, 1992b). An emphasis on controlling school and classroom work through externally applied assessment schemes makes it difficult to produce this kind of practice.

Peter Senge (1992) explains why organizational controls operating through extrinsic rewards and sanctions undermine the development of learning organizations:

> Making continual learning a way of organizational life . . . can only be achieved by breaking with the traditional authoritarian, command and control hierarchy where the top thinks and the local acts, to merge thinking and acting at all levels. This represents a profound re-orientation in the concerns of management—a shift from a predominant concern with controlling to a predominant concern with learning. (p. 2)

His assertion is borne out by research on necessary factors for restructuring schools. David (1990) describes the restructuring districts she studied:

> Teachers and principals are asked to experiment and to continuously assess the effects of their experiments. . . . District leaders encourage school staff to learn from their successes and their mistakes. School staffs are urged to experiment without fear of punishment for failures. These districts are moving from the known to the unknown, so risks are an essential part of progress. All the districts face the challenge of getting teachers and principals to imagine new ways of organizing their roles and their work. They recognize that risk taking requires knowledge of what to do and how to judge it as well as support and flexibility. (pp. 226–227)

Thus, support for learning and risk-taking are strengthened by opportunities for evaluating the results of that learning, when a safe environment for innovation has been created. Engaging teachers in assessment is a critical aspect of that process. That engagement becomes a powerful vehicle for professional development, supporting teachers in looking at and understanding student learning, in investigating the effects of teaching on learning, and in transforming their practices so that they become more effective. It is this insight into what students are really doing, thinking, and learning that is one of the greatest contributions of authentic assessment to teacher development.

This insight is greatly encouraged by opportunities for teachers to evaluate and document students' work in ways that help the teachers attend to what students can do, how they approach their work, and what types of teaching approaches seem to support what kinds of learning. In the parlance of many currently proposed performance assessment schemes, this kind of insight might be supported by participation in "scoring" activities; however, the kind of teacher participation needed for full attention to student learning must extend beyond evaluations of discrete pieces of work against a common grid or rubric. A focus on distinct tasks scored against necessarily narrowed and standardized criteria can be periodically helpful, but a more comprehensive view of teaching, learning, and the diverse capacities of students is needed to ensure that teachers have the understandings they need to help students learn. This learner-centered information can only be derived from extensive involvement in looking at children and their work from many different vantage points.

Kanevsky (1992), a teacher, explains the Descriptive Review process, a collaborative means for evaluating student learning and growth:

> The assessment we use determines the way we see children and make educational decisions. . . . Because the Descriptive Review is a collaborative process, it can contribute to the current efforts to restructure schools. The Descriptive Review process allows teachers to hear individual voices and to pursue collaborative inquiry. As teachers draw upon their experiences and knowledge, they begin to envision new roles for themselves and new structures for schools. They are also creating a body of knowledge about teaching and learning that starts with looking at a particular child in depth and ends with new insights and understandings about children and classrooms in general.
>
> Teachers must have opportunities to participate in an educational community; to examine what they care about and what is important for children; to have ongoing, thoughtful conversations about teaching and learning in order to plan meaningful restructuring. (p. 57)

CONCLUSION

I have argued here that, for all the promise of more authentic and performance-based forms of assessment, their value depends as much on how they are used and what supports for learning accompany them as on the new technologies they employ. Changing assessment forms and formats without changing the ways in which assessments are used will not change the outcomes of education. In order for assessment to support student learning, it must include teachers in all stages of the process and be embedded in curriculum and teaching activities. It must be aimed primarily at supporting more informed and student-centered teaching rather than at sorting students and sanctioning schools. It must be intimately understood by teachers, students, and parents, so that it can help them strive for and achieve the learning goals it embodies. It must allow for different starting points for learning and diverse ways of demonstrating competence. In order for schooling to improve, assessment must also be an integral part of ongoing teacher dialogue and school development.

In short, we must rethink the uses of assessment, since we have entered an era where the goal of schooling is to educate all children well, rather than selecting a "talented tenth" to be prepared for knowledge work. In addition, we must publicly acknowledge that inequalities in access to education must be tackled directly if all students are to be well-educated. Testing students will not provide accountability in education while some students receive only a fraction of the school resources that support the education of their more privileged counterparts. For all students to receive high-quality instruction from highly qualified teachers, financial investments in schooling must be equalized across rich and poor communities.

With these supports, authentic assessment strategies can help schools become educational communities committed to self-determined common values. When this happens, all members of the community become learners struggling to construct knowledge that they can individually and collectively use to achieve their goals. The development and practice of authentic assessment casts teachers in the role of problem-framers and problem-solvers who use their classroom and school experiences to build an empirical knowledge base to inform their practice and strengthen their effectiveness. When supported by adequate resources and learning opportunities for teachers, authentic assessment increases the capacity of schools to engage in a recursive process of self-reflection, self-critique, self-correction, and self-renewal. As schools thus become learning organizations, they can increase their capacity to ensure that all of their students learn. Under these conditions, assessment may work on behalf of equity in education, rather than perpetuating the "savage inequalities" (Kozol, 1991) that now exist.

REFERENCES

Allington, R. L., & McGill-Franzen, A. (1992). Unintended effects of educational reform in New York. *Educational Policy, 6*, 397–414.

Ancess, J., & Darling-Hammond, L. (in press). *Authentic assessment as an instrument of learning and evaluation at International High School.* New York: Columbia University, Teachers College, National Center for Restructuring Education, Schools, and Teaching.

Archbald, D. A., & Newman, F. M. (1988). *Beyond standardized testing: Assessing authentic academic achievement in the secondary school.* Reston, VA: National Association of Secondary School Principals.

Bailey, T. (1989). *Changes in the nature and structure of work: Implications for skill requirements and skill formation* (Technical Paper No. 9). New York: Columbia University, Teachers College, National Center on Education and Employment.

Barr, R., & Dreeben, R. (1983). *How schools work.* Chicago: University of Chicago Press.

Barrs, M., Ellis, S., Hester, H., & Thomas, A. (1988). *The primary language record.* London: Inner London Education Authority Centre for Language in Primary Education.

Boyer, E. L. (1983). *High school.* New York: Harper & Row.

Carnegie Council on Adolescent Development. (1989). *Turning points: Preparing youth for the 21st century.* New York: Carnegie Corporation of New York.

Carnevale, A. P., Gainer, L. J., & Meltzer, A. S. (1989). *Workplace basics: The skills employers want.* Alexandria, VA: American Society for Training and Development.

Centre for Language in Primary Education. (1990). *The reading book.* London: Inner London Education Authority.

Cohen, D. K., & Spillane, J. P. (1992). Policy and practice: The relations between governance and instruction. In G. Grant (Ed.), *Review of research in education, Vol. 18* (pp. 3–50). Washington, DC: American Educational Research Association.

College Entrance Examination Board. (1985). *Equality and excellence: The educational status of black Americans.* New York: Author.

Commission on Chapter I. (1992). *High performance schools: No exceptions, no excuses.* Washington, DC: Author.

Commission on the Skills of the American Workforce. (1990). *America's choice: High skills or low wages.* Rochester, NY: National Center on Education and the Economy.

Cooper, E., & Sherk, J. (1989). Addressing urban school reform: Issues and alliances. *Journal of Negro Education, 58,* 315–331.

Cremin, L. (1961). *The transformation of the school: Progressivism in American education, 1876–1957.* New York: Vintage Books.

Cubberly, E. P. (1919). *Public education in the United States: A study and interpretation of American educational history.* Boston: Houghton Mifflin.

Darling-Hammond, L. (1990). Teacher quality and equality. In J. Goodlad & P. Keating (Eds.), *Access to knowledge: An agenda for our nation's schools* (pp. 237–258). New York: College Entrance Examination Board.

Darling-Hammond, L. (1991). The implications of testing policy for quality and equality. *Phi Delta Kappan, 73,* 220–225.

Darling-Hammond, L. (1993). Creating standards of practice and delivery for learner-centered schools. *Stanford Law and Policy Review, 4,* 37–52.

Darling-Hammond, L. (in press). Inequality and access to knowledge. In J. Banks (Ed.), *Handbook of multicultural education.* New York: Macmillan.

Darling-Hammond, L., Ancess, J., & Falk, B. (in press). *Authentic assessment in action: Case studies of students and schools at work.* New York: Teachers College Press.

Darling-Hammond, L., & Ascher, C. (1990). *Accountability in big city schools.* New York: Columbia University, Teachers College, National Center for Restructuring Education, Schools, and Teaching, and Institute for Urban and Minority Education.

Darling-Hammond, L., & Snyder, J. (1992a). Traditions of curriculum inquiry: The scientific tradition. In P. Jackson (Ed.), *Handbook of research on curriculum* (pp. 41–78). New York: Macmillan.

Darling-Hammond, L., & Snyder, J. (1992b). Reframing accountability for learner-centered practice. In A. Lieberman (Ed.), *The changing contexts of teaching: 91st Yearbook of the National Society for the Study of Education* (pp. 11–36). Chicago: University of Chicago Press.

Darling-Hammond, L., Snyder, J., Ancess, J., Einbender, L., Goodwin, A. L., & Macdonald, M. (1993). *Creating learner-centered accountability.* New York: Columbia University, Teachers College, National Center for Restructuring Education, Schools, and Teaching.

Darling-Hammond, L., & Wise, A. (1985). Beyond standardization: State standards and school improvement. *Elementary School Journal, 85*, 315–336.

David, J. (1990). Restructuring in progress: Lessons from pioneering districts. In R. Elmore (Ed.), *Restructuring schools: The next generation of educational reform* (pp. 209–250). San Francisco: Jossey-Bass.

Davis, D. G. (1986, April). *A pilot study to assess equity in selected curricular offerings across three diverse schools in a large urban school district: A search for methodology.* Paper presented at the annual meeting of the American Educational Research Association, San Francisco.

Dreeben, R. (1987). Closing the divide: What teachers and administrators can do to help black students reach their reading potential. *American Educator, 11*(4), 28–35.

Dreeben, R., & Barr, R. (1987, April). *Class composition and the design of instruction.* Paper presented at the annual meeting of the American Education Research Association, Washington, DC.

Dreeben, R., & Gamoran, A. (1986). Race, instruction, and learning. *American Sociological Review, 51*, 660–669.

Eckland, B. K. (1980). Sociodemographic implications of minimum competency testing. In R. M. Jaeger & C. K. Tittle (Eds.), *Minimum competency achievement testing: Motives, models, measures, and consequences* (pp. 124–135). Berkeley, CA: McCutchan.

Educate America. (1991). *An idea whose time has come: A national achievement test for high school seniors.* Morristown, NJ: Author.

Falk, B., & Darling-Hammond, L. (1993). *The primary language record at P.S. 261.* New York: Columbia University, Teachers College, National Center for Restructuring Education, Schools, and Teaching.

García, G., & Pearson, D. (in press). Assessment and diversity. In L. Darling-Hammond (Ed.), *Review of research in education, 20.* Washington, DC: American Educational Research Education.

Gardner, H. (1983). *Frames of mind.* New York: Basic Books.

Gardner, H. (1991). *The unschooled mind.* New York: Basic Books.

Glaser, R. (1981). The future of testing: A research agenda for cognitive psychology and psychometrics. *American Psychologist, 36*, 923–936.

Glaser, R. (1990). *Testing and assessment: O tempora! O mores!* Pittsburgh, PA: University of Pittsburgh, Learning Research and Development Center.

Goodlad, J. I. (1984). *A place called school: Prospects for the future.* New York: McGraw-Hill.

Gordon, E. (no date). *Implications of diversity in human characteristics for authentic assessment.* Unpublished manuscript, Yale University.

Gordon, B., & Sum, A. (1988). *Toward a more perfect union: Basic skills, poor families, and our economic future.* New York: Ford Foundation.

Gould, S. J. (1981). *The mismeasure of man.* New York: W. W. Norton.

Haney, W., & Madaus, G. (1986). *Effects of standardized testing and the future of the national assessment of educational progress.* Chestnut Hill, MA: Center for the Study of Testing, Evaluation, and Educational Policy.

Holmes, C. T., & Matthews, K. M. (1984). The effects of nonpromotion on elementary and junior high school pupils: A meta-analysis. *Review of Educational Research, 54*, 225–236.

Hornbeck, D. (1992, May 6). The true road to equity. *Education Week*, pp. 33, 25.

Jaeger, R. M. (1991, June 5). *Legislative perspectives on statewide testing: Goals, hopes, and desires.* Paper presented at the American Educational Research Association Forum, Washington, DC.

Kamin, L. (1974). *The science and politics of IQ.* New York: John Wiley.

Kanevsky, R. D. (1992). The descriptive review of a child: Teachers learn about values. In *Exploring values and standards: Implications for assessment* (pp. 41–58). New York: Columbia University, Teachers College, National Center for Restructuring Education, Schools, and Teaching.

Koretz, D. (1988). Arriving in Lake Wobegon: Are standardized tests exaggerating achievement and distorting instruction? *American Educator, 12*(2), 8–15, 46–52.

Kornhaber, M., & Gardner, H. (1993). *Varieties of excellence: Identifying and assessing children's talents.* New York: Columbia University, Teachers College, National Center for Restructuring Education, Schools, and Teaching.

Kozol, J. (1991). *Savage inequalities: Children in America's schools.* New York: Crown.

Lee, V., & Bryk, A. (1988). Curriculum tracking as mediating the social distribution of high school achievement. *Sociology of Education, 61,* 78–94.

Legislative Research Commission. (1990). *A guide to the Kentucky Education Reform Act of 1990.* Frankfurt, KY: Author.

Linn, R. L. (1987). Accountability: The comparison of educational systems and the quality of test results. *Educational Policy, 1*(2), 181–198.

Madaus, G., West, M. M., Harmon, M. C., Lomax, R. G., & Viator, K. A. (1992). *The influence of testing on teaching math and science in grades 4–12.* Chestnut Hill, MA: Boston College Center for the Study of Testing, Evaluation, and Educational Policy.

Madaus, G. F. (1985). Public policy and the testing profession—You've never had it so good? *Educational Measurement: Issues and Practice, 4,* 5–11.

Mann, D. (1987). Can we help dropouts? Thinking about the undoable. In G. Natriello (Ed.), *School dropouts: Patterns and policies* (pp. 3–19). New York: Teachers College Press.

Massachusetts Advocacy Center and the Center for Early Adolescence. (1988). *Before it's too late: Dropout prevention in the middle grades.* Boston: Author.

McKnight, C. C., Crosswhite, F. J., Dossey, J. A., Kifer, E., Swafford, S. O., Travers, K. J., & Cooney, T. J. (1987). *The underachieving curriculum: Assessing U.S. school mathematics from an international perspective.* Champaign, IL: Stipes.

Mercer, J. R. (1989). Alternative paradigms for assessment in a pluralistic society. In J. A. Banks & C. M. Banks (Eds.), *Multicultural education* (pp. 289–303). Boston: Allyn & Bacon.

National Assessment of Educational Progress. (1981). *Reading, thinking, and writing: Results from the 1979–80 National Assessment of Reading and Literature.* Denver: Education Commission of the States.

National Association for the Education of Young Children. (January, 1988). NAEYC position statement on developmentally appropriate practice in the primary grades, serving 5 through 8 year-olds. *Young Children, 47*(1), 64–84.

National Center for Education Statistics. (1982). *The condition of education, 1982.* Washington, DC: U.S. Department of Education.

National Center for Education Statistics. (1985). *High school and beyond: An analysis of course-taking patterns in secondary schools as related to student characteristics.* Washington, DC: U.S. Government Printing Office.

National Center on Education and the Economy. (1989). *To secure our future: The federal role in education.* Rochester, NY: Author.

National Council on Educational Standards and Testing. (1992). *Raising standards for American education.* Washington, DC: Author.

New York Council on Curriculum and Assessment. (1992). *Building a learning-centered curriculum for learner-centered schools: Report of the Council on Curriculum and Assessment.* Albany: New York State Education Department.

Oakes, J. (1985). *Keeping track: How schools structure inequality.* New Haven: Yale University Press.

Oakes, J. (1986). Tracking in secondary schools: A contextual perspective. *Educational Psychologist, 22,* 129–154.

Oakes, J. (1990). *Multiplying inequalities: The effects of race, social class, and tracking on opportunities to learn mathematics and science.* Santa Monica, CA: RAND.

O'Day, J. A., & Smith, M. S. (1993). Systemic school reform and educational opportunity. In S. Fuhrman (Ed.), *Designing coherent education policy: Improving the system* (pp. 250–311). San Francisco: Jossey-Bass.

Resnick, L. B. (1987a). *Education and learning to think.* Washington, DC: National Academy Press.

Resnick, L. (1987b). Learning in school and out. *Educational Researcher, 16,* 13–20.

Rosenbaum, J. E. (1980). Social implications of educational grouping. In D. C. Berliner (Ed.), *Review of Research in Education, 8* (pp. 361–401). Washington, DC: American Educational Research Association.

Senge, P. M. (1992). *Building learning organizations.* Framingham, MA: Innovation Associates.

Shepard, L. (1993). Evaluating test validity. In L. Darling-Hammond (Ed.), *Review of Research in Education, Vol. 19* (pp. 405–450). Washington, DC: American Educational Research Association.

Shepard, L., & Smith, M. L. (1986). Synthesis of research on school readiness and kindergarten retention. *Educational Leadership, 44*(3), 78–86.

Shepard, L. A., & Smith, M. L. (1988). Escalating academic demand in kindergarten: Counterproductive policies. *Elementary School Journal, 89,* 135–145.

Sizer, T. (1985). *Horace's compromise.* Boston: Houghton Mifflin.

Smith, F. (1986). *High school admission and the improvement of schooling.* New York: New York City Board of Education.

Sternberg, R. J. (1985). *Beyond IQ.* New York: Cambridge University Press.

Trimble, K., & Sinclair, R. L. (1986, April). *Ability grouping and differing conditions for learning: An analysis of content and instruction in ability-grouped classes.* Paper presented at the annual meeting of the American Educational Research Association, San Francisco.

Tyack, D. (1974). *The one best system.* Cambridge, MA: Harvard University Press.

U.S. Department of Education. (1991). *America 2000: An education strategy.* Washington, DC: Author.

Watson, B. (in press). *Essays from the underside.* Philadelphia: Temple University Press.

Wehlage, G. G., Rutter, R. A., Smith, G. A., Lesko, N., & Fernández, R. R. (1990). *Reducing the risk: Schools as communities of support.* New York: Falmer Press.

Wheelock, A. (1992). *School accountability policies: Implications for policy making in Massachusetts.* Paper prepared for the Massachusetts Department of Education.

Wigdor, A. K., & Garner, W. R. (Eds.). (1982). *Ability testing: Uses, consequences, and controversies.* Washington, DC: National Academy Press.

Wiggins, G. (1989). Teaching to the (authentic) test. *Educational Leadership, 46*(7), 41–47.

Wise, A. E. (1979). *Legislated learning.* Berkeley, CA: University of California Press.

Wolf, D. P., & Baron, J. B. (in press). A realization of a national performance-based assessment system. In D. Stevenson (Ed.), *Promises and perils of new assessments.* Hillsdale, NJ: Lawrence Erlbaum Associates.

CHAPTER THIRTEEN

Social Evaluation of Curriculum

Michael W. Apple
Landon E. Beyer

In this essay, we want to demonstrate some of the inherent limitations of the usual ways educational evaluation is conducted. In particular, we wish to challenge the dominance of curriculum evaluation based on achievement test results and to suggest a set of questions and strategies that will be more responsive to the actual socioeconomic reality of schools. In so doing, we will propose ways of engaging in the social evaluation of curriculum that go beyond the more individualistically and psychologically oriented models in use within programmatic evaluation efforts today.

We will argue that because evaluation is a process of *placing value* on a procedure, process, goal, or outcome (Apple, 1974), that alternatives to the current ways we do place value on curricula can be developed only by seeing how values now work through our activity and expanding the ways we look at these procedures, processes, goals, or outcomes to include the ideological and economic "functions" of our educational system.[1]

Our discussion construes evaluation somewhat differently than it has often been construed in the past. Evaluation can be seen and usually is seen by many educators as demonstrating whether or not a specific program,

[1]Throughout this essay, we will be using the concept of the social "functions" of education. We do *not* mean to imply either that these functions are all schools do or that schools always successfully perform the social roles that they are called upon to perform. As one of us has argued at length elsewhere (Apple, 1982b), there are serious conceptual and empirical difficulties in a totally functional analysis of education.

text, and so forth, given "the limitations of student background and ability," is successful and then giving feedback to participants, administrators, or funding agencies about this relative success. A comparison between the stated goals of curricular programs and how far the students have gone is not inherently always wrong. After all, there may be times that goal directedness and efficiency are important. However, most of the procedures developed to deal with these concerns, while often technically sophisticated, remain relatively unreflective about the interests, values, and ideologies in the curriculum or even embodied in the concerns themselves. Given this, we take one fundamental task of evaluation in education to be unpacking what schools and curricula actually do socially.

TECHNICAL CONCERNS AND SOCIAL INTERESTS

Most evaluations of school curricula depend on measures of the achievement scores of pupils to determine the success of a specific curricular offering. They rest on particular assumptions regarding efficiency, cost effectiveness, ability, and mean gain in student achievement. Curricula "work" if they "produce" higher test scores, for less money, in a measurable and relatively uncomplicated way. We break down the knowledge we want to teach into atomistic units of behaviors (ignoring in the process the potent practical, conceptual, and political limitations of such a reductive approach), give pretests, determine "ability," teach, then test, and start the whole cycle over again. The focus is on technical questions (Did we get from point A to point B?), not on whether B, or the process of getting there, is ethically or politically just.

This emphasis on what has been called process/product thinking has had a long history. For the better part of this century educators have searched long and hard for a general set of technical procedures that would guide curriculum planning and evaluation. In large part, this has reduced itself to attempts at creating *the most efficient method* of doing curriculum work. This stress on method has not been without its negative consequences. At the same time that process/product rationality grew, the fact that curriculum planning and evaluation was through and through a political enterprise withered. The questions we asked tended to divorce us and our work from the ways the unequal economic and cultural apparatus of our society operated. A "neutral" method meant both our own neutrality and that of the knowledge we selected and tested, or so it seemed. The fact that the methods we employed had their roots in industry's attempts to control labor and increase productivity and profit, in the popular eugenics movement, and in maintaining particular class and status group interests became increasingly invisible. At the same time, educators seemed to assume that the development of these supposedly neutral methods would somehow eliminate the need to deal with the difficult issues of whose knowledge should be or already was preserved and transmitted in schools, and what the social impact of this knowledge and our evaluations of it would be. While a number of alternative traditions continued to try to keep this kind of political question alive, by and large the faith in the inherent neutrality of our institutions, the knowledge that was taught, and our planning and evaluation efforts was ideally suited to help legitimate the structural bases of inequality.

The key to this last sentence is the concept of legitimation. Like the late philosopher Ludwig Wittgenstein, we are claiming that the meaning of a good deal of our evaluative methods and theories is in their use. And the use in this case has often been twofold. The traditions that have come to dominate education assist in the reproduction of inequality while at the same time serving to legitimate both the institutions that recreate it and our actions within them. This is not to claim that *individual* children are not often helped by our methods and practices; nor is it to argue that all our day-to-day actions are misguided. Rather, we want to point to the fact that macroeconomically and macroculturally our efforts may serve functions that bear little resemblance to even our best intentions.

Part of the problem rests on the issue of neutrality. As we will see, our theories and methods of research and evaluation do not protect us as much as we might like from serving hidden social interests.

All too many evaluators and researchers tend to neglect the fact that their work already serves social interests. These interests and values tend to be constituted by the very questions they often ask. Let us give one example. In the midst of the data-gathering phase of a program to "rehabilitate" juvenile offenders, one of the questions asked was, "Why do these people steal?" A logical extension of this is the development of a program to reeducate these people. This sounds quite straightforward and neutral. However, it is here that one can begin to see values working through one's research and evaluation efforts. For, given the evident maldistribution of income in the United States (recent government reports suggest that the gap between rich and poor is increasing at approximately 7% per year above the inflation rate), given the massive and almost ignored unemployment and underemployment rate among minority youth, and given the intense psychological manipulation by corporate advertising to consume more and more, one could just as easily ask, "Why don't more people steal?" The question of "Who benefits?" looms large here.

Our point is not to claim neutrality for the second question; rather it is to illuminate the second-order nature of our research and evaluation questions. They have their biases in particular tacit conceptions of social justice, conceptions that tie us to social arrangements in important ways.

REDEFINING OUR UNIT OF ANALYSIS

The foregoing discussion of how the very questions we ask are connected to ideological values and outcomes points to the importance of seeing the enterprise of schooling itself as connected to these same ideological values and outcomes. Unfortunately, as we noted earlier, the very theoretical framework most educators have employed has made it difficult to face these connections honestly. Questions of who benefits, about what might be called the latent social effects of the curricula and social organization of schools, are not overtly dealt with in our dominant evaluative procedures because of the very conception of schools that guides the evaluation enterprise.

Let us examine this in more detail. Theory does not merely determine what we observe. It determines what we cannot observe as well. As Wright (1979) has noted, our questions "are always embedded in conceptual structures and if these structures lack certain pivotal elements . . . certain questions cannot or will not be asked." In particular, questions of what constitutes a proper unit of analysis are often specified by our unconscious theoretical presuppositions (pp. 57–58). And it is here that we need to make serious headway if we are to more fully understand curriculum. For just as our questions do not stand alone, but can be seen to be linked to social relations outside of them, so too is the school itself, as an isolated entity, not a proper unit of analysis if we are interested in the social functions of curricula. If our unit of analysis is only the school, then the issues surrounding curriculum evaluation can stand alone and less of a serious challenge can be made against the process/product path it has taken in the past. If, however, the school is interpreted as inextricably connected to powerful institutions and classes outside of itself, then our unit of analysis must include these connections. We are arguing, hence, that one commits a serious category error by thinking about the school as if it and its programs and problems existed independently. And such an error can have disastrous consequences for evaluation.

Thus, a first step in going beyond the usual disconnected framework, and toward a more relational analysis of curriculum and evaluation, is to accept one fundamental social fact, one that may be hard to deal with given where many of us are employed, but one that is accurate nonetheless. At one level, this can be stated easily. The way our institutions are organized and controlled is not equal. What this means is important. A number of lines of recent social research have devoted themselves to providing us with impressive documentation of the extent to which our society remains at heart unequally responsive by class, race, and gender. In brief, the evidence suggests the following: that we do not live in a meritocratic order; that as the sociologist of medicine Vincente Navarro has documented (1976), slogans of pluralism aside, in almost every social arena from health care to anti-inflation policy, one can see a pattern in which the top 20 percent of the population consistently benefits more than the bottom 80 percent (see also Castells, 1980); that while schools may often be avenues for individual mobility (though this is more accidental than we might suppose), there has been little consistent loosening of the ties between origins and attainments through schools over time (Olneck & Crouse, 1978); and finally, that schools are not now nor have they ever been immune to social pressures, economic, racial, and sexual ideologies, or these patterns of differential benefits (Karabel & Halsey, 1977).

We may not all agree with the social implications of this evidence; however, the accumulated evidence over the past few years should make us less than complacent about assuming that schools are socially neutral, meritocratic institutions, tied into a pluralistic and meritocratic social order, an order which by policy and practice is organized to distribute educational and economic goods and services equally. The evidence suggests that this is simply not true. Schools are not isolated entities, divorced from the maintenance of economic and cultural inequality. Exactly the opposite is sometimes the case. This assertion is so general as to be less than helpful, unless we become more specific about how schools are situated in this wider array of institutions.

Recent research on the social, ideological, and economic role of our educational apparatus has pointed to three activities that schools engage in. We can label these functions as assisting in accumulation, legitimation, and production. First, schools assist in the recreation of an unequally responsive economy by helping to create the conditions necessary for capital accumulation. They do this in part through their internal sorting and selecting of students by "talent," thus roughly reproducing a hierarchically organized labor force. As students are hierarchically ordered—an ordering often based on the cultural forms of dominant groups (Bourdieu & Passeron, 1977; Ogbu, 1978)—different groups of students are often taught different norms, skills, values, and dispositions by race, class, and sex. These tend to embody those values that are "required" by their projected rung on the labor market. In this way, schools help meet the needs of an economy for a stratified and at least partially socialized body of employees. Clearly, this does not mean that what goes on in schools is mechanistically determined by economic forces (Apple, 1982b). Just as clearly, as anyone who has worked in an inner-city school realizes, many students do not accept the values that the school teaches in this "hidden curriculum" (Apple, 1982b; Willis, 1977). It is still essential, though, to realize that there are some important ties between an economy and the social outcomes of schools.

Second, schools are important agencies of legitimation. That is, they distribute social ideologies and help create the conditions for their acceptance. Thus, schools tend to describe their internal workings as meritocratic (inaccurately, so it seems) and as contributing to widespread social justice. (See Rosenbaum, 1976; on the school's role in legitimation, see Meyer, 1977.) In this way, they foster a social belief that the major institutions of our society are equally responsive by race, sex, and class. Unfortunately, as we have noted, the available data suggest that this is less the case than we might like to think.

Finally, the educational apparatus as a whole constitutes an important set of agencies for production. This is quite complex, but basically what it means is this. Our kind of economy requires high levels of technical/administrative knowledge for the expansion of markets, the artificial creation of new consumer needs, the control and division of labor, and for technical innovation to increase or hold one's share of a market or increase profit margins. Schools and universities help in the production of such knowledge. This, in part, explains why most school systems and the curricula within them are organized toward the university and why there is so much of a growing emphasis on establishing programs for gifted students in a time of economic recession. Students who can ultimately contribute to the production of this knowledge are sponsored by the school. Those who cannot are labeled as somehow deviant or are formally or informally tracked in schools. (See Apple, 1979; on the relationship between the control of knowledge and the economy, see Braverman, 1974, and Noble, 1977.)

These three functions—accumulation, legitimation, and production—must be understood if we are to grapple with what schools do and, especially, with what they are capable of doing. Such understandings are essential if we are to deal with problems in evaluation in a more complete, sophisticated way. One of the important facts about these functions is that they may be contradictory. That is, they may work against each other at times. For instance, education is caught between selecting and sorting an "adequately socialized" work force and at the same time acting as if it were part of an open system. The school's need to legitimate ideologies of social justice (and to make its own operation legitimate to its clientele) may therefore be objectively at odds with the equally (and given current economic conditions, now more) compelling pressure on it to serve the changing needs of industry.

We have gone on at some length here, not to bore you either with the burdens of theoretical accounts of our institutions or the details of what we are beginning to know about the connections schools may have to the reproduction of an unequal society, but to suggest something of no little significance. Only by placing our research and evaluation efforts within a more thorough analysis of these social functions, these connections, can we make progress in understanding what is happening in schools.

Making the connections between school curricula and the larger society our unit of analysis implies reorienting our methods of inquiry. First, this change in unit of analysis would involve carefully scrutinizing a program one is evaluating in light of its wider social role, in light of the three socioeconomic functions we just examined. This would mean that our initial task would require that we ask what have come to be called "prior questions." Thus for any evaluative activity in curriculum, the prior question should be, "evaluation for what social, economic, and ideological purpose?"

Let us give an example of the importance of asking the prior question of "evaluation for what social purpose?" Let us assume that we are engaged in the evaluation of a program to keep minority and poor teenagers in high school. We wish to ask whether and on what grounds it is "successful." But, successful according to what? As Jencks et al. (1979) have shown, the economic returns for blacks, as opposed to whites, who complete elementary and secondary schools is still *twice* as great for whites as for blacks (Jencks et al., 1979). Further, completing secondary school gives relatively few advantages to students from economically disadvantaged backgrounds. As these researchers put it:

> Apparently, high school graduation pays off primarily for men from advantaged backgrounds. Men from disadvantaged backgrounds must attend college to reap large occupational benefits from their education. (p. 175)

In other words, getting those minority and poor students to stay in school simply has little economic rewards associated with it, no matter what our commonsense assumptions would lead us to expect.

This example documents an interesting point. To take seriously some claim for the retention, elimination, or modification of such a curricular program, in order for our evaluation to make sense socially, our unit of analysis must be extended beyond the achievement scores of the pupils. It must include the social connections between the school's role in accumulation in producing students of this type (with their probable economic trajectories) and the tacit legitimation of an ideology of opportunity ("if only you would finish high school everything would be all right"), when the opportunity structure of the economy may objectively preclude that as an actual statistical probability (Wright, 1979).

Taking the unit of analysis to be the isolated school system, classroom, program, or achievement scores of students would preclude this kind of investigation. Yet look at what the extended socioeconomic appraisal that we have argued for does. It immediately raises the competing ideological and political claims made upon the school. It forces us to confront the latent ideological and economic outcomes of the institution and asks us to make certain that our programs, curricula, policies, research, and evaluations are not covering things that we may not want to go on. This appraisal would obviously involve a good deal of debate at the policymaking level and between the school and its varied clientele. Yet the dominant ways we evaluate school programs tend to preclude serious consideration of competing ethical, political, or economic claims in large part because of their technical orientation and their focus on the achievement or IQ scores of the students (Apple, 1979).

In the example of the evaluation of the dropout program above, we can see how this occurs. A political and economic issue is transformed into a less powerful one. Here we are left to argue about the relative merits of a specific curricular program—Are the test scores of the students raised? Do they stay in school longer? and so on—as if this was cut off from the real distribution of power and benefits in our society. In this case, evaluators have taken the problems as defined by both the administrative managers of the institutions and elite groups in society as the major issues. Yet taking, rather than making, our problems can lead to acceptance of elite values and policies in such a way that, as Edelman (1977) reminds us, the material aspects, the benefits, of these programs and policies "are likely to favor dominant groups" while the symbolic aspects of such programs and policies may tend to "falsely reassure mass publics that their interests are being protected" against dominant groups (Edelman, p. xxi). As we in fact sought to show, closer scrutiny of the evidence of the social effects of such curricular programs might indicate that the problem is *not* dropouts. It is not getting kids to stay in school longer. This is how the problem is defined for us. A more searching appraisal, a more intensive examination of how value is placed on it, would place the issue squarely where it belongs, in the unequal economic apparatus of the larger social order. Any curricular evaluation that ignores this misses the reality of the connections between our curricular programs and that larger society. The evaluation of the program that we have proposed, examining it in light of the connections the curriculum has to external socioeconomic structures, makes it much more difficult to miss this reality.

TOWARD SOCIAL EVALUATION INSIDE THE SCHOOL

In the prior section of this paper we illuminated some of the inherent problems with technical and achievement-oriented evaluation models. We argued that enlarging our unit of analysis so that it included the real ties among the institutions, programs, and curricula we are evaluating and their varied social functions was an essential step in having a more thorough understanding of what schools do. In this section, we want to briefly suggest alternative questions to ask, as well as those areas of school curricula that these questions need to interrogate, that take our prior points into account. Finally, we will argue for a greater emphasis on ethnographic studies in evaluation and give an example of a study that combines several of our points.

So far we have looked at curricular programs from the outside. While this has been of no small moment, we have not gone inside the school itself to examine the actual content and social relations embodied *within* the curriculum and their relation to the structure of inequality. Yet no social evaluation of curricula can be complete unless it also gets inside the black box of the school and investigates what is actually taught and what the concrete experiences of students are within the programs. In the space available here, we can only point to the kinds of issues that need to be raised, though a much more detailed analysis can be found elsewhere (Apple, 1979, 1982a; Beyer, 1983).

Three basic areas of curricula need to be scrutinized to see the connections between curricula and ideological and economic structures. These include (a) the day-to-day interactions and regularities of school life—what has come to be called the "hidden curriculum"—that teach important norms and values related to the world of work and to class, race, and gender divisions in our society; (b) the formal corpus of school knowledge, that is, the overt curriculum itself, that is planned and found in the various materials and texts and filtered through teachers; and, finally, (c) the fundamental perspectives, procedures, and theories—such as social labeling practices that "blame the victim," a vulgar and reductive positivism, industrial models such as systems management, and so on—that educators use to plan, organize, and evaluate what happens in schools. Each of these elements should be examined to see to what extent the day-to-day meanings and practices that are so standard in classrooms (while clearly there to help individual children) may tend to be less the instruments of help and, unfortunately, more a part of a complex process of the reproduction of the unequal class, race, and gender relations in our society (Apple, 1979, p. 14).

Since the third area, the one about the perspectives, procedures, and theories we usually employ, has already been partially discussed in our treatment of the evaluation of both the dropout and juvenile rehabilitation programs, let us turn our attention to the overt and hidden curricula.

It has become increasingly clear that a selective tradition operates in school curricula. Out of an entire universe of knowledge in history, science, social studies, language, the arts, and so on, only some is selected for teaching in our schools. Because of this, curriculum evaluation needs not only to be guided by a concern for how we might get students to acquire more knowledge (the dominant question in our efficiency-minded field), but by another set of questions as well. For *prior* to measuring whether or not students are "able" to learn or have learned a particular set of facts, skills, or dispositions, we should want to know *whose* knowledge it is, *why* it is organized and taught in this particular way, to this particular group (Apple, 1979, p. 7). This would require us to examine what the institution considers "legitimate" knowledge and teaching and testing strategies and unpack their actual social outcomes. How do curriculum, teaching, and evaluation function in the accumulation, legitimation, and production roles played by the school? Is this what we as parents and educators really want to go on? Notice again that these sorts of queries require us to recapture the ethical, political, and economic sensitivity that has been lost over the years in our analysis of curriculum, as well as taking much more seriously data similar to Jencks's and Navarro's findings about the unequal returns from most of our social and cultural institutions.

But what about the hidden curriculum? What questions should guide our investigations in this area? Here it is important to remember that not every group receives the same tacit social messages; nor are the effects of this tacit teaching the same. Thus, the following issues are significant. What ideological norms and values does everyone get? What is differentially taught by race, gender, and class simply by living in the school day after day for most of one's preadult life?

Some simple examples of why we might want to interrogate the formal and informal knowledge found within the institution may be helpful here. For instance, in most schools there is little labor history (Anyon, 1979). Instead, we teach military history and the history of the presidents. Women, blacks, browns, and so on, are still strikingly misportrayed as well. The form, not only the content, of curricula—that is, the way the knowledge is organized—tends more and more to be individualized and prepackaged into standardized sets of material with one standard correct answer. It often offers little opportunity for cooperation or serious group inquiry. We also find behavior modification techniques (with their emphasis on only doing exactly what someone in authority says, for a small reward) more widely used in black, brown, and poor neighborhoods. In more economically advantaged areas, pedagogical and curriculum strategies are less likely to be dominated by such techniques and may be more likely to allow for more intellectual curiosity, multiple answers, more flexible behavioral norms, and so forth.

We may also find that the categories and procedures we use in our curriculum organization and evaluation are also strongly related to unequal socioeconomic relations. Thus, we establish "remedial curricula" for "slow" learners and then find that being slow and being remediated is often related to the history of racial oppression and to poverty. Further, we find that it is not unusual that once a student is placed in a remedial group, the objective chances of doing markedly better are small. The label of "slow" sticks. For it seems that if we look at the macro level, when we establish "bluebird," "blackbird," and "buzzard" groups, once you are a buzzard you stay a buzzard.

If these various examples are widespread (and they seem to be) we are learning a good deal about what the overt and hidden curricula and our ways of evaluating students and programs may be doing socially. They may in fact be strongly related to both reproducing particular social and economic divisions in society and providing a helping ideology that legitimates these divisions.

AGAINST MECHANISTIC SOCIAL EVALUATION

Questions and examples of the type we just discussed are powerful tools in evaluating the school and its programs. However, these kinds of prior questions can lead to a mechanistic style of social evaluation where we assume that the school is always successful in performing its social functions. This would be unfortunate. No social institution, no set of ideological forms and practices, is ever totally monolithic. And students, for instance, will not necessarily always accept what the school teaches. Therefore, we cannot take for granted that students are passive receptacles into which the school pours ideological content and values[2]; nor should we assume that students do not have some creative responses to the sorting and selecting functions of the school. In fact, recent research points to the critical nature of asking what students reject, since the research documents the ability of many students to reinterpret dominant ideologies in the overt and hidden curricula. The students often act in ways that make a simple conclusion about the social effects of curricula inside the black box difficult to make.

One thing is certain. If we are to find out what is accepted and what is rejected, if we are to really see what impact the curricula, social relations, and evaluative practices of the school have on the students themselves, accepted evaluations based on achievement scores and other forms of testing are simply inadequate. This means that a different style of evaluation, one that is more sensitive to the social role of the school, needs to be sponsored. Process/product evaluation does not enable us to get at the lived experience of students, to show *why* curricula fail, why programs are accepted or rejected, how conceptions of ability and achievement actually cover a much more complicated relationship between what a student experiences and acts on on the one hand and dominant ideologies and economic relations on the other. Instead, what we need is a greater emphasis on ethnographic analyses that would show the complex interaction between the strengths of the culture the students bring with them to school, the formal and informal curricula, and the unequal society outside the institution.

The crucial importance of not relying on "objective" test or achievement data to evaluate the effects of curricula is demonstrated quite well in a recent ethnographic study by Willis (1977). Willis focuses on a group of working-

[2]Anyone who has taught in an inner-city school knows the intense resistance that goes on. Even more subtle forms of resistance occur in more middle-class schools in many areas. (See, e.g., McNeil, 1977.)

class high school students in a heavily industrialized city. He shows how, even in a school that tries to develop curricula to meet the needs of its students, for many of the students its curricular programs usually fail. Achievement is not raised; the students remain cynical.

Why this occurs and a large part of its actual social effect is exceptionally interesting and would be totally missed by an emphasis on test scores. It has less to do with the students' ability than we might think. Rather, it has an immense amount to do with the vibrant culture of the students themselves and their place in the social division of labor and the class structure. The knowledge that the school wants the students to learn and the hidden curriculum of punctuality, individual achievement, and authority relations are *both* rejected by the students. What the school considers legitimate knowledge bears little resemblance to the actual world of work, to life "on the street," to the facts of labor that these students experience from their parents, friends, and their own part-time jobs. Willis shows that because of this, the youths reject book learning and glorify physical labor and "being cool." They spend a good deal of their time in school creatively finding ways of beating the system and getting out of doing school work. By rejecting the "legitimate" culture of the school, by affirming manual work and physicality, they also affirm their own background. At the same time, they also act in a way that actually constitutes a realistic assessment that *as a class*, finishing their schooling or trying hard will not enable them to go much further than they already are.

This is a paradoxical situation. By rejecting the overt curriculum, the students are rejecting "mental labor." Thus, they harden and make even more legitimate a distinction that lies at the heart of the social relations of production in our unequal economy, the separation between mental and manual labor. While they are affirming and acting on the strengths of their own lived culture, a culture which almost unconsciously recognizes the low statistical probability of high school really paying off in the end, they are also closing off whatever paths to advancement schools may in fact offer, and are reinforcing unfortunate ideological distinctions at the same time. Yet, by rejecting the authority relations of the hidden curriculum, by learning to control their own time and space and beat the system, they are also learning skills that will give them more informal control at their own work places later. The social effects of the hidden and overt curricula are, hence, quite complicated.

Notice what this ethnographic study does. It does not assume a mechanistic process in the school; yet at the same time it places the connections among the school, the students, the curricula, and the larger social/economic framework at the heart of its analysis. It even enables us to more fully answer traditional questions about curricular success or failure by not only focusing on test data but by illuminating how and why these data are produced.

Social evaluations of curricular programs in our inner cities, among poor black, Hispanic, and Native American populations, in industrialized working class areas, in the rural areas of the South and West, and elsewhere could profitably draw upon similar kinds of analyses.

CONCLUSION

At the heart of the suggestions we have made here, as it is at the heart of Willis's provocative study, is the knowledge of what our society is like structurally. We have claimed that given this knowledge, evaluators are compelled to take more seriously how the social meanings within the curriculum and the social impact of school programs work in supporting dominant groups within contemporary society in various ways. Only by becoming more aware of these varied functions in which the school is called upon to engage, can we go further here. We have also warned against becoming so overly mechanistic, however, that we forget that real people, including many educators, may act against the accumulation, legitimation, and production functions of our educational institutions.

In short, our questions have been guided by a concern for who ultimately gains the most from the hidden and overt curricula and the evaluative practices that are found in our schools. If Navarro's findings are correct, we might expect to find that a good deal of our own practices might in fact ultimately provide benefits that are just as unequal. Taking up the questions and strategies we have provided in this essay could open up ways of altering such inequalities.

REFERENCES

Anyon, J. Ideology and United States history textbooks. *Harvard Educational Review*, 1979, *49*, 361–386.

Apple, M. The process and ideology of valuing in educational settings. In M. Apple, M. Subkoviak, & H. Lufler (Eds.), *Educational evaluation: Analysis and responsibility*. Berkeley, Calif.: McCutchan, 1974.

Apple, M. *Ideology and curriculum*. Boston: Routledge & Kegan Paul, 1979.

Apple, M. (Ed.). *Cultural and economic reproduction in education: Essays on class, ideology, and the state*. Boston: Routledge & Kegan Paul, 1982. (a)

Apple, M. *Education and power*. Boston: Routledge & Kegan Paul, 1982. (b)

Beyer, L. Aesthetic curriculum and cultural reproduction. In M. Apple & L. Weis (Eds.), *Ideology and practice in schooling*. Philadelphia: Temple University Press, 1983.

Bourdieu, P., & Passeron, J. *Reproduction in education, society and culture*. Beverly Hills, Calif.: Sage Publications, 1977.

Braverman, H. *Labor and monopoly capital*. New York: Monthly Review Press, 1974.

Castells, M. *The economic crisis and American society*. Princeton, N.J.: Princeton University Press, 1980.
Edelman, M. *Political language*. New York: Academic Press, 1977.
Jencks, C., Bartlett, S., Corcoran, M., Crouse, J., Eaglesfield, D., Jackson, G., McClelland, K., Mueser, P., Olneck, M., Schwartz, J., Ward, S., Williams, J. *Who gets ahead?* New York: Basic Books, 1979.
Karabel, J., & Halsey, A. H. (Eds.). *Power and ideology in education*. New York: Oxford University Press, 1977.
McNeil, L. *Economic dimensions of social studies curriculum: Curriculum as institutionalized knowledge*. Unpublished doctoral dissertation, University of Wisconsin–Madison, 1977.
Meyer, J. The effects of education as an institution. *American Journal of Sociology*, 1977, *83*, 55–77.
Navarro, V. *Medicine under capitalism*. New York: Neale Watson Academic Publications, 1976.
Noble, D. *America by design*. New York: Alfred Knopf, 1977.
Ogbu, J. *Minority education and caste*. New York: Academic Press, 1978.
Olneck, M., & Crouse, J. *Myths of meritocracy: Cognitive skill and adult success in the United States* (Institute for Research on Poverty Paper #458-78). Madison: University of Wisconsin, March 1978.
Rosenbaum, J. *Making inequality: The hidden curriculum of high school tracking*. New York: John Wiley, 1976.
Willis, P. *Learning to labour: How working class kids get working class jobs*. Lexington, Mass.: D. C. Heath, 1977.
Wright, E. *Class structure and income determination*. New York: Academic Press, 1979.

SUGGESTED LEARNING EXPERIENCES

1. Request and review copies of curriculum evaluation plans employed by several different school districts. Compare and contrast these evaluation plans with the recommendations by Eisner and Apple and Beyer.

2. Request and review copies of school improvement plans used by local school districts, county offices of education, or state departments of education. Compare and contrast these plans with the recommendations by Eisner and Apple and Beyer.

3. In collaboration with several of your peers, develop criteria for evaluating school practices in a culturally diverse society.

Author Index

R

S

T

U-V

W

Y-Z

Subject Index